# Emotional Well-Being in Educational Policy and Practice

Schools in numerous countries around the world have become key sites for interventions designed to enhance the emotional well-being of children and young people, offering new forms of pedagogy and curriculum knowledge informed in ad hoc and eclectic ways by various strands of psychology, counselling and therapy.

Responding to C. Wright Mills' famous injunction for a 'sociological imagination', this unique interdisciplinary collection of papers explores ideologies and imperatives that frame contemporary education policy and practice around emotional well-being, ideas and assumptions about the state of childhood today, and the changing nature of the curriculum subject and associated forms of knowledge.

In bringing together British and American advocates of behavioural interventions in social and emotional learning, alongside critics who draw on historical, philosophical and sociological perspectives, it highlights new and important debates for policy makers, the designers, implementers and evaluators of interventions and those who participate in them.

This book was originally published as a special issue of *Research Papers in Education.*

**Kathryn Ecclestone** is Professor of Education at the University of Sheffield, UK. Her research, teaching and publications explore the impact of education policy on everyday teaching, assessment practices and curriculum knowledge, with a particular interest in the effects of wider 'therapeutic culture' and concerns about emotional well-being on education policy and practice in Britain and internationally.

# Emotional Well-Being in Educational Policy and Practice
Interdisciplinary Perspectives

*Edited by*
**Kathryn Ecclestone**

LONDON AND NEW YORK

First published 2014
by Routledge
2 Park Square, Milton Park, Abingdon, Oxon, OX14 4RN

and by Routledge
711 Third Avenue, New York, NY 10017

*Routledge is an imprint of the Taylor & Francis Group, an informa business*

© 2014 Taylor & Francis

All rights reserved. No part of this book may be reprinted or reproduced or utilised in any form or by any electronic, mechanical, or other means, now known or hereafter invented, including photocopying and recording, or in any information storage or retrieval system, without permission in writing from the publishers.

*Trademark notice*: Product or corporate names may be trademarks or registered trademarks, and are used only for identification and explanation without intent to infringe.

*British Library Cataloguing in Publication Data*
A catalogue record for this book is available from the British Library

ISBN13: 978-0-415-72849-2

Typeset in Times New Roman
by Taylor & Francis Books

**Publisher's Note**
The publisher accepts responsibility for any inconsistencies that may have arisen during the conversion of this book from journal articles to book chapters, namely the possible inclusion of journal terminology.

**Disclaimer**
Every effort has been made to contact copyright holders for their permission to reprint material in this book. The publishers would be grateful to hear from any copyright holder who is not here acknowledged and will undertake to rectify any errors or omissions in future editions of this book.

# Contents

| | |
|---|---|
| *Citation Information* | vii |
| *Notes on Contributors* | ix |
| Introduction: Emotional well-being in education policy and practice: the need for interdisciplinary perspectives and a sociological imagination<br>*Kathryn Ecclestone* | 1 |
| 1. Effective evidence-based interventions for emotional well-being: lessons for policy and practice<br>*Tracey Bywater and Jonathan Sharples* | 7 |
| 2. Marking time: some methodological and historical perspectives on the 'crisis of childhood'<br>*Kevin Myers* | 27 |
| 3. Developing social and emotional aspects of learning: the American experience<br>*Maurice J. Elias and Dominic C. Moceri* | 41 |
| 4. The contribution of religious education to the well-being of pupils<br>*Stephen Pett* | 53 |
| 5. We need to talk about well-being<br>*Ruth Cigman* | 67 |
| 6. From emotional and psychological well-being to character education: challenging policy discourses of behavioural science and 'vulnerability'<br>*Kathryn Ecclestone* | 81 |
| 7. Educating the emotions from Gradgrind to Goleman<br>*Thomas Dixon* | 99 |
| 8. What difference does it make? Philosophical perspectives on the nature of well-being and the role of educational practice<br>*Beverley Clack* | 115 |
| *Index* | 131 |

# Citation Information

The chapters in this book were originally published in *Research Papers in Education*, volume 27, issue 4 (September 2012). When citing this material, please use the original page numbering for each article, as follows:

**Introduction**
*Emotional well-being in education policy and practice: the need for interdisciplinary perspectives and a sociological imagination*
Kathryn Ecclestone
*Research Papers in Education*, volume 27, issue 4 (September 2012) pp. 383-388

**Chapter 1**
*Effective evidence-based interventions for emotional well-being: lessons for policy and practice*
Tracey Bywater and Jonathan Sharples
*Research Papers in Education*, volume 27, issue 4 (September 2012) pp. 389-408

**Chapter 2**
*Marking time: some methodological and historical perspectives on the 'crisis of childhood'*
Kevin Myers
*Research Papers in Education*, volume 27, issue 4 (September 2012) pp. 409-422

**Chapter 3**
*Developing social and emotional aspects of learning: the American experience*
Maurice J. Elias and Dominic C. Moceri
*Research Papers in Education*, volume 27, issue 4 (September 2012) pp. 423-434

**Chapter 4**
*The contribution of religious education to the well-being of pupils*
Stephen Pett
*Research Papers in Education*, volume 27, issue 4 (September 2012) pp. 435-448

**Chapter 5**
*We need to talk about well-being*
Ruth Cigman
*Research Papers in Education*, volume 27, issue 4 (September 2012) pp. 449-462

CITATION INFORMATION

**Chapter 6**
*From emotional and psychological well-being to character education: challenging policy discourses of behavioural science and 'vulnerability'*
Kathryn Ecclestone
*Research Papers in Education*, volume 27, issue 4 (September 2012) pp. 463-480

**Chapter 7**
*Educating the emotions from Gradgrind to Goleman*
Thomas Dixon
*Research Papers in Education*, volume 27, issue 4 (September 2012) pp. 481-496

**Chapter 8**
*What difference does it make? Philosophical perspectives on the nature of well-being and the role of educational practice*
Beverley Clack
*Research Papers in Education*, volume 27, issue 4 (September 2012) pp. 497-512

Please direct any queries you may have about the citations to
clsuk.permissions@cengage.com

# Notes on Contributors

**Tracey Bywater** is Reader at The Institute for Effective Education, University of York, UK. Her area of interest lies in the design and implementation of complex intervention evaluations to assess 1) the effect on behavioural and health outcomes for disadvantaged or vulnerable children, 2) intervention delivery, process and fidelity and 3) cost-effectiveness. She has published widely in this area; her latest publication is *Behavioural and cognitive-behavioural group-based parenting programmes for early-onset conduct problems in children aged 3 to 12 Years* (Review), (2012).

**Ruth Cigman** is Senior Research Fellow in Philosophy of Education at the Institute of London, UK. She has published widely on ethics and philosophy of education, with a focus on moral psychology, inclusive education and medical ethics education.

**Beverley Clack** is Professor in the Philosophy of Religion at Oxford Brookes University, UK. She is a co-author with Brian R. Clack of *The Philosophy of Religion: A Critical Introduction* (revised 2nd edition, 2008); author of *Sex and Death* (2002) and co-editor of the journal *Feminist Theology*. Currently she is writing two books on psychoanalysis.

**Thomas Dixon** is Senior Lecturer in History and Director of the Centre for the History of the Emotions at Queen Mary, University of London, UK. His books include: *From Passions to Emotions: The Creation of a Secular Psychological Category* (2003) and *The Invention of Altruism: Making Moral Meanings in Victorian Britain* (2008).

**Kathryn Ecclestone** is Professor of Education at the University of Sheffield, UK. Her research, teaching and publications explore the impact of education policy on everyday teaching, assessment practices and curriculum knowledge, with a particular interest in the effects of wider 'therapeutic culture' and concerns about emotional well-being on education policy and practice in Britain and internationally.

**Maurice J. Elias** is Professor of Psychology and Internship Coordinator and Director of Clinical Training for the PhD Program in Psychology at Rutgers, the State University of New Jersey, USA, and Academic Director of Rutgers Civic Engagement and Service Education Partnerships Program. His research interests focus on improving school climate for academic and life success and he writes a blog on social, emotional and character development for www.edutopia.org. His most recent book is for educators and parents: *Talking Treasure: Stories to Help Build Emotional Intelligence and Resilience in Young Children.*

## NOTES ON CONTRIBUTORS

**Dominic C. Moceri** is a fourth-year clinical psychology PhD student at Rutgers, the State University of New Jersey, USA. His research interests are quantifying the implementation, sustainability and scalability of evidence-based practices in various settings, with an emphasis on school-based prevention and promotion interventions. His master's thesis on the system of sustainable implementation model was recently accepted to the *Journal of Community Psychology*.

**Kevin Myers** is Senior Lecturer in Social History and Education at the University of Birmingham, UK. His research interests are in the history of the educational sciences.

**Stephen Pett** is a part-time MPhil student at the University of Birmingham, UK, transferring to PhD to research the relationship between RE, happiness and well-being. He works for RE Today Services, writing classroom resources for RE teachers.

**Jonathan Sharples** is Manager of Partnerships at the Institute for Effective Education, University of York, UK. His interests and expertise lie in bringing together policy-makers, researchers and practitioners to enhance the use of evidence within education. His recent publications include *Effective classroom strategies for closing the gap in educational achievement for children and young people living in poverty, including white, working class boys* (Technical Report), (2010).

# INTRODUCTION

## Emotional well-being in education policy and practice: the need for interdisciplinary perspectives and a sociological imagination

Kathryn Ecclestone

Over the past 10 years or so, a very powerful political and social consensus has emerged that we have a crisis of well-being, that it is getting worse, and that governments need to intervene. In March 2007, Geoff Mulgan, former head of the Number Ten Policy Unit, subsequently head of the think-tank the Young Foundation, now head of the National Endowment for Science Technology and the Arts, and co-founder of the Action for Happiness movement in April 2011, wrote in the Times that 'well-being will be the major focus of government in the twenty first century, in the way that economic prowess was in the 20th and military prowess in the nineteenth'. The goal of 'well-being', with a particular emphasis on a mental health interpretation permeated the previous government's strategies across health, work and pensions, education, with statutory requirements for local authorities to promote children and young people's mental health and well-being through Every Child Matters (ECM) (see Bywater and Sharples this volume).

A major impetus for politically sponsored intervention has been the previous Labour government's 'Third Way' ideology, which shifted social policy from redistribution of material and social resources towards a concern about the symbiotic relationship between the psychological and emotional effects of inequality and socio-economic disadvantage (e.g. Giddens 1998; Social Exclusion Unit 1999). Subsequent policy initiatives such as SureStart, ECM and the Social and Emotional Aspects of Learning Strategy for schools (SEAL) reflect a reframing of 'social justice' and 'inclusion' towards addressing feelings and behaviours associated with lack of aspiration, self-esteem and confidence as part of poor emotional well-being. In response, such programmes aim to provide a springboard to educational and social success. Notions of equality and social justice in this psychological orientation have led to research that explores 'the intergenerational transmission of socio-economic status and the extent of social mobility' and, through this, the factors that create 'equality of opportunity for happiness' (e.g. Fritjers et al. 2011, 2).

Following this political shift, David Cameron commented in his first speech as leader of the Conservative party in 2006 that there should be a focus on general well-being rather than just Gross Domestic Product:

> there's more to life than money ... Wellbeing can't be measured by money or traded in markets. It's about the beauty of our surroundings, the quality of our culture, and, above all, the strength of our relationships ... Improving our society's sense of well-

being is, I believe, the central political challenge of our times. (quoted by Lexmond and Grist 2011, 10)

Measurement is now a central goal. In November 2010, the Coalition government built on research commissioned from the London School of Economics by the previous government and announced a £2 million-a-year research project for the Office for National Statistics to establish credible measures of subjective well-being (see Dolan et al. 2011). This has generated a great deal of related research and development activity. Reports by think-tanks such as the Young Foundation and the New Economics Forum (NEF) collate ideas and evidence from a range of local projects across ageing, mental and physical health, and education to present a 'compelling' case for government and its agencies, locally and nationally, to encourage individuals, families and communities to develop well-being and to use locally appropriate, robust measures of it (e.g. Bacon et al. 2010; NEF 2011).

Fuelling the drive to find better measures and interventions is a consensus reflected in numerous high-profile policy reports and academic texts which argue that Britain is facing an unprecedented crisis of well-being, with 'widespread anxiety' about the effects of social and technological change, materialism, declining social networks, a test-driven education system and an irrelevant, outdated curriculum. According to many policy-based, professional and popular commentators in the UK, the USA, Canada, Singapore, Finland and Australia, and in global organisations such as the WHO and United Nations Children's Fund factors have created a crisis of childhood, with deteriorating levels of well-being, mental health, and motivation for, and engagement in, formal education (e.g. Sharples 2007; House and Lowenthal 2009; Sodha and Gugleimi 2009; Cigman, Myers, Bywater and Sharples this volume).

From 2003, pressure at the highest levels in the previous British government from numerous interest groups and individuals, including the Children's Society and Lord Richard Layard, Professor of Economics at the London School of Economics and co-founder of the Action for Happiness movement, led the then Department for Children Schools and Families to explore the potential for more robust interventions beyond the SEAL strategy. In October 2007, Baroness Greenfield chaired the All-Party Parliamentary Group on Scientific Research in Learning and Education to explore 'Well-being in the classroom' (Sharples 2007).

Under the previous government, an increase in interventions for emotional and psychological well-being in educational and welfare organisations was accompanied by 'resilience' projects in youth work, adult and community education, parenting and mental health programmes (e.g. Hart, Blincow, and Thomas 2007; Aranda forthcoming). More recently, riots in British cities in August 2011 appear to be fuelling a revival of older concerns about young people's moral and character development and renewed interest in teaching moral values and virtues as part of a broader set of character 'capabilities' (Ecclestone this volume). One effect of these related developments is that public and private organisations, charities and research centres offer a diverse range of 'products' in the form of instruments, activities and programmes, guidance and evidence, and equally diverse definitions of well-being.

Yet, British education policy has been subject to constant fluctuation for decades and much might be expected to change with a Coalition government heavily influenced by a Conservative political ideology. The first of a spate of changes was to rename the Department for Children, Families and Schools (a move by the

Labour government that had removed 'education' from the remit of its government department for the first time since 1873) as the Department of Education (DfE). In March 2011, the DfE ended formal political sponsorship of the previous government's Social and Emotional Learning strategy for primary and secondary schools, which had borrowed heavily from American research and practice, accompanied by recent rumours of hostility towards formal initiatives within the DfE (Northern 2012).

It is not surprising that supporters of interventions for emotional well-being fear that a return to a 'traditional' subject curriculum will herald the end of formal sponsorship of them. Nevertheless, the Secretary of State for Education supports the development of emotional intelligence, a key strand in emotional well-being, not just for children, but for teachers and institutional heads too, and as Bywater and Sharples argue in this volume, schools now have more autonomy to decide for themselves which programmes they might adopt. There are also early signs that some 'free' schools want to provide an outlet for a focus on personal, emotional and social development, rather than traditional subject disciplines, following the Royal Society of Arts' 'capabilities curriculum': for example, a free school proposing this is proposed in Oxford.

The complexity and pace of policy and practice, together with a largely unchallenged consensus that intervention is a progressive role for social policy, led to a seminar series funded by the Economic and Social Research Council, 'Changing the subject?: inter-disciplinary perspectives on emotional well-being and social justice' (Ecclestone et al. 2010), and to related dissemination and engagement seminars for policy think-tanks, practitioners and academics. This work attempted to bring together supporters of interventions and those who challenge or criticise them in order to explore contested concepts, assumptions and practices (Ecclestone et al. 2010). The series produced a set of propositions that formed the basis of a proposal to the editors of *Research Papers in Education* for a special edition to address them:

(1) There is much conceptual confusion, with interchangeable constructs, and elision between 'well-being' and 'emotional well-being' at the levels of policy, promotion of interventions, everyday practice and discourse.
(2) Most of the debate and related research has been largely uncritical: there may be technical disagreements about 'evidence' for particular interventions or objections to underlying principles, but there are few substantive challenges to underlying claims and assumptions about the need for intervention.
(3) In the face of enthusiastic promotion of interventions, it is difficult to evaluate the quality of different sources of evidence cited to prove both a need for interventions and subsequent effectiveness.
(4) Most of the interventions and related research derive their rationale from cognitive and positive psychology, thereby privileging a measurable construction and downplaying challenge or more nuanced ideas about well-being.

From different disciplinary perspectives, this special edition of *Research Papers in Education* addresses these propositions. A spur for deciding which perspectives should have a platform was the famous injunction by Mills (1959) that a 'sociological imagination' should incorporate the insights of history and psychology so that social science might illuminate the ways in which people's 'private troubles' become public and political imperatives, and the 'varieties of men and women' and images of human nature that come to prevail in a particular society and historical period (Mills 1959).

In responding to Mills' aims for social science, it is important to acknowledge a deliberate bias in the papers towards perspectives from history, religious education, philosophy and sociology, which is intended to counter a policy and practice terrain dominated by behavioural psychology, where government funding for universities, as Beverly Clack argues, now favours science over the humanities. Yet, as she argues in relation to philosophers, if academics from the humanities are to have any influence on policy and public understanding, they have to respond more accessibly and engagingly than many have hitherto. Philosophical questions lead Ruth Cigman to explore the legitimate role of schools in fostering well-being and to question the taken for granted assumption that well-being is a positive human condition, which schools can not only develop but enhance. Also focusing on the curriculum and pedagogic implications of developing well-being, Stephen Pett reasserts a role for religious education as far more than an instrument for teaching it as a set of skills, arguing that Religious Education can draw on positive psychology to foster children's ability to consider questions about human well-being.

In a counter to the historical amnesia that besets much social and education policy, Kevin Myers challenges estimates about a crisis of child well-being, drawing on evidence about changing uses of instruments and measures of well-being in different historical times. In another challenge to historical amnesia, Thomas Dixon shows that Victorian debate about the role of schools in training and measuring children's emotions has powerful resonances today, not least in the emergence of 'modern day Gradgrinds'.

Finally, in response to a consensus that 'private troubles' in the form of emotional and psychological well-being become public issues that require the attention of behavioural science, Kathryn Ecclestone invokes Wright Mills' injunction to use a sociological imagination in her exploration of the ways in which a revival of old concerns about 'character' raises new questions about both the legitimacy of interventions and the images of human nature that justify them.

Yet, while this special edition sets out to challenge the powerful consensus that schools should intervene in children's emotional well-being, it does not confine itself to critical perspectives. Two papers present a powerful, evidence-based case for universal interventions that promote emotional well-being as part of social and emotional learning or competence, and for the efficacy of certain interventions. Maurice Elias and colleagues in the Collaborative for Academic, Social, and Emotional Learning, an organisation that has played a prominent role in American policy, research and professional development for evidence-based interventions, offer lessons from the USA experience. In the British context, Tracey Bywater and Jonathan Sharples summarise the evidence base, which they argue British schools should take seriously in deciding which interventions to use and highlight the influence of the American experience in shaping British policy and practice.

As all the papers show in different ways, the propositions that led to the compilation of this special edition of *Research Papers in Education* illuminate ongoing concerns for research, policy and practice in a context, where concepts, practices and policies are likely to take new forms whilst continuing old themes and interests.

The papers also remind us that whatever the hue of government, perennial questions about the purpose and legitimate role of schools prevail lie at the heart of debate about emotional well-being and its new manifestations in a revival of 'character'.

## References

Aranda, Kay, Zeeman, L., Scholes, J., and Morales, A. S.-M. 2012. The resilient subject: Exploring subjectivity, identity and the body in narratives of resilience. *Health.*

Bacon, Nicola, Marcia Brophy, Nina Mguni, Geoff Mulgan, and Anna Shandro. 2010. *The state of happiness: Can public policy shape people's wellbeing and resilience?* London: The Young Foundation.

Dolan, Paul, Richard Layard, and Metcalfe R. Richard. 2011. *Measuring subjective well-being for public policy.* London: Office for National Statistics.

Ecclestone, Kathryn, Beverly Clack, Dennis Hayes, and Vanessa Pupavac, V. 2010. *Changing the subject?: Interdisciplinary perspectives on emotional well-being and social justice.* End of Award Report for Economic and Social Research Council funded seminar series RES-451–26-054, University of Birmingham.

Fritjers, Paul, Johnston, D.W., and Shields, M. 2011. Destined for (Un) Happiness: Does childhood predict adult life satisfaction? Discussion paper No. 5819, Institute for Labour Studies, University of Bonn, June.

Giddens, Anthony. 1998. *The third way: The renewal of social democracy.* Oxford: Polity Press.

Hart, Alison, Blincow Derek, and Thomas Helen. 2007. *Resilient therapy: Working with children and families.* London: Routledge.

House, Richard, and Del Lowenthal, eds. 2009. *Childhood, well-being and a therapeutic ethos.* London: Routledge.

Lexmond, Jan, and Mat Grist. 2011. *The character inquiry.* London: DEMOS.

Mills, C. Wright. 1959/1979. *The sociological imagination.* London: Penguin Books.

New Economics Forum. 2011. *Measuring our progress: The power of well-being.* London: NEF.

Northern, Sally. 2012. Whatever happened to happiness? *The Guardian*, January 17, 32.

Sharples, J. 2007. *Transcript of the keynote seminar of the all-party parliamentary group on scientific research in learning and education, 'Well-being in the classroom', Portcullis House,* 23 Oct 2007. Oxford: Institute for the Future of the Mind, University of Oxford.

Sodha, Sonia, and S. Guglielmi. 2009. *A stitch in time: Tackling educational disengagement.* London: DEMOS.

# Effective evidence-based interventions for emotional well-being: lessons for policy and practice

Tracey Bywater and Jonathan Sharples

*Institute for Effective Education, University of York, York, UK*

> School-based programmes developed to promote social and emotional well-being aims to reduce the risk of academic failure and other negative outcomes, such as antisocial behaviour and mental health problems. This article maps the British political trajectory from understanding the importance of social and emotional well-being, to delivering programmes in schools that enhance it. It summarises the outcomes of a selective review of effective school-based interventions and draws out lessons for policy and practice regarding choice and implementation of programmes. Amongst universal and targeted evidence-based interventions, multi-modal/component approaches appear useful in promoting cross-context competence and well-being. However, the scaling up of effective programmes remains unsuccessful and there is a lack of cost-effectiveness or cost-benefit analyses surrounding effective programmes. Despite these drawbacks there is a greater understanding of what constitutes 'evidence' and how it can facilitate policy-makers' selection process when identifying a promising or effective programmes. There is a need to address ongoing outcome and process evaluation, and delivery and resource factors in order to ensure fidelity in programme implementation, and replication of positive outcomes.

## Introduction

In 2004, 10% of children aged 5–16 had a clinically diagnosed mental disorder. Boys were more likely to have a disorder, as were children from disrupted families, children with parents with no educational qualifications and children from poorer families in disadvantaged areas (Office for National Statistics 2004). Other studies show that children's social and emotional well-being is influenced by individual factors, family background, peers, social groups, the school environment, the community and society within which they live (e.g. Lane et al. 2004). As young school children move towards greater independence and autonomy, they become increasingly influenced by factors external to the family. Schools are therefore an excellent environment in which to promote social and emotional learning (SEL) and well-being (Appleton and Hammond-Rowley 2000).

In this paper, we use the term *social and emotional well-being* as defined by the National Institute for Health and Clinical Excellence (NICE 2008), comprising three dimensions with associated indicators:

(1) Emotional well-being (including happiness and confidence, and the opposite of depression).
(2) Psychological well-being (including autonomy, problem solving, resilience and attentiveness/involvement).
(3) Social well-being (good relationships with others, and the opposite of conduct disorder, delinquency, interpersonal violence and bullying).

SEL is the process of developing the ability to recognise and manage emotions, develop caring for others, make responsible decisions, problem solve using non-conflict strategies and establish positive relationships (The Collaborative for Academic, Social, and Emotional Learning [CASEL] 2005). Children who demonstrate high levels of social and emotional well-being are likely to do better at school and in life, and educators are recognising the importance of integrating social, emotional and academic factors for effective learning (CASEL 2005). Satisfying children's emotional needs increases motivation to learn and commitment to school, improves attention and attendance rates and reduces suspension and expulsions (Malecki and Elliott 2002) and impacts on patterns of health inequalities in adulthood (Graham and Power 2004).

Children with emotional and social problems are more likely in later life to experience lower educational attainment, teenage pregnancy, unemployment, drug and alcohol misuse, violence and crime (Adi et al. 2007). An integrated approach, using universal and targeted interventions, could prevent negative behaviours and subsequent costly consequences for the education, health and social services, and the criminal justice system (NICE 2008). The costs of crime alone contributed to individuals with conduct problems is £65 billion per year (Sainsbury Centre for Mental Health 2009).

School-based activities to develop and protect social and emotional well-being should, in light of other influential factors, form one element of a broader, multi-agency strategy (NICE 2008). Other elements may include, for example, the development of policies to improve family life and the social and economic circumstances of children living in disadvantaged circumstances, and good service provision such as childcare in the early years. Recent reports by Tickell (2011) on the implementation of the Early Years Foundation Stage in England, and also Fields (2010), state the importance of closing the achievement gap between disadvantaged children and their more advantaged peers, and SEL programmes could facilitate the achievement of this aim.

In this paper, we look briefly at the risk and promotional factors salient to developing social and emotional well-being. We then provide policy background, from the UK perspective, on social and emotional well-being and the subsequent development of a universal government initiative to enhance child well-being. This is followed by examples of well-evidenced, and promising, interventions that have demonstrated effectiveness in increasing social and emotional well-being. Interventions aimed to promote prosocial skills and behaviours, to reduce bullying and disruptive behaviours, and those to improve mental well-being will be included.

The emphasis is on SEL approaches (to promote well-being) currently available in the UK with school-aged children. We then discuss potential issues which affect outcomes or potential scale up of programmes, thereby presenting lessons for policy and practice.

### *Influences on social and emotional well-being*

Socially and emotionally competent individuals typically succeed in life as they are self-aware with a grounded sense of self-confidence, socially aware and empathic, can handle their own emotions and pursue long-term goals, are effective in establishing and maintaining relationships, and are resistant to inappropriate social pressure, and are responsible decision-makers by respecting others.

### Individual factors

Individual factors such as cognitive/developmental impairment, impulsiveness, attention deficits and hyperactivity are risk factors against developing or maintaining social and emotional well-being (Sutton, Utting, and Farrington 2004). Interventions for school-aged children that improve parent–child relationships and children's own cognitive, self-control and social skills can promote well-being and subsequently prevent, or reduce, emotional difficulties and potential antisocial behaviour (Sutton, Utting, and Farrington 2004).

### Family and parenting factors

Risk factors for negative child well-being outcomes include poor parental supervision, inconsistent, neglectful or harsh discipline and a failure to set clear expectations for children's behaviour (Hawkins, Welsh, and Utting 2010). Conversely, positive parenting practices such as effective praise, limit-setting and positive interactions promote self-esteem and social and emotional well-being. Family factors continue to exert an important influence even when children of 9 or 10 begin to value their friends as highly as their parents (Reid and Patterson 1989).

### School factors

Geographical location and community factors such as levels of disadvantage can influence well-being. However, schools can positively influence well-being through their ethos, organisation, teaching and disciplinary practices and pastoral care (Farrington and Welsh 2007), thereby encouraging motivation to learn (CASEL 2005). Underachievement emerging during junior school is an important factor for negative life outcomes, with children who perform poorly more likely to truant, and be at risk of negative outcomes such as unemployment (Anderson et al. 2005).

### Peer influences

Positive peer relationships play a promotional role by providing opportunities for practicing cooperation, negotiation, compromise, conflict resolution, problem solving and social support (Hartup 1996). Children who associate with antisocial or delinquent peers tend to be those rejected by their wider group of peers (Farrington and Welsh 2007). Emotionally withdrawn children may have difficulties in social skills, social information processing (Harrist et al. 1997), peer group acceptance (Hymel, Bowker, and Woody 1993) and teacher–child relationship (Ladd and Burgess 1999).

## UK policy context around SEL

UK government's interest in interventions that develop social and emotional competencies, are relatively new, emerging largely as a policy shift towards more integrated children's services under the former Labour government.

Following the Children's Act of 2004, the Every Child Matters (ECM) agenda set out an ambitious framework to reform education and children's services by reframing young people's needs around five key outcomes: being healthy, staying safe, enjoying and achieving, making a positive contribution and achieving economic well-being (DfES 2004a). The ECM agenda placed a duty on local authorities to ensure greater cooperation and integration between statutory agencies (e.g. education, social services, health and police) and other bodies such as the voluntary and community and private sector (DfES 2004b).

Theoretical and semantic issues surrounding social and emotional competence were outlined in the Department for Education and Schools' (DfES) commissioned report, 'What works in developing children's emotional and social competence and wellbeing?' (Weare and Gray 2003). Subsequently a school-based programme was developed in response to the growing evidence (mainly from the USA) of the positive impacts of SEL. The Social and Emotional Aspects of Learning (SEAL) programme was an ambitious attempt by the DfES (and later the Department of Children Schools and Families [DCSF]) to provide universal SEL support for all pupils at primary level. Disseminated as a programme through the National Strategies (a series of central UK government teaching initiatives), the programme was described as 'a comprehensive approach to promoting the social and emotional skills that underpin effective learning, positive behaviour, regular attendance, staff effectiveness and the emotional health and well being of all who learn and work in schools'. SEAL took a less prescriptive stance than many existing (US) SEL programmes, in that it adopted an enquiry-led approach that encouraged children to explore and develop their own understandings around SEL.

The Primary SEAL guidance stated that children should be evaluated on 42 social, emotional and behavioural skills, yet methodology and direction on how to formally evaluate progress was missing. The DfES commissioned a review of approaches and instruments to assess SEL (Edmunds and Stewart-Brown 2005), but the review failed to make recommendations of explicit standardised instruments to assess SEAL outcomes. SEAL has not been rigorously evaluated in a randomised controlled trial (RCT), that is, by comparing schools implementing SEAL to those without SEAL. The 2003–2005 pilot of Primary SEAL in 25 local authorities was, however, evaluated using simple pre- and post-intervention questionnaires demonstrating positive age-related improvements in social skills and relationships (Hallam, Rhamie, and Shaw 2006). SEAL take-up by primary schools has been good, but variable levels of implementation and fidelity are noticeable. A rigorous evaluation of SEAL is needed, to include full outcome, process and cost-effectiveness evaluations, and ensure that we are supporting our children in the best way possible, without being wasteful of resources.

In 2007, the issues around child well-being were placed dramatically in the media and policy spotlight following Jonathan Bradhaw's influential report for UNICEF, in which the UK was ranked bottom out of 21 industrialised nations in a comprehensive comparison of child well-being (UNICEF 2007). Child well-being was measured across six different domains (material well-being, health and safety, education, relationships, behaviours/risks and subjective reporting), drawing on 40 separate indicators relevant to children's lives. The UNICEF report prompted a much wider, high-profile debate around the role of SEL interventions with policymakers, researchers, teachers and parents arguing the benefits, and even potential harms, of explicitly developing social and emotional skills through such programmes (APPG 2007). In an updated study, the UK has risen marginally in its ranking, although this is most likely due to an expansion of the study to include developing nations (Bradshaw and Richardson 2009).

In 2007, a secondary school version of the SEAL programme was under development by the Labour government. The publication of the UNICEF findings prompted an accelerated rollout of this initiative, without a full evaluation of effectiveness. By the time a national evaluation of secondary SEAL was completed in 2010, approximately 70% of schools were reported to be implementing the SEAL programme to some extent (and 90% of primary schools). The secondary SEAL evaluation highlighted variability in methods and quality of programme implementation. It was suggested these variable approaches were due to SEAL being envisaged as a loose enabling framework for school improvement, whereby schools apply the programme flexibly within their own context, rather than as a structured programme with relevant levels of support, training and fidelity to implementation (APPG 2007; Humphrey, Lendrum, and Wigelsworth 2010). In terms of impact, the analysis of pupil-level outcome data indicated that secondary SEAL failed to impact significantly upon pupils' social and emotional skills, general mental health difficulties, prosocial behaviour or behaviour problems. Set against the context of the wider evidence base around effective SEL programmes, it was argued that future school-based SEL initiatives should offer more structure and consistency in terms of programme delivery and careful monitoring of fidelity of implementation (Humphrey, Lendrum, and Wigelsworth 2010).

So where does the above place us today? Despite the development of government policies and initiatives over the past decade, progress in the implementation of *effective* evidence-based interventions for promoting children's SEL within schools remains slow. The removal of the National Strategies by the new UK government (Conservative and Liberal Democrat coalition) means that SEAL is no longer being disseminated as a central government initiative. This political shift, coupled with pressures on schools to adopt a more 'traditional curriculum', means less attention is being placed on SEL at a national government level.

Interestingly, the current move towards decentralisation provides schools, colleges and children's centres with greater freedom in terms of which teaching methods and programmes to adopt, including SEL interventions (DfE 2010). In this context, it is crucial that practitioners are given high-quality information around effective SEL interventions in order to make informed choices. Encouragingly, accessibility to relevant information on, for example, research findings, programme implementation and materials, is becoming easier, with clear, user-friendly reports and the development of databases or 'toolkits' to enable easy access to research-proven programmes. For example, MP for Nottingham North, Graham Allen, recently led a review that based its recommendations around evidence-based approaches to children's services and early intervention (Allen 2011). The report, 'Early intervention: next steps', recommends that 19 programmes with rigorous evidence of effectiveness should be supported and expanded, including a number of SEL programmes, some of which are covered in this paper. The proposals include the development of an independent 'Early Intervention Foundation', which would expand and improve the provision for evidence-based SEL programmes across the UK.

The uptake and promotion of SEL interventions in the UK will become increasingly influenced by decisions made by educational professionals and practitioners, rather than policy-makers. These practical decisions will be influenced heavily by how confident professionals are that SEL will be effective, and cost effective, within their particular context.

### *Effective interventions*

A recent review of 213 studies involving school-based *universal* interventions found SEL programmes to significantly enhance protective factors and help build children's resilience, when compared to control children. Those who participated in a programme demonstrated improved social and emotional skills, attitudes, behaviour and academic performance (Durlak et al. 2011). Similarly, a review of 80 studies involving school-based *targeted* programmes, found positive effects on social–emotional skills, attitudes towards self, school and others; social behaviours; conduct problems; emotional distress and academic performance (Payton et al. 2008). Outcomes for programmes in both reviews were maintained for a minimum of six months after the intervention.

This paper presents a selective, non-meta-analytic review, of programmes available in the UK to promote SEL and well-being.

## Method
### *Search strategy*

A search was conducted to identify evidence-based programmes relating to SEL and well-being for school-aged children.

The Durlak et al. (2011) and Payton et al. (2008) reviews, and other relevant reviews and databases including the Allen Report (2011), Blueprints for Violence Prevention (Mihalic et al. 2002a), Best Evidence Encyclopaedia, CASEL, Cochrane Collaboration, and the Children's Workforce Development Council Commissioning Toolkit, were searched. Professional networks, service providers and programme developers/websites were then targeted to establish which were available within the UK. The ISRCTN website was also searched for UK trials (ongoing and completed) of identified programmes. The programmes outlined below do not form an exhaustive list, but are a selection of those with best available evidence.

### *Programme inclusion criteria*

- Have achieved quality (or promising) status on a rigid set of criteria, such as Blueprints' Model criteria.
- Promotes SEL or well-being.
- Appropriate for school-aged children.
- Available in the UK.

## Programme exclusion criteria

- The negatives of the above.

In describing a selection especially relevant to the UK, we describe programmes with robust evidence that have been evaluated by RCT. We make a distinction between *universal* interventions primarily focused on whole schools, year groups or classes and *targeted* (or indicated) programmes for individual children who are displaying early signs of emotional or behavioural problems and have therefore been identified as requiring additional support, and *multi-modal* programmes that comprise multiple components, delivered across contexts or agencies, such as parent programmes delivered within schools alongside programmes for children.

### Universal school-based programmes

*Promoting Alternative Thinking Strategies (PATHS)* (http://www.channing-bete.com/prevention-programs/paths/paths.html) is an American cognitive-behavioural programme for promoting social and emotional competencies and reducing aggression, while enhancing academic attainment among primary school children. The curriculum provides teachers with systematic, developmentally based materials. RCTs in the USA and Netherlands have shown reduced levels of aggressive behaviour and increased self-control, tolerance for frustration and use of conflict resolution strategies (Mihalic et al. 2002b; Kam et al. 2004; Riggs et al. 2006). An adapted version of PATHS for Northern Ireland (Together4All) has been evaluated by RCT in 12 schools; positive findings included increased empathy, cooperation and conflict resolution, and reduced aggression among participants compared with a control group (Ross et al. in preparation). In England, a RCT of PATHS with 56 schools is due to conclude in 2012. Preliminary short-term results show improved child behaviour and social and emotional competence in schools delivering PATHS compared to 'non-PATHS' schools (Morpeth and Bywater 2011). PATHS has also been trialled in Flintshire, Wales (Appleton and Hammond-Rowley 2000).

*Incredible Years (IY) Classroom Dinosaur Programme* (www.incredibleyears.com) was originally developed to treat clinic-referred children (ages 3–7 years) diagnosed with oppositional defiant disorder or early-onset conduct problems. The programme was adapted to enable teachers to deliver it to whole classes. Programme methods include videotape modelling, role play and practice of targeted skills and reinforcement for targeted behaviours. The classroom-based Dinosaur Curriculum comprises 30 classroom lessons per year, with content divided into seven units: Learning school rules; How to be successful in school; Emotional literacy, empathy and perspective taking; Interpersonal problem solving; Anger management; Social skills; and Communication skills. Lesson plans cover each of these areas at least twice a week, in 15–20-minutes large group circle time followed by 20 minutes of small group skill practice activities. In the US RCT in disadvantaged Head Start schools intervention children demonstrated more social and emotional self-regulation and fewer conduct problems than control children (Webster-Stratton, Reid, and Stoolmiller 2008). The Classroom Dina Programme is implemented across Wales with some attendance at training being previously funded by the Welsh government, and it is delivered in every primary school in the county of Gwynedd.

The multi-level Norwegian *Olweus programme* (http://olweus.org/public/bullying_research.page) uses a 'whole school' approach by altering the institutional ethos of primary and secondary schools to reduce bullying problems. The programme includes class discussions about bullying and peer relations. Pupils who bully, or are victims of bullying, receive additional individual interventions. In Norway, the programme was found to reduce bullying by 50% with additional reductions in anti-social behaviour, theft, vandalism and truancy during at a two-year follow-up (Olweus 1999). A UK antibullying programme evaluated in Sheffield, England, drew on the Norwegian work and involved 6000 pupils aged 8–16 years in 16 primary and seven secondary schools (Smith and Sharp 1994). Results showed a 17 and 5% reduction in bullying in primary and secondary schools, respectively. The Sheffield approach subsequently informed a government-led strategy for tackling bullying in schools nationally.

*KiVa* (http://www.kivakoulu.fi/there-is-no-bullying-in-kiva-school) is an antibullying programme developed in Finland, and also includes universal and targeted approaches. The 20-hour curriculum includes class discussions, group work, short films, role-playing exercises and an interactive computer game. In the targeted component, trained staff members work with teachers to resolve bullying incidents. A RCT in 78 Finnish schools showed that pupils in participating schools were significantly less likely to be bullied than those in control schools (Salmivalli, Kärnä, and Poskiparta 2011). KiVa is now implemented by 82% of schools in Finland. The programme is for primary and secondary school children and has been translated into English for age groups 4–6 and 10–12 years. Although it has not yet undergone rigorous evaluation in the UK KiVa trainings are being introduced in to the UK in 2012.

### Targeted school-based programmes

*The American Incredible Years Therapeutic (small group) Dinosaur Programme* (www.incredibleyears.com) was designed for clinically-referred children with behavioural problems. It reduces conduct problems and improves children's peer relationships and problem solving skills. It is delivered to targeted groups of six children over 18–22 weeks in two-hour sessions, and uses the same curriculum as the IY Classroom Dina Programme. Teachers identify children, for example, by using a screener such as the Strengths and Difficulties Questionnaire (Goodman 1997). It has shown encouraging results when delivered in UK schools (Hutchings et al. 2011) and is currently undergoing evaluation by RCT in 20 UK schools (Bywater et al. 2011).

### Multi-component/modal programmes

Collaborative working across agencies has seen parenting programmes being delivered in school environments to improve home–school links while promoting social and emotional and academic skills, while other programmes offer a multi-level or multi-agency approach.

*The Incredible Years Series* (www.incredibleyears.com) includes interventions for parents (of children aged 0–12 years), teachers and primary school children – all of which have been found to be effective in the USA and further afield. The series was developed to prevent or treat, conduct problems and antisocial behaviour by promoting children's social and emotional well-being. The parent programmes have been found to be effective in the UK (Hutchings et al. 2007; Bywater et al. 2009) and Ireland (McGilloway et al. 2012) and cost effective in the UK and Irish context (Edwards et al. 2007; Charles, Bywater, and Edwards 2011; O'Neill et al. 2011; Furlong et al. 2012). The Teacher Classroom Management programme introduces teachers to effective classroom management strategies, which includes proximal praise, rewarding good behaviour. The programme is effective in the UK and Ireland (Hutchings et al. 2007; McGilloway et al. 2012). The two child programmes were outlined in previous sections.

Although the programmes can be delivered successfully and effectively as 'stand-alone' programmes to achieve the greatest impact, it is recommended that child, parent and teacher programmes be delivered simultaneously (Webster-Stratton and Reid 2010). In the UK, all 22 authorities in Wales have trained service staff to deliver the parent programme, with staff from 19 authorities trained to deliver the child and teacher programmes. The Welsh government has previously funded attendance at trainings.

*Families and Schools Together* (FAST) (www.familiesandschools.org), developed in the UK, brings together families, schools, the community and local services. It uses a combination of different approaches such as kid's clubs, parent sessions and structured peer time, to enhance family functioning and reduce school failure, violence, delinquency, substance abuse and family stress (Terrion 2006). There are five versions of the programme from 'baby' to 'teen' FAST. FAST RCTs in disadvantaged communities in the USA have demonstrated improvements in academic performance and classroom behaviours, including aggression and social skills, and family adaptability for children aged 4–9 years, up to two years following intervention (Kratochwill et al. 2004, 2009; McDonald et al. 2006). FAST is delivered in five local authorities/geographical sites across the UK and an RCT in Britain is planned for 2012. Save The Children's aim is to establish over 430 FAST groups across the UK, improve the educational achievement and life chances of 50,000 children, and train over 8000 new FAST programme facilitators by 2014.

*The Family Links Nurturing Programme* (http://www.familylinks.org.uk/about/nurturing-programme.html) was developed in the USA to promote emotional literacy in parents and children. The approach is based on four basic principles; self-awareness and self-esteem, appropriate expectations, positive discipline and empathy. It provides tools to help adults and children understand and manage feelings and behaviour, improve home and school relationships, and self-confidence. There are two main programmes. The *Parents Nurturing Programme* is a 10-week group programme (2 h/week) for parents of children up to 18, which discusses core parenting issues, like constructive praise and criticism, problem solving and negotiation, but also wider issues such as those around sex. The *Schools and Early Years Nurturing Programme* for children aged 3–13 is delivered for up to one hour per week every term. The programme was initially piloted in the UK by an Oxford based charity. It can be referred to as a 'promising' programme and is developing an evidence base (Eaude 2006). It is currently being evaluated by RCT in Wales (Simkiss et al. 2010).

Table 1 presents a summary of these programmes, which all have international evidence of effectiveness by rigorous research design. PATHS, IY and the Olweus Programmes have all achieved the status of a Blueprint Model Programmes, that is, have been independently evaluated by RCT, demonstrating evidence of effect with

Table 1. UK available programmes at a glance. All have undergone RCT evaluation elsewhere; this table establishes whether RCT UK evidence is available.

| Programme | Type (origin) | For ages (years) | Primary aim and outcomes | Length of programme | UK RCT findings | Cost analysis in UK or Ireland | Process analysis in UK |
|---|---|---|---|---|---|---|---|
| PATHS | Universal (USA) | 4–6 | To promote social and emotional well-being.<br><br>Outcomes:<br><br>• Recognition of emotions<br>• Problem solving<br>• Social/anti-social behaviour<br>• Self-control | Lessons 3–5 times per week | Increase in social and emotional competence | √ | √ |
| Incredible years series | Multi-modal comprising standalone programmes (USA) | 0–12 | To promote social and emotional well-being and reduce conduct problems<br><br>Outcomes:<br><br>• Recognition of emotions<br>• Problem solving<br>• Social/antisocial behaviour<br>• Self-control<br>• Family stress<br>• Parent/teacher skills | | | | |

| | | | | | | | |
|---|---|---|---|---|---|---|---|
| | Universal | 3–8 | | Child: 2 lessons per week Teacher: teacher sessions 1/month for 6 months. Uses strategies daily in class | No RCT as yet in UK Increase in positive teacher and child behaviour. Decrease in negative teaching and teacher stress | X √ | X √ |
| | Targeted | 3–8 | | Child: 18–24 2 h weekly session | Pilot trials show increased social and problem solving skills. RCT outcomes due 2013 | X | √ ongoing to complete 2013 |
| | | 0–12 | | Parent: 8–18 2 h weekly sessions | Reduction in negative parenting and child behaviour, increase in positive parenting and child social and emotional competencies | √ | √ |
| Families and Schools Together | Multi-modal (UK) | 0–18 | Empowering families and children by promoting protective factors. Build home, school and community links. | | No RCT as yet in UK – planned for 2012 | X | X |
| | Parent programmes | 0–3 | Outcomes: | 8 weeks | | | |
| | School and parent/child programme | 3–18 | • Academic performance • Social/antisocial behaviour • family stress • positive relationships | 8 wks 2.5hrs/wk then monthly multi-family group meetings (2.5–4 h) for 2 years led by parents | | | |
| KiVa | Universal (Finland) Multi-level – individual, class and school | 4–12 | To reduce/prevent bullying. Outcomes: • Bullying levels • Depression/anxiety • Peer interaction/perception | 20hr curriculum | Materials translated. No RCT as yet in UK | X | X |

(*Continued*)

Table 1. (*Continued*).

| Programme | Type (origin) | For ages (years) | Primary aim and outcomes | Length of programme | UK RCT findings | Cost analysis in UK or Ireland | Process analysis in UK |
|---|---|---|---|---|---|---|---|
| Olweus Programme | Universal (Norway) Multilevel – individual, class and school | 6–15 | To reduce/prevent bullying<br><br>Outcomes:<br><br>• Bullying levels<br>• Social/antisocial behaviour<br>• Positive school attitude | Weekly classroom meetings | No RCT as yet in UK | X | X |
| The Family Links Nurturing Progr amme | Multi-modal (USA)<br><br>Parent programme<br><br>Schools and early years | <18<br><br>3–13 | To promote self-awareness, esteem and confidence and understand and manage feelings and behaviour.<br><br><br>Outcomes:<br><br>• Social/antisocial behaviour<br>• Self-esteem<br>• Emotional literacy<br>• Conflict resolution<br>• Depression/anxiety<br>• Parent skills | 10 weeks 2 h/week<br>45–60 min/week every term | Awaiting outcomes – RCT completed 2011 | √<br><br><br>Completed 2011 | √<br><br><br>Completed 2011 |

sustained effect, and multiple site replication. The FAST programme has achieved the 'highest' rating, and Family Links a 'promising' rating on the Children's Workforce Development Council's Commissioning Toolkit of parenting programmes, through strong evaluation evidence, which are underpinned by evidence-based theories that are accurately reflected in the programme's materials and activities. KiVa is an example of Canadian 'best practice' on the Canadian Public Health Agency because of the programme, research, evaluation and outcome quality.

The table highlights the lack of consistency on prime outcome measures, and length of follow-up (see the systematic reviews by Durlak et al. (2011) and Payton et al. (2008) for a discussion on these limitations).

## Selecting an evidence-based programme is not enough to guarantee success

Developing the UK evidence base for effective interventions is extremely important for improving child well-being. However, in order for the interventions to achieve results similar to those in rigorous evaluation trials they must also be well executed, that is, delivered with fidelity. It is important to establish whether the programme developers or trainers have a framework in place to provide professional development, such as onsite observation and provision of objective feedback on delivery and skills, and ongoing training or supervision. Programmes should include tools to facilitate implementation such as protocols, manuals, guidelines, and materials to not only deliver the programme well but to monitor implementation and fidelity levels. The programmes outlined above are amongst the most thorough in their attention to these issues, however variability still exists across programmes, and not all trials have assesses process of delivery and the interaction with effect.

Systematic investigation of working processes such as changing needs, resources, intervention application, or delivery, all impact on intervention outcome (Gitlin and Smyth 1989). At the end point, we cannot be sure if it is the intervention, the process, or both, that influenced outcome effects without assessing both strands.

Complex interventions, such as those delivered in schools, have several interacting components and present unique problems for evaluators in addition to usual practical and methodological difficulties. The UK Medical research Council (MRC) (2009) state that it is necessary to evaluate the following dimensions of complexity to fully assess any meaningful intervention and/or process effects:

- Number of components and interactions between them – theoretical understanding is needed of *how* the intervention causes change, so that weak links in the causal chain can be identified and strengthened.
- Number and difficulty of behaviour changes required by those delivering or receiving the intervention – lack of impact may reflect implementation failure rather than genuine ineffectiveness; a thorough process evaluation is needed to identify implementation problems.
- Number of groups or organisational levels targeted by the intervention – variability in individual level outcomes may indicate a need for larger sample sizes to take account of the extra variability, or cluster – rather than individual-randomised designs.

- Number and variability of outcomes – a single primary outcome may not be most appropriate; a range of measures may be required.
- Degree of flexibility or tailoring of the intervention – ensuring strict fidelity to a protocol may be inappropriate; the intervention may work better if adaptation to local setting is allowed.

Issues may arise relating to the difficulty of standardising intervention delivery, within local contexts, such as making adaptations or accommodations to the programme or delivery service to ensure that both programme and services are ready for delivery, the logistical difficulty of applying experimental methods to service or policy change and the complexity of the causal chains linking intervention with outcome (MRC 2009).

The University of Illinois, USA and the CASEL have developed a more specific model to guide schools in implementing and sustaining SEL programmes (Devaney et al. 2006). The model comprises 10 implementation steps grouped into three phases – readiness, planning and implementation – and six sustainability factors. A rubric tool, based on this model, helps schools rate their implementation quality on each of the steps and factors. The tool and model are being used in a three-year pilot initiative to implement SEL programmes in Illinois, with encouraging results. The MRC (2009) and CASEL's (Devaney et al. 2006) guidance could support UK stakeholders when undertaking the actions recommended by NICE (2008) to promote children's well-being in schools. (see Table 2).

Process evaluation is critical when trialling an intervention programme, and ongoing evaluation and monitoring is crucial throughout scale-up to maintain intervention integrity and effectiveness, for example, to monitor that programmes are not delivered by insufficiently trained staff with inadequate resources (Mihalic et al. 2002a). A process evaluation may highlight barriers to successful implementation such as: inaccurate conceptualisation of programme underpinnings into programme components; overburdened and overwhelmed staff; lack of programme support for adequate, continuing, staff development and for programme implementation or

Table 2. Summary of CASEL's implementation model.

| Implementation stage | Steps in implementation model |
| --- | --- |
| Readiness | 1. Head commits to school-wide programme |
| | 2. Engage stakeholders and form steering committee |
| Planning | 3. Develop and articulate a shared vision |
| | 4. Conduct needs and resources assessment |
| | 5. Develop action plan |
| | 6. Select evidence-based programme |
| Implementation | 7. Conduct initial staff development |
| | 8. Launch programmes in classrooms |
| | 9. Expand and integrate school-wide programme |
| | 10. Revisit activities and adjust for improvement |
| Sustainability factors | 1. Provide ongoing professional development |
| | 2. Evaluate practices and outcomes for improvement |
| | 3. Develop infrastructure to support social emotional learning |
| | 4. Integrate the learning framework school-wide |
| | 5. Nurture partnerships with families and communities |
| | 6. Communicate with stakeholders |

supervision/monitoring; school or region limited capacity or resources to implement the programme or strategy successfully, e.g. lack of staff, time or finances (Devaney et al. 2006).

## *Cost-effectiveness*

Empirical educational research typically focuses on intervention effects, policies and programmes whilst ignoring costs (Rice 2002). If school-based SEL programmes are to be seriously considered for scale up, costs of implementation, cost-effectiveness and potential long-term cost-benefits should be a priority. It seems foolhardy to evaluate an intervention, find it is effective in achieving positive outcomes, but found not to be cost effective during roll-out, and is thereby abandoned through lack of resources, or worse its delivery is continued, with various 'corners cut', in an attempt to reduce implementation costs, which may yield the intervention useless.

Potential costs involved in developing a whole school approach would include additional planning, preparation and assessment, with both staff and resource implications, particularly with regard to supply teachers to provide cover for permanent staff while training or conducting assessments. For a targeted approach, costs could include: payment for external/cross-agency trained staff to deliver sessions; crèche facilities for parenting groups and administration costs. A thorough detailed micro-costing analysis, will inform decision-makers and practitioners of intervention delivery costs (Charles et al. in press).

In addition to establishing delivery costs, the calculation of an incremental cost-effectiveness ratio, is recommended to establish whether an intervention is more, or less, cost effective than a comparator or no intervention. For example, how much it costs to improve peer relations in schools by one point on a specified outcome measure such as the Strengths and Difficulties Questionnaire (Goodman 1997). A sensitivity analysis can then be conducted to test the economic analysis and to demonstrate at what point the intervention may no longer be cost effective, for example if the implementation cost suddenly increased by 10% would the intervention still be cost effective?

There are currently few empirical cost-effectiveness evaluations assessing the impact of school SEL programmes in the UK (McCabe 2007a), although the IY Teacher Classroom Management in Ireland has undergone such an evaluation (McGilloway et al. 2010). A recent UK study (of mainly US programmes and costs) has estimated the costs of a representative intervention, including teacher training, programme coordinator and materials as £132 per child per year (2009 prices) (McCabe 2007b), suggesting the intervention offers good value for money.

Long-term cost benefits can be calculated to establish future savings, or return on investment. Based on the (mainly US) evidence, school-based SEL programmes achieve a 9% reduction in transition between conduct 'health states' (McCabe 2007b). Reducing the assumption of impact from 9 to 3% produces cost savings to the National Health Service after only four years; assuming an impact of just 1% across the 'health states', the model is cost saving to the public sector after five years.

## Conclusions

This paper has summarised a selection of effective school-based SEL programmes, available in the UK, that target influential factors in promoting/protecting child social and emotional well-being. The evidence suggests that school approaches can compensate, to some level, for certain socio-economic and cultural factors outside the school, and impact on educational achievement. To ensure learning occurs across context a multi-modal approach is recommended.

Although there is increasing UK interest in school-based SEL programmes, there is a paucity of evidence-based 'home-grown' programmes, with the exception of (a) FAST, which was developed (and implemented widely) in the UK, but only, thus far has robust (RCT) evidence of effectiveness in the USA and (b) SEAL which was implemented as the UK government initiative and has been taken up by schools without any robust evaluation with comparison groups. In contrast, US programmes such as IY and PATHS have been rigorously tested by RCT within the UK and Ireland, yet have not been rolled out to any great extent as yet, with perhaps the exception of IY in Wales.

Choosing a programme 'that works' is not enough to guarantee success; implementing the programme with fidelity takes time and resources, but is necessary to achieve the desired, proven outcomes. A shift from being narrowly focused on 'clinical effectiveness' and outcomes to being more inclusive of cost and process evaluations should result in more promising approaches, with a good potential for long-term financial and societal savings.

**Key messages for policy and practice**

- Given the patterns of multiple influences on school-aged children multi-modal/component interventions provide a holistic approach to enhancing well-being.
- Practitioners and policy-makers in the UK can choose from an expanding suite of effective programmes for school-aged children.
- Although a suite of effective programmes now exists, scale up remains an issue. Barriers to successful implementation, particularly with regard to fidelity and cost need to be addressed.
- There is a need to build the UK evidence base of 'home-grown' as well as internationally transportable programmes with proven long-term positive effects. New programmes should undergo a thorough development phase, pilot testing, rigorous evaluation by RCT, with embedded cost and process evaluations.
- There is a strong case that school-based SEL programmes are cost saving for the public sector, with education services likely to recoup the cost of the intervention in five years. Lack of investment in well-being (mental health) promotion in schools is likely to lead to significant costs for society.

## References

Adi, Yaser, Amanda Killoran, Kulsum Janmohamed, and Sarah Stewart-Brown. 2007. *Systematic review of the effectiveness of interventions to promote mental wellbeing in children in primary education*. Report 1: Universal approaches (non-violence related outcomes). London: National Institute for Health and Clinical Excellence.

Allen, Graham. 2011. *Early intervention: The next steps*. Independent Report. http://www.dwp.gov.uk/docs/early-intervention-next-steps.pdf.

All-Party Parliamentary Group (APPG). 2007. *Well-being in the classroom* seminar, All-Party Parliamentary Group on Scientific Research in Learning and Education. Futuremind. http://www.futuremind.ox.ac.uk/downloads/transcript_well_being_08_v6.pdf.

Anderson, Barry, Sarah Beinart, David Farrington, Jonathan Langman, Pat Sturgis, and David Utting. 2005. *Risk and protective factors*. London: Youth Justice Board.

Appleton, P.L., and S. Hammond-Rowley. 2000. Addressing the population burden of child and adolescent mental health problems: A primary care model. *Child Psychology and Psychiatry Review* 5: 9–16.

Bradshaw, J., and D. Richardson. 2009. An index of child well-being in Europe. *Child Indicators Research* 2, no. 3: 319–51.

Bywater, T., J. Hutchings, D. Daley, C. Eames, R. Tudor-Edwards, and C. Whitaker. 2009. A pragmatic randomised control trial of a parenting intervention in sure start services for children at risk of developing conduct disorder: Long term follow-up. *British Journal of Psychiatry* 195: 318–24.

Bywater, T., J. Hutchings, C. Evans, L. Parry, and C. Whitaker. 2011. Research protocol: Building social and emotional competence in young high-risk school children: A pragmatic randomised controlled trial of the incredible years therapeutic (small group) dinosaur curriculum in Gwynedd primary schools, Wales. *Trials*, doi:10.1186/1745-6215-12-39.

Charles, J., T. Bywater, and R.T. Edwards. 2011. Parenting interventions: A systematic review of the economic evidence. *Child: Care, Health and Development*. doi:10.1111/j.1365-2214.2011.01217x.

Charles, J., R.T. Edwards, T. Bywater, and J. Hutchings. In press. A micro-costing of the incredible years toddler parenting group with families of toddlers at risk of developing conduct disorder. *Prevention Science*.

Collaborative for Academic, Social, and Emotional Learning (CASEL). 2005. *Safe and sound: An educational leader's guide to evidence-based social and emotional learning programs – Illinois edition*. Chicago, IL: Author.

Department for Education (DfE). 2010. *The importance of teaching*. Nottingham: Department for Education.

Department for Education and Skills (DfES). 2004a. *The Children Act Report 2003*. Annesley: DfES. https://www.education.gov.uk/publications/standard/publicationDetail/Page1/DfE-1053-2004.

Department for Education and Skills (DfES). 2004b. *Every child matters: Change for children*. Annesley: DfES.

Devaney, Elizabeth, Mary U. O'Brien, Hank Resnik, Susan Keister, and Roger Weissberg. 2006. *Sustainable school wide social and emotional learning (SEL): Implementation guide and toolkit*. Chicago, IL: CASEL.

Durlak, J.A., R.P. Weissberg, D.A. Dymnicki, R.D. Taylor, and K.B. Schellinger. 2011. The impact of enhancing students' social and emotional learning: A meta-analysis of school-based universal interventions. *Child Development* 82: 405–32.

Eaude, T. 2006. *Sustaining emotional literacy: An evaluation for the trustees of family links of the medium- to long- impact of the nurturing programme in schools*. Family Links Organisation. http://www.familylinks.org.uk/userfiles/file/2006Tony%20Eaudesummary.pdf.

Edmunds, Laurel, and Sarah Stewart-Brown. 2005. *Assessing emotional and social competence in primary school and early years settings: A review of approaches, issues and instruments*. London: DfES.

Edwards, R.T., A. ÓCéilleachair, T. Bywater, D.A. Hughes, and J. Hutchings. 2007. Parenting programme for parents of children at risk of developing conduct disorder: Cost-effective analysis. *British Medical Journal*. doi:10.1136/bmj.39126.699421.55.

Farrington, D., and B. Welsh. 2007. Saving children from a life of crime. *Youth Violence and Juvenile Justice* 7, no. 2: 156–7.

Field, Frank. 2010. *The foundation years: Preventing poor children becoming poor adults*. The report of the Independent Review on Poverty and Life Chances. London: Department of Health.

Furlong, M., S. McGilloway, T. Bywater, J. Hutchings, M. Donnelly, S.M. Smith, and C. O'Neill. 2012. Behavioural/cognitive-behavioural group-based parenting interventions for children age 3–12 with early onset conduct problems (Review), Cochrane Library. http://onlinelibrary.wiley.com/doi/10.1002/14651858.CD008225.pub2/abstract.

Gitlin, Andrew, and John Smyth. 1989. *Teacher evaluation: Critical education and transformative alternatives*. Lewes: Falmer Press.

Goodman, R. 1997. The strengths and difficulties questionnaire: A research note. *Journal of Child Psychology, Psychiatry, and Allied Disciplines* 38, no. 5: 581–6.

Graham, Hilary, and Chris Power. 2004. *Childhood disadvantage and adult health: A life-course framework*. London: Health Development Agency.

Hallam, Susan, Jasmine Rhamie, and Jackie Shaw. 2006. *Evaluation of the primary behaviour and attendance pilot*. London: DCSF.

Harrist, A.W., A.F. Zaia, J.E. Bates, K.A. Dodge, and G.S. Pettit. 1997. Subtypes of social withdrawal in early childhood: Sociometric status and social-cognitive differences across four years. *Child Development* 68, no. 2: 278–94.

Hartup, W.W. 1996. The company they keep: Friendships and their developmental significance. *Child Development* 67: 1–13.

Hawkins, J.D., B.C. Welsh, and D. Utting. 2010. Preventing youth crime: Evidence and opportunities. In *A new response to youth crime*, ed. D.J. Smith. Cullompton, Devon: Willan.

Humphrey, Neil, Ann Lendrum, and Michael Wigelsworth. 2010. *Secondary social and emotional aspects of learning (SEAL): National evaluation*. Nottingham: Department for Education.

Hutchings, J., T. Bywater, D. Daley, F. Gardner, K. Jones, C. Eames, R. Tudor-Edwards, and C. Whitakker. 2007. A pragmatic randomised control trial of a parenting intervention in sure start services for children at risk of developing conduct disorder. *British Medical Journal* 334: 678–82.

Hutchings, J., T. Bywater, N. Gridley, C. Whitaker, P. Martin-Forbes, and S. Gruffydd. 2011. Introducing the incredible years therapeutic social and emotional skills programme: A pilot study with high risk children. *School Psychology International*. Sage. http://spi.sagepub.com/content/early/2011/08/13/0143034311415899.

Hymel, S., A. Bowker, and E. Woody. 1993. Aggressive versus withdrawn unpopular children: Variations in peer and self-perceptions in multiple domains. *Child Development* 64: 879–96.

Kam, C.M., M. Greenberg, and C. Kusche. 2004. Sustained effects of the PATHS curriculum on the social and psychological adjustment of children in special education. *Journal of Emotional and Behavioural Disorders* 12, no. 2: 66–79.

Kratochwill, Thomas R., Kimberley Eaton Hoagwood, Jennifer L. Frank, Jessica Mass Levitt, Serene Olin, Lisa Hunter Romanelli, and Noa Saka. 2009. Evidence based interventions and practices in school psychology: Challenges and opportunities for the profession. In *Handbook of school psychology*, ed. T.B. Gutkin and C.R. Reynolds, 497–521. New York, NY: Wiley.

# EMOTIONAL WELL-BEING IN EDUCATIONAL POLICY AND PRACTICE

Kratochwill, Thomas, Lynn McDonald, Holly Young-Bear-Tibbitts, and Joel Levin. 2004. *Families and schools together: An experimental analysis of a parent-mediated early intervention program for at-risk American Indian children* (Final Report). Madison, WI: University of Wisconsin, Wisconsin Center for Education Research.

Ladd, G.W., and K.B. Burgess. 1999. Charting the relationship trajectories of aggressive, withdrawn and aggressive/withdrawn children during early grade school. *Child Development* 70, no. 4: 910–29.

Lane, Eleanor, Frances Gardner, Judy Hutchings, and Brian Jacobs. 2004. Eight to thirteen years: Risk and protective factors; effective interventions. In *Support from the start: Working with young children and their families to reduce the risks of crime and antisocial behaviour*, ed. C. Sutton, D. Utting, and D. Farrington, 57–68. London: Department for Education and Skills.

Malecki, C.K., and S.N. Elliott. 2002. Children's social behaviours as predictors of academic achievement: A longitudinal analysis. *School of Psychology Quarterly* 17: 1–23.

McCabe, Christopher. 2007a. *A systematic review of the cost effectiveness of universal mental health promotion interventions in primary schools*. Report to the NICE Public Health Interventions Programme.

McCabe, Christopher. 2007b. *Estimating the cost effectiveness of a universal mental health promotion intervention in primary schools: A preliminary analysis*. Report to the NICE Public Health Interventions Programme.

McDonald, L., D.P. Moberg, R. Brown, I. Rodriguez-Espiricueta, N.I. Flores, M.P. Burke, and G. Coover. 2006. After-school multifamily groups: A randomized controlled trial involving low-income, urban, Latino children. *Children and Schools* 8, no. 1: 25–34.

McGilloway, S., T. Bywater, G. Ni Mhaille, C. Comiskey, M. Donnelly, Y. Leckey, and P. Kelly. 2012. Preventing conduct problems through parenting in disadvantaged areas: A pragmatic randomised controlled trial. *Journal of Consulting and Clinical Psychology* 80, no. 1: 116–27.

McGilloway, Sinead, Hyland, Lynda, NiMhaille, Grainne, Lodge, Anne, O'Neill, Donal, Kelly, Paul, Leckey, Yvonne, Bywater, Tracey, Comiskey, Catherine, and Michael Donnelly. 2010. *Positive classrooms, positive children*. A randomised controlled trial to investigate the effectiveness of the Incredible Years Teacher Classroom Management programme in an Irish Context (short-term outcomes). Summary Report. Archways, Ireland.

Medical Research Council (MRC). 2009. Developing and evaluating complex interventions: New guidance. Medical Research Council. www.mrc.ac.uk/complexinterventionsguidance.

Mihalic, Sharon, Fagan, Abigail, Irwin, Katherine, Ballard, Diane, and Delbert Elliot. 2002a. *Blueprints for violence prevention replications: Factors for implementation success*. Centre for the Study and Prevention of Violence, University of Colorado.

Mihalic, Sharon, Diane Ballard, Amanda Michalski, Jonathan Tortorice, L. Cunningham, and Susan Argamaso. 2002b. *Blueprints for violence prevention, violence initiative: Final process evaluation report*. Boulder, CO: Center for the Study and Prevention of Violence, Institute of Behavioral Science, University of Colorado.

Morpeth, Louise and Bywater, Tracey. 2011. *Finding out what works in the real world: Evaluating a social-emotional programme (PATHS) and a parenting programme (Incredible Years)*. Paper presented at the IEE Inaugural Conference, September 9, in York, England. http://www.york.ac.uk/iee/index.htm.

National Institute for Health Clinical Excellence. 2008. *Promoting children's social and emotional wellbeing in primary education*. NICE public health guidance 12.

Office for National Statistics. 2004. *The health of children and young people*. London: Office of National Statistics.

Olweus, Dan. 1999. Norway and Sweden. In *The nature of school bullying. A cross-national perspective*, ed. P.K. Smith, Y. Morita, J. Junger-Tas, D. Olweus, R. Catalano, and P. Slee, 2–48. London: Routledge.

O'Neill, D., S. McGilloway, M. Donnelly, T. Bywater, and P. Kelly. 2011. A cost-benefit analysis of early childhood intervention: Evidence from a randomised controlled trial of the incredible years parenting program. *The European Journal of Health Economics*. doi: 10.1007/s10198-011-0342-y.

Payton, John, Roger P. Weissberg, Joseph A. Durlak, Alison B. Dymnicki, Rebecca D. Taylor, Kristan B. Schellinger, and Molly Pachan. 2008. *The positive impact of social and emotional learning for kindergarten to eight-grade students. Findings from three scientific reviews*. Chicago, IL: Collaborative for Academic, Social, and Emotional Learning (CASEL).

Reid, J.B., and G.R. Patterson. 1989. The development of antisocial Patterson of behaviour in childhood and adolescence. *European Journal of Personality* 3: 107–19.

Rice, Jennifer. 2002. Cost analysis in education policy research: A comparative analysis across fields of public policy. In *Cost-effectiveness in educational policy*, ed. H.M. Levin and P.J. McEwan, 21–35. Larchmont, NY: Eye on Education.

Riggs, N., M. Greenberg, C. Kusche, and M.A. Pentz. 2006. The mediation role of neuro-cognition in the behavioral outcomes of a social–emotional prevention program in elementary school students: Effects of the PATHS curriculum. *Prevention Science* 7, no. 1: 91–102.

Ross, Steven, Sheard, Mary, Slavin, Robert, Cheung, Alan, Elliott, Louise, Hanley, Pam, and Louise Tracey. (in preparation). *Evaluation of the together 4 all programme for schools*, Final Report.

Sainsbury Centre for Mental Health. 2009. *The chance of a lifetime: Preventing early conduct problems and reducing crime*. London: A Better Way.

Salmivalli, C., A. Kärnä, and E. Poskiparta. 2011. Counteracting bullying in Finland: The KiVa program and its effects on different forms of being bullied. *International Journal of Behavioral Development* 35, no. 5: 405–11. doi: 10.1177/0165025411407457.

Simkiss, D.E., A. Helen, H.A. Snooks, N. Stallard, S. Davies, M.A. Thomas, B. Anthony, S. Winstanley, L. Wilson, and S. Stewart-Brown. 2010. Measuring the impact and costs of a universal group based parenting programme: Protocol and implementation of a trial. *BMC Public Health* 10: 364.

Smith, P., and S. Sharp. 1994. *School bullying: Insights and perspectives*. London: Routledge.

Sutton, Carole, Utting, David, and David Farrington. 2004. *Support from the start: Working with young children and their families to reduce the risks of crime and antisocial behaviour*. Research Report 524. ISBN: 1 84478 203 4. London: Department for Education and Skills.

Terrion, J. 2006. Building social capital in vulnerable families: Success markers of a school-based intervention program. *Youth Society* 38, no. 2: 155–76.

Tickell, Clare. 2011. *The early years: Foundations for life, health and learning*. An Independent Report on the Early Years Foundation Stage to Her Majesty's Government.

UNICEF. 2007. Innocenti Report Card 7 Child Poverty in Perspective: An Overview of Child Well-being in Rich Countries.

Weare, Katherine, and Gay Gray. 2003. *What works in developing children's emotional and social competence and wellbeing?* (456). London: DfES Research Report.

Webster-Stratton, Carolyn, and Jamila Reid. 2010. The incredible years parents, teachers and children training series: A multifaceted treatment approach for young children with conduct problems. In *Evidence-based psychotherapies for children and adolescents*, 2nd ed., ed. J. Weisz and A. Kazdin, 194–210. New York, NY: Guilford.

Webster-Stratton, C., J. Reid, and M. Stoolmiller. 2008. Preventing conduct problems and improving school readiness: Evaluation of the incredible years teacher and child training programs in high-risk schools. *Journal of Child Psychology and Psychiatry* 49, no. 5: 471–88.

# Marking time: some methodological and historical perspectives on the 'crisis of childhood'

Kevin Myers

*School of Education University of Birmingham, Birmingham, UK*

> Historical amnesia besets the consensus that Britain faces an unprecedented 'crisis of childhood', and of child well-being. Drawing on evidence about changing uses of instruments and measures of well-being over time, this article explores and critiques claims about historical change and trends over time that are central to the imagined crisis of childhood in both diagnostic and therapeutic terms. It argues that diagnostic labels about the state of children's well-being arising from changing methodologies and measures, and the therapeutic and pedagogical models they create, cannot be isolated from social conditions. This means that claims about a crisis of childhood, and the kinds of interventions that follow, require critical debate and cautious application. In the current climate of crisis, however, such reflection and debate are notable only by their absence.

## Introduction

In recent comparative measurements of children's well-being, the UK has consistently performed poorly when compared to other nation states. In 2007, a United Nations Children's Fund (UNICEF) report ranked children's well-being in the UK as being the worst of 21 developed nations on measures such as health, poverty and the quality of family and peer relationships. In 2009, a similar European Union table of child well-being ranked the UK 24th out of 29 nation states and in May 2011 a report issued by the charity Save the Children placed the UK 23rd out of 43 developed countries (Bradshaw and Richardson 2009; Save the Children 2011). A follow-up UNICEF study in 2011 found British parents unable or unwilling to spend adequate time with their children and identified an excessive materialism as a causal factor in children's unhappiness (UNICEF 2011).

In domestic political and public discussion, these international comparisons have served to underpin a growing conviction that contemporary childhood is in a state of crisis. In her examination of media reporting of children's lives, the sociologist Mary Kehily identifies a common narrative organised around the claim that extensive social and cultural change over the last 50 years or so has left childhood despoiled (Kehily 2010). This article is an attempt to further explore and critique the claims about historical change, and trends over time, that are central to the imagined crisis of childhood in both diagnostic and therapeutic terms.

Diagnostically historical analysis is a crucial element of the claim that the experience of childhood has become more turbulent, anxious, isolated and, overall, less happy over the last five decades or so. In one of the most influential 'crisis of childhood' texts published over the last decade or so, Sue Palmer dated 'the past' to as recently as the mid-1980s. In that past time children grew up surrounded by 'old certainties' and were allowed to develop through a 'time-consuming and old-fashioned process of nurturing that small, highly intelligent primates have needed through the ages' (Palmer 2006, 1–21). In stark contrast, Palmer presents the past two decades as marking a fundamental rupture in the experience of post-1945 childhoods. Technological and social changes have transformed family structures and working patterns; relationships are more fluid and marriage, specifically, is both less common and less stable; the world is experienced in a qualitatively different manner, one which is both faster than in the past and which allows 'less and less contact with children's own cultural past'. Moreover, Palmer is far from alone in this analysis. A much wider body of policy and academic literature echoes these themes which are now widely promoted and supported (Layard and Dunn 2009).

Popular discussions of the crisis of childhood echo political and policy debates and prominently feature parental anxieties in which the past is recalled as a simpler, more certain and somehow easier time (Nelson 2010). This discussion often takes place in the most general of terms and is couched around what is presented as a paradox; that greater wealth has not led to greater happiness. Instead, according to depictions of this paradox excessive competition, selfishness and materialism have led to increased isolation, the devaluation of human relationships and the loss of those skills that enabled those relationships to flourish (Offer 2006; UNICEF 2011; Wilkinson and Pickett 2009).

Therapeutically, one prominent and highly influential response has been to argue that there now exist scientific tools to modify (or intervene) in the crisis of childhood. The new and interdisciplinary 'science of happiness', for example, which claims to draws its insights from a novel synthesis of psychology, neuroscience, sociology, economics and philosophy, seeks to identify, categorise and measure the component parts of happiness (see Ecclestone, Pett, and Cigman (this volume) for discussion). From this research, the notion that we can prevent future problems with mental health and emotional well-being has led to a range of therapeutic interventions that can, it is claimed, be applied across children's journey to adulthood both at home and in their experiences of public education, health and social care. Instructions for, and applications of, well-being can be found in the literature relating to parenting, foster care, formal and informal education, mental health and various counselling and therapeutic techniques and the care system (Gureasko-Moore, DuPaul, and White 2006; Maxwell et al. 2008; National Institute for Health and Clinical Evidence 2006).

However, both therapeutically and diagnostically there is room for some scepticism around the central themes of the crisis discourse. Therapeutically, much of the literature on novel pedagogical approaches, whether it is the application of brain gym, the widespread development of circle time and the emergence of cognitive behavioural therapy in schools or whole-school programmes for developing resilience and well-being, presents a story of strong claims by advocates, small samples, inadequate peer review and uncertainty about outcomes (see Ecclestone et al. 2010). Nevertheless, counter-arguments of robust evidence for effectiveness of particular interventions are also strongly presented (see Bywater and Sharples; Elias et al., this volume). Diagnostically, there certainly exists persuasive evidence to demonstrate that the extensive socio-economic changes of the last 50 years or so have significantly altered the experiences of children and young people as they grow up. However, and as Furlong and Cartmel have argued, such changes do not necessarily 'represent an epochal shift' (Furlong and Cartmel 2007, 2). Moreover, claims that there has been a profound rupture in the experience of growing up, and one that causes unprecedented levels of misery are often based on questionable historical thinking, on data that is subject to variable interpretation and on a silencing of the difficulties that are intrinsic to social scientific accounts of change over time, especially when some of the variables being measured are conceptually problematic and historically novel.

In order to illustrate these difficulties, this article investigates the quality of the evidence for, and the problems of, tracking children's decline in mental health over the past four decades. In particular, it explores the claim that psychosocial disorders have become more prevalent in young people as the result of social and economic change. Psychosocial disorders are defined here as mental illness caused or influenced by life experiences, and maladjusted cognitive and behavioural processes. These disorders include depression, eating disorders and suicidal behaviours (Rutter and Smith 1995). The argument is presented in three sections.

The first section, on history and nostalgia, notes the significance of time in social science analyses of change. It argues that whilst a sense of temporal dislocation has been a characteristic feature of social science analysis for two centuries or more, anxieties about loss and change have been heightened by methodological changes in the post-war period which, unwittingly, have identified the child as a particular object for nostalgia. This may help explain the proliferation of social science accounts of childhood in crisis.

The second section, measuring decline, considers more closely the quality of the empirical evidence in one component part of the childhood in crisis discourse. In particular, it reviews attempts to define and measure psychosocial disorders in children and young people. In doing so, it makes concrete some of the complexities of measuring change over time. The third section, on contexts and contests, argues that any discussion of children's contemporary mental health needs to be set firmly in a historical perspective that relates the discovery and application of scientific findings to wider social change. It argues that any adequate explanation of the apparently increasing numbers of children and young people with psychosocial disorders requires a richer understanding of professional change and of the politics of scientific method than is apparent in the current 'crisis of childhood'.

## On history and nostalgia

A central concern for all modern social science has been the experience of social change. Ever since the French Revolution of 1789, and particularly the arguably decisive decade of the 1830s across industrialising European nations, social scientists have been concerned to catalogue, to understand and to administer the problems caused by social change. In seeking to understand political economic and social upheavals, temporality and the relationships between past and present, have been a central part of the social scientific genre and an important object of enquiry. This is easy enough to register in a vocabulary underpinned by temporality, by 'transitions', 'developments' and 'contrasts', and by the social scientific tendency to proclaim the existence of 'new times' and 'new kinds' of societies.

Some of the most influential social theory of recent times follows this tendency. Ulrich Beck's *Risk Society* (1992) is typical in its declaration of a break with modernity, a transformation of the foundations of change and an end to the experience of historical continuity (Beck 1998, edn: 9–10, 14, 92; see also, e.g. Giddens 1990). In this thesis, the order and predictability imposed by the institutions of modernism, by the nation state, the nuclear family, local communities and the hierarchies of class, gender and race that operated in them are shaken to their foundations by the aggressive expansion of corporate capitalism that imposes both new opportunities and new risks. Beck's is arguably only the most influential of a whole range of recent work that has identified some kind of decisive change and the ushering in of a new historical epoch. For Giddens, for example, this is the new age of 'high modernity' or, for Sennett the new capitalism brings with a new regime of time that corrodes character (Giddens 1990; Sennett 1998, 138). This manner of thinking proved influential not just in academia but also in the media, with think tanks, policy-makers and a general public for whom the sense of a new historical time held powerful appeal.

This grand sociological idiom, with historical developments and change as an explanatory device, has a long history of course. Marx, Durkheim and Weber, the destruction of tradition and the birth of new kinds of societies were also central concerns and a melancholy sense of dislocation, and of nostalgia for old traditions and solidarities, is not difficult to identify. In fact, anxieties around the losses imposed in periods of rapid social change have been a characteristic feature of social science analysis for at least two centuries.

If this is an unremarkable observation, Mike Savage's recent work suggests something more interesting and novel central to arguments in this article. Savage has argued that that the epochal arguments now so characteristic of the social sciences received decisive support from a methodological turn to interviewing in the expansion of the social sciences after 1945 period (Savage 2010).

One of the features of the growth of post-war social science was the adoption of interviews with individuals. In important studies of housing, town planning, immigration, education and a range of other topics interviewing subjects became central to the research practices of social scientists (Savage 2010, 180–7; Wilmott and Young 1957). If this was a commendable attempt to better understand marginalised communities, it also meant that individuals became important sources, and often the dominant source, for the identification and explanation of social change. Savage's argument is that in these shifts change became internal to the source itself, and immanent to the data. It may not be incidental that popular histories of this period, constructed partly from this material, have struggled to avoid the accusation of a romantic rescue of ordinary people assailed by the battle between the old and new and, as David Kynaston puts it, 'glancing anxiously over the shoulder at a disappearing past'. (Kynaston 2010, 14, 697). When individuals, who are inextricably embedded in the process of social change, become dominant sources for the existence and meaning of those changes, it is not surprising that epochal arguments became increasingly prevalent.

This tendency to narrate change was arguably compounded in the development of large-scale social surveys and of cohort studies in which repeat interviews were conducted with selected individuals over time. Whatever the precise form of these interviews, as closed questionnaires, semi-structured interviews or open-ended discussions, they all sought to identify and explain changes in attitudes, behaviours or experiences over time. In other words, and more or less explicitly, cohort studies were concerned with measuring the experience and perception of change through the life course, from the promise of childhood to the realities and perhaps, the inevitable disillusions, of adult living. They were, argues Savage, profoundly important in focusing attention on the developmental capacity of the individual, measured and tested through time, but also isolated from their immediate context (Savage 2010, chap. 8).

Cohort studies could thus hardly avoid capturing some of the ambitions for, and investment in, children that were integral to the post-war political settlement. They were the instrument through which the promises embodied in the film Children's Charter, of more equal life chances, of a meritocracy in which all talents would be recognised and all potential harnessed, of cradle to grave state provision, were to be measured (Cunningham 2000; Savage 2010). Cohort studies at once reflected both a romantic ideal of childhood, as a privileged state, deserving of special care and protection, and a more utilitarian idea that children were human becomings, the object of State investment in order to ensure economically productive adults and wider social stability (Hendrick 1997). As the birth rate declined, as average family size became smaller, and as the rhetoric of opportunity in the affluent society became more widespread, more was invested in the figure of the child, politically, materially and emotionally (Stearns 2010).

Seen in this light it can be argued that the emergence of interviewing and of cohort studies as key methodologies for measuring social change, and their repeated interviewing with sample populations, underlined the individualism, and perhaps the melancholy, of the 'psychological society' (Smith 1997, chap. 16; Thomson 2006). A cohort was moment of possibilities, invested with the progressive hopes of post-war Britain's New Jerusalem but, as structural factors bear down on the life course, nostalgia for that child, and the hopes invested in it, became increasingly apparent. If this argument sounds plausible it also remains somewhat speculative and it requires a more concrete example.


**Measuring decline**

In their 2009 report for the Children's Society entitled *A Good Childhood*, economist Richard Layard and psychiatrist Judy Dunn reviewed an impressive range of empirical evidence of children's experiences of growing up in contemporary society. It is entirely typical that claims about the unprecedented challenges facing children feature prominently in the preface and then are set out in the first chapter entitled 'Is there a problem?' The chapter begins by noting that children in Britain are materially better-off, more educated and less physically sick than ever before. However, it also notes widespread unease about the commercial pressures, violence, stresses and emotional distress that children can experience. Layard and Dunn say clearly that 'some of this unease is exaggerated and reflects unwarranted angst about the greater freedom that children now enjoy'. Yet they also say that there is 'genuine fear' and that 'survey evidence supports these fears' (Layard and Dunn 2009, 1–2).

The first evidence cited concerns children's emotional health and was used to support the claim that 'more young people are anxious and troubled'. The sources for this claim, and its elaboration in the observation that an 'increasing proportion of 15–16 year olds experiencing significant emotional difficulties', are an Office for National Statistics study based on child psychiatric morbidity data (Green et al. 2005) and another, much cited paper by Collishaw et al. (2004) entitled 'Time trends in adolescent mental health'. Whilst the former study was concerned with a short and recent time period, the latter is of particular interest here because it attempted to measure whether conduct, hyperactive and emotional problems have become more common in children over a 25-year period. Widely cited in epidemiological, psychological, psychiatric, educational and sociological literature, Collishaw et al. have been treated as providing authoritative evidence for the increasing prevalence of psychosocial disorders. It therefore provides an important opportunity for assessing the quality of historical thinking that has typically underpinned the current debates around the crisis of childhood.

Published in the respected *Journal* of *Child Psychology and Psychiatry*, 'Time trends in adolescent mental health' is a serious piece of scholarship that carefully sets out the context for the paper, describes in detail the research methods used, tabulates the results and includes a discussion that sets out clearly, albeit briefly, the strengths and limitations of the research. The tone of the paper is circumspect. In fact, Collishaw et al. begin by referring, not to the fact, but to the 'commonly held belief' that 'young people are more badly behaved and more troubled by emotional difficulties than those in the past' (Collishaw et al. 2004, 1327). Their comparisons of parental questionnaires from surveys of the general population in 1974, 1986 and 1999, led to the conclusion that there were marked increases in aggressive behaviours over the whole period for all family types and across all social categories, and that there were also marked increases in emotional problems and hyperactive problems for both boys and girls in the period 1986–1999. Nonetheless, they stress these findings are tentative and they admit frankly that 'methodological limitations make it difficult to provide conclusive answers' (Collishaw et al. 2004, 1327).

However, and because of the alarmist tone of public debate, those limitations and their consequences for assessing the experiences of young people over time are very rarely discussed or articulated in non-technical language. In response to this overlooked problem, part of the purpose of this article is to provide just that kind of discussion.

One important methodological limitation on measurements of children's well-being across time concerns the use of questionnaires for gathering data on conduct, hyperactive and emotional problems. Collishaw et al. (2004) utilise data from two cohort studies, the national child development study (NCDS) that began in 1958 and the 1970 British cohort study (BCS70), and the 1999 British Child and Adolescent Mental Health Survey based largely on questionnaires. Parents in both the 1958 and 1970 cohort studies answered questions taken from the Rutter A Scale and Collishaw et al. used data taken from the 16-year follow-up studies (1974 for the NCDS and 1986 for BCS70).

The Rutter scales have become influential in international social and health research. They were partly behind the descriptive and categorical changes both to the International Classification of Disease published by the World Health Organisation and to the Diagnostic and Statistical Manual published by the American Psychiatric Association (Rutter 1989). The scales were originally devised for a comprehensive, and now famous, study of *Education, Health and Behaviour* conducted in the Isle of Wight in 1964–1965. Aiming to 'give a comprehensive picture of "handicap" in a total population who lived in a defined geographical location and who were in the middle years of schooling' Rutter and the research team distributed questionnaires to all teachers and parents (Rutter, Tizard, and Whitmore, 1970, 3). These questionnaires, and the diagnostic interviews that followed for those parents that reported significant behavioural problems, or whose children were already in care, being seen at a Child Guidance Clinic or had been before the Courts. The same methodologies, and similar questions, were used in the 1970 BCS70. In turn, BCS70 provides much of the baseline data used to inform claims about the prevalence of psychosocial disorders in young children. Its methods are, therefore, of foundational significance for current debates around children's well-being and it is worth exploring them further.

Rutter's parental questionnaire had three sections. The first asked parents to identify which of six minor health problems their child had suffered from over the course of the last year. Included in this category were not only those that might still unequivocally be considered health problems, headaches and vomiting, for example, but also those indeterminate behaviours that were to become grouped as symptoms of disorder (bed-wetting, biliousness and soiling, tears on arrival at or truanting from school). A second section asked about habits and incidence of speech, stealing (with some options designed to elucidate the location, objects and number of thieves), eating and sleeping. A third, and final section, listed 18 descriptions of the child's behaviour and asked the parents to indicate whether the description 'certainly applied', 'somewhat applied' or 'did not apply'. Similar, though not identical, questions appeared in the follow-up studies. A similar questionnaire was provided to teachers who were asked to decide whether 26 behavioural descriptions 'did not apply', 'applied somewhat' or 'definitely applied' to each individual child in their class (Rutter, Tizard, and Whitmore, 1970, 151, 152, 412–418).

Once this screening had identified possible children with what were then termed 'handicap', standardised interviews with the identified children and their parents, but actually almost always just mothers, took place. Interviews with mothers, and what they were taken to reveal about both the particular child and family attitudes and relationships more generally, had long been a key part of the diagnostic process in child psychiatry. Yet, and as Rutter and Graham noted, interviews with children had received little methodological investigation in the period up to the late 1960s. Whilst interviews with children, and observations of their play had been common in the psychoanalytical attempt to discover unconscious attitudes and internal conflicts, they had rarely been used to establish the presence and type of disorder. Standardised but informal interviews of around 30 min, conducted by 'registrars with at least six months experience', therefore constituted something of a methodological departure (Rutter, Tizard, and Whitmore 1970, 153, 154, 168–170).

Rutter's own evaluation regarded the child interviews as 'a reasonably sensitive diagnostic interview' but he noted frankly that it was markedly better at achieving an overall psychiatric diagnosis that conformed with other sources of data, than at identifying specific behaviours that contributed to a specific disorder (Rutter, Tizard, and Whitmore 1970, 169). This may not be surprising given that some of these items were highly specific (e.g. smiling) or highly subjective, or to use Rutter's term, inferential (emotional responsiveness and relationship with examiner). It is also worth noting, as Rutter did, that the interviews were particularly poor when assessed for their ability to identify particular affective items that were taken as a sign of disorder. Psychiatrists had difficulty establishing the extent to which certain signs of abnormal emotionality, anxiety and depression for example, but particularly 'tremulousness', 'tearfulness', 'apprehension' and 'anxious expression' were significant indicators of disorder for individual children (Rutter, Tizard, and Whitmore 1970).

The efficacy of these research methodologies has, of course, been the subject of extended debates, both in education and in health research. This literature makes clear that, even when questions remain largely stable over time, subtle changes in the wording or ordering of questions can have dramatic impacts on findings (For one account, see Drew, Raymond, and Weinberg 2006). Moreover, there have been changes to the administration of the questionnaires and the interviews. The range of actors employed in completing the questionnaires and the interviews includes various officials from health and educational agencies (health visitors, teachers and so on) and parents. It is not necessary to enter some of the more philosophical debates around whether there exists a neutral medical language to accept that the eliciting of this kind of information through verbal exchange is highly sensitive to context (Epstein 1992; Greenhalgh and Hurwitz 1998). Changes in wordings, or associations, or the collection of data has the potential to affect results. Moreover, and arguably more significantly, the meaning of behaviour for individuals changes through time. Not only have there been changes in the social acceptability of various behaviours but the ways in which emotions and feelings are recognised and discussed have undergone significant shifts in the post-1945 period.

The data that chart the apparent increase in psychosocial disorders may simply reflect the rise of what some sociologists call the therapy society (De Swann 1990; Wright 2011). The increasing willingness to openly discuss emotions and feelings, the tendency to cast behaviours in psychological frames of reference and the increasing availability of a psychological discourse to understand the self may be important causal factors in changing responses to questionnaire and interview questions. The fact that the meaning and understanding of behaviour changes over time is especially important with the category of psychosocial disorder because definitions of child mental illness have been subject to radical revision over at least the past 50 years. Indeed, the first, 1952, edition of the hugely influential Diagnostic and Statistical Manual, the classificatory system of mental disorders published by the American Psychiatric Association, listed only one diagnosis, the Adjustment Reaction of Childhood/Adolescence, that applied specifically to young people (APA 1952) The second edition, published in 1968, included a very significant category now defined much more by behaviour and less by biology. The 'characteristic manifestations' of Behaviour Disorders of Childhood–Adolescence, included 'such symptoms as overactivity, inattentiveness, shyness, feeling of rejection, over-aggressiveness, timidity and delinquency' (APA 1952, 50, 51). Seven specific disorders were grouped under this category; hyperkinetic reaction, withdrawing reaction, overanxious reaction, runaway reaction, unsocialised aggressive reaction, group delinquent reaction and other reaction of childhood.

By the time of the publication of the Diagnostic and Satistical Manual (DSM) IV in 1994, seven times longer than DSM II, the category 'Disorders usually first diagnosed in infancy, childhood or adolescence' had 10 sub-categories which included 'mental retardation' and nine other kinds of disorders some of which are described as learning, motor skills, feeding and eating, tic, elimination and pervasive developmental disorders (including Autism and Asperger's). A new sub-category, attention-deficit and disruptive behaviour disorders, now set out the psychosocial disorders that are the focus for attention in this article. The category was further subdivided into attention deficit hyperactivity disorder, oppositional defiant disorder and conduct disorder. Along with the exponential expansion of these disorders went a parallel rise in the numbers diagnosed children. Estimates of the prevalence of clinically significant psychiatric disorders in the late 1960s and early 1970s were around 5–7%. Conservative contemporary estimates put the figure at around 10% but some are as high as 20% (Meltzer et al. 2000).

Diagnostic revisions over time do not invalidate the attempt to ask or answer questions about trends in young people's health and behaviour over time, but they do make measuring time trends problematic. It is an elementary methodological point, but one worth repeating, that without a consistent definition of psychosocial disorders it is difficult to be certain that the same phenomenon is being measured over time. Claims around increases in psychosocial disorders in young people have to wrestle with the fact that psychological constructs lack consistent definition and, at the very least, this makes them difficult to measure.

Such difficulties make it particularly important to think critically about the measurement of time trends in the human sciences. Yet this is a topic that seems somewhat underexamined in research design and methods literature where time is sometimes ignored, often simplistically referred to in terms of period effects, or, at best, presented as an important but complex challenge to researchers (Bechhofer and Patterson 2000). Mike Savage's recent work offers an important supplement to this literature by noting the shift towards the use of survey data to measure time trends (Savage 2008, 2010). Even if a small but significant literature on secondary data analysis, noticeably stronger for quantitative rather than qualitative research, has accompanied this shift, few of these complexities seem to have informed claims around the crisis of childhood. Of course, survey data are not responsible for the development of moral panics around children's mental health in the early twenty-first century. Nevertheless, divorced from any adequate discussion or understanding of what social scientists call age, period and cohort effects, it has certainly aided the development of persistent moral panics around children's mental health.

## Children's mental health and illness: contexts and contests

The Rutter scales, and the attempt to establish a 'clinical-diagnostic' approach to child psychology and psychiatry, belong to a particular moment in history (Rutter, Tizard, and Whitmore 1970, 176). It was arguably a late flourishing of that North American and European phenomenon, 'new psychology', which studied psychological problems of deviance, illness and adjustment under the term mental hygiene. By the interwar period the hygiene movement had begun to break down the categorical distinction between the pathological and the normal, between mental illness and mental health and replaced it with something like a continuum on which all individuals could be positioned (Stewart 2011; van Drenth and Myers 2011). In some respects at least, particularly in relation to attempts to counter the pathologisation of individuals' mental ill-health, these are the antecedents of the contemporary positive psychology (see Ecclestone, Cigman this volume).

It is significant that it was through the establishment of child guidance clinics that mental hygiene became significant in England (Stewart 2011). Their multidisciplinary teams, consisting of psychiatrists, psychologists and psychiatric social workers, became integrated into the National Health Service after 1948 and, especially where children were concerned, led to a willingness to accept social experiences

EMOTIONAL WELL-BEING IN EDUCATIONAL POLICY AND PRACTICE

and conditions as significant and causal, but also preventable, for at least some apparently medical conditions. In fact, this kind of generalist approach, that mixed medical expertise with a concern for social circumstances, became an important disciplinary claim for psychiatrists around Europe in the post-1945 period (Gijswijt-Hofstra and Porter 1998) and they help explain the adoption of a multi-axial system of classification for mental disorders in the 1970s (Rutter 1969).

Rutter's studies were a late but still component and influential part of these trends. With only 'some exceptions', he argued, 'disorders of emotions and behaviour in childhood do not constitute "diseases" or "illnesses" which are *qualitatively* different from the normal' (Rutter, Tizard, and Whitmore 1970, 148). Instead, disorders were judged to be present only when there was a prolonged abnormality of behaviour, emotions or relationships which caused prolonged impediment to the child's daily life or distress and disturbance to family and/or community life. As has already been shown, this broad definition was accompanied by an emphasis on empirical research, an attempt to understand children's problems holistically and a concern for scientific validity that articulated itself in the championing of controlled conditions, longitudinal studies and randomised control trials (Graham, Minnis, and Nicolson 2009). In fact, Rutter's positive evaluation of his Isle of Wight epidemiological study helped to promote the scientific rigour of child and adolescent psychiatry. It lay behind the foundation of a new and specialist department of child and adolescent psychiatry, the publication of a landmark textbook and the research methods it championed directly informed the revisions to the International Classification of Diseases and the adoption of a multi-axial classification system. It is also no exaggeration to say that the study, and its use of questionnaires and interviews and its specific championing of longitudinal study, influenced the design and collation of health and social research for a generation (Graham, Minnis, and Nicolson 2009).

It is possible, and tempting, to read these developments as a story of inevitable progress in which child science was freed from its Freudian origins and psychoanalytical speculation slowly gave way to a more clinical and robust science. However, historians of medicine have long warned of the twin dangers of teleology, of anticipating the present in viewing the past, and triumphalism, of celebrating scientific heroes and discarding those who seemed to have got things wrong (Smith 1997). It therefore comes as no surprise to read one recent review of the historical categorisation of behaviour disorders arguing that there was a lack of 'any clear empirical support' for changing diagnostic criteria and telling a story of tiny samples and a limited evidence base that was nonetheless promoted by an influential network of medics (Mallett 2006). The shift towards empirical methods and descriptive diagnosis has elsewhere been evaluated as successful in 'identifying and exploring certain psychosocial disorders' (van Ginneken 2004, 240) but its wider significance is rarely noted in contemporary literature, whether it refers to research design, methods or as a background to contemporary claims about children's behaviour. Yet, this methodological change was important.

Although Rutter's studies may have continued in an older tradition of trying to infer illness from observed behaviour because he continued to give children tasks to perform, there was also increasing attention to children and their parents as sources of key diagnostic information. Eliciting this information was a topic that attracted considerable methodological attention in order that it could be regarded as credible and as scientifically robust. But, and as Smith has written, in the search for scientific legitimacy experimental social psychology translated 'human relations into behavioural variables' that both simplified social relations and created a new kind of social relationship; the person in a laboratory' (Smith 1997, 769). If children and their parents in Rutter's studies were not in a physical laboratory, they did become new kind of partners in the diagnostic process. This required them to answer a series of questions or scales that recorded specific kinds of behaviour and feelings over time but also removed those feelings and behaviours from the specific contexts, or the 'social worlds' of children, that gave them meaning. Such approaches were increasingly a topic of interest, and a source of sustained difficulty, for some critical and post-structural psychologists (Henriques et al. 1984; Richards and Light 1986).

Indeed, and despite the promises inherent in the compound *psychosocial* disorders, the social and its concern for context and meaning remained a notably shallow category. An important and substantive study of psychosocial disorders of 1995, coedited by Michael Rutter and presented as interdisciplinary, included no sociologists or critical psychologists, brushed aside arguments that some psychosocial disorders may be functional (or rational responses) for individuals or groups in specific social locations, and entirely ignored the possibility that changes in research methodologies may partly explain changing diagnoses of disorder (Rutter and Smith 1995, 1–23). Yet, by the post-war period an increasingly popularised psychology had already begun to change the way in which parents and children thought about themselves and their relationships. In advice books and manuals, on radio and television, (male) experts, Bowlby and Spock who were usually very far from the practical and mundane tasks of child-rearing, explicitly addressed women in a psychological language. A language of self was also central to the cultural revolution of the 1960s as psychological discourse and its constructs were employed to identify and explain emotions, behaviour and identity.

Thus, when children and parents answered questionnaires or even spoke to interviewers they did not give neutral answers but spoke through a language sponsored by professionals and whose foundational assumption was that mental health was a fragile state. In turn, that assumption may have encouraged parents to frame children's mundane difficulties in professional terms and subject them to professional help and intervention (De Swann 1990). That an increasingly significant element of this intervention has been pharmaceutical and reliant on powerful medications have increased fears, and promoted fierce debate, about the exploitation of parents by exploitative drug companies who have promoted disease and disorder in the pursuit of profit (Bailly 2005).

The rising numbers of children and young people suffering from psychosocial disorders is a matter to take seriously. It is also a matter in which the contested definition of those disorders and the contexts in which they emerged, should not be forgotten. Even the possibility that rising rates of psychosocial disorder may simply be an artefact of changing research methodologies should act as a caution for those who wish to portray a previous time as a different world in which parents were more confident and children much happier. Nostalgia is seductive but it is not a substitute for serious historical thought.

## Conclusions

This article has explored some of the methodological difficulties of measuring change over time, and the possibility that children's widely reported contemporary unhappiness may, in part at least, be an artefact of wider changes over the last five decades or so. This does not mean that empirical research is inherently flawed or that progress, in terms of an increase in factual knowledge and understanding about children's behaviour and learning, has not already happened or is not possible. It does suggest, however, that in relation to claims about the state of children's emotional well-being, such knowledge cannot be divorced from an understanding of wider social change. New aims and methods of governance, new models of childhood, changing research methodologies, novel structures of feeling and emotion, the increasing power of medicine and of pharmaceutical treatments have all impacted in complex ways to produce a generation of children at risk.

However, this complexity, this richer sense of social change, is absent in contemporary political and policy debate. Instead, in those arenas, ideas about epochal change and long-term decline reign. They are linked to critiques of excessive materialism and to a kind of psychological narcissism that is said to have irrevocably damaged young people. In political and public debates apparently scientific diagnoses of declining standards of children's well-being appear to be both more neutral and, in so far as they present themselves as universal, as a critique of social change rather than specific groups in society. But this appearance of neutrality is an illusion. The human sciences are categorically different to the natural sciences and the diagnostic labels they develop and the therapeutic and pedagogical models they create cannot be isolated from social conditions. Since this is the case, claims about the crisis of childhood, and the kinds of interventions that follow from it, at least require critical debate and cautious application. In the current climate of crisis, however, such reflection and debate is notable only by its absence.

Instead, apparently expert knowledge seems to dominate relationships between adults and children. Identified simultaneously as vulnerable and dangerous, as objects of pity and fear, the child is on a potentially perilous journey to adulthood. It is this kind of knowledge, of a vulnerable object accumulating risk, buffered by forces outside its control and susceptible to lasting emotional damage, that precedes and colours contemporary, attitudes to childhood. The idea that childhood is a special phase of life, and that specific events or processes are causal and predictive for later outcomes, is linked to a dominant notion of children's staged development, happening 'upwards' in a process of linear accumulation. In this model, which has been dominant in both sociology and psychology, time operates solely in a chronological fashion and specific early childhood experiences are said to determine later outcomes for the adult. Persuasive though these arguments may be, they have not been strong enough to dispense with more psychoanalytical views of development in which relationships between past and present, and change over time, is more complex, and arguably more realistic, than one of simple determination. As Cathy Urwin argued some time ago, 'the psychic implications of environmental contingencies cannot be read off directly, nor can they be entirely predicted' (Urwin 1986, 258).

Reviewing two centuries of Enlightenment child science Historian Adriana Benzaquen came to a similar conclusion. 'While we think the knowledge we bring to our encounter with the child eases our access to him or her' she writes, it actually often served to 'cloud our perception' (Benzaquen 2006, 269). Social science certainly has the potential to illuminate the condition of childhood but requires a more critical and reflexive debate, and one informed by a sophisticated sense of social change and a deeper understanding of children's agency, than is evident in the current debate around the crisis of childhood.

## References

American Psychiatric Association. 1952. *Diagnostic and statistical manual of mental disorders*. Washington, DC: APA.

Bailly, L. 2005. Stimulant medication for the treatment of attention-deficit hyperactivity disorder: evidence-b(i)ased practice? *Psychiatric Bulletin* 29: 284–7.

Bechhofer, Frank, and Lindsay Patterson. 2000. *Principles of research design in the social sciences*. London: Routledge.

Beck, U. 1992/98. *Risk society: Towards a new modernity*. London: Sage.

Benzaquen, Adriana. 2006. *Encounters with wild children: Temptation and disappointment in the study of human nature*. Montreal: McGill University Press.

Bradshaw, J., and D. Richardson. 2009. An index of child well-being in Europe. *Child Indicators Research* 2, no. 33: 319–51.

Collishaw, S., B. Maughan, R. Goodman, and A. Pickles. 2004. Time trends in adolescent mental health. *J Child Psychology and Psychiatry* 45, no. 8: 1350–62.

Cunningham, P. 2000. Moving images: Propaganda film and British education, 1940–1945. *Paedagogica Historica* 36, no. 1: 389–406.

De Swann, Abram. 1990. *The management of normality*. London: Routledge.

Drew, Pual, Geoffrey Raymond, and Darin Weinberg. 2006. *Talk and interaction in social research methods*. London: Sage.

Ecclestone, Kathryn, Beverley Clack, Dennis Hayes, and Vanessa Pupavac. 2010. Changing the subject?: Interdisciplinary perspectives on emotional well-being and social justice. End of Award Report for Economic and Social Research Council funded seminar series RES-451-26-054 , in University of Birmingham.

Epstein, J. 1992. Historiography, diagnosis and poetics. *Literature and Medicine* 11, no. 1: 23–44.

Furlong, Andy, and Fred Cartmel. 2007. *Young people and social change: New perspectives*. Maidenhead: Open Univesity Press.

Giddens, Anthony. 1990. *The consequences of modernity*. Cambridge: Polity.

Gijswijt-Hofstra, Marijke, and Roy Porter, eds. 1998. *Cultures of psychiatry and mental health care in postwar Britain and the Netherlands*. Amsterdam: Wellcome.

Graham, Phillip, Helen Minnis, H and Malcolm Nicolson, eds. 2009. The development of child and adolescent psychiatry from 1960 until 1990. Witness seminar at the Centre for the History of Medicine, May 12, 2009, University of Glasgow. http://vambo.cent.gla.ac.uk/media/media_196525_en.pdf.

Green, H., et al. 2005. *Mental health of children and young people in Great Britain 2004*. London: Palgrave.

Greenhalgh, Trishs, and Brian Hurwitz, eds. 1998. *Narrative based medicine: Dialogue and discourse in clinical practice*. London: BMJ Books.

Gureasko-Moore, S., G.J. DuPaul, and G. White. 2006. The effects of self-management in general education classrooms on the organizational skills of adolescents with ADHD. *Behavior Modification* 30, no. 2: 159–83.

Hendrick, Harry. 1997. *Children, childhood and English society 1880–1990*. Cambridge: Cambridge University Press.

Henriques, Julian, Wendy Hollway, Cathy Urwin, Couze Venn, and Valerie Walkerdine. 1984. *Changing the subject: Psychology, social regulation and subjectivity*. London: Methuen.

Layard, Richard, and Judy Dunn. 2009. *A good childhood: Searching for values in a competitive age*. London: Penguin.

Kehily, M. 2010. Childhood in crisis? Tracing the contours of 'crisis' and its impact upon contemporary parenting practices. *Media, Culture and Society* 32, no. 2: 171–85.

Kynaston, David. 2010. *Family Britain, 1951–57*. London: Bloomsbury.

Mallett, C.A. 2006. Behaviorally-based disorders: The historical social construction of youths' most prevalent psychiatric diagnoses. *History of Psychiatry* 17, no. 4: 437–60.

Maxwell, C., P. Aggleton, I. Warwick, E. Yankah, V. Hill, and D. Mehmedbegovic. 2008. Supporting children's emotional wellbeing and mental health in England: A review. *Health Education* 108, no. 4: 272–86.

Meltzer, H., R. Gatward, R. Goodman, and T. Ford. 2000. *Mental health of children and adolescents in Great Britain*. London: HMSO.

National Institute for Health and Clinical Evidence (NICE). 2006. *Parent training/education programmes in the management of children with conduct disorders*. London: NICE.

Nelson, Margaret K. 2010. *Parenting out of control: Anxious parents in uncertain times*. New York, NY: New York University Press.

Offer, Avner. 2006. *The challenge of affluence: Self-control and well-being in the United States and Britain since 1950*. Oxford: Oxford University Press.

Palmer, Sue. 2006. *Toxic childhood: How the modern world is damaging our children and what we can do about it*. London: Orion.

Richards, Martin, and Paul Light, eds. 1986. *Children of social worlds: Development in a social context*. Cambridge: Polity.

Rutter, M. 1969. A tri-axial classification of mental disorders in childhood, an international study. *Journal of Child Psychology and Psychiatry* 36, no. 10: 41–61.

Rutter, M. 1989. Child psychiatric disorders in ICD-10. *Journal of Child Psychology and, Psychiatry* 19: 99–118.

Rutter, Michael, and David John Smith, eds. 1995. *Psychosocial disorders in young people: Time trends and their causes*. Chichester: Wiley.

Rutter, M., J. Tizard, and K. Whatmore. 1970. *Education, health and behaviour*. London: Longman.

Savage, M. 2008. Changing class identities in post-war Britain: Perspectives from mass-observation. *Sociological Research Online*, 12: 3, www.socresonline.org.uk/12/3/6.html.

Savage, M. 2010. *Identities and social change in Britain since 1940: The politics of method*. Oxford: Oxford University Press.

Save the Children. 2011. *State of the World's Mothers*. Westport, CT: Save the Children.

Sennett, Richard. 1998. *The corrosion of character: The personal consequences of work in the new capitalism*. London: Norton.

Smith, Roger. 1997. *The Norton history of the human sciences*. New York, NY: W.W. Norton and Co.

Stearns, Peter N. 2010. *Childhood in world history*. London: Routledge.

Stewart, J. 2011. The dangerous age of childhood: Child guidance and the 'normal child' in Britain, 1920–1950. *Paedagogica Historica: International Journal of the History of Education* 47, no. 6: 785–803.

Thomson, Mathew. 2006. *Psychological subjects: Identity, culture and health in twentieth-century Britain*. Oxford: Oxford University Press.

UNICEF. 2011. *Child well being in the UK, Spain and Sweden*. Florence: UNICEF.

Urwin, C. 1986. Developmental psychology and psychoanalysis: Splitting the difference. In *Children of social worlds: Development in a social context*, ed. M. Richards and P. Light, 257–86. Cambridge: Polity.

van Drenth, A., and K. Myers. 2011. Normalising childhood: policies and interventions concerning special children in the United States and Europe 1900–1960. *Paedagogica Historica: International Journal of the History of Education* 47, no. 6: 719–27.

van Ginneken, Japp. 2004. Social orientations. In *A social history of psychology*, ed. P. van Drunen and J. Jansz, 220–40. Oxford: Blackwell.

Wilkinson, R., and K. Pickett. 2009. *The spirit level: Why more equal societies almost always do better*. London: Allen Lane.

Wright, K. 2011. *The rise of the therapeutic society: Psychological knowledge and the contradictions of cultural change*. Washington, DC: New Academia.

# Developing social and emotional aspects of learning: the American experience

Maurice J. Elias and Dominic C. Moceri

*Department of Psychology, Rutgers University, Tillett Hall, Piscataway, NJ, USA*

> Developments in American policy, research and professional development to promote social and emotional learning in schools have drawn on work carried out by the Collaborative for Academic, Social, and Emotional Learning (CASEL), encouraged by the popular and political catalyst of Daniel Goleman's work on emotional intelligence. Based on CASEL's exploration and articulation of the implications of emotional intelligence for schools, this article defines 'social and emotional learning' as part of character development and draws on empirical studies of successful implementation to outline principles of effective intervention. In a context where, despite political rhetoric about a flourishing and progressive education system, a seemingly intractable achievement gap affects particular social and ethnic groups, the article evaluates key influences and ongoing barriers to successful realisation of the goals of social and emotional learning in American schools.

## Introduction

The publication of Goleman's (1995) worldwide best-selling book, emotional intelligence, was the catalyst that created the emergent field of social emotional learning (SEL). To be sure, scientists, educators, parents, employers and others were long aware of the importance of social, social-cognitive and emotional development for human functioning (Bar-On, Maree, and Elias 2007). Nevertheless, Goleman's book was a high-profile, popular catalyst which crystallised and unified many strands of research, theory and practice, including insights from neuroscience which highlighted the central role of emotion in all human functioning. Others have subsequently elaborated, both empirically and theoretically, the role that emotion plays in learning, and in education more generally (Lemerise and Arsenio 2000; Saarni 2007).

Goleman's work led to the creation of Collaborative for Academic, Social, and Emotional Learning (CASEL), then known as the Collaborative for the Advancement of Social and Emotional Learning, to more fully explore and articulate the implications of emotional intelligence for schools. Among the empirical pillars of Goleman's work on emotional intelligence were data from several school-based interventions designed to improve SEL that, in so doing, also generated improvements in positive behaviours, learning-to-learn behaviours, self-efficacy and academic performance, as

## EMOTIONAL WELL-BEING IN EDUCATIONAL POLICY AND PRACTICE

well as declines in problem behaviours such as aggression, withdrawal, anxiety and substance abuse (Goleman 1995).

**What is SEL?**

Perhaps it is worth taking a step backward to examine the definition of SEL. Goleman did not use the term, SEL; that was articulated in the founding of CASEL, and CASEL introduced the field of SEL in the book, *Promoting Social and Emotional Learning* (Elias et al. 1997). CASEL's thinking about SEL was built on a foundation of research from groups, such as the Consortium on the School-Based Promotion of Social Competence (Elias et al. 1996) and the Conduct Problems Prevention Research Group (2002) that predated the term emotional intelligence but clearly contributed to its articulation.

From this research, CASEL identified a core set of social and emotional skills that underlie performance on a wide range of life tasks (Elias et al. 1997). SEL was defined as the process of acquiring knowledge, skills, attitudes and beliefs to identify and manage emotions; to care about others; to make good decisions; to behave ethically and responsibly; to develop positive relationships and to avoid negative behaviours. SEL is connected to academic achievement, because it embodies skills necessary for succeeding in the classroom, in the life of the school, in the family, in the community, in the workplace and, indeed, in life in general.

These skill areas are now grouped into what is commonly known as 'the CASEL Five':

(1) *Self-awareness* – recognising one's emotions and values, and being able to realistically assess one's strengths and limitations.
(2) *Self-management* – being able to set and achieve goals, and handling one's own emotions so that they facilitate rather than interfere with relevant tasks.
(3) *Social awareness* – showing understanding and empathy for the perspective and feelings of others.
(4) *Relationship skills* – establishing and maintaining healthy relationships, working effectively in groups as both leader and team member, and dealing constructively with conflict.
(5) *Responsible decision-making and problem solving* – making ethical, constructive choices about personal and social behaviour.

Drawing from research in brain-behaviour relationships, social learning theory and developmental and prevention science, these skill areas are similar to the main dimensions of emotional intelligence identified by Bar-On (2007) and Salovey (2007) and to those adopted by major school-based competence promotion curriculum innovators (Elias and Arnold 2006).

However, SEL implies more than a set of skills; it implies a pedagogy for building those skills and an intervention structure to support the internalisation and generalisation of the skills over time and across contexts. Indeed, SEL implies that there is a developmental trajectory for these key skills and that how they are instructed by parents, educators, peers and other key influences in a child's life. The teaching of SEL is guided by two core insights: emotions affect how and what we learn, and relationships provide a foundation for all lasting learning (Elias et al. 1997; Saarni 2007).

It is worth noting, for the historical record, that CASEL's influence coincided with a fateful meeting held by the CASEL Leadership Team and a group of school superintendents from around the USA at the Fetzer Institute in Kalamazoo, Michigan. The topic of conversation was, 'If SEL is so important to learning and to academic success, why aren't schools embracing it more?' The answer was uniform and fascinating: schools are so focused on academic achievement that they cannot take time away for social and emotional factors. Unless CASEL's work is more centrally tied to academic achievement, it will not catch on widely.

The outcome of deliberations following this feedback was a change in CASEL's name, to the Collaborative for Academic, Social, and Emotional Learning. The acronym remained the same, but the name incorporated the academic link explicitly. And CASEL's fortunes, and the influence and penetration of SEL in the language of education, school psychology, school counselling, school social work, school-based research and prevention and related fields, has grown steadily.

As Dunkelblau (2009) has articulated, SEL has undergone a transition recently due to a functional accommodation with work undertaken in the tradition of character or moral education. Founded several years prior to CASEL, The Character Education Partnership (CEP; www.character.org) has operationalised its 11 principles of character into a rubric used to designate winners of its National School of Character (NSOC) award. It is worth noting that the field of character education preceded the founding of CEP, just as the SEL field predated the founding of CASEL. The reason these two traditions did not intersect sooner reflected two major trends in the early years of character education: (1) tendency to not systematically evaluate interventions and (2) the use of pedagogical strategies nor reflective of a social-learning/cognitive-behavioural approach (Elias et al. 2007).

However, the NSOC concept underlines an important emphasis of CEP that has found its way into SEL practice: the context in which skills are developed matters a great deal. CEP defines 'character' in terms of two major dimensions, moral character, which is knowing the morally proper action to take and performance character, which is having the skills and dispositions to enact one's moral character (CEP 2010). An NSOC winner has a school culture that emphasises and has structures to create the best from staff and teachers in both dimensions.

Performance character, of course, bears many similarities to SEL, and CEP recommendations for performance character draw from SEL-related research. Historically, movements for character and moral education have emphasised 'knowing the good', often with the implicit assumption that actions should follow this knowledge, or at least that a great deal of effort would not be needed to create that congruence (Dunkelblau 2009). However, evaluations of programmes and advances in research and theory, particularly about emotional and social development, have made it clear that the road from intention to action is complex and that an array of skills are needed to navigate the road toward successful interventions successfully (Berkowitz and Bier 2006).

Similarly, SEL proponents have come to realise that in a school culture characterised by negative interpersonal relationships, low expectation of students, no clear sense of shared positive purpose and few mechanisms for the development of supportive communities among educator or students. SEL skills may not be employed well or, worse, may be employed for questionable ends. Therefore, greater attention has been paid to the integration of social, emotional and character development and the need to organise school programming and structures to address core values/essential life habits and the skills needed to enact those habits (Elias 2009; Lickona and David-son 2007). One tool used by some schools to define core values is the concept of 'touchstones' (Elbot and Fulton 2008). Touchstones are developed over a time through a collaborative and inclusive whole school process and lead to one or more 'we' statements that embody the focal direction of the school and then are accompanied by a more elaborated 'mission statement' and code of conduct. Examples of touchstones include 'We pursue excellence in scholarship and character' and 'We are a learning place, where dreams are born, caring is shown, and leaders are made'.

## The conceptual link between SEL and school and life success

Based on existing empirical evidence, Zins et al. (2004) provide a general model of how evidence-based SEL programming operates to have a positive long-term effect on success in school and life. Their choice of the latter as the main dependent variable is important, because they realised that success in school alone is not the end product; indeed, as school success has become defined narrowly, in terms of academic test score performance, there is considerable reason to not equate school success with life success unconditionally.

Zins et al. (2004) note that high-quality programmes must be embedded within safe, caring, well-managed and cooperative classroom environments, as well as wider settings that provide equitable opportunities for positive participation and recognition. These programmes must explicitly teach the CASEL five set of social–emotional skills systematically and developmentally. From this set of factors, students come to feel significant engagement, attachment and commitment to their schools, feel empowered to enact their skill set. As a result, skills are built in ongoing ways within caring contexts to which students feel strong connections and which afford pathways for success. This creates more disincentive for engaging in dysfunctional behaviour than might otherwise be the case, and increases the likelihood of positive distal outcomes, such as success in school and life.

At a more detailed level, it makes sense that students who increase their social–emotional competencies will become more self-aware and develop better academic self-efficacy as they see a better correlation between effort and outcome; this sets up a reinforcing cycle in which students who try harder, motivate themselves, set goals, effectively manage their stress, make responsible decisions about approaching and engaging in their school work and homework and use sound decision-making to build and keep positive adult and peer relationships and overcome setbacks will indeed accomplish more academically, socially and emotionally. Ultimately, life success arises not from programmes being implemented in isolation but from a convergence of a combination of interpersonal, instructional, climate and environmental supports, sustained over time (Zins et al. 2004).

What is not known is how much convergence of which dimensions over what period of time, with what levels of consistency are sufficient to produce positive life outcomes. And family and socio-economic factors certainly moderate these relationships. However, what is uniformly recognised by those who study and implement interventions is that social-emotional and character development (SECD) can be strongly influenced by the schools and represents a modifiable risk and protective factor that seems more accessible than socio-economic change at the community level or through affecting a wide swath of parents and families in the community (Torff 2011).

## Principles of intervention

Several other conceptual and empirical benchmarks are important in understanding the growth and perspective on social and emotional influences on learning from an American perspective. In an instructive study, Gager and Elias (1997) examined implementation of SEL-related programmes statewide in New Jersey, with particular attention to how the same programmes are in urban disadvantaged vs. more advantaged communities. The question being raised was about implementation and potential limitations of effects. The findings showed clearly that even those programmes best supported by empirical evidence were as likely to be unsuccessfully implemented as well implemented. Indeed, success across difficult socio-environmental contexts depended on the degree of implementation integrity.

We use the term, 'implementation integrity', to denote that research has created a rich literature on the conditions needed for SEL and related programmes to achieve their intended outcomes. These conditions often exceed those recommended by programme developers; hence, 'implementation fidelity' may actually not be sufficient, particularly in highly challenging school contexts. Table 1 presents a summary of this known literature. As one can see, such factors as continuity and implementation supports are often difficult to address at the level of individual classrooms. Indeed, efforts to successfully enhance students' SECD are really systems-level interventions. However, because it is essential to systematically build performance character-related skills in students, a determination must be made of

Table 1.    Characteristics of successful SEL-related efforts in schools.

Theoretical: contain sound theoretical justification, address risk and protective factors identified in research, and have empirical support of efficacy

Skills based: include strong behavioural, emotional and cognitive components that focus on the acquisition of specific skills and ensure opportunities for practicing those skills in relevant contexts

Thematic: espouse a set of core values, essential life habits, guiding themes or other overarching principles that provide direction for application of skills

Developmental: contain a scope and sequence outlining the expected developmental trajectory of skills and themes and associated supportive processes over multiple years

Coordinated: provide multiple, coordinated interventions in multiple settings to address interrelated goals

Diverse: incorporate cultural sensitivity and cultural norms as appropriate

Sufficient: contain sufficient length and intensity/'dosage' to ensure the desired effects and include booster sessions and linkages to other developmentally sequenced approaches when appropriate

Relational: promote the development of positive relationships in classrooms, schools and other settings, as well as between subgroups in the setting

Contextual: Address necessary changes in setting and communities, including changes in formal policies and specific practices, especially around school climate and discipline/positive recognition systems, and developing resources for positive development and encouragement of student engagement and voice

Continuous: convey and provide for appropriate training for staff and ongoing mentoring and support to ensure effective implementation and sustainability

Ecological: are integrated into the fabric of the setting and are not perceived as an 'add on'

Evaluable: include ongoing processes to ensure continuous monitoring of implementation, indicators of outcomes, assessment of changing needs and creation of processes for incorporating and assessing improvements the extent to which it has been possible to create programmes that operationalise best-practice instructional procedures toward the goal of systematically teaching students the CASEL five set of SEL skills. A discussion of a relevant investigation and its outcome follows.

In 2003, CASEL examined 242 nationally available prevention and positive youth development programmes. From these, 80 were found to have systematic information about their content and processes and evaluation results sufficient for more detailed analysis. They were rated on their instructional practices, implementation support structure, link of SEL curriculum and instruction to congruent practices at the school, family and community level, and outcome data, including the degree of rigour of experimental evidence. CASEL (2003) determined that 22 of the programmes were sufficiently high across dimensions to merit being named as 'CASEL SELect Programs'. Introductions to many of these programmes, their primary principles and examples of their practices for immediate use by teachers have been compiled by CASEL (Elias and Arnold 2006). While it might seem that 22 is a relatively small number of programmes, a number of these have significant implementation systems in the USA (e.g. Responsive Classroom, Social Decision Making, Open Circle) and internationally, including the UK (PATHS, Second Step, Lions-Quest).

Thus, to summarise, theory and research on SECD have converged to suggest that this construct is important for understanding children's social functioning and academic success. Much has been learned about the conditions under which SECD can be fostered, and a number of programmes have been developed that have demonstrated the capacity to teach students the CASEL Five skill set. It is also clear that it is likely that only comprehensive SECD efforts can yield schools of character, which create truly empowering settings for students. However, there are some realities in American education that stand in contrast to this relatively good news about SEL and related efforts. Among the most prominent and persistent of these will be addressed next.

## Application of SEL to the achievement gap

In American schools, there has been a decades-long achievement gap. It is sometimes defined as a 'black-white' gap, a minority-Caucasian gap and a 'black/Hispanic-Caucasian' gap, but many feel that it is more properly defined as a poverty-related gap, i.e. a gap between students with economic resources and those lacking in those resources. While data from the National Assessment of Educational Progress (the largest nationally representative and continuing assessment of student achievement in the USA), reveals that the racial achievement gaps have been narrowing since the 1970s, the gaps persist (Perie, Moran, and Lutkus 2005). Looking at this from a wider perspective, one can identify communities in which students are less likely to have adequate test scores and achievement levels and graduation rates, vs. others, and the defining feature is typically the socio-economic resources of those communities (Rothstein 2004).

These gaps are more prominent in, though not exclusive to, urban education but of course are neither inherent features of racial group, cultural group, poverty or urban settings. Rather they are the result of a complex series of interacting factors that Haberman (1991) labelled as 'the pedagogy of poverty'. Education can be seen as what Masterpasqua (1981) has defined as a development right, and as such, a democratic society is weakened when there are disparities in the delivery of educational services to subgroups within the population. Clearly, students living in high-risk urban environments, particularly those populated largely by ethnic minority groups, are receiving a less adequate education than their more advantaged peers.

Kozol (2005) has laid bare the modern application of what Haberman (2004) called the pedagogy of poverty – instruction focused on rote learning, teaching to the test, and rigid adherence to a dry, focused, non-integrative curriculum that is often shorn of such 'frills' as art, music and social studies (as well as recess). There is a pervasive disconnect between the human dignity of those in the system, their creative potential, and the reality of the rigid, demeaning rule structures placed on the operation of schools. The system is characterised by a 'blaming the victim' mentality, with teachers, parents and students being the regular targets. Hope is in short supply, aspirations are truncated and potential is too rarely seen and encouraged. The stakes – risking low scores on standardised tests – are seen as too high to attempt any extended innovations. We know that these are not the conditions under which children develop a love of learning, nor are they likely to learn materials deeply and in ways they can put to use to bring about better things for the world around them.

For a nation that appears to pride itself on education, the continued existence of the achievement gap is both an embarrassment and an incongruity. The No Child Left Behind legislation, that heralded a very strict regimen of academic testing and focus on language arts and mathematics, has not led to the expected levels of success (Elias 2009). It is instructive to examine relevant research on why this has taken place and what alternatives might be considered.

First, in examining the academic achievement gap, it is important to utilise some form of ecological systems theory. While there are various accounts of this theory, we find·it useful to refer to three types of nested systems in which individuals are embedded: microsystems, organizational systems and macrosystems (Kloos et al. 2011). Microsystems involve face-to-face and small-group interactions. They are intensive and proximal to individuals and encompass such things as family interaction, classroom interaction, peer groups and after school/extracurricular groups or teams. Microsystems have rules, interaction dynamics, and goal, incentive and maintenance structures that are not defined at the individual level, though they affect all individuals involved. Organizational systems similarly have their own properties, and these are larger units within which microsystems are embedded. These include schools, workplaces, out-of-school programmes, health care organizations, and, some would say, extended families. Macrosystems refer to laws, customs, public attitudes, policies and media influences that create a strong context within which actions are taken at all other levels of the ecological system. A fourth system, the chronosystem, defined as how things do or do not change over time, is also critically important. Needless to say, approaches that only look at the individual student level are bound to have great inaccuracies. Yet, it is just this approach that characterises the pedagogy of poverty.

### *Research on ecological influences on learning*

Strayhorn (2010) examined standardised math achievement for black high school students through an ecological lens. He conducted hierarchical linear regression analyses, in which prior math achievement and individual level differences were controlled for before adding microsystem and organizational system-level variables (represented by family- and school-related factors). Together the effect size for the family- and school-related factors was twice the effect size as the individual factors.

Expanding upon the importance of family-level indicators, Orr (2003) used data from 1979 through 2002 of the National Longitudinal Survey of Youth (NLSY79), to show that wealth goes above and beyond income. Wealth had a larger effect on children's mathematics achievement than other indicators of socioeconomic status (e.g. parent education, occupation and income). Additionally, the gap between wealth in white families and black families was larger than the gap in income.

Congruently, the chronosystem for black children appears to be more stable than the chronosystem for white children in ways that may perpetuate achievement gaps. Timberlake (2007) used data from 1976 through 1997 of the Panel Study of Income Dynamics to demonstrate that not only were black children more likely to be born into poor neighbourhoods than white children but they were also more likely to remain in a poor neighbourhood as they grew up, even after holding place of birth constant. While this study did not look at academic achievement directly, this means that black students are more likely to spend this academic life in low-income schools as school funding in the USA primarily comes from the local neighbourhood.

A wider picture can be obtained by examining the macrosystem by looking at how the US fares in the Programme for International Student Assessment (PISA) tests (Elias 2011). It has been well documented that American schools do nor perform favourably compared to those in many other developed countries; interestingly, these countries are uniform in having policies and practices that do not embody all of the elements of No Child Left Behind. In fact, clearly implicated in the PISA findings but underappreciated by policy-makers and educational practitioners in the USA is the role of SECD factors as influencing performance in schools across the socio-economic spectrum.

### Research on SEL influences on learning

Elias and Haynes (2008), looking at a sample of 282 predominantly black and Latino third graders from a low-performing urban district across six elementary schools, found that social–emotional competence and change in social–emotional competence predicted end-of-year academic grades, after controlling for prior grades. The findings were strongest for black students. Also implicated in the findings was the predictive role of student perceptions of teacher support. The results were found for both reading and math scores, and it is noteworthy that teachers did know that the students' scores would be examined for the purpose of the study. These findings are especially important when considering that the third grade is the end of a critical period for reading acquisition, and that social–emotional factors provided a significant increment in academic performance over and above past academic performance. That is, students who had not been doing well academically showed academic gains when they also had, or improved in, social competence skills.

The most important study showing the role of social–emotional factors in achievement was conducted by Durlak et al. (2011). The researchers conducted a meta-analysis of 213 school-based, universal SEL programmes involving 270,034 students from kindergarten through high school age. The findings showed that, when compared to controls, SEL programme participants showed enhanced social–emotional competencies, positive attitudes about themselves, other students and their schools, and improvement in a range of problem behaviours. Most importantly for our current consideration, participation in systematic SEL programmes led to an average of 11-percentile-point gains in academic achievement. Not surprising, these effects were moderated by the extent to which best implementation practices – those fully at odds with the pedagogy of poverty – were applied.

There are some caveats and implications from this study. First, the vast majority of interventions were effectively delivered by school staff, which shows the scalability of the SEL approach. Second, the research does not give impetus to whether one should focus on social, cognitive or emotional skill development. Virtually, all effective programmes involve an intentional integration of these elements, as well as behavioural performance, considering their operation as a totality. Thus, no impetus is given to those seeking to streamline SEL programmes. Third, the research did not systematically look at whether parallel attempts were under way in schools to create coherent set of values. Other research summaries (e.g. Berkowitz and Bier 2006) suggest that this is the case and additional relevant research will be discussed shortly. Finally, while it appears that SEL programmes are successful at all educational levels (elementary, middle and high school) and in schools of all socio-economic status, the data are most sparse from high schools and in rural areas.

If, as noted earlier, SEL programmes reduce barriers to learning by building students' essential learning to learn skills, evidence also exists that creating an overall school climate allowing disadvantaged students to affirm their positive values also has a positive impact on learning and potential for closing the achievement gap. Cohen (2006) looked at the impact of a brief values-affirming intervention on a mixed population of black and white students in a lower-middle class population of seventh graders. The intervention significantly benefited nearly 70% of black students; those performing poorly and moderately equally benefited and both benefited more than the highest performing students, who themselves still showed benefits. Interestingly, corresponding effects were not found for white students. The effects even generalised to grade point average in a course in which the intervention did not occur. Overall, the average performance gap for students who did not receive the intervention was .75 grade points, and the average intervention effect was .30. Thus, the authors point to a 40% reduction in the achievement gap. In a two-year follow up Cohen et al. (2009) found that, the black students continued to be positively affected, sustaining their positive gains. Interestingly, an attempt to provide a booster did not show any effects, leading the investigators to conclude that, while a 'values-affirmation intervention closed the achievement gap not only over one school term, but throughout African Americans' tenure in middle school' (402), '[e]ffective psychological interventions depend on the presence of positive and sufficient structural, material, and human resources' (403).

### *Implications and future directions*

While there is much additional research to be done, it is also clear that many important findings have not been systematically applied within American education. Given the relative strength of the research, particularly as summarised by Durlak et al. (2011) and Berkowitz and Bier (2006), and the wide range of highly applicable SECD-related interventions (Elias and Arnold 2006; www.character.org for the National Schools of Character), one cannot attribute the situation to empirical shortfalls. There is no strong data base for the test and drill approach of No Child

Left Behind, for approaches to curriculum and instruction and school climate that are not strongly engaging of students, or for such widespread interventions as after school academic programmes, longer school days, longer school years or supplemental reading programmes. In fact, it is likely that SECD factors play a significant role when such approaches are indeed found to work. SECD is at the foundation of everything that happens in education. Relationships and strong emotions influence learning and it is patterns of interpersonal interaction that determine the effectiveness of classrooms, other school settings, and the school as a whole.

We believe that two fundamental reasons for the reluctance of educators to adopt SECD as a focal emphasis in schools and as the gateway to academic success are unfamiliarity with how SECD efforts look and feel in schools, and the almost complete absence of SECD and school climate considerations from the preparation of future teachers, school support personnel and administrators, as well as school board members. The dissemination of video and richly evocative written examples becomes an important strategy, and it is fortunate that excellent and accessible examples exist (www.edutopia.org; www.CASEL.org; www.character.org; http://earnedwisdomtech.org/). These must be shown and discussed in many forums, until a tipping point is created. Our view is that demand will create supply, i.e. that once educators appreciate the value of SECD and school climate approaches, educator preparation programmes will be modified to include greater emphasis on these areas. We will know that a successful transition has taken place when the American education system is more concerned with preparing students for the tests of life, rather than a life of tests.

## References

Bar-On, Reuven. 2007. How important is it to educate people to be emotionally intelligent, and can it be done? In *Educating people to be emotionally intelligent*, ed. Reuven Bar-On, Jacobus G. Maree, and Maurice J. Elias, 1–14. Westport, CT: Praeger.

Bar-On, Reuven, Jacobus G. Maree, and Maurice J. Elias, eds. 2007. *Educating people to be emotionally intelligent*. Westport, CT: Praeger.

Berkowitz, Marvin W., and Mindy C. Bier. 2006. What works in character education: A research-driven guide for educators. Center for Character and Citizenship. http://www.characterandcitizenship.org/research/whatworks.htm.

Character Education Partnership. 2010. Performance values: Why they matter and what schools can do to foster their, development. (www.character.org).

Cohen, J. 2006. Social, emotional, ethical and academic education: Creating a climate for learning, participation in democracy and well-being. *Harvard Educational Review* 76, no. 2: 201–37.

Cohen, J., E. McCabe, N.M. Michelli, and T. Pickeral. 2009. School climate: Research, policy, practice, and teacher education. *Teachers College Record* 111, no. 1: 180–213.

Collaborative for Academic, Social, and Emotional Learning. 2003. *Safe and sound: An educational leader's guide to evidence-based social and emotional learning programs*. Chicago, IL: CASEL. http://www.casel.org/pub/safeandsound.php (accessed May 14, 2012).

Conduct Problems Prevention Research Group. 2002. The implementation of the Fast Track program: An example of a large-scale prevention science efficacy trial. *Journal of Abnormal Child Psychology* 30, no. 1: 1–17.

Dunkelblau, Edward. 2009. *Social–emotional and character development: A laminated resource card for teachers, for students, for parents*. Port Chester, NY: National Professional, Resources. www.nprinc.com.

Durlak, J.A., R.P. Weissberg, A.B. Dymnicki, R.D. Taylor, and K.B. Schellinger. 2011. The impact of enhancing students' social and emotional learning: A meta-analysis of school-based universal interventions. *Child Development* 82, no. 1: 405–32.

Elbot, Charles, and David Fulton. 2008. *Building an intentional school culture*. Thousand Oaks, CA: Corwin Press.

Elias, M.J. 2009. Social–emotional and character development and academics as a dual focus of educational policy. *Educational Policy* 23, no. 6: 831–46.

Elias, M.J. 2011. The relationship between respect and test scores. *Education Week*, May 4. http://www.edweek.org/ew/articles/2011/05/04/30elias.h30.html?r=1153177048.

Elias, Maurice J., and Harriet A. Arnold, eds. 2006. *The educator's guide to emotional intelligence and academic achievement: Social-emotional learning in the classroom*. Thousand Oaks, CA: Corwin Press.

Elias, M.J., and N.M. Haynes. 2008. Social competence, social support, and academic achievement in minority, low-income, urban elementary school children. *School Psychology Quarterly* 23, no. 4: 474–95. doi: 10.1037/1045–3830.23.4.474.

Elias, Maurice J., Joseph E. Zins, Roger P. Weissberg, Karin S. Frey, Mark T. Greenberg, Norris M. Haynes, Rachael Kessler, Mary E. Schwab-Stone, and Timothy P. Shriver. 1997. *Promoting social and emotional learning: Guidelines for educators*. Alexandria, VA: Association for Supervision and Curriculum Development.

Elias, M.J., S.J. Parker, Virginia M. Kash, and E. Dunkelblau. 2007. Socioemotional learning and character and moral education in children: Synergy or fundamental divergence in our schools? *Journal of Research in Character Education* 5, no. 2: 167–82.

Elias, M.J., R. Weissberg, J. Zins, P. Kendall, Kenneth J. Dodge, R. Leonard, M. Perry, C. Hawkins, J. David, and D. Gottfredson. 1996. Transdisciplinary collaboration among school researchers: The Consortium on the School-Based Promotion of Social Competence. *Journal of Educational and Psychological Consultation* 7, no. 1: 25–39.

Gager, P.J., and M.J. Elias. 1997. Implementing prevention programs in high risk environments: Application of the resiliency paradigm. *American Journal of Orthopsychiatry* 67, no. 3: 363–73.

Goleman, Daniel. 1995. *Emotional intelligence*. New York, NY: Doubleday.

Haberman, M. 1991. The pedagogy of poverty versus good teaching. *Phi Delta Kappan* 73, no. 4: 290–4.

Haberman, Martin. 2004. Urban education the state of urban schooling at the start of the 21st century. http://www.educationnews.org/urban-education-the-state-o-furb.htm.

Kloos, Bret, Jean Hill, Elizabeth Thomas, Abraham Wandersman, Maurice J. Elias, and James Dalton. 2011. *Community psychology: Linking individuals and communities*. 3rd ed. Belmont, CA: Wadsworth.

Kozol, J. 2005. Apartheid in America? *Phi Delta Kappan* 87, no. 4: 264–75.

Lemerise, E.A., and W.F. Arsenio. 2000. An integrated model of emotion processes and cognition in social information processing. *Child Development* 71, no. 1: 107–18.

Lickona, Thomas, and Matthew Davidson. 2007. Smart and good high schools. www.cortland.edu/character.

Masterpasqua, F. 1981. Toward a synergism of developmental and community psychology. *American Psychologist* 36, no. 7: 782–6.

Orr, Amy J. 2003. Black–White differences in achievement: The importance of wealth. *Sociology of Education* 76, no. 4: 281–304.

Perie, Marianne, Rebecca Moran, and Anthony D. Lutkus. 2005. *NAEP 2004 trends in academic progress: Three decades of student performance in reading and mathematics* (NCES 2005–464). http://nces.ed.gov/pubsearch/pubsinfo.asp?pubid=2005464 (accessed May 14, 2012).

Rothstein, Richard. 2004. *Class and schools: Using social, economic, and educational reform to close the black-white achievement gap*. Washington, DC: Economic Policy Institute.

Saarni, Carolyn. 2007. The development of emotional competence: Pathways for helping children to become emotionally intelligent. In *Educating people to be emotionally intelligent*, ed. Reuven Bar-On, Jacobus G. Maree, and Maurice J. Elias, 15–35. Westport, CT: Praeger.

Salovey, Peter. 2007. Integrative summary. In *Educating people to be emotionally intelligent*, ed. Reuven Bar-On, Jacobus G. Maree, and Maurice J. Elias, 291–8. Westport, CT: Praeger.

Strayhorn, T.L. 2010. The role of schools, families, and psychological variables on math achievement of Black high school students. *The High School Journal* 93, no. 4: 177–94.

Timberlake, J.M. 2007. Racial and ethnic inequality in the duration of children's exposure to neighborhood poverty and affluence. *Social Problems* 54, no. 3: 319–42.

Torff, B. 2011. Teacher beliefs shape learning for all students. *Phi Delta Kappan* 93, no. 3: 21–3.

Zins, Joseph E., Roger P. Weissberg, Margaret C. Wang, and Herbert J. Walberg, eds. 2004. *Building academic success on social and emotional learning: What does the research say?* New York, NY: Teachers College Press.

# The contribution of religious education to the well-being of pupils

Stephen Pett

*School of Education, University of Birmingham, Birmingham, UK*

> Religious education (RE) is under serious political and professional pressure to justify its existence and, for some, positive psychology seems to offer a more compelling route to well-being. In response, this article establishes a case for the inherent value of the subject whilst showing that the well-being of pupils, in the broader sense of human flourishing that engages us with ideas of meaning and purpose, is an integral part of the aims of RE. The article defends this role by establishing a view of happiness as concerned with the transcendent, and well-being arising from an interest in meaning and purpose in life. It concludes that RE can learn from positive psychology without being subservient to it in order to play a significant part in a worthwhile education.

## Introduction

Current interest in developing the well-being and happiness of members of society raises questions about purposes, pedagogy and curriculum content in mainstream schooling. These are relevant to setting the scene for exploring the specific contribution of religious education (RE) to pupil well-being. First, what do we mean by the terms happiness and well-being? They embrace such a wide range of concepts that it is difficult to make connections across disciplines, yet some theoretical coherence is necessary if we are to make sense of the call for well-being interventions in education. Second, should pupil well-being be on the government's agenda at all? Some critics have raised ideological questions over the desirability of the state and schools intervening in individuals' well-being, and whether this approach represents a compulsory 'therapeutic' agenda that should not be imposed on pupils (Ecclestone and Hayes 2008). Third, are happiness and well-being legitimate aims of education? This raises further questions about what pedagogies should be used to meet these aims, and whether many of the interventions currently used to develop emotional well-being are little more than a reductionist form of training omitting the moral dimensions of emotional well-being (Suissa 2008), or a psychological experiment being imposed on children without good evidence (e.g. Craig 2007). There are also questions about the extent to which interventions overlook the social and economic factors in well-being and present it, instead, as an individual, psychological problem (e.g. Ecclestone this volume).

This article responds to these questions by exploring the role of RE as part of the broader contribution of education to the well-being of pupils. This requires clarity about what understanding of 'well-being' is promoted in various interventions, and a careful distinction between emotional well-being as training in a set of emotional skills, attributes and attitudes, and a broader sense of well-being linked with human flourishing and ideas of meaning and purpose. This provides a basis for exploring how RE relates to the language of happiness and well-being in contemporary education discourse and what contribution RE makes in this process.

Yet, in evaluating the role of RE, it is crucial to recognise the significant political challenges. The coalition government has reiterated its support for RE and the subject retains its place as a compulsory element of the curriculum, with syllabuses devised and agreed within each local authority (LA). However, Department for Education policies of cutting LA responsibilities and funding, and the promoting of academies, undermine this apparently strong position. There are no effective mechanisms in place to ensure compliance with the law on RE, leaving its position within schools potentially subject to the vagaries of individual head teachers' preference. The exclusion of General Certificate of Secondary Education religious studies (RS) from the English Baccalaureate dealt an additional blow to the subject. Research from the National Association of Teachers of RE (2011) shows that schools were already cutting hours for RE and RS, and even cutting staff, within weeks of the announcement of the English Baccalaureate.

In the face of this challenge to the legitimacy of RE, it might be tempting to use its contribution to pupil well-being as a pragmatic defence to prevent its demise. However, in this paper I argue for the inherent value of the subject based on a careful rationale, whilst also showing that the well-being of pupils, in the broader sense of human flourishing and ideas of meaning and purpose, is integral to the aims of RE. I defend this role by establishing a view of happiness as concerned with the transcendent and well-being arising from an interest in meaning and purpose in life. I then explore the possible contribution of the content and pedagogical process of RE. It is not my contention that RE is the only place in the curriculum where this can be done, but I argue that it plays a significant part in the 'good education' promoted by Cigman (this volume) and Suissa (2008).

## Competing definitions and interventions

The task of relating well-being to different disciplines faces the difficulty of pinning down a satisfactory understanding of the term and the distinction between religious and philosophical notions and psychological ones is crucial. Coleman (2009), in a special edition of the *Oxford Review of Education* on the subject of well-being in education, notes that just in the pages of that edition, 'well-being' is used in relation to 'academic resilience and buoyancy', 'freedom and choice', 'happiness', 'the meaningful life' and 'social and emotional aspects of learning', among others. Within this range of meanings, many terms are elided without discussion or critical evaluation, such as 'well-being' and 'emotional well-being', in particular (Ecclestone this volume). It is clear that the ideas span different constituencies and different ideological and educational concerns. In addition, many of the proponents of interventions to develop emotional well-being as measurable skills and attributes and to underpin these with psychological concepts and practices themselves invoke broader notions of human flourishing (e.g. Layard 2007; Seligman 2011).

In order to try and place the role of RE within the well-being debate, Figure 1 seeks to map the ways in which well-being is understood by different groups or thinkers. It compares a range of views of happiness as its basis, since much positive psychology research has been expressed in terms of its impact on happiness. Often the term happiness has been used conterminously with well-being, such as in Eid and Larsen (2008), where the chapter titles cover the 'science of subjective well-being' and the 'science of happiness'. The book honours the contribution of Ed Diener to the 'science of subjective well-being' and his contribution examines the myths that have developed around 'subjective well-being' – the myths mixing up happiness and well-being e.g. *Myth No 1: Happiness has an unchanging individual 'setpoint'. Myth No 2: causes of well-being can be understood as a pie-chart of influences* (2008, 494–6).

Most writers look to distinguish between happiness and well-being and Figure 1 shows the move from a psychological view of happiness, with a starting point of a hedonic view of happiness, to a philosophical or transcendent view, being concerned with ultimate human meaning and purpose. Figure 1 also gives some suggestions as to the placing of current interventions on this continuum, according to the view of happiness/well-being that they appear to hold.

Coleman (2009) recommends the classification of well-being in the systematic review carried out by National Institute for Health and Clinical Excellence (NICE) (2008). He suggests that if all studies used their classification then some confusion would be reduced. NICE differentiates between emotional, psychological and social well-being:

For the purposes of this guidance, 'social and emotional wellbeing' encompasses:

- happiness, confidence and not feeling depressed (emotional well-being),
- a feeling of autonomy and control over one's life, problem-solving skills, resilience, attentiveness and a sense of involvement with others (psychological well-being) and
- the ability to have good relationships with others and to avoid disruptive behaviour, delinquency, violence or bullying (social well-being) (NICE 2008, 6).

Whilst it would be helpful to delineate the term well-being in this way, this outline omits the significant elements of life-satisfaction, flourishing and transcendence, with their accompanying need for a theory of value. As MacMahon shows in his history of happiness, philosophical and religious notions of well-being in terms of both life satisfaction and flourishing have given way over the past 60 years or so to other ideas derived from popular psychology (McMahon 2006). Yet, it is the contribution of philosophy and religion that illuminate what it means to be satisfied and to flourish. Religions and philosophies can provide a framework required for people to be able to evaluate the moment to moment feelings of well-being, the overall assessment of whether one's life attains a level of well-being and the value of having goals of self-actualisation. The idea of well-being relating to having an overall sense of meaning and purpose clearly requires someone to have an idea of what constitutes a good life (see also Cigman this volume; Clack this volume).

Figure 1 indicates that some of the current interventions, programmes such as Social and Emotional Aspects of Learning and Promoting Alternative Thinking Strategies (PATHS), regard happiness and well-being as hedonic or as an emotional state. The Penn Resilience Programme and the course at Wellington College

| *Psychological view of happiness* | | *Philosophical view of happiness* | |
|---|---|---|---|
| **Happiness as hedonic**<br>In this view, pleasure outweighs unhappiness and pain. Happiness is seen as the opposite of unpleasantness and is found in pleasant experiences. | **Happiness as emotional state**<br>This view sees happiness as an emotion, comparable to tranquillity. Happiness is effectively a mood, the opposite of depression and anxiety. | **Happiness as life-satisfaction**<br>In this view, someone makes an overall appraisal of his or her life and views it as positive, in relation to their goals and ideals of life. | **Happiness as eudaimonic**<br>In this view, happiness is about flourishing and self-actualisation; it is about developing resilience in the face of life's challenges and making the most of life. | **Happiness as well-being: the transcendent**<br>This view suggests that the most profound sense of happiness is tied in with a search for meaning. The importance of seeking ultimate meaning and purpose in life leads to a transcendent view of life – that its significance extends beyond the material. |

**Some key contributors**

| **Layard**<br>"By happiness I mean feeling good – enjoying life and wanting the feeling to be maintained." (Layard 2005, 12) | **Haybron**<br>Happiness is an emotional state but is clearly only part of what matters for well-being. (Haybron 2008, 6)<br>**Csikszentmihalyi**<br>The idea of 'flow', of being caught in the moment. (Csikszentmihalyi 1990) | **Sumner; Tiberius** (in Haybron)<br>Happiness is more than a simple judgement about subjective well-being – it include our *ideals* about how to respond to life. (Haybron 2008) | **Aristotle; Seligman**<br>*Eudaimonia*: an activity of the soul in accordance with excellence; needs to be assessed at the end of life rather than in response to moments of happiness. Aristotle, *Nichomachean Ethics* | **Vernon; Cottingham**<br>This view implies that there is a moral dimension to the question of happiness: the question is not just "has my life been good?" but what *is* goodness? |
| | | Both life-satisfaction and eudaimonic views of happiness require a theory of **value** in order to come to a judgement. | | |

**How commentators fit into this scheme**

Haybron (2008): feeling happy ⟶ having a happy life ⟶ being happy

Nettle (2005): feeling of joy/pleasure ⟶ judgements about feelings ⟶ quality of life

Seligman (2002): pleasure/gratification ⟶ strength/virtue ⟶ meaning/purpose; lasting fulfilment

Cottingham (2009): (prerequisites include welfare) contentment ⟶ dignity (the ability to exercise choice) ⟶ achievement; virtue ⟶ meaningfulness

**Education strategies/interventions/subjects**

| Techniques for handling feelings, such as Social and Emotional Aspects of Learning (SEAL) | Techniques developing the ability to identify and articulate feelings e.g.<br>• UK Penn Resilience Programme<br>• SEAL<br>• PATHS (Promoting Alternative Thinking Strategies)<br>• Meditation<br>• Ideas of "Flow" | Programmes for teaching happiness, e.g. Wellington School | *Building Learning Power* approach from Guy Claxton (flow and resilience)<br>Potential in:<br>• Citizenship<br>• PSHEE<br>• Ethics<br>• History<br>• Music | RE e.g. human development model<br>Potential in:<br>• Art<br>• Literature<br>• Critical pedagogy |

Figure 1.  Mapping happiness and well-being.

referred to in Ecclestone (this volume) overlap with this hedonic and emotional state view, but also include elements of life-satisfaction. Holding these views of happiness and well-being are likely to lead to these kinds of skills-based programmes.

## The absence of RE in the happiness and well-being debate

The role of RE has been missing from the current debate, partly because much of the talk of happiness and well-being in schools has been at the level of hedonic and emotional state views of happiness. However, there are several reasons why it is appropriate to consider the place and role of RE in the promotion of pupil well-being, in the deeper philosophical sense of relating to the transcendent and to questions of meaning and purpose.

Firstly, the content of RE includes ancient wisdom from world religions, demonstrating centuries of human concern with social justice as well as personal well-being. Seligman, a prime mover in the field of positive psychology, draws on key virtues arising from the world's major religious and philosophical traditions: wisdom and knowledge, courage, love and humanity, justice, temperance and spirituality and transcendence (Seligman 2002, 132–3). Snyder and Lopez's *Handbook of Positive Psychology* (2005) examines the impact of, for example, humility, compassion, forgiveness, gratitude, love and empathy on well-being. Post and Neimark (2007) focus on the effect of gratitude, celebration, respect and listening, among other expressions of self-giving, and argue the scientific case for generosity.

All these values are the stuff of religions, although obviously not exclusive to them. Part of the role of RE in examining these virtues might be to contrast the tendency of secular positive psychology to polarise emotions and values into positive and negative, with the more nuanced views held within religions. In positive psychology, 'negative' emotions of anger or loneliness are to be removed and 'positive' virtues of patience and love to be cultivated. Whilst not denying the value of patience and love, within the Jewish tradition expressed in the Psalms and the Book of Job, for example, rage and despair are permitted, as well as hope.

Central to several RE pedagogies is the importance of older school pupils developing skills related to the key disciplines by which religion is studied, including textual study, hermeneutics, history, sociology, ethnography, philosophy, theology and psychology of religion. For example, the current statement for level eight on the Qualifications and Curriculum Authority (QCA) levels of attainment for RE, used by most LAs in England to inform their locally agreed syllabuses for RE, reads as follows:

> Pupils use a comprehensive religious and philosophical vocabulary to analyse a range of religions and beliefs. They contextualise interpretations of religion with reference to historical, cultural, social and philosophical ideas. They critically evaluate the impact of religions and beliefs on differing communities and societies. They analyse differing interpretations of religious, spiritual and moral sources, using some of the principal methods by which religion, spirituality and ethics are studied. They interpret and evaluate varied forms of religious, spiritual and moral expression.
>
> Pupils coherently analyse a wide range of viewpoints on questions of identity, belonging, meaning, purpose, truth, values and commitments. They synthesise a range of evidence, arguments, reflections and examples fully justifying their own views and ideas and providing a detailed evaluation of the perspectives of others. (QCA 2004).

In the light of an endorsement of the impact of religious faith and values offered by positive psychology, it seems reasonable to extend the list of disciplines to include positive psychology as part of the content of RE curricula, both for its insights and also to allow its critique in the light of the teachings of religions. There may also be a place in considering its impact more fundamentally in developing a relevant RE pedagogy.

Secondly, despite the clear links above, not all advocates of happiness lessons in schools acknowledge the religious and philosophical roots of the findings of positive psychology. Layard attributes the finding that 'if you care more about other people relative to yourself, you are more likely to be happy', to Stanford positive psychologist Sonja Lyubomirsky (Layard 2007). Even at the most prosaic level, many RE pupils in schools would be able to spot the links between this finding and the teaching in Christianity to 'love your neighbour as you love yourself', a text that has parallels in most other religious traditions. Pupils might well go beyond this to explore the extent to which the current advocacy of happiness and well-being is a secular alternative to religion.

Layard goes on to say that caring for others

> is not something that we can necessarily bring about by saying to people 'care about other people because you will be happier' because that kind of motivation may not work. But it is a very important fact and background to all of education and all of morality. (Sharples 2007)

The *Action for Happiness* organisation, founded by Layard, advises that a key to happiness is 'If you want to feel good, be good'. In RE lessons, it is precisely the motivation that someone may have to 'be good' or to 'love your neighbour' that might be explored and its impact evaluated, within religious and non-religious worldviews. Layard's questionable assertions that 'Generally, what makes us happy is good for us ...' and 'most, but not all, moral behaviour makes us feel better' are also suitable for evaluation within RE lessons (Layard 2005, 224). Whether the fact that something makes us feel better has any value in making moral decisions is an appropriate topic for RE, as well as evaluating whether happiness is the most important goal, or even a worthwhile one.

The third reason why it is worth examining the contribution of RE to the well-being agenda is to do with the debate about the aims and purposes of RE within its own community. There is an ongoing discussion as to the role of faith communities in developing curricula for RE and the place of the teachings of religions within RE. Pedagogies such as Andrew Wright's religious literacy approach regard the religions' self-understanding and internal interpretation of beliefs as primary, and so RE should listen to the voices of the faith communities to see how they wish their faith to be presented. Other pedagogies, such as Michael Grimmitt's human development model and Clive Erricker's constructivist approach, take the view that the educational aim of pupils' personal development takes precedence over the views of organised religion in the shaping of RE. For Grimmitt and Erricker, who view RE as instrumental in pupils' personal development, pupil well-being can be seen as a fundamental part of the aims for the subject.

If these arguments are valid, RE may play an important role in promoting well-being, not least because has a potentially coherent subject and knowledge base and is more integrated pedagogically than the kinds of interventions commonly added to curriculum programmes, such as PATHS, or teaching happiness as a series of skills. Whilst these can contribute to the hedonic and emotional state views of happiness, they generally omit the depth and complexity of the view of happiness as related to questions of meaning and purpose.

## Happiness, well-being, positive psychology and world religions: common ground

A brief account of some distinguishing features of Jewish, Christian and Hindu thinking about happiness and well-being, alongside Greek philosophical thinking, will serve to establish the links between these traditions and the findings of positive psychology. The diagnoses of the human condition may differ both within and across these traditions, but the ethical outworking of all three have significant common ground and the RE classroom offers an ideal place for the exploration of such ideas.

Examining religious and philosophical traditions reveals varied ideas about the nature of happiness and well-being. The Jewish Bible identifies the 'happy' or 'blessed' person as one who takes refuge in God, follows God's paths, obeys his commands and pursues virtue, and who shows concern for justice for the poor and needy. This call for justice is reflected in the wider hopes for Israel which often centre on the idea of rest, of peace, of wholeness and of completeness. The term *shalom* implies a psychological wholeness reflected in a life of justice and plenty, of battles won and a righteous peace. There are repeated themes of the importance of family and the tribe, of serving God as an ultimate aim, of submission to God, of acknowledging failings and adopting true humility, of pleading for and receiving forgiveness and of expressing gratitude to God for many good things, and, in the case of Job, terrible things too (Job 1:21). These emotions and attitudes constitute a life lived well in the face of the terrors of war, famine, plague and death, so that even Job, who does not have a theology of life after death, can rail and rant against the vicissitudes of life, and yet come to a state of calm acceptance:

> Then Job replied to the LORD: 'I know that you can do all things; no plan of yours can be thwarted. My ears had heard of you but now my eyes have seen you'. (Job 42:1–2, 5 New International Version)

All of these attitudes are rediscovered as constituents of happiness or well-being in the findings of twenty-first century positive psychology (Post and Neimark 2007; Myers 2008).

As the Jewish canon was coming to a close the Greeks had a different view on life. Herodotus has King Croesus asking if he is not the happiest man alive. Solon, lawgiver of Athens, replies that it is not possible to make such a judgement until he knows if Croesus' life comes to a good end. In contrast with Job's ultimate submission to a trustworthy Deity, Croesus can only lament the vagaries of fate. 'No one who lives is happy', he cries. No one can be happy, unless they happen to be fortunate enough to get through life's trials (McMahon 2006). 'Happen' and 'fortunate' are both apposite terms, since it is entirely dependent upon what befalls a person whether one can be called happy.

It is in Herodotus' account that we encounter a crucial term for the Greek understanding of happiness: *eudaimonia*. Derived from the Greek *eu* (good) and *daimon* (god, spirit and fortune), *eudaimonia* is usually referred to as *flourishing*. However, the term includes the element of fortune that is present in Solon's conclusion. When Aristotle claims that happiness (*eudaimonia*) is a product of human flourishing, there is more of a sense that the happy person is one who is able to exercise a measure of control over the randomness of their lives through the practice of virtue (McMahon 2008). Of course, Aristotle is not unaware of the role of good fortune in allowing a person to pursue happiness, but he would deny that true happiness can come about as a result of mere luck (Kenny 1992, 57). It is difficult to avoid the conclusion, however, that the luxury of pursuing these virtues was really only open to the elite of Athenian society. Control over one's situation was a luxury – only the wealthy could protect themselves from some of the worst of the perils of life.

The perils of life were embraced in the Christian gospels. The themes of humility, submission to God, serving others, pursuing justice and mercy – all these build on the qualities desired in the Jewish scriptures, as does the primacy given to self-sacrificial love throughout the gospels. Jesus' Jewish roots are clear and would have resonated with his audience. However, the subversive tone of Jesus' teachings would not have been missed either. If fullness was found through emptying oneself, if joy was to be found in serving others and if riches could only be found through generosity then there would be plenty of unhappy people pursuing self-satisfaction, status and wealth.

The New Testament develops the theme of judgement. Ultimately, happiness is a future hope and reward to last forever. This perspective made the suffering of life less significant, albeit not less painful. Whilst Aristotle faces the ultimate irony that as he gains in happiness through virtue pursued through life, so he gets closer to death, which robs him of everything, the Christian attains the ultimate happiness at death (McMahon 2008, 83). Death is 'the culmination of earthly pain and the onset of infinite beatitude' (McMahon 2006, 106). There is joy and delight in serving God and following Jesus, service which can result in people growing in the 'fruit of the Spirit': love, joy, peace, patience, kindness, goodness, gentleness, faithfulness and self-control. And this is through all kinds of suffering, because the ultimate reward is a state in which there is 'no more death or mourning or crying or pain' (Revelation 21:4). The list of the virtues produced by the Holy Spirit in the Christian's life would not look out of place as the chapter headings in a handbook of positive psychology.

Eastern religions respond to the search for happiness differently. The diagnosis of the human condition for Christianity concerns human sin and the cure includes the need for divine forgiveness and restoration. Eastern religions, on the other hand, stress our ignorance of our true status; for example, our divinity (in Advaita Vedanta) or our assumed status as enduring substances (in Therevada Buddhism). The cure for these is to know our true status, to attain oneness with Brahman through *moksha* or to realise the transitory nature of existence on the way to enlightenment. In many discourses within Hinduism, for example, the ultimate aim is not to experience happiness eternally but to escape from *samsara*, the inherent suffering of continued life, death and rebirth. Until *karma* is extinguished, our individual soul is bound to reincarnation endlessly. The pursuit of happiness becomes a pursuit to lose yourself. For some Hindu discourses, the aim is for the individual consciousness, *atman*, to lose connection with the body and merge into the universal soul, Brahman, as the drop of water dissolves into the ocean.

Within the Hindu traditions there are various methods to attain the ultimate aim of losing oneself, although the attainment of final liberation, *moksha*, is not the only aim of life. *Arta* is the aim of earning money through honest means, in order to support an individual's family, contribute to the welfare of society and give alms to the poor. The pursuit of fame, power and business success is worthy aims. Alongside *arta* is *kama*, the enjoyment of beauty and pleasure in life including, notably, sex and sexuality. This desire for pleasure may be a form of pure hedonism, but woven through it for most Hindus following the path of *karma marga* (the way of action) is the duties of raising and supporting a family and practising charity and hospitality.

The third aim of life is *dharma*, which involves doing one's duty according to one's age and stage in life, and according to one's position in society. Many Hindus see the idea of duty as bound up with the ultimate nature of life. Hinduism is *sanatana dharma* – eternal law. Following this ancient and universal law involves emphasis on ahimsa (non-violence), *satya* (the pursuit of truth), *asteya* (not stealing), *sauca* (purity) and control of the senses (Jamison 2006). Fulfilling these duties is pre-eminent for many Hindus, with the ultimate intention of escape from the cycle of life, death and rebirth – but finding happiness en route, as a by-product of virtue. It is detachment from desiring happiness that brings happiness (Schoch 2007). According to Vivekananda, 'What we want is neither happiness nor misery. Both make us forget our true nature; both are chains, one of iron, another of gold' (cited in Klostermaier 2000, 130).

Exploring the varying impact of these responses to the human condition is the stuff of the RE classroom, where pupils can try to make sense of their meaning in the lives of believers and also discern whether they may have value within their own lives. Such an approach opens up questions of meaning and purpose within the examination of religious and philosophical ideas, rather than presenting a series of skills as the route to well-being. It takes both the academic subject and the human subject seriously.

## Well-being as meaning and purpose: the proper concern of RE?

As outlined in the opening paragraphs of this paper, there is something of a crisis in the RE community as it faces pressure from coalition government policy on education. This crisis has also begun to cause the RE community to reconsider its purpose, in order to defend itself against the (perhaps unintentional) consequences of policies such as the English Baccalaureate, academies, free schools and the like.

Since the move away from confessional religious instruction to the phenomenological teaching of religion in the 1960s–1970s, a range of pedagogies for RE have been developed, exploring ways of approaching and defending the subject within a secular education system. Grimmitt's book *Pedagogies of RE* (2000) outlines nine pedagogies, with overlapping aims. It would be possible to caricature the division between these, whereas there is considerable common ground; however, there is a contrast between two basic approaches, which might be summed up as nominalist and genericist approaches.

The nominalist position rejects the notion that there is such a thing as religion, only specific and incompatible 'religious' systems. The self-understanding of Islam, for example, includes a view of being the one true religion that effectively negates all others (Wright 1997). Wright holds to the nominalist position, seeing RE as being a way of developing 'religious literacy', which allows pupils to recognise and evaluate the conflicting truth claims of religions. For Wright, impact on pupil well-being is incidental to a pursuit of questions of truth, in order to deepen understanding of what it means to be a believer in that tradition. For the nominalist, the RE curriculum is in the service of the faith communities, who might be consulted on establishing the key concepts, beliefs and practices they consider essential for an understanding of their faith. This is in contrast with the genericist approach, which argues that RE is primarily in the service of the child.

The genericist view sees religions as representing diverse expressions of a common human religious experience, the examination of which is of value as part of the humanising process of education. As such, the RE curriculum should be constructed on the basis of the process of humanisation, not according to the internal self-understanding of the religions and beliefs to be studied. The nominalist generally rejects this approach, as imposing a liberal religious ideology. However, the genericist approach has had widespread influence and is the most fruitful one in terms of its contribution to pupil well-being.

The 'human development' model is articulated most fully by Grimmitt in *RE and human development* (1987). Grimmitt, an influential teacher trainer and researcher at the University of Birmingham over 30 years, offered a substantial justification of the place of RE within a secular education system. Regarding education as 'a process by, in and through which pupils may begin to explore what it is, and what it means, to be human', Grimmitt explores the role of education in general in the human development of adolescents and the contribution of RE to this humanising project (1987, 198).

Grimmitt seeks to offer an 'acceptable basis for teaching religion in schools' as a 'prerequisite to the formulation of curriculum proposals' (1987, 15). To do this requires a careful examination of the value assumptions underpinning how societies view knowledge, values and the child, including how children learn. He believes that any rationale for RE should not hide the fact that this is a *secular* study of religion,

> drawing upon a variety of disciplines … governed by those educational principles which relate to the manner in which all subject disciplines in the curriculum, including religion, should be investigated (i.e. in a manner which assists the development of cognitive perspective or rationality, promotes understanding of the structure and procedures of the disciplines, recognises the integrity, autonomy and voluntariness of the pupil, etc.). (1987, 46)

His work underpins two attainment targets widely adopted since 1994 by the majority of the locally agreed syllabuses for RE from over 150 LAs, namely 'learning about religion' and 'learning from religion'. However, despite the widespread use of this dual aim of RE – that pupils' own personal development is an integral intention in the light of their encounter with religion and belief – Grimmitt himself is critical of the way 'learning about religion' and 'learning from religion' have moved from being a pedagogical strategy to becoming a pedagogical principle applied to the teaching of religions for their own sake, in line with the nominalist approach.

This is somewhat removed from Grimmitt's original approach, which saw 'learning about and learning from' religion as a strategy to enable pupils to engage with religious materials chosen as the result of a complex curriculum structured around core human givens, core values, substantive religious categories (such as providence, the sacred, law, soul, etc.), shared human experience (such as compassion, suffering, truth, guilt, beauty, etc.) and traditional belief systems. This called for the 'instrumental use of religion to address those crucial themes of human development which enable us to learn what it means to be human', incorporating into the RE curriculum only those aspects of religion which would enable the human givens Grimmitt identified to be addressed (cited in Teece 2008a).

As Teece (2008a) explains,

> what is important for the learner is not knowledge of religion per se, as a reified 'Traditional Belief System', but the way in which a religious believer perceives the world and how these insights can inform how the learner sees the world.

Religious subject matter is chosen in order to provide 'an opportunity for reflection on, and re-evaluation and re-interpretation of the self' (Grimmitt 1991, 77). In order to do this, there needs to be a pedagogy which brings the 'religious life-world' and the 'adolescent life-world' into a dialectical relationship. By studying religions in a way that juxtaposes their 'content' with the 'content' of the pupils' life worlds, pupils are not just informed about religious beliefs and values but are helped 'to *use* the religious beliefs and values as instruments for the critical evaluation of their own beliefs and values' (1987, 141). This interaction between pupils and religious content therefore requires the pedagogical strategy of learning *about* religion (including beliefs, teachings and practices of religious traditions and faith responses to ultimate questions) and learning *from* religion, 'the application of *religious insights* to an understanding of personal issues and experiences' (1987, 219).

It is common practice in good RE to study a religion, making links with and beyond pupils' own experience, setting up interactions that enable pupils to evaluate their own responses to the beliefs and values. The application of religious insights to understanding ideas of meaning and purpose is thus central to the human development model of RE, and therefore, I believe, makes a deeper contribution to pupil well-being than applying a series of skills in handling emotions, beneficial though these skills may be in certain circumstances.

## The value of happiness and well-being in education

There have been some telling criticisms of the well-being agenda and the introduction of happiness lessons. Positive psychology researchers acknowledge that they cannot measure happiness (in terms of meaning and purpose), but then go on to devise measures of happiness (limited to happiness as hedonic, emotion or possibly life satisfaction). Happiness scientists promote meaning and engagement as the pinnacle of the good life, but then fall back on weaker definitions about positive feelings because that is all they can measure (Schoch 2007). Seldon and Layard see happiness as a universal motivation in education, but whilst they reject a focus on the measurable in schools, such as progress in exam results, they replace it with a focus on the 'measurable' aspects of happiness (Smith 2008).

Suissa points out that such interventions fail to capture the role of normativity and questions of value around the idea of a 'meaningful life', stating that simplistic advice like 'take control' or 'avoid relationships that cause conflict' is not educational, as education's normative dimension has a concern with values at its heart (Suissa 2008, 578–80). She agrees with Smith that education is a deeper enterprise, and that 'appreciation of the idea of "the shape of life" and its meaning for ourselves and others cannot be reached through a pre-packaged list of techniques' (Smith 2008, 211; Suissa 2008, 582). This is supported by Haybron's assertion that for human beings to be able to come to a conclusion about their happiness and well-being requires both 'transparency' (that we are able to know what is best for us) and 'aptitude' (that we are able to choose well from the rich variety of options open to us) (Haybron 2008, 13–4). Haybron questions both assumptions, a view that would not be out of place in a religious interpretation of human nature, whether from the western or eastern traditions.

Suissa also argues that the fact that certain states of affairs correlate with happiness has nothing to do with education, against Layard's assertion. Suissa points out that Layard follows Mill's utilitarian view which was intended as guidance for the social management of communities, whereas education is about individuals becoming agents able to make moral choices (Suissa 2008). Some go further, claiming that the application of such programmes for all pupils rather than a select few who may need such training reflects a diminished image of pupils as emotionally vulnerable, undermining pupils' autonomy and choice, as well as an emptying out of the importance of knowledge in the curriculum (Ecclestone and Hayes 2008).

I think that some of these criticisms are clarified by the distinction I make between psychological and philosophical views of happiness. Advocates of happiness in schools use the language of philosophical views, but in practice address the psychological views. They see the flourishing, meaningful life as the ultimate aim but produce interventions that work at the level of pleasure and emotion. Critics' calls for a deeper educational view of happiness could be met by examining the complexities of questions of meaning and purpose, of values and commitments, raised in the human development model of RE, retaining the importance of knowledge within the subject whilst also viewing pupils as agents able to make moral choices, however, imperfectly (*pace* Haybron).

## To what extent does RE contribute to the well-being of pupils?

The human development model of RE is concerned with getting pupils to explore key concepts, ideas, beliefs, traditions, questions, values and commitments arising from the study of religion and belief and to discern their possible application to their own lives. Teece (2008b) presents a view of religions as transformative from the work of John Hick. Religions offer ideas about what it means to be human and they call for, and effect, transformation in the lives of followers. In a pedagogy exploring transformative religion and belief, contributing to pupils' own consideration of meanings and purposes in life including the ethical and transcendent dimensions, both the 'religion' and the 'education' in RE are thus transformative.

This, then, is the relationship with happiness and well-being. RE does not replace the interventions which seek to give those children who need them the skills, such as emotional resilience, to cope with specific situations. These should not be mistaken as routes to happiness, however. RE allows for complexity of individual choices and values, it retains the pupil's autonomy, it reveals that responses to life are not neat and predictable, as shown by the depth and variety of religious and philosophical responses, both theistic and atheistic. RE also allows space for consideration of those beliefs that deny that our lives have any ultimate meaning or purpose. Grimmitt's pedagogy makes RE a part of the curriculum in which questions are opened up and pupils are given the wherewithal to seek answers.

As Suissa (2008, 588) says, 'There is no need … to "put happiness on the curriculum", for on any meaningful account of education as involving, centrally, challenge, disruption and an ability to appreciate complexity – it is already there'. In a similar manner, Cigman (this volume) cites Whitehead in arguing that '"life in all its manifestations" is the proper subject matter of education'. I do not suggest that RE is the only subject in the curriculum that contributes to this meaningful account of education, but I do argue that the teaching of RE essentially involves 'challenge, disruption and an ability to appreciate complexity'. Religion and belief are an important 'manifestation' of life and therefore worth studying. The teaching of RE contributes to pupils' awareness and understanding of questions of meaning and purpose, exploration of which plays a significant part in ideas of happiness and well-being as transcendent. RE does not teach or develop happiness, but it opens up the kinds of thinking and understanding that may start pupils on a path to a life of purpose and meaning.

## References

Coleman, J. 2009. Well-being in schools: Empirical measure, or politician's dream. *Oxford Review of Education* 35, no. 3: 281–92.
Cottingham, John. 2009. Emotional well-being, fragmentation and identity. Presentation to Changing the subject?: Interdisciplinary perspectives on emotional well-being and social justice, economic and social research council funded seminar series RES-451-26-054, University of Nottingham, 19–21 November 2009.
Craig, Carol. 2007. *The potential dangers of a systematic, explicit approach to teaching social and emotional skills (SEAL)*. Glasgow: Centre for Confidence and Well-being.
Csikszentmihalyi, Mihaly. 1990. *Flow: The psychology of optimal experience*. New York, NY: Harper and Row.
Ecclestone, Kathryn, and Dennis Hayes. 2008. *The dangerous rise of therapeutic education*. London: Routledge.
Eid, Michael, and R.J. Larsen, eds. 2008. *The science of subjective well-being*. New York, NY: Guilford Press.
Grimmitt, Michael. 1987. *RE and human development*. Great Wakering: McCrimmons.
Grimmitt, M. 1991. The use of religious phenomena in schools: Some theoretical and practical considerations. *British Journal of RE* 13, no. 2: 77–88.
Grimmitt, Michael. 2000. *Pedagogies of RE*. Great Wakering: McCrimmons.
Haybron, Daniel M. 2008. *The pursuit of unhappiness*. Oxford: OUP.
Jamison, Ian. 2006. *Hinduism*. Deddington: Philip Allan Updates.
Kenny, Anthony. 1992. *Aristotle on the perfect life*. Oxford: OUP.
Klostermaier, Klaus K. 2000. *Hindu writings*. Oxford: Oneworld.
Layard, Richard. 2005. *Happiness: Lessons from a new science*. London: Penguin.
Layard, Richard. 2007. Happiness and the teaching of values. Edited version of 2007 Ashby Lecture, University of Cambridge. http://cep.lse.ac.uk/pubs/download/cp227.pdf (Accessed February 2012).
McMahon, Darrin M. 2006. *Happiness: A history*. New York, NY: Grove Press.
McMahon, Darrin M. 2008. The pursuit of happiness in history. In *The science of subjective well-being*, ed. M. Eid and R.J. Larsen, 80–93. New York, NY: Guilford Press.

Myers, David G. 2008. Religion and human flourishing. In *The science of subjective well-being*, ed. M. Eid and R.J. Larsen, 323–43. New York, NY: Guilford Press.

National Institute for Health and Clinical Excellence. 2008. *Promoting young people's social and emotional wellbeing in secondary education*. London: NICE.

NATRE. 2011. An analysis of a survey of teachers on GCSE change and RE in light of the EBacc changes. http://www.natre.org.uk/docstore/NATRE%20EBacc%20Survey2%20report_final.pdf (accessed February 2012).

Nettle, Daniel. 2005. *Happiness: The science behind your smile*. Oxford: OUP.

Post, Stephen, and Jill Neimark. 2007. *Why good things happen to good people*. New York, NY: Broadway Books.

QCA. 2004. *Religious education: The non-statutory national framework*. London: Qualifications and Curriculum Authority.

Schoch, Richard. 2007. *The secrets of happiness*. London: Profile Books.

Seligman, Martin E.P. 2002. *Authentic happiness*. London: Nicholas Brealey.

Seligman, Martin E.P. 2011. *Flourish*. London: Nicholas Brealey.

Sharples, Jonathan. 2007. Well-being in the classroom. Report on the All-Party Parliamentary Committee, Portcullis House, London, 27 October 2007. Oxford: University of Oxford.

Snyder, Charles R., and Shane J. Lopez, eds. 2005. *Handbook of positive psychology*. Oxford: OUP.

Smith, R. 2008. The long slide to happiness. *Journal of Philosophy of Education* 42, nos. 3–4: 559–73.

Suissa, J. 2008. Lessons from a new science? On teaching happiness in schools. *Journal of Philosophy of Education* 42, no. 3–4: 575–90.

Teece, G. 2008a. Michael Grimmitt and human development: A significant contribution to RE pedagogy. *Resource* 30, no. 3: 9–13.

Teece, G. 2008b. Learning from religions as 'skilful means': A contribution to the debate about the identity of religious education. *British Journal of RE* 30, no. 3: 187–98.

Vernon, Mark. 2008. *Wellbeing*. Stocksfield: Acumen.

Wright, A. 1997. Mishmash, religionism and theological literacy. *British Journal of RE* 19, no. 3: 143–56.

# We need to talk about well-being

Ruth Cigman

*Department of Humanities and Social Science, Institute of Education, London, UK*

> In this paper, I explore the enhancement agenda, which aims to enhance well-being nationwide and particularly among young people. Although it is said by its proponents to embody the ideas of Aristotle, I argue that its true theoretical underpinning is the polarised thinking of positive psychology. The sharp distinction between positive and negative emotion at the heart of this psychology is alien both to Aristotle and William James, another alleged 'ancestor' of positive psychology. It is supplemented by further polarised thinking about the 'point' of education, which according to enhancement thinkers is well-being *as opposed to* knowledge. This leads to a radical but untenable position that sees school subjects as answerable to a well-being test, and asks for those that fail the test to be consigned to the curricular scrap heap. To counter this, we need to restore the idea of mastery, supporting this with a robust but not necessarily traditionalist concept of value that gives teachers the confidence to teach, and pupils the confidence to learn.

## Introduction

> ... it was this broad covenant with children-in-theory ... to which I was unable to resort when Kevin finally tested my maternal ties to a perfect mathematical limit on *Thursday.*

Shriver (2003), *We need to talk about Kevin*

The enhancement agenda, prominent in education today, aims to enhance so-called positive emotions in children (optimism, resilience, confidence, curiosity, motivation, self-discipline, self-esteem, etc.) and inhibit negative ones. Supported by a substantial body of empirical research and numerous policy initiatives, in some respects it is to be welcomed. It is good to stand back from the uncritical obsession with goals that characterises many forms of education. It should be noted however that, healthy as it is to deny philosophers a monopoly on discussions about well-being, the topic remains an inescapably philosophical one.

Recognising this, there has been a tendency in recent years to draw heavily on the philosophy of Aristotle. Aristotle is attractive because, unlike most Utilitarian philosophers, he locates well-being firmly within an ethical frame. Living well, according to Aristotle, is not merely living pleasurably, but taking pleasure in thinking, feeling and acting well. To aspire to this on behalf of children seems a laudable educational goal, particularly at a time when reports of children's depression, educational failures and disaffection make regular headlines news (see Ecclestone this volume; also Claxton 2002; House and Loewenthal 2009).

However well-being is complex, and the well-intentioned desire to promote this may require more than a cursory look at Aristotle. Moral philosophy, for Aristotle, is *essentially* practical. He wanted to make us into expert archers with a clear mark to aim at, and he taught us a great deal about what it means *in practice* to cultivate the virtues, moderate the emotions and deliberate about difficult ethical issues. (see Aristotle 1972). All this goes well beyond the Aristotelian ideas in circulation today about well-being as a form of quasi-biological flourishing.

Aristotle's influence is apparent in the National Curriculum Handbook for Teachers in England (DFEE 1999); Every Child Matters (DfES 2004) and many other policy documents. It is explicit in the happiness agenda that Anthony Seldon and others have developed for independent schools, where classes are designed to develop resilience and optimism as a basis for effective learning (see Layard 2005; Morris 2009). Seligman, similarly, identifies Aristotle as the philosophical inspiration for his influential theory of positive education. The notion of positivity now resonates inside and outside educational settings (see Seligman 2002; Seligman et al. 2009).

Educational policy in the UK thus reflects a heady mix combining the ideas of Aristotle and positive psychology in central ways. Positive emotions are presented by the latter as measurable, enhancible *and* central to an Aristotelian account of well-being. However, positive psychology's sharp distinction between positive and negative emotion is alien to Aristotle, not to mention William James, another alleged ancestor of positive psychology. Aristotle's ideas do not necessarily translate well into policy or empirical psychology, and I shall argue that much of importance has gone missing.

The enhancement agenda is supplemented by further polarised thinking about the 'point' of education, which according to enhancement thinkers is well-being *as opposed to* knowledge. This leads to a radical but (I argue) untenable position that sees school subjects as answerable to a well-being test, and asks for those that fail the test to be consigned to the curricular scrap heap. To counter this, I suggest that we need to restore the idea of mastery, supporting it with a robust but not necessarily traditionalist concept of value that gives teachers the confidence to teach, and pupils the confidence to learn.

## Theoretical underpinnings: positive thinking, Aristotle and the problem of generality

It would be odd to suggest that a person could live well and be well if they were gloomy and miserable all the time (Brighouse 2006, 138). We tend to agree with James (1982), who wrote eloquently of the evils of the 'pining, puling, mumping mood' and asked: 'What is more injurious to others? What less helpful as a way out of the difficulty? It but fastens and perpetuates the trouble which occasioned it, and increases the total evil of the situation (102)'. These sorts of remarks strongly influenced his co-patriot positive psychology movement, which claims to bring optimism and resilience to millions.

However, William James was not a polarised thinker; he did not laud positive thinking at the expense of the negative, though a careless reader may get this impression. Like his brother Henry, James was an outstanding master of prose and time spent in the company of his books quickly shows the folly of extracting sentences here and there as though they express universally valid truths. To do so, quite simply, is to miss the contour of his writings, which entice us towards ideas and also destabilise our thoughts, appearing to demand at times that we believe incompatible things. William James, in short, is a master of irony, which means that his commitment to the truth of his ideas is often uncertain; he wants us to *think richly* before we believe.

The following passage, for example, is pure positive psychology; or so it would seem.

> Much of what we call evil is due entirely to the way men take the phenomenon. It can so often be converted into a bracing and tonic good by a simple change of the sufferer's inner attitude from one of fear to one of fight; its sting so often departs and turns into a relish when, after vainly seeking to shun it, we agree to face about and bear it cheerfully, that a man is simply bound in honor, with reference to many of the facts that seem at first to disconcert his peace, to adopt this way of escape. Refuse to admit their badness; despise their power; ignore their presence; turn your attention the other way; and so far as you yourself are concerned at any rate, though the facts may still exist, their evil character exists no longer. Since you make them evil or good by your own thoughts about them, it is the ruling of your thoughts which proves to be your principal concern. (Ibid. 101–2)

One could hardly improve on this as a manifesto for positive thinking, and it is plausible to suggest that positive psychology has refined and systematised these ideas scientifically, creating techniques for recognising, disputing and removing pessimistic thoughts. We all understand the horrors of the 'pining, puling, mumping mood', and the importance at times of coaxing people (ourselves and others) towards a more positive and in many cases more truthful appreciation of reality. However, there is dark side, as James explains:

> ... happiness, like every other emotional state, has blindness and insensibility to opposing facts given it as its instinctive weapon for self-protection against disturbance. When happiness is actually in possession, the thought of evil can no more acquire the feeling of reality than the thought of good can gain reality when melancholy rules. To the man actively happy, from whatever cause, evil simply cannot then and there be believed in. He must ignore it; and to the bystander he may then seem perversely to shut his eyes to it and hush it up. (Ibid. 101)

Optimists – 'actively happy' people – can be blind and insensible, and there are clearly dangers attached to this condition. In a rare moment of philosophical succinctness, James writes:

> ... since the evil facts are as genuine parts of nature as the good ones, the philosophic presumption should be that they have some rational significance, and that systematic healthy-mindedness, failing as it does to accord to sorrow, pain, and death any positive and active attention whatever, is formally less complete than systems that try at least to include these elements in their scope. (Ibid. 170–1)

So there are limitations to what James calls healthy-mindedness (a phrase that is itself partly ironic), and a careful reader understands that James is not primarily interested in healthy- versus sick-minded philosophy, positive versus negative thinking and optimism versus pessimism. He is interested in system building, ideals and their limitations. He says:

> The deliberate adoption of an optimistic turn of mind thus makes its entrance into philosophy. And once in, it is hard to trace its lawful bounds. Not only does the human instinct for happiness, bent on self-protection by ignoring, keep working in its favor, but higher inner ideals have weighty words to say. (Ibid. 102)

Optimism can be valuable, but it can also be dangerous. The difficult part is tracing its 'lawful bounds': judging *how far* we should oppose the 'pining, puling, mumping mood' in favour of a brighter, more positive outlook. How happy and hopeful *ought* we to be, and on what occasions? Life, as James observes, contains pain, death and disease, other people's as well as our own. Parodying the extremes of optimism, he asks whether 'Cheer up, old fellow, you'll be all right erelong, if you will only drop your morbidness!' is always a reasonable response (Ibid. 148). In modern idiom, when should teachers encourage children to 'snap out of it', and when is it kinder to acknowledge and even share their misery?

The idea of 'tracing lawful bounds' is profoundly Aristotelian, as is the idea that living well involves a continual preparedness to make difficult, contextual judgements. Pride is not a virtue, in the Aristotelian scheme; *proper* pride is the virtue, and it means neither indulging nor suppressing one's pride but keeping it within 'proper bounds'. Nor is anger a vice; *excessive* anger is the vice, as is its deficiency, the failure to be roused by injustice or offence. The key to well-being, for Aristotle, is the disposition to respond appropriately – at the levels of thought, feeling and action – to the *particular* circumstances in which we find ourselves. Fear, shame, anger, pride, pity and indeed hope, are all parts of human life; problems set in when they are too strong or weak, too intense or mild, relative to the circumstances in which they occur.

The great difficulty for human beings – a difficulty that may impede not only our moral characters but our entire well-being – is 'tracing the lawful bounds' of our responses, and particularly our emotions. We draw on this idea when we say a person went over the top or dramatised a situation or accuse them of under reacting, being walked-over, buttoned-up, a shrinking violet. Rather as James' thought is misrepresented when his richly articulated ideas are reduced to neat assertions ('positive thinking is good'), so Aristotle's ideas about ethics are misrepresented if it is thought that virtue is easily taught. We are not virtuous in an Aristotelian way by following rules about how to act. We are virtuous by making difficult judgements about *how* to respond *when*, without going over the top, being buttoned-up, etc.

This is the important ethical territory in which children have a great deal to learn. They do not enter this territory by being encouraged to hope or be happy grandly and indiscriminately. According to Aristotle, they need wise guides to cultivate their emotions, keep their infantile excesses in check, engender good emotional habits and gradually help them to understand *why* certain responses are deficient or excessive, why *this* response is more appropriate than *that* in *this* situation, and help them to take pleasure in feeling, thinking and acting well. So develops the practical reason that is at the heart of the ethical life, essential, in Aristotle's view, for well-being.

Many philosophers feel, and I agree, that Aristotle gives a rich and fundamentally accurate account (merely sketched here, of course) of how human beings become virtuous and lead good lives. He does not say that virtue is *sufficient* for a good life; he does not deny, as many Greek thinkers did, our lack of self-sufficiency, our vulnerability to fate. He says a certain amount of good fortune is needed, as well as virtue, and explains why the latter is so difficult to achieve.

Positive psychology promotes an ideal without cautioning us, as James does, against turning our backs on the negative realities of our own and others' lives, or coasting in realms of abstraction. The positive ideal is embodied in much contemporary policy-making, intended to bring resilience, optimism, self-esteem and other 'life skills' to children through national interventions. But are these always useful? Consider self-esteem. The Social and Emotional Aspects of Learning (SEAL) programme teaches children to reach positive conclusions about themselves, saying things like 'I accept myself for who and what I am'. But a child who has just bullied another child should not necessarily be encouraged to say this; it could reinforce a dangerous arrogance or conceit. Like pride (to which it is related), self-esteem can be improper or proper, i.e. excessive, deficient or just about right. When it is 'taught' as a 'life skill', we may be missing the vital detail, the needs of particular children in the circumstances of their lives (see Cigman 2009).

The same sorts of questions arise with resilience. Thinking physically for a moment, we know that resilient materials withstand shocks, retain or resume their original state on impact, are resistant to foreign bodies. It is *good* to be resilient, but as with self-esteem, how resilient should we be? How would you feel if your resilient spouse withstood not only the misery of his own chemotherapy, but also the misery of yours? Just like materials, resilient people can be tough, and from an emotional point of view this may not be ideal, for it is human sometimes to weep and accept vulnerability. When, where and why is resilience good? How can resilience programmes gauge and monitor such things? How can we feel at ease with them if they fail to do so? How can we be sure that their effects are truly beneficial?

In the report mentioned earlier, Yvonne Roberts urges us to adopt an enhancement agenda (as I call it) in education. Policy-maker, Geoff Mulgan sums up the argument at the opening of his Preface (Mulgan 2009, 6):

> Over the last two decades a gulf has opened up between what education systems provide and what children need. Education systems rightly provide children with skills in numeracy and literacy and academic qualifications. But the emphasis on a set of core academic skills, and a culture of intensive testing, has too often squeezed out another set of skills – how to think creatively, how to collaborate, how to empathise – at the very time when they are needed more than ever.

Basing her argument on wide-ranging research, including research in positive psychology, Roberts explores the theme of life skills, particularly skills needed for twenty-first century life, of which she argues grit or resilience is key (Roberts 2009). Discussing the Penn Resiliency programme, based on positive psychology, which the Young Foundation uses in schools, she writes:

> It is a cognitive behavioural intervention for adolescents that teaches them gradually to change the beliefs that are fuelling their maladaptive emotions ... It encourages them to keep a sense of perspective; to 'think outside the box' and more flexibly

about the multiple and varied causes of problems ('self disputing') and to restrict the tendency to 'catastrophise' that fuels negative thoughts. (21–2)

It sounds appealing and I have no doubt that, as its proponents claim, this programme has helped many children, at least temporarily. Roberts herself approves the programme unreservedly, but reading further into the text, one wonders why. Talking about children who are lagging behind in their developmental abilities (as do some in every classroom), she asks:

> What protective or competence-enhancing factors might help to build resilience in children so far behind in their developmental abilities? [Researchers] argue that there are no universal protective factors. Instead, these may vary according to the age of the child and developmental outcome being targeted. 'Paradoxically, the promotive processes in one context may prove to be risky in another,' they say ... The researchers conclude: 'The major implication of multiple risk models is that interventions need to be as complex as development itself.' This view echoes ... John Dewey's belief that learning is the interaction between a young person and their environment, which means that the experience is different for each individual. (39)

Dewey's particularism echoes Aristotle's, and William James expresses the same sorts of ideas when he warns us against undiscriminating hostility towards the 'pining, puling, mumping mood'. The Penn Resiliency Programme, like positive psychology generally, turns this hostility into what James calls a 'higher ideal' with 'weighty words to say'. Roberts appears to be so in thrall to this ideal that she is oblivious of her own *crucial* quotation, '... the promotive processes in one context may prove to be risky in another', said by the scientists of whom she approves. But they are talking about the *risks of generalities* to particular children, some of whom presumably 'catastrophise' negative thoughts because they have experienced catastrophes in their own homes. Such children need sensitive handling; we may be confident that the best teachers will be alert to such issues (though it is hard to see how this can be guaranteed), but we cannot be confident about all.

At the very least, these observations should encourage us to take a closer look at the enhancement agenda in education. I am not saying that children should not be taught emotional and social skills in the classroom. I am suggesting that Aristotle shows how complex this really is, and that we should be cautious about national interventions conducted without proper appreciation of this complexity. In the next sections, I explore the idea that well-being should be enhanced independently of the passionate, creative teaching of subject disciplines, for it is on this idea that SEAL and happiness classes depend. First, however, we must raise a fundamental question: what's the point of school?

## What's the point of school?

We are highly preoccupied at the present time with the question of what education is *for*, what its basic aims should be, and proposed answers to these questions run through numerous policy documents, books, articles and public debates. The basic themes of this discussion are articulated in the passage by Geoff Mulgan quoted above, where he talks about a gulf between what education systems provide and what children need. The UK schools, he reminds us, are not doing well. Our children are depressed and disaffected, their test scores are low and employers complain that they leave school without basic skills. There is obviously a gulf between need and provision that policy-makers must attend to.

My first task is to analyse this discourse, not defend or reject a position. Argument comes later; what I believe we need to understand initially is how polarities stack up. The enhancement agenda embodies an argument; it says that well-being ought to be the basic aim of education *as opposed to* knowledge for its own sake, or intrinsically valuable knowledge. It says that the latter (Hamlet, equations, etc) is what we typically provide, whereas well-being is what children need. Debates about the point of school typically place the well-being/knowledge choice before us, which is generally associated with left and right wing, progressive and traditional, thinking. Fortunately, as we shall see, these divisions are becoming impossible to sustain.

In the interests of analysis, then, imagine a dual column screen before our collective consciousness. The first column is headed 'enhancement agenda'; the second is headed 'knowledge agenda'. This screen, I shall argue, represents much of the current discourse about schools, and we need to inspect some of the detail.

Geoff Mulgan and Yvonne Roberts are in the first column, as is Claxton, who opens his book *What's the point of school?* (2008) like this:

> The purpose of education is to prepare young people for the future. Schools should be helping young people to develop the capacities they will need to thrive. What they need, and want, is the confidence to talk to try things out, to handle tricky situations, to stand up for themselves, to ask for help, to think new thoughts ... But they are not getting it. There is no evidence that being able to solve simultaneous equations, or discuss the plot of Hamlet, equips young people to deal with life. (vi)

This passage explicitly sets up the polarity. The point of schools *is* to enhance children's capacities to lead good twenty-first century lives (what children need); it is *not* to waste their time with equations, Hamlet and other useless knowledge (what schools provide). Claxton says later on: '"Knowledge" is not what's true; it's what helps' (77). He means that for educational purposes we need to distinguish not between true and false claims, knowledge and error, but between useful and useless knowledge. This emphasis on utility is characteristic of thinkers in the enhancement column.

Another thinker in this column is philosopher John White, who writes:

> In England ... there is a national curriculum built around largely traditional subjects. Thinking about aims is pushed to the margins or welded awkwardly onto an existing structure. But this gets things the wrong way round. School subjects are not ends in themselves, but vehicles ... to attain further purposes. (White 2011, 135)

What are these further purposes? White explains:

> ... schools should be mainly about equipping people to lead a fulfilling life ... In one way this sounds banal: isn't this what we all expect of them? In another, it is anything but. If we were really aiming at fulfilment and had a blank sheet to plan how to go about it, schools ... would become very different places. (Ibid. 1)

So school subjects are vehicles; disciplinary knowledge, as for Claxton, is instrumental. The crucial question then becomes: which knowledge does and does not promote well-being? These ideas are radical: policy-makers should start with a blank sheet on which they list useful knowledge only, knowledge that enhances well-being, and everything else should go on the curricular scrap heap. What should concern us, says White, is not whether a child is:

> proficient in French, or knows about the atomic structure of matter, or [can] solve algebraic equations ... The starting point is that she should have the positive qualities needed for a flourishing life. (Ibid. 131)

Here is the polarisation again. What should concern us primarily are the positive qualities needed for a flourishing life *as opposed to* proficiency in any subject discipline. This prompts a simple question: cannot educators have more than one concern, more than a single, all-encompassing aim?

Turning to column two, the knowledge agenda column, the first thing we notice is that, although some thinkers clearly belong here, what they are opposing is not well-being as an educational aim, but well-being as an *overriding* educational aim. They are not saying that proficiency in a discipline should concern us *as opposed to* well-being or flourishing. Rather, they are saying that these are bound up with each other in crucial ways.

J.S. Mill, for example, found in Wordsworth's poems both intrinsically valuable knowledge and a 'medicine for my states of mind' when he suffered from profound depression:

> From them I seemed to learn what would be the perennial sources of happiness, when all the greater evils shall have been removed. (Mill 1944, 104)

By 'learning from them' (Wordsworth's poems), Mill does not mean dry, analytical or factual learning; indeed he sees this as the cause of his own breakdown. (He received from his father an intense classical education, which included studying Greek at the age of three.) Knowledge of poetry, as of the other arts, *necessarily* involves cultivation of the feelings and the discovery of Wordsworth's poetry thus led him to assert in an Aristotelian spirit:

> The cultivation of the feelings became one of the cardinal points in my ethical and philosophical creed. (Ibid. 101)

So knowledge for its own sake is not *distinct* from knowledge for well-being; rather, assuming that the first cultivates the feelings as it should, these are intimately, insolubly, linked. The linkage is Aristotelian: the cultivation of feelings in association with thinking and understanding is at the heart of Aristotle's account of well-being, as I discussed earlier. In educational terms, this means that knowledge of the humanities and even scientific knowledge, in their deepest forms, have emotional cores. They develop in association with curiosity, discipline, love of truth and beauty, not to mention (at times) fear, pity, anger and shame – in fact, the entire gamut of human emotions. This is most obvious in relation to literature and history, where reflection on human folly and wisdom (including emotional excesses and deficiencies as discussed earlier) are of the essence. Good teaching *provokes* and *elicits* children's emotional responses; it cultivates these in distinctively Aristotelian ways.

Philosopher Richard Peters was a traditionalist; he characterised education as the transmission of intrinsically valuable knowledge. Like Mill, he made it clear that that this dry-sounding idea is actually about passion and our 'quality of living':

> 'There is a quality of life which lies always beyond the mere fact of life' [according to A.N. Whitehead]. The great teacher is he who can convey this sense of quality to another, so that it haunts his every endeavor and makes him sweat and yearn to fix what he thinks and feels in a fitting form ... It is education that provides that touch of eternity under the aspect of which endurance can pass into dignified, wry acceptance, and animal enjoyment into a quality of living. (Peters 2010, 74)

For Peters, the gulf that matters is that which exists between children's need to discover a 'quality of living' and the provision by teachers of information, pedantry and dry facts. A.N. Whitehead, a mathematician whose *The Aims of Education* (1967) influenced Peters, also attacks the tendency to desiccate knowledge:

> There is no royal road to learning through an airy path of brilliant generalisations ... There is only one subject matter for education, and that is Life in all its manifestations. Instead of this single unity, we offer children – Algebra, from which nothing follows; Geometry, from which nothing follows; Science, from which nothing follows; History, from which nothing follows; a Couple of Languages, never mastered; and lastly, most dreary of all, Literature, represented by plays of Shakespeare, with philological notes and short analyses of plot and character to be in substance committed to memory. (6–7)

What is striking about this passage is that it captures an ideal that virtually everyone shares. Education should be about 'Life in all its manifestations': this is what children need to learn about, what many schools do not provide. Given our testing obsessions at the present time, the passage prompts us to ask whether we have progressed very far beyond Gradgrind after all. Are we teaching a kind of geometry, history and literature, *from which nothing follows*? The answer, from almost everyone who currently claims an interest in education, is a resounding 'yes'. *Much* of the time, we agree, this is what teaching has been reduced to; and recent educational policies are responsible for this.

We are unanimous, then, about the baneful gulf between Life and Education, and as we realise this, the enhancement and knowledge columns begin to collapse. Not only Mill and Peters, but Claxton, Mulgan, Roberts and White, must applaud Whitehead's argument in this passage. However, the *conclusions* of the first and second groups are different, which is why we need to talk about separate columns.

Unlike the enhancement thinkers, Whitehead is not suggesting that algebra, history, Shakespeare etc. are useless. He does not propose a distinction between different kinds of *knowledge content*, some of which does, some of which does not, enhance well-being. Rather, he distinguishes between *ert* and *inert* knowledge, knowledge that does and does not deal with Life in all its manifestations:

> In training a child to activity of thought, above all things we must beware of what I will call 'inert ideas' – that is to say, ideas that are merely received into the mind without being utilised, or tested, or thrown into fresh combinations. (Ibid. 1)

Whitehead does not prompt us to ask: should we teach history or IT? Literature or media studies? Natural history or sport psychology? He prompts us to consider whether we transmit knowledge in lively or moribund, ert or inert forms. It is not Hamlet that is useless; it is Hamlet as plot summary, philological notes, imagery grid and testable Key Stage 3 resource. Shakespeare as rich poetic drama has the power to enhance our lives 'perennially', as Wordsworth did for Mill.

When we consider the form in which knowledge is dished up to GCSE and A-level students, it seems obvious that ertia and inertia, rather than enhancive and unenhancive knowledge content, is the distinction educators and policy-makers need to examine. Children are bored and depressed by high-stakes bullet pointed lists, which desiccate fascinating material, present hoops to jump through and place pupils in terrifying competition with one another. It is my belief that if we could address this problem clear sightedly, the debate about which knowledge passes and fails the well-being test would be seen as pointless, as it is. The problem is that no-one appears to have a clue what the test amounts to. How do we *decide* and *agree* which knowledge content has and has not the power to enhance well-being? Whose well-being are we talking about? Isn't it a truism to say that people *vary*, thrive on different subjects and activities? The proper conclusion seems to be that children should be offered a range of excitingly taught, intrinsically valuable knowledge.

It is interesting that, on the last point, left wing journalist Melissa Benn and Conservative Education Minister Michael Gove concur. It is unsurprising that Gove favours a knowledge agenda; more surprising is the discovery that egalitarian Benn does the same:

> Young people need not just efficient instruction but the opportunity for exploration – of ideas, history, literature, poetry, music, art, film, politics. These are the things that make and keep us human, and if we don't learn how to begin to think about these things when young, we may never return to them as adults. (Benn 2011)

Benn is not asking us to put these subjects on hold while we debate their enhancive powers. She believes they are valuable in rather the way Mill, Peters and Whitehead believe they are valuable: because they are rooted in our humanity. Implicit here is a willingness to identify certain knowledge as *intrinsically* valuable, which enhancement thinkers are unwilling to do. The question posed by the latter – which kinds of knowledge content enhance well-being? – risks cutting the connection with individual lives through overgeneralisation. As Benn implies, placing traditional knowledge on the curricular scrap heap because it is believed to fail the well-being test can mean loss and deprivation for countless individuals whose lives will never be enriched by it.

**Mastery of the disciplines**

I have presented contemporary educational discourse as dominated by two crumbling columns: a strange and perplexing image. Enhancement thinkers see well-being as the *overriding* educational aim; they mount an assault on the idea of knowledge for its own sake, which is cast as a luxury for the elite unless it is shown to serve enhancive aims. Knowledge advocates are not so exclusive. They agree that well-being (happiness in a perennial sense, quality of living, Life with a capital L) is at the heart of education, and say that knowledge in its richest, most *emotional* sense is bound up with this.

Note that the knowledge agenda does not depend on instrumental thinking, though it can sometimes sound this way (as when Mill talks about poetry as 'medicine for the mind'). Rather, it says that intrinsically valuable knowledge *enriches* life. This is a humanistic educational aim that does not pretend to be scientific. We can agree that this is important without being tempted to conduct a survey, for it rests ultimately on our thoughts and judgements about what makes human lives worthwhile.

So we have knowledge as a humanistic educational aim in one column – here well-being has a central place – and well-being as an overriding educational aim, to which knowledge aims are beholden, in the other. The latter lends itself to science; it encourages the question 'which kinds of knowledge do/do not enhance well-being?' which I have suggested is obscure and possibly meaningless. It is expressed in Claxton's idea that equations, Hamlet and much else besides *fail to equip young people for life.*

The exclusivity of the enhancement agenda, by contrast with the inclusivity of the knowledge agenda, betrays something of philosophical importance. Advocates of the first are clearly *uncomfortable* with the idea of intrinsically valuable knowledge. For the philosopher Wittgenstein, discomfort with ideas should be the mainspring of philosophy, that is, of fruitful reflection. It should prompt what he called 'philosophical investigations' rather than leading directly to conclusions with which we feel more (as we now say) in our comfort zone. He thought that, without examining the underlying discomfort, the latter are likely to be misguided. (see, e.g. Wittgenstein 1953.)

Mulgan says in the Preface to Yvonne Roberts' report:

> There is a remarkably broad consensus on what would be in the curriculum if it started with children's present and future needs rather than what's familiar to policymakers and teachers. What's required includes systematic reasoning, creativity, collaboration and the ability to communicate as well as mastery of the disciplines. (Ibid. 7–8)

This is like John White's point about starting with a blank sheet, though the idea of a 'remarkably broad consensus' about what to put here might strike many as optimistic. What mainly interests me about this passage is the last phrase, mastery of the disciplines. It has a tacked-on, uncomfortable feel, and examining the report that follows, one understands why. Disciplines are not discussed by Roberts, though the life skills of *discipline* and *self-discipline* are discussed a great deal. From an enhancement perspective, disciplines are antediluvian things that have not been submitted to the rigours of the well-being test (particularly the twenty-first century well-being test). They are based on the quaint idea of intrinsically valuable knowledge, knowledge for its own sake, which lacks a sound rationale in the modern world.

It lacks this, or is believed to do so, for two reasons. One is discomfort with the ideas of moral objectivity or absolutism, expressed in protests like: who's to say that Shakespeare is valuable? This protest often combines the idea that *nothing* is intrinsically valuable, for values are relative, with the idea that cultures other than our own may produce poets whose work is *as* valuable as that produced in the West. That these ideas do not sit easily together is clearly a problem; many philosophers, as a consequence, see relativism as a self-defeating position (see, e.g. Williams 1985, chap. 9).

The second source of discomfort is a social problem that may be more acute in Britain than in almost any other country: disaffection. Children in the UK schools often demand a clear understanding of why they are learning what. Many simply refuse to engage with learning if they cannot 'see the point', and our awareness of this difficult and in many ways counter-educational situation cannot but influence our reflections about the 'point' of school. Not only must we convince ourselves; we must convince children that there is some 'point' to what we are teaching them. The authority required to impart this conviction is often strenuously challenged. Whitehead says:

> All practical teachers know that education is a patient process of the mastery of details, minute by minute, hour by hour, day by day. (Ibid. 6)

I agree that teachers know this (it is at least *part* of what education involves), but how hard is their task when children cannot see the point of this process, when our testing obsessions make our educational offerings moribund, when many teachers are so paralysed by relativist and cultural inhibitions that *they* are often doubtful about the point of traditional disciplines? How, in these circumstances, can we expect children to endure the 'patient process' that Whitehead describes? Positive psychology teaches us to avoid pain unless its rewards are pretty much guaranteed ('evidence-based'); but the humanistic enrichment of life guarantees nothing. It vaguely assures us that there are likely to be rewards, no more, and what kind of argument is this for nihilistic, impatient, anti-authoritarian and frequently depressed children?[1]

Yet we all know that, hard as learning may be, it can also be unbelievably exciting. The quaint idea of 'mastery of disciplines' will not go away – even Mulgan cannot quite give it up – for engagement with Shakespeare or Wordsworth can be not only arduous, not only 'useless', but thrilling and life-enhancing (as the depressed Mill was to discover). It can take us over, lift our moods, do what positive psychologists *rightly* draw attention to when they talk about 'flow' (Csikszentmihalyi 2002). The crucial point is that educational disciplines must be taught 'ertly' rather than 'inertly', and there are countless extraordinary teachers today, passionate about their disciplines, struggling to engage children with 'Life in all its manifestations'. For an outstanding teacher this effort, as Peters says (quoted above), 'haunts his every endeavour and makes him sweat and yearn to fix what he thinks and feels in a fitting form'. The enhancement agenda's denigration of disciplines, of *intrinsically* valuable knowledge, is a denigration of such a teacher's life-long passion.

## Concluding remarks

The polarisation of enhancement and knowledge casts a shadow over educational policy and debate. It is potentially damaging to children – it makes many into casualties of misguided generalisations – and it threatens the future society that enhancement thinkers are so anxious to serve. I have suggested that at the heart of this situation is discomfort with the idea of intrinsically valuable knowledge. Enhancement thinkers try to shock us out of our complacency about traditional disciplines (as they see it) by asking: what ends do they serve? If not the ultimate end of promoting well-being, why bother with them at all? The demand for justification

EMOTIONAL WELL-BEING IN EDUCATIONAL POLICY AND PRACTICE

cultivates doubt about educational experiences that set people alight, and generates a kind of nihilism that does teachers and pupils no good at all.

Fortunately, the demand often has no purchase, because poetry, history, fine arts etc enrich many people's lives in inestimable ways. If something enriches your life, you may be unable to articulate what this means or describe your feelings to others, but the demand for justification loses its sting. It may, however, undermine your confidence as a teacher, and this can have devastating implications for future generations. What we know is that disciplinary knowledge fails to enrich every life; that knowledge and ideas are easily desiccated by educators; that intense testing makes desiccation virtually inevitable; that the *main* casualties of all this tend to be children with social and economic disadvantages; that disaffection, which can be toxic, often ensues.

I close with two suggestions. First, we should pay more attention to the idea of mastery, uncomfortable though its associations may be. (For a start, it is offensively gendered.) One can be a master of anything that involves the gradual acquisition of knowledge and skill: car mechanics and tree surgery as well as medieval literature. This acquisition may be more or less arduous and painful, but it is valuable for virtually everyone. It requires the personal qualities beloved by John White and others (patience, self-discipline, resilience etc.), without prioritising these over knowledge in meaningless ways. Learning, acquiring mastery, *is* sometimes painful, but it can also be infinitely pleasurable and satisfying, as well as bringing self-respect and economic rewards. The question we need to ask is whether the enhancement agenda is not a distraction from the patient engagement with learning that we should aspire to for children. This can bring the lasting satisfactions of mastery – a crucial aspect, for many, of well-being – and is an ideal site for the Aristotelian cultivation of feeling that lies at the heart of his conception of the good life.

My second suggestion is that we can only pursue such questions if we stand up to nihilism, expressed in Claxton's idea that Hamlet lacks educational value because it fails to equip children for life. Take this idea into a classroom, and you will no doubt find a bunch of bored and disaffected children who, like yourself, cannot see the point of Shakespeare. Take Peters' 'sweat and yearning' to convey a 'quality of living', and Hamlet could change their lives. The *conviction of value* is essential for teachers, who will only help children to aspire to mastery and tolerate painstaking learning if they can transmit this. These issues need urgent examination, for nihilism about educational value is at the heart of the enhancement agenda see Cigman (2000). Distrust of value is set against positive thinking, which lauds some values over others in polarised ways, and neglects the complex insights of Aristotle.

I want to end with Mill (the disaffected Utilitarian), describing the effects of Wordsworth on his life. I use this passage to suggest that the enhancement theorist's sceptical demand for justification can be met in one way only. It is met *humanistically*, by listening carefully to what people say about the importance of certain knowledge in their lives. The demand for justification comes from enlightenment, science-based thinking, and it cannot be assumed that questions of intrinsic value will yield to this demand. Hamlet is not *justified*; it is reflected on, responded to and above all, accepted or rejected as a source of learning. My suggestion is that, as we learn from Hamlet if we allow ourselves to, so we may learn a great deal about education from passages like the following:

79

What made Wordsworth's poems a medicine for my state of mind, was that they expressed, not mere outward beauty, but states of feeling, and of thought coloured by feeling, under the excitement of beauty. They seemed to be the very culture of the feelings, which I was in quest of. In them I seemed to draw a source of inward joy, of sympathetic and imaginative pleasure, which could be shared in by all human beings … (Mill 1944, 104)

## Note

1. In 2007, a UNICEF report placed UK children at the bottom of a 21-nation well-being league.

## References

Aristotle. 1972. *Nichomachean ethics*. Trans. D. Ross. London: Oxford University Press.
Benn, Melissa. 2011. In a class of their own. *The Guardian*. Comment section. October 25.
Brighouse, Harry. 2006. *On education*. New York, NY: Routledge.
Cigman, R. 2000. Ethical confidence in education. *Journal of Philosophy of Education* 34, no. 4: 643–57.
Cigman, R. 2009. Enhancing children. *Journal of Philosophy of Education* 42, no. 3–4: 539–57.
Claxton, Guy. 2002. *Building learning power: Helping young people become better learners*. Bristol: TLO Ltd.
Claxton, Guy. 2008. *What's the point of school?* Oxford: One World.
Csikszentmihalyi, M. 2002. *Flow: The psychology of happiness*. London: Rider.
Department for Education and Skills. 2004. Every child matters: Change for children. http://www.dcsf.gov.uk/everychildmatters/about/aims/aims/
Department for Education and Employment/ Qualifiations and Curriculum Authority. 1999. National curriculum handbook for teachers in England. https://www.education.gov.uk/publications/eOrderingDownload/QCA-99-457.pdf
House, R., and D. Loewenthal, eds. 2009. *Childhood, well-being and a therapeutic ethos*. London: Karnac.
James, William. 1982. *The Varieties of Religious Experience*. London: Fount.
Layard, Richard. 2005. *Happiness: Lessons from a new science*. London: Penguin.
Mill, John. S. 1944. *Autobiography*. New York, NY: Columbia University Press.
Morris, Ian. 2009. *Teaching happiness and well-being in schools, learning to ride elephants*. London: Continuuum.
Mulgan, Geoff. 2009. Preface to Roberts, Y. 2009. Grit: The skills for success and how they are grown. http://www.youngfoundation.org/files/images/publications/GRIT.pdf.
Peters, R.S. 2010. Education as initiation. In *Philosophical analysis and education*, ed. R.D. Archambault. Oxon: Routledge.
Roberts, Yvonne. 2009. Grit: The skills for success and how they are grown. http://www.youngfoundation.org/files/images/publications/GRIT.pdf.
Seligman, Martin. 2002. *Authentic happiness*. London: Nicholas Brealey.
Seligman, M., R. Ernst, J. Gilham, K. Reivich, and M. Linkins. 2009. Positive education: Positive psychology and classroom interventions. *Oxford Review of Education* 35, no. 3: 293–311.
Shriver, Lionel. 2003. *We need to talk about Kevin*. New York, NY: Counterpoint.
White, John. 2011. *Exploring well-being in schools*. Oxon: Routledge.
Whitehead, A.N. 1967. *The aims of education*. New York, NY: Free Press.
Williams, Bernard. 1985. *Ethics and the limits of philosophy*. London: Fontana.
Wittgenstein, L. 1953. *Philosophical investigations*. Oxford: Blackwell.

# From emotional and psychological well-being to character education: challenging policy discourses of behavioural science and 'vulnerability'

Kathryn Ecclestone

It is difficult to challenge a strong consensus that governments must intervene in a worsening crisis of emotional and psychological well-being. The article relates rising estimates of problems and corresponding calls for intervention in educational settings to the increasingly blurred boundaries between a cultural therapeutic ethos, academic research and policy. The recent revival of an old discourse of 'character' reinforces a search for better measurement as the basis for behaviour change strategies reflected in government interest in new ideas from behavioural science. In response to C. Wright Mills' injunction that a sociological imagination should try to understand how social change reflects changing images of the human subject, the article explores the educational implications of these development. It argues that the depiction of well-being and character as a set of behaviours and the parallel drive to measure them are rooted in a diminished view of an essential human vulnerability. This legitimises the imposition of psychological interventions that avoid moral and political questions about the nature of well-being and character and the conditions needed to develop them.

## 1. Introduction

At a conference organised by the Young Foundation and the Macquarie Bank on 7 February 2012, Brigadier Rhonda Cornum told a receptive audience of community resilience project leaders, teacher educators and the media that the US army's $125 million investment in 'reliable global assessment instruments' and 'emotional fitness' training could be a basis for universal interventions in the UK, on the grounds that 'if we know how to make everyone better, I think we would all agree that we should' (Cornum 2012). Introducing the event, ex-Labour government Minister for Transport and now adviser to the Macquirie Bank, Gus McDonald, commended Prime Minister Cameron for his stated commitment that policy-makers should base effective intervention on 'the best that science teaches us about how people behave and what drives their well-being'.

Political interest in applying behavioural psychology to education and other areas of social policy has ebbed and flowed since the 1920s, both in the USA and here (e.g. Myers 2011; Stewart 2009, 2011; Thomson 2006). Yet, while all governments hope to shape good citizenship, the current British Government's much-touted slogan 'from nanny to nudge' suggests an intensifying desire to find scientific evidence for more sophisticated strategies for behaviour change. Formed in 2010 as part of the Cabinet Office, the behavioural insight unit is exploring behavioural economics, social psychology and neuroscience for better ways of getting citizens to make better lifestyle choices, take on a more active role in areas traditionally run by local and national government (such as housing, youth work and social care) and develop their own and others' well-being (e.g. John et al. 2011; Sullivan 2011).

Cultural and political concerns about the emotional state of citizens are manifested in numerous countries through initiatives in education, welfare, legal and rehabilitation systems, survivor movements, political apologies and post-war reconstruction. A growing body of sociological analysis argues that they emanate from, and also fuel, a powerful cultural 'therapeutic ethos'. Through this ethos, ideas, claims and practices of psychologists, therapists and psychiatrists permeate popular culture, politics and social and educational policy settings and create new common sense assumptions about the state of the self, and accompanying vocabularies and practices (e.g. Brunila 2012; Durodie 2009; Ecclestone 2011; Ecclestone and Hayes 2008; Ecclestone et al. 2010; Furedi 2003; Lau 2012; Moon 2009; Nolan 1998, 2008; Pupavac 2001, 2009; Wright 2008). As I argue below, a cultural therapeutic ethos is integral to the current slip from discourses and associated practices of emotional and psychological well-being into a revival of an old discourse of character, and broader government interest in new ideas from behavioural science.

It is important to reiterate at the outset of my exploration of these developments that 'well-being' and 'emotional and psychological well-being' as a subset of it, embrace related but different concepts and concerns, and draw in diverse perspectives about important attributes, attitudes, dispositions and 'skills' that need developing (e.g. Coleman 2009; Ecclestone 2011; Watson, Carl, and Philip 2012). I use 'emotional and psychological well-being' as an umbrella that draws in an extensive set of 'constructs' seen as amenable to development. These include resilience, stoicism, an optimistic outlook, an ability to be in the moment (or 'in flow'), feelings of satisfaction, being supported, loved, respected, skills of emotional regulation, emotional literacy (or emotional intelligence) as well as empathy, equanimity, compassion, caring for others and not comparing yourself to others (e.g. Huppert 2007; Layard 2007; Seligman et al. 2009). As I show below, a renewed discourse of character embraces all these constructs whilst adding other attributes and dispositions as virtues in a long list of 'character capabilities' (e.g. Lexmond and Grist 2011).

I begin my analysis by exploring the increasingly blurred boundaries between political and public consensus about a crisis of emotional and psychological well-being and the common sense assumptions of a cultural 'therapeutic ethos'. I argue that this blurring normalises informal and formal assessments of people's emotional and psychological states, thereby legitimising universal programmes that aim simultaneously to prevent future problems and enhance present well-being. I then go onto argue that the revival of an old discourse of 'character' incorporates concerns with morals and virtues within a psychological depiction that embraces all the constructs of well-being within a more inclusive set of 'capabilities', and hopes to find ways to measure them. Behind these developments lies political interest in using new ideas from behavioural science as a basis for more sophisticated interventions a and

## EMOTIONAL WELL-BEING IN EDUCATIONAL POLICY AND PRACTICE

measures. In the final section, I argue that such hopes are rooted in a cultural sensibility that presents emotional vulnerability, not as an existential condition, but as a determining characteristic of the contemporary self which requires therapeutically based intervention. I conclude by proposing that this determinist view of human beings psychologises moral dimensions to well-being and character in a social project that aims to engineer them through state-sponsored behaviour training.

## 2.  Consensus and crisis

### 2.1.  *Responding to emotional and psychological vulnerability*

Positive psychology, or what its followers call the 'new science of happiness' has become highly influential in policy and practice, reinforced by bodies such as the World Health Organisation. This presents well-being as part of positive mental health in which we realise our own abilities, cope with the normal stress of everyday life, work productively and contribute positively to the community. Its acknowledged founder, Martin Seligman, ex-president of the American Psychological Association and promoter of high profile interventions for the US army and British Government, argues that learned optimism is at the heart of well-being, alongside psychological and emotional components listed above. He and supporters argue that these can be taught and transferred to life situations (e.g. Seligman 2011; Seligman et al. 2009). Richard Layard, a prominent British supporter suggests that science enables us to challenge existential beliefs that life involves suffering. Launching the Action for Happiness movement in April 2011, he argued:

> Happiness is good for you ... Everyone wants to be happy, yet many are not. This has been the human condition for as long as anyone can remember – Samuel Beckett said that the tears of the world are a constant quantity. But what if the tears of the world are not so constant? What if it really is possible for individuals and whole societies to shape and boost their happiness? (www.happiness.org.uk)

In addition to its compelling challenge to fundamental existential beliefs, a crucial appeal of positive psychology is its rejection of traditional solutions to well-being such as redistribution of wealth or promotion of economic growth. Instead, policymakers' resurrection of the old adage that 'money can't buy happiness' fits well with a view that capitalist materialism and alienation are key causes of its contemporary poor state (e.g. James 2007a; Layard 2005). In contrast, an epidemiological perspective correlates mental health with relative levels of wealth and inequality (Wilkinson and Pickett 2009). These contrasting arguments lend weight to arguments for intervention and measures for well-being. In further debate, the Institute of Economic Affairs argues that both analyses and their implications for economic growth are wrong, and it cautions against official measures and interventions (Booth 2012).

Conflicting views about the role of government and the economy in emotional and psychological well-being do not challenge powerful arguments for intervention made in studies which quantify factors that contribute to it. A typical estimate is that about 40% of its underlying 'constructs' are genetic or trait-based, 15% are affected by material conditions and social relationships and the rest are amenable to intervention (Huppert op. cit.). Other studies suggest that genetic or trait-based factors comprise 50%, but the overall argument for promoting 'equality of opportunity for happiness' is the same (Fritjers, Johnston, and Shields 2011). A powerful impetus for intervention is fear that cycles of emotional and material deprivation, life chances and poor self-esteem are not only interwoven but create damaging emotional and psychological legacies for future generations. Since 1997, a cornerstone of social policy shared across political parties is that government must intervene in order to *'replace a vicious cycle with a virtuous cycle'* (Duncan-Smith and Allan 2009, 9; see also Social Exclusion Unit 1999).

Over the past 15 years or so, a strong consensus has emerged that certain universal interventions prevent future mental illness whilst helping those with early problems (e.g. Bailey 2010; Bywater and Sharples this volume; Cornum 2012; Huppert 2007; Layard 2005). Calls for public investment go hand in hand with another compelling tenet of the new science, namely its rejection of individual psychopathology which has traditionally underpinned targeted strategies. By identifying measurable social and individual characteristics of subjective well-being, positive psychology aims to build upon the individual and communal assets that foster them in a form of 'emotional inoculation' (Layard op. cit.; Bailey op. cit.; Huppert op. cit.). This parallels attempt in welfare and health policy to develop 'asset-based' interventions (e.g. Foot and Hopkins 2011).

The US army resilience programme cited above is designed to prevent dramatically rising levels of post-traumatic stress disorder (Cornum 2012). Other alarming estimates of mental ill-health reinforce calls for intervention. For example, a study in 2007 for the Nuffield Foundation reported that more than a million children have problems, doubling the numbers of a generation ago. A survey of over 8000 children found that a third of those aged 14–16 had 'conduct disorders', such as aggressive, disruptive or anti-social behaviour, 4% aged 5–16 had emotional disorders such as stress, anxiety and depression, 2% had hyperactive behaviour or attention problems, 6% had conduct disorders and 2% had more than one type of disorder (Collishaw et al. 2007; see also Myers this volume). In promoting its resilience programme as part of a pilot project funded by the previous government in five local authorities, Hertfordshire local authority quotes Institute of Psychiatry figures in 2007 that *'the number of children with emotional and behavioural problems in the UK has doubled in the past 25 years ...'* (Bailey 2010). Others offer different estimates (e.g. Bywater and Sharples this volume).

In parallel, popular texts reinforce consensus about a crisis. For example, a self-help guide to diagnosing mental health claims that 40% of the British public will *'undergo psychological difficulties at some time'*, defining someone with a mental disorder as having *'disabling psychological symptoms, an emotional or behavioural problem or dysfunction in thinking, acting or feeling ... all of which can cause distress and may impair how someone functions'* (Connelly-Stephenson 2007, 6). Psychiatrist Oliver James argues that 24% of Britons will suffer emotional distress (James 2007b). In a book on emotional literacy for teachers and parents, educational psychologist Peter Sharp claims that 'approximately 1 in 4 of us will have a mental health problem at some time in our life, requiring treatment or support from the caring professions ...' (Sharp 2003, 7).

Slippery definitions and widely varying estimates of problems accompany apocryphal claims for long-term impact and costs. A commonplace assertion is that children diagnosed at five with single or multiple conduct disorders are significantly more likely to commit crimes, be unemployed, experience martial breakdown and have drug or alcohol problems (e.g. Bywater and Sharples this volume). Such problems are often quantified precisely. For example, Hertfordshire local authority claims that 'a child with a conduct disorder costs the taxpayer £70,000 in crime, social care and remedial costs by the time they are 28 compared to £7000 for a child with no such problems' (Bailey 2010, 5). As Historian Thomas Dixon shows, the Victorians had their own, albeit unquantified, concerns about the pernicious social fall-out in crime and immoral behaviour seen to arise from a failure to train children's emotions (Dixon this volume).

Contemporary advocates of intervention argue that the number needing it grows in proportion to the population diagnosed with problems (e.g. Huppert 2007). Yet, estimates overlook the official sanctioning of a large increase in professional diagnoses through successive revisions of the American Psychiatric Association's highly influential Diagnostic and Statistical Manual (DSM). In the UK, this is used for formal diagnosis by clinically qualified professionals and as a general guide by educational psychologists and other professionals. Accounts by insiders and external analysts show how DSM has changed the diagnostic criteria for post-traumatic stress disorder, anxiety and depression, expanded category disorders amongst children, turned previously rare syndromes and disorders into common ones and categorised behaviours once seen as antisocial, disruptive or merely commonplace as mental disorders: in this way, for example, post-bereavement grief and shyness have been medicalised (e.g. Horwitz and Wakefield 2007; Lau op. cit.; Myers this volume; Summerfield 2004). Use of DSM in the everyday mental health market has also expanded the range of symptoms drawn into professional remit (Lau 2012). In parallel, official technical criteria to categorise adults as 'vulnerable' or 'at risk' have shifted from the precisely delineated list created by the 1995 Law Commission to the much looser one offered by the 2006 Safeguarding Vulnerable Adults Act of 'anyone receiving treatment, health or palliative care of any description', including therapy (McLaughlin 2011, 120; also Eves 2009).

As historical analyses of changing fashions in psychiatry and clinical psychology show, diagnostic criteria and their resulting labels and assessments reflect scientific understanding in specific sociocultural conditions (Downbiggin 2011; Myers 2011; Thomson 2006). This means that although rising levels of mental ill-health are not merely social constructions, they cannot be divorced from cultural perceptions and preoccupations. At the same time, popular, political and professional interest in solutions offered by various strands of psychology, therapy and psychoanalysis are both reflected in, and fuelled by, the proliferation of popular accounts by academics about the lessons of their research for everyday life, self-assessment quizzes, pen portraits of diagnoses and symptoms, instruction and advice in self-help books and lifestyle magazines. Instructional guides include a guide to creating a 'well-being curriculum' and a clever parody of fairytales that explains disorders to parents and children (James 2007b; Morris 2009).

In everyday life and educational settings alike, a merger between academic, political and popular concerns normalises formal and informal 'diagnoses' of problems. These manifest themselves in the everyday prevalence of semi-serious claims to have 'anger management' or 'attachment issues', being 'a bit aspergers' or 'oppositional defiance disorder' or having 'an attention and hyperactivity disorder day'. Reflecting a cultural therapeutic ethos, such labels blur popular and professional understandings of our emotional and psychological selves (see Ecclestone and Hayes 2008; Furedi 2003; Nolan 1998). Studies in schools and colleges show

how this leads teachers and support staff to categorise certain children and young people as, variously, 'vulnerable', 'at risk', having 'fragile learning identities', 'no self-esteem' and being 'dysfunctional' and 'disaffected and disengaged' (Ecclestone 2010, chap. 5; Ecclestone and Bailey 2009; Gillies 2011). In these studies, such labels accompanied casual speculations about how cycles of emotional vulnerability and 'dysfunction' both arose from and created social and educational problems, anxiety about assessment tasks and difficulties in coping with various pedagogic demands. In a study of Finnish prison and young offender projects, some young men articulated therapeutic accounts of their emotional and psychological problems, learnt from sessions with youth workers (Brunila 2012).

If my analysis here is valid, everyday and cultural manifestations of assumptions about emotional and psychological legacies and their effects cannot be divorced from the parallel rise of 'treatment therapy' predicated on fears about rising levels of disorders and behaviours that warrant intervention and 'positive therapy' (or 'preventative' or 'enhancement' therapy) that turns many qualitative aspects of life and our experience of it into skills that can be taught and learned (Lau op. cit.). In a historical study of mental health, Ian Downbiggin argues that professional and popular diagnoses of new syndromes and disorders, and the interventions these create, are a paradox of diversity and inclusion that destigmatises mental health problems whilst creating new constraints on normality and new experts who tell us how to feel (Downbiggin 2011). Taken together, these cultural and professional developments contribute to a rise in professional forms of therapy and legitimise calls for state-sponsored interventions in educational settings.

## 2.2.  *The rise of behavioural interventions*

Ranging from prescriptive sequences of scripted activities to instil positive thinking and certain responses to problematic situations, to activities such as 'circle time' based on Rogerian group counselling and consciousness-raising, there is strong support for universal, generic programmes to develop emotional and psychological well-being (see Bywater and Sharples this volume). Informed variously by cognitive behaviour therapy, psychoanalysis, positive psychology, self-help, reflective thinking and counselling, officially sponsored programmes include a version of the American Penn Resilience programme, piloted by the previous British Government in five local authorities, encompassing 700 secondary school teachers and over 7000 students and the Personal and Thinking Skills programme for primary schools (e.g. Challen et al. 2011; Curtis and Northgate 2007). Less prescriptive and more eclectic is the previous government's Social and Emotional Aspects of Learning (SEAL) strategy for primary and secondary schools, introduced in 2005 and withdrawn from formal government sponsorship in 2011 (see Craig 2007; Ecclestone and Hayes 2008; Humphrey, Ann, and Michael 2010; Watson, Carl, and Philip 2012 for discussion).

Promotions and evaluations of such initiatives have tended to reflect the slippery definitions and sense of crisis that characterise the field as a whole, often eliding conduct disorders, disaffection from formal class teaching, general lack of motivation, poor social skills, emotional difficulties, bad behaviour and lack of 'emotional literacy' (e.g. Challen et al. op. cit.; Curtis and Northgate op. cit.; Hallam 2009). This means that claims about effectiveness and impact seem often to be about simple disciplinary training, such as making students more proactive in their learning, attend regularly, manage their homework and sports equipment and set realistic but challenging targets (e.g. Bailey op. cit.). Further difficulty in establishing a definitive evidence base arises from the incoherence of the field as a whole, where interest groups compete to define a problem and offer particular solutions. A key area of disagreement is whether skills-based universal interventions, child centred, holistic and relational approaches or whether teaching social and emotional learning through subjects are most appropriate (e.g. Craig 2007; Watson et al. op. cit.; Dixon 2011).

In the light of conceptual confusion, strong advocacy for intervention and competing claims about the best approach, it is difficult to see how evaluations of interventions can offer more than contradictory or inconclusive evidence. Nor, as Elias and Morceri acknowledge in this volume, do we yet know their long-term effects. Unanswered questions therefore remain about the extent and nature of problems and how best to respond. There are also ethical questions about the reductionist view of well-being that many interventions offer (see Dixon, Cigman this volume; Suissa 2008; Watson et al. op. cit.). A hitherto unaddressed question is about the images of participants reflected in policy discourses and associated practices that are used to justify behavioural interventions: as I argue below, this question also emerges through renewed interest in character development.

## 3. Building citizens of character

### 3.1. The revival of an old discourse

It is important to acknowledge that political and public debates about the role of schools in emotional development were evident before the first Education Act in 1870 but became more acute after it (see Dixon this volume). Unlike contemporary agreement that schools are key sites for intervention, there were fierce public and parliamentary debates about the respective roles of schools, the church, communities and families in 'educating' the emotions (Ibid.). In parallel, character has been an enduring focus for debate amongst numerous lobbying and pressure groups from the Victorian period to the present day (e.g. Roberts 2004; Wright 2007). In the late twentieth century, successive governments have attempted and failed to incorporate character in a 'citizenship' curriculum (Arthur 2010).

The current government's reticence about formal initiatives for emotional well-being, noted earlier, enables schools to decide on their own approach (see Bywater and Sharples this volume; Watson et al. op. cit.). It also paves the way for a revival of interest in character already evident in support for emotional well-being on the grounds that: *'there is an overwhelming case for the state to intervene in the character development of every family'* (Layard 2007). Contemporary fears about social and economic crisis and related problems with young people's character parallel those in calls during the late 1890s and early twentieth century to intervene more actively in the shaping of character (Roberts op. cit.). Like the old discourse, the revival of a character discourse is politically and educationally inclusive. Its supporters invoke the more robust and virtuous sounding elements of emotional and psychological well-being, such as emotional regulation, resilience, stoicism and altruism, responsibility, early intervention and the importance of parenting, whilst adding notions of individual choice, agency and moral development (see Arthur 2010; Lexmond and Grist 2011). Predictably, historical parallels with older ideas emerge in associations between character and the 'competitive playing fields of Eton', but their contemporary version is embellished with positive psychology.

Anthony Seldon, headteacher of Wellington School (which appointed the country's first head of a well-being curriculum in 2007) commends it as a foundation for teaching qualities such as perseverance, courage, belief in justice, loving and being loved, curiosity, wisdom and humour, alongside traditional public school discipline, sport and loyalty to 'houses' (Seldon in Lexmond and Grist, op. cit.). Positive psychologists claim a scientific basis for a set of virtues identified as key character traits. A long list includes gratitude, awe, creativity, curiosity, diligence, entrepreneurialism, forgiveness, future-mindedness, temperance generosity, honesty, humility, joy, love, purpose, reliability and thrift (e.g. Peterson and Seligman 2004).

Unlike earlier discourses of emotional and psychological well-being, the new discourse appears to encourage moral and political questions. For example, some advocates challenge traditional conservative depictions of poor achievement and social problems caused by 'bad' or irresponsible individuals and attempt, instead, to reclaim the language of values, virtues and morals as part of a liberal-Left communitarianism (Arthur, Baggini in Lexmond and Grist op. cit.). There is also resistance to reducing complex aspects of emotional development, moral and character development to 'capabilities' that avoid questions about social and personal 'good' and desirable 'ends' and privilege state intervention over the responsibilities of families, communities and non-state organisations (Arthur op. cit.; Baggini op. cit.; Kristansson 2012).

Despite talk about values, virtues, discipline and public schools, it would be a mistake to dismiss the new discourse as misplaced nostalgia for elitist stereotypes of character offered in public school and 'officer class' interpretations, or for imposing certain moral values. Instead, a broad political and educational constituency aims to identify a broad set of *capabilities (or virtues) that underpin a good and flourishing life, but which are also instrumental to success in a (comparatively) value-free sense'* (Lexmond and Grist 2011, 29). Indeed, far from imposing values and ends, the new discourse acknowledges questions about them but creates long lists of capabilities that avoid decisions about what they are. For example, some advocates argue that schemes such as SEAL offer *'one initiative that seeks to develop character through the taught curriculum'* (Gross op. cit., 91), avoiding prescriptive values by '[seeking] *to develop the underlying dispositions that will enable children to make wise choices – choices that will benefit others as well as themselves'* (Gross in Lexmond and Grist, op. cit., 94). This enables constructs associated with SEAL to transmogrify as character capabilities, such as resilience, empathy, setting learning goals, friendship, determination and application, anger management and staying in control (op. cit.). Capabilities also include a therapeutic, introspective dimension. For example, Liam Byrne, shadow secretary of state for work and pensions, argues: *'Our young people want to develop, not only their understanding of the things around them – but an understanding of the things inside them – self-confidence, self-esteem, ambition, motivation, nerve …'* (Byrne quoted by Lexmond and Grist op. cit.).

### 3.2. *The search for better measures*

Powerful precedents for conceptual confusion and a behavioural and psychological interpretation of character have been set by earlier discourses of emotional well-being. These precedents reinforce a view that we can teach complex attitudes, attributes and responses to situations whilst tempering the reductionism of 'skills' with a broader notion of 'capabilities'. This accommodates the language of virtues and values whilst avoiding the disputes about them that have always undermined previous political attempts to develop character in schools (e.g. Arthur 2005). This, together with enthusiasm for finding novel ways to measure these capabilities, encourages a behavioural training approach. For example, Lexmond and Grist argue that *'We need to get better at measuring the development of character capabilities and the range of outcomes to which they lead'* (2011, 137). Challenging narrow educational and economic measures of examination results and prosperity, they argue that these *'miss out on most of the important things in life'* and that

> capabilities important to good and successful lives (empathy, resilience, creativity, application and so on) and the outcomes that embody those good and successful lives (happiness, health, trust, beauty, connectivity and so on) are woefully undervalued by policy makers ... because they are so hard to quantify and the tools we have to measure them are so rudimentary. (op. cit., 137–8)

Proposals to find accurate measures draw in earlier initiatives such as training for parents and programmes to help children regulate their emotions and 'behave better', *'using a proven technology – not just pious exhortations'* (Lexmond and Grist op. cit., 138). Overlooking the prima facie contradiction between using 'proven technology' and laments about 'rudimentary measures', advocates hope that more robust assessments might emerge from current character projects, such as 'sophisticated tools' to measure communities' well-being (Ibid.). Other measures perhaps lie in the future, such as brain assessments of a newborn child's 'epigenetic' code to see if it is already in 'survival mode' and *'likely to be oversensitive or paranoid'* and therefore in need of different support environments, and even measures of communal epigenetic states *'that help people to overcome adversity successfully or the types of cultural institutions – family, schools, community groups and so on – that support people to buck the trend'* (Ibid.). More prosaically, some advocates derive resilience 'toolkits' that help *'shape a child's character'* from practical experience of working with young people (e.g. Hart, Derek, and Helen 2007).

While the search for effective measures of character capabilities is a key continuity from earlier attempts to teach emotional and psychological well-being, it has much older roots in Victorian and Edwardian optimism that psychology would offer effective measures of character. For example, in controversies about hopes for a 'science of character', John Stuart Mill attempted to outline a robust 'ethology' while others explored eugenics (Roberts op. cit.). In light of these older debates, it is possible to see hopes that neuroscience might provide 'epigenetic' predictors of complex human behaviours, 'emotional metrics' and 'global emotional fitness scales' as manifestations of what Raymond Tallis calls 'neuromania' (Tallis 2011). However, although such hopes might be turn out to be fanciful, the state of the science is not the salient point for arguments in this article. Instead, I argue in the next section that these hopes arise from certain ideas that seem to be emerging about the nature of those targeted for behavioural training.

## 4. The political rise of behavioural science

### 4.1. *Finding a convincing evidence base for intervention*

The presentation of emotional and psychological well-being as skills and the temptation to depict character in similar ways have been encouraged by the previous government's attempts to find scientific evidence for politically-sponsored interventions (Sharples 2007). Introducing a report from the All-Party Parliamentary Group on well-being in the Classroom in 2007, Baroness Susan Greenfield said *there is overwhelming sympathy for schools to do more to protect and promote the emotional well-being of children and young people*, calling for the group to support existing initiatives and to *make recommendations that carry considerable weight both scientifically and politically* (Ibid.). Reflecting a popular view that psychological science can now tell us how to understand and then work on our emotions, Matthew Taylor chief executive of the Royal Society of Arts (RSA) argues that this is no more problematic than using scientific insights to improve physical workouts to get fit (Taylor 2008). Similarly, an invocation of 'emotional workouts' for 'emotional fitness' to promote the US army's resilience training programme was received enthusiastically at the conference cited above.

Such aspirations resonate with political hopes that economics, behavioural/positive psychology and sociology might illuminate the interplay between our rational, irrational, conscious and unconscious behaviours and the social and individual capabilities that lead to success and happiness, thereby providing a stronger foundation for social policy. A report for the RSA argues that:

> A greater comprehension of cognitive pathways, social norms and moral motivations should join with a continuing understanding of instrumental factors in shaping government policy-making. Given the demands of co-production, and the limits to available finance, it could be argued that a shift to a more subtle range of interventions is essential to the future of public services. Our caution rests not so much over the ethical or political issues thrown up by such developments ... There is currently a gap between our understanding of general and psychological processes and capacity to ensure that these insights become effective tools for social engineering. (Stoker and Moseley 2010, 23)

Building on work started by the Labour government in 2007, the Cabinet Office's behavioural insight unit, formed in 2010, aims to develop a checklist of psychological effects that consciously and unconsciously influence our behaviour as a basis for finding better ways to change individual conduct in anti-social behaviour, pro-social behaviour and healthy and prosperous lifestyles (e.g. Dolan et al. 2011; op. cit.). Amidst these ideas, 'nudge' has caught popular and political attention as a basis for engineering what its advocates call 'choice architecture', namely the subtle signals and environments that affect our behaviour in specific contexts before we have chosen consciously to act in a certain way (e.g. John et al. op. cit.; Thayer and Sunstein 2008). According to a report for the Cabinet Office, because 'people are sometimes seemingly irrational and inconsistent in their choices', policy-makers' attention should shift from 'facts and information' and focus instead on 'manipulating' choice architecture in order to 'change behaviour without changing minds' (Cabinet Office 2010, 5).

### 4.2. *Promoting a more sophisticated approach to behaviour change*

As I observed above, British and American Government interest in behavioural psychology as a basis for attempting to define and measure behaviour is nothing new. And, as Dixon argues, Gradgrind's enthusiasm for instrumental education in 'Hard Times' would be encouraged by the drive to measure emotional well-being (this volume). Yet, contemporary behavioural scientists hope to persuade policy-makers that they need to go beyond their traditional tools of regulation, information campaigns and skills training. Instead, they need to take more account of the ways in which our best intentions are invariably sabotaged by unconscious drivers from past experience, emotional reactions to situations and other irrational aspects of ourselves. Hopes for more sophisticated approaches are exemplified by arguments in David Brooks' book *The Social Animal: The Hidden Sources of Love, Character and Achievement* which were widely debated by British think tanks and policymakers in 2011. According to Brooks, it is not that we are entirely determined by our unconscious selves and therefore, victims or dupes. Instead, shaped by the interplay of genes, culture, upbringing and education and the institutions and networks in which we live and work, it is possible for us to influence at least some of these. Following such arguments, we cannot master these factors: instead, the art of living well comes from knowing how to steer our natures and slowly remodel our characters (Ibid.). Popular interest in psychoanalysis, self-help and self-awareness reinforces a powerful therapeutic orthodoxy that better knowledge of the unconscious enables us to do this.

In this vein, and supported by policy-oriented bodies such as DEMOS and the RSA, Brooks argues for policies that strengthen 'character' and life skills, especially for those left behind by deindustrialisation and rising inequality (Ibid.). Such optimism belies an absence of evidence to delineate a pathway to such policies and the lack of, and underlying theoretical coherence in current behaviour change approaches. Positive psychology and cognitive behaviour therapy are predicated on instrumental rationalism that hopes to persuade us that learning certain thought patterns, emotional responses and habits can make us resilient, optimistic, etc. thereby enhancing relationships, educational and work achievement or merely enabling us to survive life more effectively. At the same time, therapeutically informed activities aim to enhance mindfulness about the emotional, irrational, unconscious causes of our behaviour, while nudge techniques offer 'light touch interventions' designed by 'choice architects' that aim to appeal to our unconscious desire to act in socially beneficial ways.

This theoretical eclecticism is able to draw in very diverse interests and advocates whilst also promising the possibility that more sophisticated approaches and measures might emerge from attempts to develop the psychological constructs of emotional well-being, now morphing into character capabilities. Yet, to reiterate an argument I made at the end of the last section, the salient question is not whether the underlying science and its theoretical or empirical base is robust or coherent. Instead, it is important to consider the images of human participants embedded in enthusiasm that better science might provide effective combinations of psychology as a basis for understanding and intervening in behaviour.

## 5. Challenging an essential human vulnerability

### 5.1. *The role of social science in predicting and controlling human behaviour*

The drive for better measures and interventions resurrects a warning made by Mills (1959), which is as relevant now as it was 53 years ago. For Mills, social science should not aim to predict and control human behaviour or engage in human engineering because such goals reveal an empty optimism rooted in ignorance of the roles of reason in human affairs, the nature of power and its relations to knowledge and the meaning of agency and moral action. Mills argued that talking so glibly about prediction and control assumes the perspective of the bureaucrat to whom, as Karl Marx observed, the world is an object to be manipulated. Following this argument, attempts to predict and control behaviour substitute technocratic slogans for what ought to be reasoned moral choices (Mills 1959). In a philosophical challenge to current attempts to combine behavioural and social science, Tom Nagel argues that we need to go beyond simply discovering unacknowledged influences on our conduct and adapting our behaviour accordingly. Instead, we need to learn how to respond critically: '*even if empirical methods enable us to understand sub-rational processes better, the crucial question is, how are we to use this kind of self-understanding?*' (Nagel 2011, 2).

Of course, questions about the relationship between individuals' capacity for moral understanding and government's role in changing behaviour are old philosophical concerns. Writing in 1873, John Stuart Mill offered a prescient warning against turning complex aspects of human life and experience into measurable goals or outcomes. After a nervous breakdown in his 20s when he questioned his life's work in promoting happiness as a utilitarian end, Mill changed his mind:

> I never … wavered in the conviction that happiness is the test of all rules of conduct, and the end of life. But I now thought that this end was only to be attained by not making it the direct end. Those only are happy … who have their minds fixed on some object other than their own happiness; on the happiness of others, on the improvement of mankind, even on some art or pursuit, followed not as a means, but as itself an ideal end.

> Aiming in this way at something else, they find happiness by the way. The enjoyments of life … are sufficient to make it a pleasant thing, when they are taken en passant, without being made a principal object. Once make them so, and they are immediately felt to be insufficient. They will not bear a scrutinizing examination.

> Ask yourself whether you are happy, and you cease to be so. The only chance is to treat, not happiness, but some end external to it, as the purpose of life. Let your self-consciousness, your scrutiny, your self-interrogation, exhaust themselves on that; and if you are otherwise fortunately circumstanced, you will inhale happiness with the air you breathe, without dwelling on it or thinking about it, without either forestalling it in the imagination, or putting it to flight by fatal questioning. This theory has now become the basis of my philosophy of life. And I still hold to it as the best theory for all those who have a moderate degree of sensibility and of capacity for enjoyment, that is, for the great majority of mankind. (Mill [1873] 1989, 117–8)

On the surface, although Mill's warnings appear to echo positive psychologists' promotion of a meaningful life as a pathway to authentic happiness, they contrast starkly with a contemporary depiction of many pursuits, whether learning a subject or skill, taking up a craft or sport, being altruistic or being an active listener, not as ideal ends but as instruments for skills that, in turn, enhance our emotional and psychological well-being. In light of attempts to make emotional and psychological aspects of human life targets for therapeutically informed skills training, Mill's warnings also illuminate two significant problems. First, in order to achieve these outcomes, modern behavioural science turns complex social and individual traits, attributes and dispositions into utilitarian outcomes. It then uses various forms of counselling, therapy and psychoanalysis that explore the interplay between conscious and unconscious and rational and emotional factors. In contrast, Mill suggests that well-being or character can only emerge as by-products of being absorbed in worthwhile activities and curriculum knowledge shaped by lifelong experiences (see also Suissa 2008; Cigman, Pett this volume). Second, Mill's caution against 'scrutinising examination' flies in the face of both therapeutic explorations and straightforward skills training, since both require participants to scrutinise behaviours, attitudes and dispositions, account for the feelings and emotions that drive them, speculate about how to make them more effective both now and in future, and take part in formal or informal assessments. If Mill is right a second time, all this destroys the various constructs of emotional well-being or character in the process.

Lastly, the last line of Mills' warning goes beyond what might seem to be technical concerns about effectiveness. His assertion that *'the great majority of mankind' [possess the] 'moderate degree of sensibility and ... capacity for enjoyment'* might be dismissed as elitist complacency that dismisses much human misery. It also comes, of course, from an era without access to the insights of therapy and psychology. Nevertheless, it returns me to the key question for this article, namely the underlying images of human beings that justify and normalise interventions.

Underlying a shift from a crisis of emotional and psychological well-being to concerns about character and moral development is general agreement that some form of therapeutic intervention is necessary. Behind this agreement, political and popular accounts of the contemporary self-depict, simultaneously, some people as more emotionally or psychologically vulnerable than others and all of us as potentially or actually vulnerable. According to Frank Furedi, these determinist images emerge from a prevailing cultural sensibility which sees life as inherently threatening and distressing, where *'most forms of human experience [are] the source of emotional distress ... [and people] characteristically suffer from "an emotional deficit and possess a permanent consciousness of vulnerability'* (Furedi 2003, 110).

This sensibility turns vulnerability from an existential condition, and sometimes debilitating effect or symptom of difficult life experiences, social and economic change or oppression and inequality, into an ontological characteristic (Ecclestone 2011). Reflected in policy depictions of cycles of material and psychological deprivation and everyday assessments of our emotional states, a view that, in essence, we are all vulnerable, generates hopes that science offers more effective approaches to behaviour change. It is these determinist images of vulnerability that enable scientifically based interventions to avoid moral and political questions about values and to avoid engaging the human targets of intervention in considering such questions. According to Layard, *'we live in a scientific age ... and only science can and should persuade the young about the routes to a happy society'* (quoted by Furedi 2011, 182).

The confidence of such assertions highlights a stark contrast between Victorian and Edwardian debates about the moral and ethical implications of attempts to create a science of character and their contemporary manifestation. In contrast to older concerns, the science of well-being is already rooted in attempts to make the morals and virtues that underpin 'character traits' the target of science (e.g. Peterson and Seligman op. cit.; see Kristansson op cit for critique). According to Furedi, the *'high priests'* of the science of well-being set out explicitly to replace moral values with therapeutic assumptions and practices because they fear that a secular society cannot teach morals or offer a clear moral code (2011, 185). Following this argument, attempts to use psychological science to teach well-being or character are *'an attempt to recover moral meaning through the medium of psychology ...*'. Yet, for Furedi, it will not work: '*it is likely that the confusion of psychology with morality will simply diminish the capacity [of schools] to communicate a system of shared meanings*' (Ibid., 185). In different ways, then, discourses of well-being and character both recast virtues and moral values as psychological constructs that can be trained without requiring moral engagement. According to Furedi, this is amoral because it perceives the treatment of the self as detached from a fundamental commitment to beliefs and values.

## Conclusions

Continuities between discourses of emotional and psychological well-being and character are founded on hopes that science can offer better understanding and measures of a complex, lifelong evolution of attributes, virtues, habits and attitudes. One outcome is long inclusive lists of capabilities and skills that embrace behaviours, attributes, virtues, dispositions and moral choices. The search for robust measures of psychological states and desirable behaviours combines approaches that embellish appeals to our rational assessment of the need to learn better 'skills' with therapeutically oriented assessments of subconscious and emotional aspects of our behaviour that draw on relational approaches. At best, the conceptual and evidence base is inconclusive and fragmented. At worst, it is prey to 'advocacy science' or, in its worst manifestations, to simple entrepreneurship that competes for publicly funded interventions. On a technical level, these related problems create such diverse meanings that it is impossible to decide what is being diagnosed, taught and assessed or to challenge claims made by various vested interests.

Although technical questions about the scientific evidence for claims and proposed interventions are important, I have aimed to go beyond them in order to respond to Mills' injunction that sociologists should illuminate the kinds of human nature revealed in the conduct and character of societies in particular periods. Specifically, I have argued that the contemporary politics of behaviour change are characterised by a 'diminished' view of human nature that emerges from, and reinforces, a cultural therapeutic ethos rooted in determinist assumptions about emotional and psychological vulnerability. By combining historical, psychological and philosophical insights, a sociological imagination illuminates moral and ethical questions about the legitimacy of the normative interventions and assessments that flow from these determinist assumptions. It also highlights the scale of the critical challenge involved in resisting them.

Nevertheless, despite difficulties in challenging the determinist assumptions of contemporary behavioural science, it is important to resist the ways in which it acknowledges the realities and complexities of modern life but then roots behavioural solutions in images of an essential, determining human vulnerability. Such images enables the contemporary turn to behavioural science to shift well-being as a moral and social enterprise for 'human flourishing' to a psychological terrain. This sets out explicitly to avoid moral and political debate about the material conditions, knowledge and experiences that maximise opportunities for a broad balanced cultured life, the capacity for deep reflection and the ability to allow unhappiness (or to acknowledge the importance of pessimism) (see Cigman, Pett, Clack this volume).

At a conceptual level, it is therefore important to challenge the replacement of questions about moral meaning with therapeutic values that respond to diminished images of emotional and psychological vulnerability. It is also important to explore empirically the ways in which these images manifest themselves in everyday educational practices, and to look also for resistance and counter-narratives (e.g. Ecclestone et al. 2012; Rawdin 2012). Meanwhile, I would argue that we need a political and educational challenge to a social project that hopes to engineer emotional and psychological well-being and character whilst avoiding civic engagement in the political questions this raises. The problem is that if the human targets of therapeutically informed behavioural interventions accept their underlying emotional determinism, they are in no fit state to engage in these questions.

## References

Arthur, J. 2005. The re-emergence of character education in British education policy. *British Journal of Educational Studies* 53, no. 3: 239–54.

Arthur, James. 2010. *New direction in character and values education research*. Exeter: Imprint Academic.

Bailey, Laura. 2010. *Promoting emotional resilience in children and young people*. Hemel Hempsted, Hertfordshire: Local Authority.

Booth, Paul, ed. 2012. *... And the pursuit of happiness: Well-being and the role of government*. London: Institute of Economic Affairs.

Brooks, David. 2011. *The social animal: The hidden sources of love, character and achievement*. New York, NY: Random House.

Brunila, K. in press. Hooked on a feeling: Education, guidance and rehabilitation of young people at risk, *Critical Studies in Education*.

Cabinet Office. 2010. *Mindspace: Influencing behaviour through public policy*. London: Cabinet Office/Institute for Government.

Challen, Amy, Philip Noden, Ann West, and Stephen Machin. 2011. *UK resilience programme evaluation: Final report*. London: London School of Economics and Political Science, for the Department for Education. http://www.education.gov.uk/publications/.

Coleman, J. 2009. Well-being in schools: Empirical measure or politicians' dream? *Oxford Review of Education* 35, no. 3: 281–92.

Collishaw, S., R. Goodman, A. Pickles, and B. Maughan. 2007. Modelling the contribution of changes in family life to time trends in adolescent conduct problems. *Social Science Medicine* 65, no. 12: 2576–87, Epub 2007 Sep 18.

Connelly-Stephenson, Pamela. 2007. *Head case: Treat yourself to better mental health*. London: Headline.

Cornum, Rita. 2012. *Can we teach resilience?* Keynote presentation, Young Foundation/Macquarie Group seminar 'Teaching resilience in schools', Ropemaker, London, 7th February 2012.

Craig, Carol. 2007. *The potential dangers of a systematic, explicit approach to teaching social and emotional skills*. Glasgow: Centre for Confidence and Well-Being.

Curtis, C., and R. Northgate. 2007. An evaluation of the promoting alternative thinking strategies curriculum at key stage 1. *Educational Psychology in Practice* 23, no. 1: 33–44.

Dixon, Thomas. 2011. *Feeling differently: Using historical images to teach emotional literacy in an East London school.* London: Centre for the History of the Emotions, Queen Mary, University of London.

Dolan, Paul, Richard Layard, and Metcalfe R. Richard. 2011. *Measuring subjective well-being for public policy.* London: Office for National Statistics.

Downbiggin, Ian. 2011. *The quest for mental health: A tale of science, medicine, scandal, sorrow and mass society.* Cambridge: Cambridge University Press.

Duncan-Smith, Ian, and Graham Allan. 2009. *Early intervention: Good parents, great kids, better citizens.* London: Centre for Social Justice/John Smith Institute.

Durodie, Bill. 2009. *Therapy culture revisited: The impact of the language of therapy on public policy and societal resilience*, Report of a workshop organised by the Centre of Excellence for National Security (Singapore), S. Rajaratnam School of International Studies, Nnanyang Technological University, 5–6 October.

Ecclestone, Kathryn. 2010. *Transforming formative assessment in lifelong learning.* Buckingham: Open University Press.

Ecclestone, K. 2011. Emotionally-vulnerable subjects and new inequalities: The educational implications of an epistemology of the emotions. *International Journal in Sociology of Education* 21, no. 3: 91–113.

Ecclestone, Kathryn, Beverly Clack, Dennis Hayes, and Vanessa Pupavac, V. 2010. *Changing the subject?: Interdisciplinary perspectives on emotional well-being and social justice.* End of Award Report for Economic and Social Research Council funded seminar series RES-451–26-054, University of Birmingham.

Ecclestone, Kathryn, and Joanne Bailey. 2009. *Supporting students' emotional well-being in further education: A case study.* Research report for the Westminster Centre for Excellence in Teacher Training. Oxford: Oxford Brookes University.

Ecclestone, K., C. Savage, H. Draper, and L. Lewis. 2012. *Bio-medical ethics in interventions for emotional well-being in Britain and Argentina: A comparative study of policy and practice, Bid to the nuffield foundation.* Birmingham, AL: University of Birmingham.

Ecclestone, Kathryn, and Dennis Hayes. 2008. *The dangerous rise of therapeutic education.* London: Routledge.

Eves, Alison. 2009. *Vulnerability and risk in social work, Paper given to therapy culture revisited: The impact of the language of therapy on public policy and societal resilience*, Workshop organised by the Centre of Excellence for National Security (Singapore), S. Rajaratnam School of International Studies, Nnanyang Technological University, October 5–6 2009.

Foot, Joan, and Terry Hopkins. 2011. *A glass half-full: How an asset approach can improve community health and well-being.* London: Improvement and Development Agency Healthy Communities Team.

Fritjers, P. Johnston, D.W., and Shields, M. 2011. *Destined for (Un)Happiness: Does childhood predict adult life satisfaction?* Discussion paper No. 5819, Institute for Labour Studies, University of Bonn, June.

Furedi, Frank. 2003. *Therapy culture: Cultivating vulnerability in an uncertain age.* London: Routledge.

Furedi, Frank. 2011. *Wasted: Why education is not educating.* London: Continuum.

Gillies, V. 2011. Social and emotional pedagogies: Critiquing the new orthodoxy of emotion in classroom and behaviour management. *British Journal of Sociology of Education* 32, no. 2: 185–202.

Hallam, S. 2009. An evaluation of the social and emotional aspects of learning (SEAL) programme. *Oxford Review of Education* 35, no. 3: 313–30.

Hart, Alison, Blincow Derek, and Thomas Helen. 2007. *Resilient therapy: Working with children and families.* London: Routledge.

Horwitz, Allan, and Jerome C. Wakefield. 2007. *The loss of sadness. How psychiatry transformed normal sorrow into depressive disorder.* Oxford: Oxford University Press.

Humphrey, Neil, Lendrum A. Ann, and Wigelworth Michael. 2010. *Social and emotional aspects of learning (SEAL) programme in secondary schools: National evaluation.* Manchester, NH: Department for Education.

Huppert, Felicia. 2007. *Presentation to the all-party group seminar 'well-being in the classroom'*, October 23. London: Portcullis House.

James, Oliver. 2007a. *Affluenza: How to be successful and stay sane*. London: Vermillion.

James, Laura. 2007b. *Tigger on the couch: The neuroses, psychoses, disorders and maladies of our favourite childhood characters*. London: Collins.

John, Peter, Cotterill Sarah, Liu Hahua, Liz Richardson, Alice Moseley, Graham Smith, Gerry Stoker, and Corrine Wales. 2011. *Nudge, nudge, think, think: Using experiments to change citizens' behaviours*. London: Bloomsbury.

Kristansson, K. 2012. Positive psychology and positive education: Old wine in new bottles? *Educational Psychologist* 47, no. 2: 86–105.

Lau, R. 2012. Understanding contemporary modernity through the trends of therapy and life-'skills' training. *Current Sociology* 60, no. 1: 81–100.

Layard, Richard. 2005. *Happiness: Lessons from a new science*. London: Allen Lane.

Layard, Richard. 2007. *Presentation to the all-party group seminar 'well-being in the classroom'*, October 23. London: Portcullis House.

Lendrum, A., N. Humphrey, A. Kalambouka, and M. Wigelsworth. 2009. Implementing primary SEAL group interventions: Recommendations for practitioners. *Emotional and Behavioural Difficulties* 14, no. 3: 229–38.

Lexmond, Jan, and Matt Grist, eds. 2011. *The character inquiry*. London: DEMOS.

McLaughlin, Kenneth. 2011. *Surviving identity: The rise of the 'Survivor' in contemporary society*. London: Routledge.

Mill, John Stuart. 1873/1972. *Autobiography*. London: Penguin Books.

Moon, C. 2009. Healing past violence: Traumatic assumptions and therapeutic interventions in war and reconciliation. *Journal of Human Rights* 8, no. 1: 71–91.

Morris, Ian. 2009. *Teaching happiness and well-being in schools: Learning to ride elephants*. London: Continuum.

Myers, K. 2011. Contesting certification: Mental deficiency, families and the State. *Paedogogica Historica* 47, no. 6: 749–66.

Nagel, T. 2011. Review of the social animal. *The New York Times*, May 11, Arts section.

Nolan, James. 1998. *The therapeutic state: Justifying government at century's end*. New York, NY: New York University Press.

Nolan, James. 2008. *Legal accents, legal borrowing: The international problem-solving court movement*. Princeton, NJ: Princeton University.

Peterson, Christopher, and Martin Seligman. 2004. *Character strengths and virtues: A handbook and classification*. Oxford: Oxford University Press.

Pupavac, V. 2001. Therapeutic governance: Psycho-social intervention and trauma risk management. *Disasters* 25, no. 4: 358–72.

Pupavac, Vanessa. 2009. Bosnia war victims: Vulnerability and identity, Paper given to *Therapy culture revisited: The impact of the language of therapy on public policy and societal resilience*, Workshop organised by the Centre of Excellence for National Security (Singapore), S. Rajaratnam School of International Studies, Nnanyang Technological University, October 5–6 2009.

Rawdin, C. 2012. Evaluating constructs of emotional well-being and resilience in school-based interventions, University – funded PhD studentship, University of Birmingham.

Roberts, N. 2004. Character in the mind: Citizenship, education and psychology in Britain 1880–1914. *History of Education* 33, no. 2: 177–97.

Seligman, Martin. 2011. *Flourish: A new understanding of happiness and well-being – and how to achieve them*. New York, NY: Simon and Shuster.

Seligman, M., E. Randal, J. Gilham, K. Reivich, and M. Linkins. 2009. Positive education, positive psychology and classroom interventions. *Oxford Review of Education* 35, no. 3: 293–313.

Sharp, Peter. 2003. *Nurturing emotional literacy: Guide for parents and teachers*. London: Kogan Page.

Sharples, Jonathan. 2007. *Well-being in the classroom*, Report on the All-Party Parliamentary Committee, October 27, 2007. Oxford: University of Oxford.

Social Exclusion Unit. 1999. *Bridging the gap: New opportunities for 16–19 year olds not in education or training*. London: SEU.

Stewart, J. 2009. The scientific claims of British child guidance, 1918–45. *The British Journal for the History of Science* 42: 407–32.

Stewart, J. 2011. The dangerous age of childhood': Child guidance and the 'normal child' in Britain, 1920–1950. *Paedagogica Historica: International Journal of the History of Education* 47, no. 6: 785–803.

Stoker, Gerry, and Alice Moseley. 2010. *Motivation, behaviour and the microfoundations of public services*. London: Royal Society of the Arts.

Suissa, J. 2008. Lessons from a new science? On teaching happiness in schools. *Journal of Philosophy of Education* 42, no. 3–4: 575–90.

Sullivan, Helen. 2011. *When tomorrow comes: The future of public services*, Final report, University of Birmingham/DEMOS Policy Commission. Birmingham, AL: University of Birmingham.

Summerfield, Derek. 2004. Cross-cultural perspectives on the medicalisation of human suffering. In *Post-traumatic stress disorder: Issues and controversies*, ed. G. Rosen. London: Wiley.

Tallis, Raymond. 2011. *Aping mankind: Neuromania, Dawinitis and the misrepresentation of humanity*. London: Acumen.

Taylor, Matthew. 2008. The rocky road to emotional well-being, Presentation to ESRC Seminar Series Changing the subject?: Interdisciplinary perspectives on emotional well-being and social justice, Oxford Brookes University, 7 December 2008.

Thayer, Richard T., and Cass R. Sunstein. 2008. *Nudge: Important decisions about health, wealth and happiness*. New York, NY: Yale University Press.

Thomson, Matthew. 2006. *Psychological subjects: Identity, culture and health in twentieth-century Britain*. Oxford: Oxford University Press.

Watson, Deborah, Carl Emery, and Philip Bayliss. 2012. *Children's social and emotional well-being in schools: A critical perspective*. London: The Policy Press.

Wilkinson, Richard, and Kate Pickett. 2009. *The spirit level: Why more equal societies almost always do better*. London: Allen Lane.

Wright, S. 2007. Into unfamiliar territory? The moral instruction curriculum in english elementary schools 1880–1914. *History of Education Researcher* 79: 31–41.

Wright, K. 2008. Theorizing therapeutic culture: Past influences, future directions. *Journal of Sociology* 44, no. 4: 321–36.

Wright-Mills, C. 1959/1967. *The sociological imagination*. Oxford: Oxford University Press.

# Educating the emotions from Gradgrind to Goleman

Thomas Dixon

*School of History, Queen Mary, University of London, London, UK*

Charles Dickens famously satirised the rationalism and mechanism of utilitarian educational ideas through the figure of Gradgrind in *Hard Times*. Even in the nineteenth century there were very few people, in reality, who would have agreed that the education of children should be a matter of purely intellectual, rather than emotional, instruction. The surge of interest in emotional intelligence and emotional literacy since the 1990s has given this topic new currency but, on all sides of the debate, it is mistakenly assumed that the idea of educating the emotions is something new. The present article retrieves one part of the forgotten history of emotional education by examining nineteenth-century British discussions about the proper places of passion, feeling and emotion in the classroom, in the context of debates about utilitarianism, religion and the role of the state. The views of educationalists and philosophers, including Samuel Wilderspin and John Stuart Mill, are considered and compared with more recent policy debates about 'Social and Emotional Aspects of Learning'. The article concludes by asking: who are the Gradgrinds today?

## Introduction: the culture of the heart

Now, what I want is, Facts. Teach these boys and girls nothing but Facts. Facts alone are wanted in life. Plant nothing else, and root out everything else. You can only form the minds of reasoning animals upon Facts: nothing else will ever be of any service to them.

So begins Charles Dickens's *Hard Times*, first published in 1854. The speaker is Thomas Gradgrind, politician and businessman of Coketown, somewhere in the northern manufacturing districts of England. Dickens's tragicomic caricature of a narrow-minded utilitarian has remained lodged in our collective imagination ever since as a symbol of the dire consequences of excluding emotion and imagination from the classroom.

Even contemporary readers of Dickens doubted whether any such woefully unfeeling classrooms existed in reality. The *Westminster Review* wrote in 1854: 'If there are Gradgrind schools, they are not sufficiently numerous to be generally known' (Appendix B to Dickens 1996, 336). And in the twenty-first century, it would surely be impossible to find a teacher repeating Gradgrind's mistakes.

Educators have learned about the importance of developing in children such newly minted mental capabilities as 'emotional literacy', 'emotional well-being' and 'emotional resilience'. Many have read works such as Daniel Goleman's international bestseller, first published in 1995, *Emotional Intelligence*, including its final chapter on 'Schooling the Emotions'. National governments, private consultants, educational think-tanks and charities all now promote an idea of education with emotion at its heart. In the UK, the government, in the early twenty-first century, started to put increasing emphasis on social and emotional aspects of learning (SEAL) at both primary and secondary school levels. Rose (2009), in his *Independent Review of the Primary Curriculum*, expressed the hope that the new curriculum would help children develop 'social and emotional skills' such as managing their own feelings and becoming aware of the feelings of others, and that it would thus promote 'emotional and economic wellbeing' as well as 'physical, mental and emotional health'. In its most recent phase, the promotion of emotional education has included discussions of the application of 'Positive Psychology' to educational contexts (Nussbaum 2008; Scoffham and Barnes 2011).

Among contemporary educationalists, some think that schooling is now in danger of becoming over emotional, while others want to see emotional intelligence, resilience, well-being and the rest established in a still stronger position. Supporters of the emotional curriculum, suggesting that the time has finally come for feelings and emotions to be given their due in the modern classroom, have based their arguments on a range of sources, including philosophy (Dunlop 1984; Best 1988), feminist politics (Boler 1999; Blackmorea 2011), evolutionary psychology (Spendlove 2008) and affective neuroscience (Goleman 1996; Hyland 2011). Opponents bemoan these innovations as evidence of a move away from an education centred around subject-based knowledge towards what has been called a 'curriculum of the self'; an academically less-rigorous regime, fostering introspection and emotional neediness (Ecclestone and Hayes 2009; Ecclestone 2011). What is generally taken for granted on both sides is that a belief in the central importance of the emotions to education is something new. It is not.

Lord Kames, in his *Loose Hints upon Education, Chiefly Concerning the Culture of the Heart* (1781) regretted that earlier educational theorists, with the partial exception of Jean-Jacques Rousseau, had tended to focus on the head at the expense of the heart: 'From Aristotle down to Locke, books without number have been composed for cultivating and improving the understanding: few in proportion for cultivating and improving the affections' (Kames 1781, 14–5). From the early nineteenth century, this would become a less plausible complaint. As we shall see below, the Infant School movement pioneered a form of education based on love and affection from the 1820s onwards, and in 1829 the *Quarterly Review* asserted that 'The first eight to ten years of life should be devoted to the education of the heart – to the formation of principles, rather than to the acquirement of what is usually termed knowledge', since in childhood the 'emotions are liveliest and most easily moulded', and later life will present 'an infinity of occasions where it is essential to happiness that we should feel rightly; very few where it is necessary that we should think profoundly' (Anon. 1829, 176–7). Three of the most influential mid-Victorian writers, Charles Dickens, John Stuart Mill and Herbert Spencer, all advocated emotional education between the 1830s and 1870s. The pre-Raphaelite John Lucas Tupper (1869) published a book arguing that the emotional side of children's development was the 'void in modern education', and recommending more art education as an urgent antidote, while the campaigner and journalist Frances Power Cobbe (1888) wrote an article on 'The education of the emotions', addressing herself to questions of parenting, religion, schools, universities and public ceremonies. The importance of the emotions to education continued to be endlessly forgotten and rediscovered throughout the twentieth century. Emotions were the focus of one of the most influential texts of the mental-hygiene movement in the USA (Prescott 1938; Boler 1999, 50–3), and featured prominently in two important UK government reports into primary education (Hadow 1931; Plowden 1967; Wooldridge 2006). Yet, some educationalists still felt that emotions were being overlooked (Beatty 1969; Yarlott 1972). Even in the 1980s, David Best wrote of the 'Extraordinary neglect of the education of the emotions' (1988, 239), as did Megan Boler a decade after that, interpreting the history of education in terms of a patriarchal anti-emotionalism, several years into the post-Goleman era (1999, xxiv), and two centuries after Rousseau and Kames.

Hopefully, some appreciation of the history of ideas about emotional education will save future educationalists from having to rediscover the emotions all over again. The present article offers a sketch of one part of that history, using nineteenth century British sources. Although the history of emotional education can be traced back to much earlier periods (Bantock 1986), the concern with schooling children's feelings, passions and emotions in the classroom took on its modern form in the nineteenth century, in the context of debates about utilitarianism, religion and the role of the state in monitoring, designing and ultimately providing education, especially for the children of the working classes.

The varieties of emotional schooling promoted and practised in the nineteenth century, and the utilitarianism and rote learning they were reacting against, are examined below through the writings of a range of figures, including the pioneer of the infant school movement, Samuel Wilderspin, and the philosopher John Stuart Mill. In the concluding sections, turning to developments connected with the landmark Elementary Education Act of 1870, I argue that the linguistic and conceptual shifts from Victorian ideas about moral and religious education to modern scientific and managerial concepts of social and emotional skills and competencies, reveal a complex process of secularisation and demoralisation of educational thought and practice. This process needs to be acknowledged and understood if progress is to be made in contemporary policy debates.

## Utilitarianism: men without bowels

Of what actual tendencies in nineteenth-century education was *Hard Times* a satire? Obviously the ultra-utilitarian school in Coketown, with its hard-headed and hard-hearted Gradgrind principles, implemented by a schoolmaster called M'Choakumchild, were comic creations. But contemporary reviewers recognised in this caricature some semblance of reality. Among Dickens's various targets, the two most prominent were the philosophy of utilitarianism, with its economic doctrine of self-interest and its mania for measurement, and the practice of mechanical rote learning in schools. Gradgrind's beliefs about education were, first, that reason as opposed to imagination 'is the only faculty to which education should be addressed' (56–7), secondly that education should be characterised by the accumulation of useful facts rather than the cultivation of idle fancies and, finally and most generally, that anything useful could be measured and quantified. Gradgrind applied the same principles to the raising of his own children, accordingly excluding fairy tales and nursery rhymes from their childhood reading. The keynote of this philosophy was the exclusion of wonder: 'Bring to me, says M'Choakumchild, yonder baby just able to walk, and I will engage that it shall never wonder'. The exclusion of wonder was the 'spring of the mechanical art and mystery of educating the reason without stooping to the cultivation of the sentiments and affections' (86). Dickens suggests the likely outcome of such an education by the unhappy fates that await the Gradgrind children. Young Tom is apprehended for thieving by Bitzer, previously considered by Gradgrind a model pupil. Desperately begging Bitzer to release his son rather than deliver him over to the authorities, Gradgrind asks him whether he has a heart. Bitzer replies factually: 'No man, sir, acquainted with the facts established by Harvey relating to the circulation of the blood, can doubt that I have a heart'. Gradgrind then asks whether this heart is accessible 'to any compassionate influence'. Bitzer's unfanciful reply is that his heart is accessible to reason and to nothing else (305).

Some readers, at least, thought that Dickens's attack on the utilitarians had hit the mark. 'As to the picture of the economical school', wrote the *British Quarterly Review,*

> who see the whole duty of man in buying in the cheapest market and selling in the dearest, we believe that there are not a few of them fully as bad as the picture here given of them. They are men without bowels (Appendix B to Dickens 1996, 331).

Two of the leading utilitarian philosophers of earlier generations who might have been thought to merit this designation were the 'philosophical radicals' Jeremy Bentham and his most important disciple, James Mill. Their philosophy was based on the cultivation of reason and its rigorous application to the social problem of how to define, measure and maximise happiness (Schofield 2006). In the realm of education, Bentham and Mill worked together on a treatise called *Chrestomathia*, published in its final form in 1817 (Cumming 1961, 1962, 1971; Bentham 1983). The term 'chrestomathic' meant 'conducive to useful learning' and the work set out a curriculum and teaching methods to be used in schools for the children of the 'middling and higher ranks in life'. It was an adaptation of the existing 'Lancasterian' monitorial system, according to which younger children were taught by older children, all under the direction of a single schoolmaster (Smith and Burston 1983). Bentham and Mill thought that up to 600 boys could be taught in a single schoolroom by this method, arranged in concentric rows of desks, with the master installed at the centre on a revolving chair (Cumming 1961, 22). The chrestomathic curriculum was a scheme of strictly intellectual training, explicitly excluding moral and religious instruction, music, the fine arts and literature (Bentham 1983, 89–95). Although the scheme to turn *Chrestomathia* into an actual school was ultimately abandoned, some establishments were independently founded upon similar principles, including the Hazelwood School at Edgbaston in Birmingham in 1819 and the Bruce Castle School at Tottenham in 1825, both set up by Thomas Wright Hill and his sons (Smith and Burston 1983, xvii–xviii).

At the same time that James Mill was working on *Chrestomathia* with Bentham, he was engaged in the education of his eldest son. John Stuart was born in 1806 and was educated at home according to a chrestomathic programme of his father's devising, emphasising languages, history, logic and the sciences, and excluding religion and the arts. John Stuart Mill's *Autobiography*, published in 1873, was primarily a treatise about this education and its effects on him, recounting the astonishingly rigorous intellectual training he received at the hands of his severe Calvinist-turned-utilitarian father during the 1800s and 1810s. Young John was learning ancient Greek at three; reading Plato's dialogues in Greek at seven; Latin histories at eight; Pope's English translation of the *Iliad* (20 or 30 times) around the age of 10; and in his eleventh and twelfth years writing a book-length history of the government of ancient Rome. John Stuart Mill's childhood was, in other words, an extended utilitarian experiment in the possibilities of a purely intellectual training carried out by a man who shared at least some of the beliefs and temperament of both Bentham and Gradgrind. Mill wrote of his father:

> For passionate emotions of all sorts, and for everything which has been said or written in exaltation of them, he professed the greatest contempt. He regarded them as a form of madness. 'The intense' was with him a bye-word of scornful disapprobation. He regarded as an aberration of the moral standard of modern times, compared with that of the ancients, the great stress laid upon feeling ... He resembled most Englishmen in being ashamed of the signs of feeling, and by the absence of demonstration, starving the feelings themselves. (Mill 1873, 49, 52)

An education conducted on principles such as these, and by a man such as this, was inevitably directed towards the reasoning faculty alone, to the exclusion of feeling and imagination. As we shall see below, the impact of this fancy-free educational experiment on John Stuart Mill was considerable and led him to adopt a quite different view of feeling and emotion himself.

James Mill was not the direct inspiration for the figure of Gradgrind, even though he and the Benthamites were certainly possessed of a large measure of the Gradgrind spirit (Fielding 1956). The Gradgrind approach combined utilitarian rationalist ideology on the one hand with the practice of mechanical fact cramming on the other. This latter tendency, a common feature of both the 'Lancasterian' and the 'National' schools, which both used the monitorial system, was widely observed and frequently denounced by educational commentators in the nineteenth century. In an 1834 article on 'Reform in education', John Stuart Mill, drawing on a series of lectures delivered by the Reverend Edward Biber in 1829, complained bitterly about the practice of rote learning in the National schools, which resulted in children memorising words and mottoes, without having any idea what the words meant (Biber 1830; Mill 1984). In 1861, the Newcastle Report contained many similar complaints about cramming and rote learning (Education Commission 1861). Herbert Spencer, in his first book, *Social Statics*, imagined with horror the extension of such practices into a system of state education (a development which he passionately opposed), envisaging:

> a state-machine, made up of masters, ushers, inspectors, and councils, to be worked by a due proportion of taxes, and to be plentifully supplied with raw material, in the shape of little boys and girls, out of which it is to grind a population of well-trained men and women, who shall be 'useful members of the community'! (Spencer 1851, 335)

Spencer deplored this sort of mechanical grinding out of little Gradgrinds, and especially the idea that tax payers would foot the bill for these fact factories. He also wrote, in more general terms, that any morally beneficial education must be an 'an education which is emotional', making a child not only understand but feel the difference between right and wrong. Such an education would arouse noble desires and sympathetic impulses in a way that no 'drilling in catechisms' could ever effect: 'Only by repeatedly awakening the appropriate *emotions* can character be changed. Mere ideas received by the intellect, meeting no response from within – having no roots there – are quite inoperative upon conduct, and are quickly forgotten upon entering into life' (Spencer 1851, 352).

## Love and intelligence: Samuel Wilderspin

Herbert Spencer's advocacy of an education addressed to the sympathies and impulses of the child was, of course, nothing new in 1851. That violent passions should be subdued and benevolent affections cultivated was a commonplace of moral philosophy, both ancient and modern (Dixon 2003, 2006, 2011a). One eighteenth century statement of this view, connecting it explicitly with questions about the schooling of children, is to be found in the work by Lord Kames mentioned above, *Loose Hints upon Education* (1781). In that work, Kames described the human mind as a rich soil productive of both weeds and flowers: bad passions and impressions were weeds to be rooted out, while good passions and affections were flowers to be cultivated (1–2). While it became quite conventional during the nineteenth century to argue that the whole mind needed education, imagination as well as reason, emotions as well as intellect, what was not agreed was how, where and by whom this should be achieved. In 1781, Kames had assumed that it would be overwhelmingly be the duty of the mother, in the home, through moral and religious instruction. However Kames seemed to think that in an ideal society the affections might be cultivated at school, noting with regret that there was currently 'no school, public or private, for teaching the art of cultivating the heart' (Kames 1781, 8). By the early nineteenth century, however, this was starting to change.

Samuel Wilderspin (1791–1866) was a pioneer of infant education and one of the central figures in the Infant School Society founded in 1824 (McCann and Young 1982; McCann 2008). Wilderspin has been credited with introducing the playground to nineteenth-century schools. He also endorsed the view that education was most successful when it engaged the attention and affection of the child. Wilderspin's influential book, *Infant Education: or, Practical Remarks on the Importance of Educating the Infant Poor*, first published in 1825, offered guidance, based on Wilderspin's own experience of running infant schools as well as his commitment to Swedenborgian views of religion, human nature and education, according to which infancy was a state of innocence, characterised by wonder and curiosity. Wilderspin contrasted his own system with that developed by Andrew Bell and adopted by the Church of England, explaining how his system differed both 'in spirit and practice from the National Schools':

> The fundamental principle of the Infant School system is love; it should be the constant endeavour of the master to win the affections of the children, and thus cause them to feel pleasure in submitting to his will; their attention should be excited by external natural objects, no part, however trivial, being suffered to pass unnoticed; they are by this minute mode of instruction led to a habit of observation and

thought, from which the most beneficial results may be expected. (Wilderspin 1829, 311–2)

Wilderspin added that the National Schools

deaden the faculties of the children, by obliging them to commit to memory the observations of others, few of which they comprehend: they are never invited to think for themselves and the injurious consequences arising from this radical defect, cannot but be felt through life (312).

In Wilderspin's schoolroom, by contrast, children were to be engaged in conversation about moral matters through the use of a gallery of images. Whether teaching infants the letters of the alphabet or the meaning of the Lord's Supper, Wilderspin introduced them to ideas about understanding, feeling, passion and affection. The following is one of a series of lessons proposed by Wilderspin to help children learn the alphabet. The object used as the focus of this particular lesson would have been a card bearing the letter 'X' and also a portrait of the Greek author Xenophon. Wilderspin envisaged the following conversation between the schoolmaster and his young charges:

*Q*. What letter is this?
*A*. Letter X, for Xenophon, a man's name.
*Q*. What was the particular character of Xenophon?
*A*. He was very courageous.
*Q*. What does courageous mean?
*A*. To be afraid to do harm but not to be afraid to do good or anything that is right.
*Q*. What is the greatest courage?
*A*. To conquer our own bad passions and bad inclinations.
*Q*. Is he a courageous man that can conquer his bad passions.
*A*. Yes; because they are the most difficult to conquer. (183)

These kinds of lessons were aimed at improving simultaneously the moral and intellectual condition of the 'infant poor' between the ages of 18 months and 7 years. In writing of the benefits of this approach, Wilderspin explained the good influence it would have 'on the child's moral condition, or more properly its heart': 'The better feelings of the child must gradually become most prominent, since they are constantly excited, while the bad passions are put and kept in subjection by this more and more predominating influence' (312).

Wilderspin's approach was firmly rooted in the Christian tradition of moral instruction, but his work was admired by secular as well as religious commentators. Charles Bray, for instance, a rationalist admirer of phrenology and a supporter on non-denominational education, was an enthusiastic pioneer of Wilderspin's system, which he helped to introduce to Coventry in the 1830s (Jolly 1894, xi). Bray (1872) was himself the author of a widely used and republished work on *The Education of the Feelings*, first published in 1838. John Stuart Mill wrote approvingly of the infant school movement in his 1834 article on 'Reform in education'. He admired the infant schools as places of moral culture 'designed exclusively for the cultivation of the kindly affections'; places where the 'child learned nothing, in the vulgar sense of learning, but only learned to live'. Mill quoted Biber's summary of the original aim of the infant schools to take in the infants of the poor at the tenderest age and 'to awaken them to a life of love and intelligence'. But even the infant schools, Mill reported, through the 'dullness, hardness, and miserable vanity' of some of the schoolmasters, had all too often become places 'for parroting gibberish' (Biber 1830, 172–7; Mill 1984, 70–1).

## Beauty, feeling and understanding: John Stuart Mill

If Wilderspin was one of the nineteenth century's most eloquent advocates of a particular kind of Christian moral culture of the passions and affections, John Stuart Mill was the most powerful proponent of a rather different school of thought. He offered his Victorian readers a romantic and aesthetic renovation of the utilitarian philosophy to which he had been subjected in its Benthamite form as a child. Where some educators sternly emphasised restraint of the passions, Mill promoted the gentler art of cultivating appropriate moral sentiments and aesthetic feelings. The connection between emotion and aesthetics has been a close one ever since the 'emotions' and the 'emotional' first emerged as distinct psychological domains in the nineteenth century (Dixon 2011a). One of the earliest uses of the adjective 'emotional' was in an essay by Mill published in 1834 about Plato's *Phaedrus*. In that article, Mill suggested that the English word 'emotional' was synonymous with 'aesthetic' (Mill 1978, 95). A reviewer of John Lucas Tupper's *Hiatus: The Void in Modern Education, its Causes and Antidote* (1869), already mentioned above, complained that in his book Tupper likewise treated 'emotional' and 'aesthetic' as synonymous (Anon. 1869). The young philosopher Charles Waldstein went further, making a direct connection between aesthetics, emotions and social reform, arguing that any man whose emotions were educated through public performances of drama and music, thereafter would not be inclined to 'commit a theft, a robbery, or any brutal outrage' (1878, 195). Dickens's preferred medium for the education of the imagination and affections, of course, was literature. In *Hard Times*, Gradgrind is affronted and baffled by the phenomenon of the Coketown public library at which readers, even after a fifteen-hour working day, would sit down to 'read mere fables about men and women' by Defoe and Goldsmith, and learn thereby about 'human nature, human passions, human hopes and fears' (Dickens 1996, 87). Fifteen years later, in an address to the Birmingham and Midland Institute, which provided local working men with a library, reading room, museum, art department, lectures and classes, Dickens congratulated the institute that in encouraging the artisan to think it also 'encourages him to feel' (Dickens 1869).

Dickens, Tupper, Mill and Waldstein were the Victorian ancestors of an argument, made regularly during the last century and a half, that the teaching of literature, drama, art and music in schools is essential to the cultivation of appropriate feelings and sentiments. The French educational theorist Gabriel Compayré, in reappraising the value of Herbert Spencer as an educational philosopher in the early twentieth century, complained that Spencer too often prioritised practical and intellectual training over education in literature and the fine arts, thus failing to provide for the 'training of the emotions and the sentiments of the heart' (1907, 39). Compayré's own belief was that aesthetic culture was indispensible, not a merely recreational domain: 'aesthetics are not merely the crown of civilisation; they are its foundation, one of the essential principles of intellectual life' (42–3). In more recent decades, educationalists including David Best (1988, 1992) and Geoffrey Bantock have also written about the connection between arts education and emotional development. As Bantock puts it, the arts are the mode through which feelings can best be articulated and refined; they are our 'public vehicles of the emotions' (1986, 138). Sir Jim Rose, in his *Independent review of the primary curriculum* (2009), especially recommends role-play, drama and dance as ways to develop social and emotional skills.

Although the younger Mill, unlike the younger Gradgrind, did not find himself turning to crime in later life, he nonetheless blamed his artless education for its harmful effects on his emotional development. In his early twenties, Mill experienced a mental crisis and severe depression, which he would later interpret as the direct result of his father's educational philosophy. The overdevelopment of his powers of intellectual analysis, Mill believed, had tended to wear away his feelings. His emotions were eventually saved by a course of artistic auto-didacticism during 1827 and 1828. Through the poetry of William Wordsworth, the music of the German composer Carl Maria von Weber, and the *Mémoires* of the French author Jean-François Marmontel, Mill rediscovered in himself the sources of human feeling (Mill 1873, 140–52). Tellingly, Mill recalled that it was the scene in Marmontel's *Mémoires* where the author's father died that moved him to tears (141). Reading about the death of Marmontel's father, we might surmise, effected for Mill the symbolical death of his own father; the thought that all feeling was dead within him now vanished. 'The cultivation of the feelings', Mill recalled, 'became one of the cardinal points in my ethical and philosophical creed' (143–4). Mill tried to impress on his English contemporaries something which he thought was widely appreciated in Continental Europe: that the 'habitual exercise of the feelings' leads to the 'general culture of the understanding' (59). An emotional apprehension of an object in the world, Mill argued, was entirely consistent with 'the most accurate knowledge and most perfect practical recognition of all its physical and intellectual laws and relations':

> The intense feeling of the beauty of a cloud lighted by the setting sun, is no hindrance to my knowing that the cloud is vapour of water, subject to all the laws of vapours in a state of suspension; and I am just as likely to allow for, and act on, these physical laws whenever there is occasion to do so, as if I had been incapable of perceiving any distinction between beauty and ugliness (152).

In Mill, then, we find a classic articulation of two related views about education and the emotions which, again, have been rediscovered by philosophers and educationalists in recent decades (Solomon 1976; Dunlop 1984; Best 1988; Nussbaum 2001). First, Mill's self-exploration in his *Autobiography* suggested that any overly factual and intellectual curriculum that excluded the arts would risk creating an unbalanced and unhealthy because unfeeling mind. Having made this distinction, between the arts and emotion on the one hand and scientific learning and the intellect on the other, Mill wanted to deny that there was any incompatibility between these two aspects of mental life – more feeling did not equate to less understanding.

## Science, religion and the languages of emotion after 1870

My main aim in this article, so far, has been to establish continuities between contemporary debates about emotions in education and discussions that took place during the nineteenth century. There are striking parallels in the aims and ideas of educationalists then and now, including quite widespread support for the general idea of educating the whole child, emotions as well as intellect, with a view to producing good citizens, fewer crimes and a happier society. But there are important differences too, which have come about through intertwined conceptual and social changes which can be mapped through the evolving languages of emotional education. The kind of moral and religious instruction promoted by a range of educational thinkers, from Kames to Wilderspin and many others, and practiced in Britain in schools provided by the Christian churches, involved teaching children to master their 'passions' and cultivate their 'affections'. After 1870, when the state took its first steps towards providing non-denominational education, first at elementary and then at secondary level, a new conceptual regime, derived from the nascent science of psychology, started to take over, premised on a stark contrast between intellect and the newly all-encompassing and secular category of the 'emotions' (Dixon 2003, forthcoming). These processes accelerated during the middle decades of the twentieth century, seeing a commitment to moral education being replaced by ideas about child development and child guidance based on science, psychoanalysis and medicine (Wooldridge 2006; Stewart 2009; Shuttleworth 2010). This period saw 'moral' giving way to 'social and emotional'; and 'education' or 'instruction' being replaced by 'growth', 'development', 'adjustment', and, more recently, 'management', 'skills' and 'competencies', the latter categories betraying the impact of the corporate world on educational theory and practice. Comparing the 1967 Plowden Report with the Rose Review of 2009 suggests a broad shift from biology and psychoanalysis in the former to self-help psychology, management and economics in the latter as the leading sources of ideas about the mind. The impact of Daniel Goleman's advocacy of 'emotional intelligence' in the 1990s resulted from his successful fusion of pop-neuroscience with the modern self-help ideology of global capitalism, trends which were already having a worldwide impact on social and educational thought (Boler 1999, 58–78).

Again, we can try to understand these recent developments by comparing them with what was happening in the nineteenth century. I have already noted that there was disagreement about who should be primarily responsible for educating children's emotions. The two most obvious candidates were the family (especially the mother) or the school. It made a great difference, however, whether the school was a religious or a secular institution. It was relatively uncontroversial to think that a religious institution should be in the business of the moral instruction and training of the young, but less clear that this was a role for the state to take over. Herbert Spencer, we have seen, argued strongly in favour of the view that a child must be educated through their emotions as much as their intellect, but he was violently opposed to the state providing such instruction: 'from all legislative attempts at emotional education may Heaven defend us!' (Spencer 1851, 352). Spencer's invocation of heaven was appropriate, since it was the religious question that was to prove most the most important and divisive element of the debates about the 1870 Elementary Education Act, with its proposed introduction of non-denominational state schools.

Contribution to these debates by figures with scientific and secularist leanings attempted to inaugurate a new social and conceptual configuration developed from the kind of attitudes previously promoted by philosophical radicals of the Benthamite school. Instead of denying the value of the feelings and emotions altogether, however, later Victorians such as John Stuart Mill's protégé, the philosopher–

psychologist Alexander Bain and the secularist leader George J. Holyoake, argued that emotions should be excluded from the classroom, because they fell within the proper province of religion and thus should be dealt with at home and at Sunday schools rather than in non-denominational state schools. The argument thus aimed simultaneously to see the state adopt a secular kind of schooling and also to exclude emotions from the classroom. George Holyoake stated, at the inaugural meeting of the National Education League in 1869 that the proper aim of the new state schools should not be 'education in its full sense', including all the influences of 'home, and church, and society, which form the individual character', but rather should provide the children of the working classes simply with a good 'intellectual training'. Striking a keynote that would have pleased Gradgrind, Holyoake continued: 'secular instruction, if adopted, will deal, during that brief term, merely with the mechanical routine of elementary knowledge, and the passionless facts of science'. For the rest, the state system should leave children to the teachers of religion, whose province was the domain of human experience where 'emotions arise' and 'passions are stirred which pertain to eternity'. This was the realm of 'the nurse, the mother, and the minister' (National Education League 1869, 169). Alexander Bain, in his *Education as a Science*, made exactly the same argument:

> the essence of Religion must always be something Emotional; and the culture of Emotion is not carried on advantageously in ordinary school teaching. The system that is best for securing the intellectual element, is not best for securing the emotional element. Regularity of lesson, method and sequence, a certain rigour of discipline – are all in favour of a steady progress in knowledge; but the calling out and exercising of warm affection, or deep feeling, depend on improving opportunities or events such as scarcely occur in school experience. (Bain 1879, 423)

The Irish physicist and agnostic Tyndall (1874, 60–1), and the radical educationalist and economist William B. Hodgson (Education Commission 1861, 551) had both previously endorsed similar views. It is intriguing to note, then, that the attempt to exclude emotional education from the classroom seems to be connected with Victorian secularists' attempts in the 1860s and 1870s to exclude religion. Emotion, for these latter-day Gradgrinds, was the province of 'the nurse, the mother, and the minister', and was to be banished from the schoolroom, a domain of 'mechanical routine' and the 'passionless facts of science'.

## Conclusion: Beyond the Gradgrind inheritance

It is ironic that, as attitudes to emotion changed, gradually from the 1960s and even more markedly since the 1990s, it was to brain science, evolutionary psychology, business science, economics, social psychology and psychiatry that educators and policy-makers turned for the authority and the means to reintroduce the emotions into the classroom, those very emotions that a secularist and scientific ethos had done so much to detach from the intellect during the nineteenth and twentieth centuries. 'Moral education' has been replaced by a curriculum that promotes 'social and emotional development', but any curriculum designed to promote particular feelings and emotional capacities (whether love of country, fear of terrorism, empathy, optimism, altruism, charity or happiness) is tacitly committed to a particular moral philosophy, a particular vision of the good life. Moral beliefs are now smuggled into the classroom as part of supposedly value-free and scientific pedagogical programmes rather than as components of an explicitly moral training (Boler 1999, 79–107).

I suggested at the outset that no educator in the twenty-first century was likely to repeat the mistake, memorably embodied in Gradgrind's passion for facts, of seeking to exclude feelings and emotions from the educational process. However, the repression of feeling was not Gradgrind's only mistake. Dickens also invited readers of *Hard Times* to find fault in Gradgrind's mania for science and measurement. Gradgrind was possessed by the Benthamite desire to see everything counted, quantified, statistically tabulated and mathematically analysed. The mechanical and arithmetical mindset that might be suited to running a factory or a business, Dickens suggested, was not well suited to the rather different endeavour of educating the young.

I wonder what Gradgrind's approach would be today to the question of promoting emotional well-being and resilience through education. I imagine that he would make sure he was up to date with the latest scientific terminology, and that he would be well versed in neuroscience, management science, positive psychology and their techniques for subjecting happiness and well-being to quantitative measurement (Nussbaum 2008). He would insist that public policy in this area be based only on facts; facts derived from empirical datasets; facts generated by randomised controlled trials; facts expressed in terms of hardwired neurological affect programmes. He would seek, from any programme of emotional education, a package of activities that could be mechanically, identically, practiced in every classroom in the land, regardless of the fanciful foibles of individual teachers or the cultural inheritance of individual children. His favoured programme would be monitored constantly through the use of 'emotional metrics' and 'global assessment tests' measuring emotional fitness and emotional health (Cornum 2012). He would thus impose a single pedagogical scheme and a universal emotional language. In short, our modern Gradgrind would hope to see a veritable machine of state-sponsored emotional education set in motion, grinding out useful members of the community from the raw material of little boys and girls.

If any of this sounds familiar, then it is perhaps a salutary warning that there are many among those who favour emotional education today, as well as among those who resist it, who are Gradgrind's true heirs. The scientific study of the emotions, of course, has its place, but its underlying methodological assumptions that such things as 'human nature' or 'basic emotions' exist universally, does not suit it to educational thought or practice. In classrooms in the real world, each child's emotions are produced through particular cultural, linguistic and intellectual schemes, within particular social systems, as part of a singular biographical narrative, not by the triggering of hardwired basic affective responses. As Dickens put it in a sentence in the original manuscript of *Hard Times* omitted from the final text:

> It may be one of the difficulties of casting up and ticking off human figures by the hundred thousand that they have their individual varieties of affection and passions which are of so perverse a nature that they will not come under any rule into the account. (Dickens 1996, 458)

What is required, then, perhaps, is a framework for emotional education in which children can produce their own meanings, and develop their own emotional languages, rather than having imposed upon them a universalising scheme based on

## EMOTIONAL WELL-BEING IN EDUCATIONAL POLICY AND PRACTICE

the version of human nature promoted by the most fashionable science of the moment (Dixon 2011b).

Studying the history of ideas about the culture of the heart confronts us with certain basic philosophical questions, fundamental to the decisions we collectively take about education, and have taken in the past, but which often remain hidden. Let me end by posing these questions anew: What do we think is the relationship between intellect and emotion? Is there a dichotomy between them or was John Stuart Mill right that cultivating the feelings and training the intellect can and should go hand in hand? What are the proper roles of feeling and emotion in the well lived life? What are the best sources of understanding and knowledge about emotions? If we think that feeling rightly is as important as thinking profoundly and that both need to be learned, who should be responsible for providing the required emotional training: parents, schools, community groups, religious organisations, or can all be left to nature? Should happiness and well-being be aimed at directly, through programmes in emotional literacy and resilience, or indirectly through the teaching of, for instance, literature, drama, music, art and moral philosophy? Do we believe in a universal human nature and hardwired basic emotions, and, if not, what alternative models of mental life and development are available to us?

## References

Anon. 1829. Review of an account of some of the most important diseases peculiar to women, by Robert Gooch M.D. *Quarterly Review* 41: 163–83.

Anon. 1869. The void in modern education. *Pall Mall Gazette*, March 24.

Bain, Alexander. 1879. *Education as a science*. London: C. Kegan Paul and Co.

Bantock, G.H. 1986. Educating the emotions: An historical perspective. *British Journal of Educational Studies* 34: 122–41.

Beatty, Walcott H. 1969. Emotions: The missing link in education. *Theory into Practice, Teaching the Young to Love* 8.2: 86–92.

Bentham, Jeremy. 1983. *Chrestomathia* (Original publication 1815–17), ed. M.J. Smith and W.H. Burston. Oxford: Clarendon Press.

Best, David. 1988. Education of the emotions: The rationality of feeling. *Oxford Review of Education* 14: 239–49.

Best, David. 1992. *The rationality of feeling: Understanding the arts in education*. London: Falmer Press.

Biber, Edward. 1830. *Christian education, in a course of lectures delivered in London, in Spring 1829*. London: Effingham Wilson.

Blackmorea, Jill. 2011. Lost in translation? Emotional intelligence, affective economies, leadership and organisational change. *Journal of Educational Administration and History* 43: 207–25.

Boler, Megan. 1999. *Feeling power: Emotions and education*. New York, NY: Routledge.

Bray, Charles. 1872. *The education of the feelings: A moral system, revised and abridged for secular schools* (First published 1838). 4th ed. London: Longmans, Green, Reader and Dyer.

Cobbe, Frances Power. 1888. Education of the emotions. *Fortnightly Review* 49: 223–36.

Compayré, Gabriel. 1907. *Herbert Spencer and scientific education,* trans. Maria E. Findlay. London: George G. Harrap and Co.

Cornum, Rhonda 2012. Can we teach resilience? Keynote presentation, Young foundation/ Macquarie group seminar 'Teaching resilience in schools', February 7, 2012, in Ropemaker Place, London.

Cumming, Ian. 1961. *Useful learning: Bentham's Chrestomathia, with particular reference to the influence of James Mill on Bentham.* Auckland: University of Auckland Education Series.

Cumming, Ian. 1962. The Scottish education of James Mill. *History of Education Quarterly* 2: 152–67.

Cumming, Ian. 1971. Enemies to wonder: James Mill and the diffusionists. *Paedagogica Historica: International Journal of the History of Education* 11: 351–68.

Dickens, Charles. 1869. *Address delivered at the Birmingham and Midland Institute, on the 27th September, 1869.* Birmingham: Josiah Allen.

Dickens, Charles. 1996. *Hard times* (Original, publication 1854), ed. Graham Law. Peterborough, Ontario: Broadview Press.

Dixon, Thomas. 2003. *From passions to emotions: The creation of a secular psychological category.* Cambridge: Cambridge University Press.

Dixon, Thomas. 2006. Patients and passions: Languages of medicine and emotion, 1789–1850. In *Medicine, emotion, and disease, 1750–1950,* ed. Fay Bound Alberti, 22–52. Basingstoke: Palgrave Macmillan.

Dixon, Thomas. 2011a. Revolting passions. *Modern Theology* 27: 298–312.

Dixon, Thomas. 2011b. *Feeling differently: Using historical images to teach emotional literacy in an East London School.* Centre for the History of the Emotions, Queen Mary, University of London. http://www.qmul.ac.uk/emotions/docs/54589.pdf.

Dixon, Thomas. Forthcoming. 'Emotion': History of a keyword in crisis. *Emotion Review.*

Dunlop, Francis. 1984. *The education of feeling and emotion.* London: George Allen and Unwin.

Ecclestone, K. 2011. Emotionally-vulnerable subjects and new inequalities: The educational implications of an 'epistemology of the emotions'. *International Studies in Sociology of Education* 21: 91–113.

Ecclestone, Kathryn, and Dennis Hayes. 2009. *The dangerous rise of therapeutic education.* London: Routledge.

Education Commission (Newcastle Report). 1861. *Report of the assistant commissioners appointed to inquire into the state of popular education in England, 1861,* 3. London: HMSO.

Fielding, K.J. 1956. Mill and Gradgrind. *Nineteenth-Century Fiction* 11: 148–51.

Goleman, Daniel. 1996. *Emotional intelligence: Why it can matter more than IQ.* London: Bloomsbury.

Hadow, Sir W.H. (Chair) 1931. *Report of the consultative committee on the primary school.* London: HMSO.

Hyland, Terry. 2011. *Mindfulness and learning: Celebrating the affective dimension of education.* Dordrecht: Springer.

Jolly, William. 1894. Introduction. In *The education of the feelings: A system of moral training, for the guidance of teachers, parents, and guardians of the young. 5th ed,* ed. Charles Bray, ix–xvi. London: Longmans, Green and Co.

Kames, Henry Home, Lord. 1781. *Loose hints upon education, chiefly concerning the culture of the heart.* Edinburgh: John Bell.

McCann, Phillip, and Francis A. Young. 1982. *Samuel Wilderspin and the infant school movement.* London: Croom Helm.

McCann, W.P. 2008. *Wilderspin, Samuel (1791–1866). Oxford dictionary of national biography* (Online edition). Oxford University Press.

Mill, John Stuart. 1873. *Autobiography.* London: Longmans, Green, Reader, and Dyer.

Mill, John Stuart. 1978. Notes on some of the more popular dialogues of Plato: The Phaedrus. In *The collected works of John Stuart Mill.* XI (Original publication 1834) ed. John M. Robson. Essays on philosophy and the classics, 62–96. Toronto: University of Toronto Press.

Mill, John Stuart. 1984. Reform in education. In *The collected works of John Stuart Mill*. XXI (Original publication 1834), ed. John M. Robson. Essays on equality, law and education, 61–74. Toronto: University of Toronto Press.

National Education League. 1869. *Report of the first meeting of the members of the national education league, held at Birmingham on October 12 and 13, 1869*. London: Simpkin, Marshall, and Co.

Nussbaum, Martha. 2001. *Upheavals of thought: The intelligence of emotions*. Cambridge: Cambridge University Press.

Nussbaum, Martha. 2008. Who is the happy warrior? Philosophy poses questions to psychology. *Journal of Legal Studies* 37, no. S2: S81–S113.

Plowden, Bridget Horatia. 1967. *Children and their primary schools: A report of the central advisory council for education (England)*, 1 (The report). London: HMSO.

Prescott, Daniel A. 1938. *Emotion and the educative process*. Washington, DC: American Council on Education.

Rose, Jim Sir. 2009. *The independent review of the primary curriculum: Final report*. London: Department for Children, Schools and Families.

Schofield, Philip. 2006. *Utility and democracy: The political thought of Jeremy Bentham*. Oxford: Oxford University Press.

Scoffham, Stephen, and Jonathan Barnes. 2011. Happiness matters: Towards a pedagogy of happiness and well-being. *Curriculum Journal* 22: 535–48.

Shuttleworth, Sally. 2010. *The mind of the child: Child development in literature, science, and medicine, 1840–1900*. Oxford: Oxford University Press.

Smith, M.J., and W.H. Burston. 1983. Editorial introduction. In *Chrestomathia*, ed. Jeremy Bentham, xi–xxix. Oxford: Clarendon Press.

Solomon, Robert C. 1976. *The passions: Emotions and the meaning of life*. New York, NY: Doubleday.

Spencer, Herbert. 1851. *Social statics: Or, The conditions essential to happiness specified, and the first of them developed*. London: John Chapman.

Spendlove, David. 2008. *Emotional literacy*. London: Continuum.

Stewart, John. 2009. The scientific claims of British child guidance, 1918–1945. *British Journal for the History of Science* 42: 407–32.

Tupper, John L. 'Outis' 1869. *Hiatus: The void in modern education, its causes and antidote*. London: Macmillan.

Tyndall, John. 1874. *Address delivered before the British association assembled at Belfast*. London: Longmans, Green, and Co.

Waldstein, Charles. 1878. *The balance of emotion and intellect: An essay introductory to the study of philosophy*. London: C. Kegan Paul and Co.

Wilderspin, Samuel. 1829. *Infant education: Or, Practical remarks on the importance of educating the infant poor, from the age of eighteen months to seven years: Containing hints for developing the moral and intellectual powers of children of all classes*. 4th ed. London: W. Simpkin and R. Marshall.

Wooldridge, Adrian. 2006. *Measuring the mind: Education and psychology in England, c. 1860–c.1990*. Cambridge: Cambridge University Press.

Yarlott, Geoffrey. 1972. *Education and children's emotions: An introduction*. London: Weidenfeld and Nicolson.

# What difference does it make? Philosophical perspectives on the nature of well-being and the role of educational practice

Beverley Clack

*Department of History, Philosophy and Religion, Oxford Brookes University, Oxford, UK*

> This paper suggests ways in which philosophy as a discipline and practice offers the possibility of a richer account of well-being than currently informs policy initiatives in this area. Sources derived from philosophy – and particularly moral philosophy – support a shift away from understanding well-being as something grounded primarily in the emotions, towards an understanding of its relationship to the well-lived life. Refocusing the debate in this way suggests, moreover, a view of education as a practice that transcends the classroom and that is, in effect, a lifelong pursuit.

## Introduction

> Whether we are caught in the grasp of an inexorable law of fate, whether it is God who as lord of the universe has ordered all things, or whether the affairs of mankind are tossed and buffeted haphazardly by chance, it is philosophy that has the duty of protecting us. (Letter XVI; Seneca 1969, 64)

The Roman philosopher Seneca's description of the different ways in which the nature of human life might be construed seems an odd place to start an article on well-being and educational practice. Even more strange might seem his conclusion. Having detailed the trials and tribulations attending to human life, Seneca concludes, not that governments or the religious or scientists are best placed to offer protection against the pains of existence, but that those most suited to the task are the philosophers.

As a philosopher of religion who wishes to show the significance of philosophical discourse to the concerns of people outside the academy, my intention in this paper is to apply Seneca's words to the well-being agenda that has, in recent years, shaped aspects of educational policy and practice. In so doing, I want to suggest that philosophy provides sources and methods useful for shaping a richer account of well-being than that which currently informs aspects of this agenda. In part, this involves shifting the focus of such initiatives away from promoting *emotional* well-being towards providing sources for 'the well-lived life'. Refocusing the debate in this way necessitates an additional move: education as a practice is viewed in this paper as something that transcends the classroom, for it is something which is, in

## EMOTIONAL WELL-BEING IN EDUCATIONAL POLICY AND PRACTICE

effect, a lifelong pursuit. Educational practice, while grounded in schools, colleges and universities, also transcends these institutions, and I intend to show how it can help establish meaningful ways of living by referring to a discipline that can seem rather rarefied but which provides methods and sources for the lifelong cultivation of the well-lived life.

### Educating for happiness: the well-being agenda

The early years of the twenty-first century saw economists and politicians noting that increased affluence in western economies was not matched by a similar increase in individual levels of happiness. In light of this surprising and counter-intuitive fact, attempts to promote a greater sense of well-being became a key driver of public, social and educational policy.[1] In developing policy in this area, governments have not always found it useful to turn to philosophers. Jonathan Wolff points out that one of the problems for philosophers when they venture into the public domain is their tendency to ignore the constraints placed on policy-makers: 'Philosophers have been known to write as if an entire issue is an intellectual one, and once the best reasons are set out for the best policy the philosophers' work is done' (2011, 192). Wolff advises that we start from the realities of where we are, not from some idealised view of where we *should* be, and cites with approval Bernard Williams' dictum: 'what is the best form of society we can get to, starting from here?' (Williams 2005, 23; Wolff 2011, 192). Bearing this in mind, I want to suggest some ways in which a philosophical approach might prove useful when considering the role of education in the promotion of well-being.

Philosophy is a critical practice that has, I believe, something to contribute to these policy debates. It is particularly useful when considering the well-being debate as it enables the unacknowledged assumptions that lie beneath commonly accepted accounts of 'well-being' to be challenged with a view to considering the practices and beliefs that might lead to a different approach where well-being is understood as arising from the meaningful life. In particular, it is worth turning a critical eye to the often unacknowledged assumption that 'well-being' and 'happiness' are two sides of the same coin.

Influential voices in the area of policy have tended to make this connection, as is evident from the economist Richard Layard's (2005) *Happiness: Lessons from a New Science*. A key advisor to the Labour government on happiness and member of the House of Lords, Layard's account suggests ways of promoting greater emotional well-being in the general public. To do this, policies must be designed that help people to *feel* happy. Happiness, according to Layard, should be defined in the following way:

> [B]y happiness I mean feeling good – enjoying life and wanting the feeling to be maintained. By unhappiness I mean feeling bad and wishing things were different. (2005, 13)

Well-being, read through a Layardian lens, becomes linked to the cultivation of feelings of happiness, and thus what is really meant by well-being is 'emotional well-being'; emotional well-being in turn, being informed by behavioural psychology (see Ecclestone this volume).

## EMOTIONAL WELL-BEING IN EDUCATIONAL POLICY AND PRACTICE

Kathryn Ecclestone and Dennis Hayes' critique of therapeutic education suggests something of the effect that an emphasis on the emotions drawn from mental health and behavioural psychology has had on educational policy and practice (2009). Attention is focused on how to cultivate emotional well-being in children. By learning effective strategies for its associated constructs (stoicism, resilience, optimism, mindfulness and emotional intelligence), education ceases to be something primarily concerned with the development of the intellect and becomes aligned instead with the diagnosis, training and assessment of the emotions. More than that, Ecclestone and Hayes argue that education is now modelled as a form of therapy designed to elicit particular emotional responses from children; responses and strategies which are highly normative. As they put it:

> Therapeutic education replaces education with the social engineering of emotionally literate citizens who are also coached to experience emotional well-being. (2009, xiii)

Educational practice against this backdrop becomes largely a means of developing positive feelings, the child being taught ways of regulating and managing the emotions, and, importantly, of how to ameliorate negative ones. This approach was at the core of the previous government's strategy for social and emotional learning in primary and secondary schools, through an eclectic array of universal and targeted activities (see DfEs 2005; also Ecclestone this volume). Training the child's emotions as well as their intellect in this way necessitates changing the school curriculum. Teaching and assessment methods have also to be changed in order to accommodate such approaches to emotional management; and this is the case for *all* children as a preventative measure for future problems with mental health, as well as for children diagnosed with (or deemed to have) emotional and behavioural problems. In this way, stoicism, resilience, optimism, altruism, emotional regulation and mindfulness – the psychological constructs deemed necessary for emotional well-being – are viewed as attitudes and associated behaviours to be acquired by all through learning the kind of skills familiar to cognitive behavioural therapies.

### The invisibility of philosophy

At the heart of attempts to cultivate the attitudes of mind deemed necessary for a sense of well-being have been scientific resources. Turning to science, particularly psychology and (increasingly) neuroscience, for solutions is hardly surprising, reflecting cultural assumptions about those methods and practices deemed most valuable and effective. The notion that science, broadly understood, can solve all our problems pervades Layard's vision of the world. This is a world that we are largely in control of, thanks to the technological achievements of science:

> By using our brains we have largely conquered nature. We have defeated most verte-brates and many insects and bacteria. In consequence, we have increased our numbers from a few thousand to a few billion in a very short time – an astonishing achievement ... The great challenge now is to use our *mastery over nature* to master ourselves and to give us more of the happiness that we all want. (2005, 27, my emphasis)

Emphasising the solutions of science suggests the arts and humanities in general and philosophy in particular have little to contribute to the peculiar problems of contemporary living. The review conducted by Lord Browne into the future funding of higher education, delivered in October 2010, did little to challenge such views. Browne's free market model for higher education included the suggestion that the government contribution to teaching should be withdrawn for all subjects save science, technology, engineering and maths. With the Comprehensive Spending Review adopting this idea, it is difficult to escape the conclusion that the withdrawal of state funding for the arts is based upon an assumption that there is little economic or social value to be had in promoting such subjects.[2]

Academics working in the field of arts and humanities must take some responsibility for this state of affairs. Our subjects have become increasingly rarefied, failing to speak to the concerns and experiences of those outside the academy. Successive Research Assessment Exercises (RAEs) are partly responsible for this, encouraging academics to speak to themselves rather than to the broader community (see Ecclestone editorial, this volume).

Despite their undoubted influence, the RAE and the new Research Excellence Framework cannot, however, be blamed entirely for the invisibility of philosophy in contemporary debate about the role of educational settings in developing emotional well-being and for understanding well-being more generally. Philosophy has long been caught in a more general bind caused by the increasing professionalisation of academic disciplines. The emphasis on analysing language which shaped the development of analytic philosophy came out of the desire to connect philosophy more explicitly with the positivist forms of science popular at the turn of the twentieth century.[3] This vision of philosophy as a kind of science continues to shape the practice of the subject in many UK departments, as well as determining what makes for 'proper' philosophy.[4]

Aligning itself with the methods of science may make philosophy look like a respectable subject, but it does so at the price of losing its connection to the existential questions that historically drove it. It is these existential questions that make philosophy of importance not just to academics but to a broader audience outside the academy. Similarly, philosophers of religion in an Anglo-American context[5] have tended to limit the scope of its endeavour. The concern has been to establish the credibility of key religious beliefs and concepts, and in many cases this has resulted in the discipline acting implicitly as a form of apologetic for the dominant expression of western religion, Christianity. Addressing the concerns of religious insiders – albeit through the lens of technical philosophical argument – has led to an increased detachment of the subject from the ordinary concerns of human life; namely, the struggle with the vulnerability of being human, the problems of suffering, issues of mortality and the other themes that have historically shaped the concerns of moral and theological philosophy.[6]

Recently philosophers of religion inspired by continental and feminist approaches have sought to return to such issues, suggesting a desire to orientate the subject to ethical concerns that connect with the day-to-day experience of ordinary human life.[7] This shift suggests something of the fruitfulness of exploring how philosophy – and specifically the philosophical approach to religion – might aid the discussion of well-being as an educational concern of importance not just for what happens in the classroom but also for the world outside educational institutions.[8] My concern is with exploring the way in which philosophy – and philosophical theology – enables deeper reflection on what it means to be human in a world like this. What I hope will come out of this discussion is a significantly enriched account of where well-being might be located that moves beyond the limitations of identifying it primarily with the management of the emotions. It also necessitates a broader account of what education is and what it involves.

## Critiquing emotional well-being

Offering a philosophical analysis of the assumptions supporting the emphasis on emotional well-being is a good place to start; not least because there is a consistent thread in the history of philosophy that suggests something of the weakness of locating one's well-being primarily in the sphere of the emotions.

For Aristotle and the Hellenistic schools that followed him, a pressing concern was to identify what made for the 'happy' or fulfilling life (*eudaimonia*).[9] While Aristotle argued that the goal of human life was happiness, he did not identify happiness primarily with the *feelings* associated with it: euphoria, ecstasy, joy, elation and so on. To live a 'happy' life was understood rather differently, revolving around how one might establish a fulfilled and fulfilling life. At the root of this kind of lifestyle was the practice that cultivated a reflective attitude (Aristotle 2002, 97–8). Fostering critical reflection enabled one to hold in balance the different aspects of life; for example, one's relationships, creativity and physical needs.

Out of this subtle balancing comes the sense that one's life is fulfilling, that it is, in this sense, 'happy'. Aristotle thus reiterates Socrates' claim that 'the unexamined life is not worth living' (*Apology*, 38a). But note that in developing his theories Aristotle does not underestimate the importance of material comfort. This should not surprise us, as Aristotle is notorious for claiming that women and slaves could not be philosophers as the reflective life required the time available only to the leisured classes (*Politics* 1252a, 16–7; also Le Doeuff 2007, 7). Elitist such a position may be; but at least it recognises that the fulfilling life requires both the cultivation of an appropriate disposition *and* a supportive external context in which such an outlook might flourish.

Given this philosophical backdrop, it is not surprising to find later philosophers resisting the formulation of happiness as an emotional response to one's life. Instead, it is seen as a bi-product of creativity, virtue, reflection or work. For John Stuart Mill, different kinds of happiness should be distinguished, for some forms are intrinsically better than others (Mill 1871, 278–81). Layard recognises Mill's contribution to this discussion, but resists his conclusion as 'paternalistic' and, by implication, elitist; what matters is cultivating experiences that maximise the *feeling* of being happy, not judging between the merit of different sources for one's happiness (Layard 2005, 23). Yet despite this comment, Layard agrees with Mill about the importance of cultivating *lasting* forms of happiness.

Now, if we wish to establish a more consistent positive outlook, there may be good reasons for eschewing the identification of happiness with happy feelings. Emotions are by their nature transitory; they come and go, ebb and flow. It is difficult to see how the *feeling* of happiness could be maintained at all times. To base the meaning of life on how we are feeling at any given moment has an additional problem associated with it. If the meaning of my life is dependent on how I *feel*, I am left vulnerable to external events and the way they affect me. For ancient philosophical schools like that of the Stoics, judging the meaning of one's life on transient emotional experiences is to leave oneself vulnerable to chance, dependent always upon the things that happen, or the way things go. For the Stoics, the answer was to cultivate mental resources that enabled one to cope with all eventualities, both good and bad. As Hadot (1995) has noted, this necessitated developing spiritual exercises which challenged the student to think seriously about a range of existential concerns, not least the reality of death. In so doing, it was possible to cultivate a particular mindset to help one cope with life's suffering.[10] But cultivating this kind of internal reflection did not necessitate becoming divorced from the external world and the importance of acting in the public sphere. The Stoics were the most politically active of the Hellenistic schools, including the philosopher Seneca (also a politician and tutor to the Emperor Nero) within their ranks.[11] It was not enough to focus on the internal world of the individual; the role of action in the external world was also deemed important for living a fulfilling life.

## Emotional well-being and the contemporary self

Pursuing this critical engagement with emotional well-being necessitates attending to the view of the self that supports it. Defining well-being in terms of the emotions draws the gaze towards the individual and their emotional responses to the things that happen to them and the things that they feel. The focus on the emotions draws attention inward, the individual almost inevitably being defined in terms that detach him or her from the broader environment of family, friends and surrounding community. The neo-liberal construction of the self by emphasising the idea of the self as a choosing, rational being supports the claim that any individual can achieve their goals, provided they take charge of their lives, their ambitions, their feelings and their desires. Well-being against this ideological and conceptual framework becomes something the individual can control through correct management of their inner life.

Emphasising the individual's responsibility for their own well-being avoids addressing the structural problems of the societies we inhabit. The debate surrounding well-being tends to focus on the individual and the resources they need in order to support their emotional management. As Richard Wilkinson and Kate Pickett forcefully argue, if we are serious about cultivating well-being, we must address the fact that societies with higher levels of economic inequality have greater levels of unhappiness and more social and mental problems than societies that are more equal. Addressing the emotions of the individual is not enough:

> The solution to problems caused by inequality is not mass psychotherapy aimed at making everyone less vulnerable. The best way of responding to the harm done by high levels of inequality would be to reduce inequality itself. (Wilkinson and Pickett 2009, 32–3)

The need to address such inequalities may seem too difficult, and the lack of political will for such solutions suggests a widespread belief that the kind of measures necessary could not realistically be achieved.[12] This lack of political confidence both inside and outside government may well explain the state's enthusiasm for promoting emotional well-being. Early years' providers and schools, in particular, become places where what has gone wrong or might go wrong in socialisation or upbringing can be put right or pre-empted. Without the radical solutions suggested by Wilkinson and Pickett, education becomes the arena for addressing by the back-door a whole host of societal ills.

In considering the sources that philosophy might provide for richer accounts of well-being, I do not intend to claim the subject as a panacea for all ills. If we accept Wilkinson and Pickett's analysis, educational interventions cannot act as alternatives to the necessary economic, political and social solutions to issues of human discontent. Instead, I want to consider what philosophy might contribute to the reshaping of ideas of well-being and the reframing of education as something that is lifelong. In discussing the question of where well-being may be found, philosophers have, historically, directed attention to the experience of being human. Taking seriously the fragility of human life and the concerns that arise from it offers the possibility of a fresh perspective on how to establish a meaningful life.

## Well-being and the well-lived life

So far, I have suggested some of the problems surrounding an account of well-being when it is formulated as '*emotional* well-being'. Taking on board the philosophical criticisms considered above, I want to develop an account of well-being as something grounded in a sense of 'the well-lived life'. This involves considering the purpose of education as well as the role that educators and educational institutions might play in helping to foster the well-lived life.

Shifting attention to the well-lived life has advantages over the formulation of well-being as something located primarily in the individual's management of their emotions. While self-reflection and self-knowledge are important features of the well-lived life, emphasising the idea of how to *live* necessitates a move away from a straightforward focus on the individual towards a sense of the individual as always grounded in community and the network of relationships that make up that community.[13] To investigate what it means to live well also involves thinking about the experience of being human in a rather different way from that which has to date dominated the well-being agenda.

In order to explain what this means, let us return briefly to the perspective that informs Richard Layard's thinking on this issue. For Layard, human life is such that it is possible to act in such a way as to maximise happiness. Science makes possible a certain kind of optimism about the human condition. We *can* be happy, and in the findings and practices of psychology and neuroscience methods are provided for achieving this goal.

Joshua Foa Dienstag's recent work on the history of pessimism (2006) suggests a different perspective on life which leads to a rather different emphasis on what constitutes the meaningful life and how it might be established. Dienstag argues that we need to take seriously the precarious nature of life in this world when reflecting on the experience of being human. Given that the world involves change, that we are vulnerable creatures at the mercy of suffering and death, it is difficult to see how 'the happy life' could really be attained. However, recognising that this is the case need not lead to unhappiness and frustration but to a deeper contentment. Taking seriously such ideas suggests something of why the shift from science to philosophy might allow for a more complex reframing of the discussion about well-being. In what follows, I want to suggest that philosophers have much to contribute to the discussion of those attitudes of mind that enable safe passage through life. However, the kind of philosophical sources that I wish to draw upon also take seriously the idea that human life and experience is frequently messy and painful. Against such a backdrop, the development of well-being becomes a lifelong project, not something that could be achieved once and for all through attaining a set of particular psychological skills.

We might start by considering the question of how to understand the world in which we 'live and move and have our being'. This necessitates dealing with the issue of loss. Human life is such that one cannot avoid engagement with loss and suffering. Religious traditions of all kinds have recognised the universal quality of such experiences and have sought to provide strategies for coming to terms with such painful realities. In recent psychoanalytic theory, similar recognition is given to the reality of loss, which is placed at the heart of each individual's experience. For Julia Kristeva, the primary loss is that of the maternal object (1988).[14] Life is defined by the attempt – always doomed to failure – of return to the first symbiotic union with the mother. In order to attain the space required for language and relationship, this cloying closeness had to be given up, desire being that which seeks something to occupy the space left by the lost mother. As a result human experience is always unsatisfying and unsatisfiable; our desires can never wholly be met for they are simply ciphers for the unattainable lost mother. This means we can never be truly happy in this life.

Even if we resist the psychoanalytic framework that forms the basis for Kristeva's analysis, we might be prepared to accept the extent to which loss of one kind or another defines much of human experience. Loss comes in many forms. The most obvious and dramatic is death, but there are other losses too: disappointment, disillusionment, rejection, failure, loss of hope or self-worth. Even the most blessed life cannot avoid having to deal with loss in one of its many forms.

For a society whose cultural assumptions are shaped by the technological achievements of science, it is tempting to think that one day science will be able to solve such problems. This kind of scientism has been challenged by philosophers and theologians. According to the philosopher Mark Johnston, scientism involves 'a certain use of the scientific world picture, particularly a metaphysical use in which it is presented as an exhaustive inventory of reality, [which] depends upon forgetting the abstractive preconditions of scientific modelling' (2009, 46). Assuming that there are no limits to the scientific project ignores the constraints of the human condition. Because we are mutable creatures in a mutable world, it is difficult to see how we can escape entirely the experiences of suffering and death that attend to being creatures of this kind.

The extent to which science can eradicate ordinary, human suffering has been challenged by Horwitz and Wakefield (2007). Modern psychiatry, they argue, has increasingly acted to pathologise normal sadness. Yet sadness is an inevitable part of human experience, and the categorisation of sadness as some kind of disorder to be treated with drugs is to ignore the role it plays in human relationships. To suggest that sadness can be eradicated is to deny the fundamentally transient experience of human life: we are born, age and die. It is also to ignore the extent to which we are social animals who are as a result open to the kind of pain (and pleasure) that comes from relationship with others. To open oneself to the other necessitates making oneself vulnerable. Just as love, joy and acceptance can be found in relationship, so can pain, suffering and rejection. As theologians such as Dorothee Soelle argue, to experience the joy of love we have to be prepared to accept the possibility of loss. Accepting vulnerability becomes part and parcel of what it means to live life to the full (Soelle 1975).

EMOTIONAL WELL-BEING IN EDUCATIONAL POLICY AND PRACTICE

That the universe does not easily support human happiness is a position with a long and distinguished philosophical pedigree. Boethius (480–524 CE) comments: 'How miserable the happiness of human life is; it does not remain long with those who are patient, and doesn't satisfy those who are troubled' (Boethius 1969, 31). The nineteenth century philosopher Arthur Schopenhauer goes further in his diagnosis. Dissatisfaction and unhappiness result when we assume that the world could be otherwise:

> Optimism is not only a false but also a pernicious doctrine ... everyone then believes he has the most legitimate claim to happiness and enjoyment. If as usually happens, these do not fall to his lot, he believes that he suffers an injustice. (Schopenhauer 1966, 584; also Dienstag 2006, 110)

Schopenhauer, in common with other pessimists, suggests that the problem arises from failing to accept the nature of things. Sure, there are ills that can be mitigated: we might think of social injustice, unkindness and certain forms of illness. But other features of life are constant: death, suffering, the loss of loved ones. And it is worth noting that the father of psychoanalysis Sigmund Freud was acutely aware of the limits of therapeutic interventions, given this cosmic backdrop. As he comments at the end of *Studies on Hysteria* to the hypothetical patient with whom he is in dialogue: 'much will be gained if we succeed in transforming your hysterical misery into common unhappiness' (Breuer and Freud 1893–1895, 305). This difficult and troubling world is not easy to navigate, and the best that we can hope for is finding meaningful activities that help us feel 'at home' in the world (Freud 1930, 140). There is no 'quick fix' to human suffering, and in his final writings he grapples with the question of whether there could ever be a complete and lasting psychoanalytic 'cure' for the things that troubled his patients' mental health (Freud 1937).

A kind of relief can come from accepting that feeling unhappy is not necessarily a bad thing. To feel sad when something or someone important to us is lost is an entirely appropriate emotion. To feel anger at injustice suggests we are engaged with those amongst whom we live. For this reason, religious education in schools forms an important part of the curriculum, for it provides a space in the curriculum for students to explore the possibility that there might be a different engagement with suffering and pain than simply the quest for their eradication. Unhappiness could be seen, not as an aberration destined to be eradicated from the student's emotional world, but as something that acts as a spur to the great questions of existence: Why am I here? Who am I? How should I live? It is with such questions that religions have grappled and sought to find answers.

We might not, of course, wish to develop a religious perspective in response to such questions. Neither might we wish to share the pessimistic outlook of Boethius, Schopenhauer and Freud; but it is worth reflecting upon the precarious nature of things to which they draw our attention. Much that we value in life is fragile and subject to loss. Reputation, status, love, friendship, life itself: all is uncertain and subject to change.[15] If we take seriously the reality of loss, the question becomes how best to deal with it. What strategies enable us to live with a sense of purpose? What kind of lifestyle has the necessary resources to deal with the disappointments, tragedies and losses that will inevitably be encountered, albeit to different degrees of severity, as we journey through life? Taking seriously pessimistic accounts of the nature of human experience need not render life meaningless, as we shall see, but it

123

does suggest that the attempt to ground a sense of meaning in a difficult and troubling world will be a task that is far from simple or straightforward.

The power of the desire to focus on the internal world when confronted with a vision of the external world as far from hospitable to humanity cannot be underestimated. Not least because when dealing with such metaphysical ills it allows us to direct our gaze to that over which we do, at least, have some degree of power: namely, the self. As Hadot (1995) argues the Hellenistic schools of the Roman period emphasised the importance of developing a mindset where rather than attempt to change the processes of the universe, one sought to place the individual's experience in the broader context of universal processes. Hence the Stoics suggested the need to cultivate a way of thinking that 'accepted fate'; that accepted the things that happen. Rather than seeing the centre of the world as 'me', my needs and concerns, they practised a way of thinking that *de-centred* the self, placing the individual's needs, concerns, fears and desires amongst the other patterns and processes of the universe.

Certain religious forms of practice suggest a not dissimilar move. One's life is best understood as located in something greater than the self. Arguably this is what lies behind the religious commitment to God or the divine. That there is something 'beyond the human' encourages a different attitude to one's life where day-to-day problems are located in the context of eternity. It becomes possible to look at one's life and attitudes with a form of detachment that enables a better perspective to develop on the things that are happening.[16]

Developing an appropriate perspective on the things that happen is important for a healthy mental life, given the way in which one's individual perspective is always peculiarly centre stage. The experience of consciousness with the self as the 'still centre of the turning world' can distort the way in which life is experienced, leading to the kind of shock and unhappiness that Schopenhauer described when things do not work out as we think they should. Historically this kind of perspective has been located in religious commitments, but one's political or social commitments can have this same quality. Developing a transcendent approach – in this broader sense – necessitates thinking about the activities that shape one's life. Something outside of the self, something larger than the self, enables a sense of the self as located in a larger framework.

What the acquisition of this transcendent perspective might involve for the practice of one's life can be exemplified in the perspective developed by the philosopher of religion and policy-maker Stewart R. Sutherland.[17] Sutherland (1969) suggests cultivating forms of reflection where the meaning of one's life is not determined by the way things go but by adherence to a set of moral principles that have a direct bearing on how one lives.

He illustrates this idea with the example of Franz Jäggerstätter, a German farmer who, during the Second War, was executed for refusing to pay taxes to the Nazi regime or to be conscripted into the German army. His refusal to participate in the regime in any way made his fate inevitable. Friends pleaded with him to reconsider, saying that it was pointless to act in this way as his death would have no affect on the regime. He refused, saying that it was impossible to serve two masters; one could not serve God and Hitler. A choice had to be made between the two.

Sutherland emphasises the values that underpin this decision. Jäggerstätter's stance is based on the distinction he makes between guilt and innocence, justice and injustice, honesty and dishonesty. For Sutherland, his willingness to die rather than compromise such ideals means that there are values that transcend the individual which cannot be destroyed, regardless of the things that happen to that individual. For our purposes, the meaning of a life is not about the extent to which the individual maximises feelings of happiness, but the extent to which their life has a sense of meaning and purpose. Jäggerstätter's life might have ended in suffering and tragedy, but it was far from meaningless because he had committed himself to a set of values outside himself that gave his suffering meaning and purpose. And his commitment to those values implied a social commitment: to ignore the pain of others was not an acceptable option. Political action emanated from a broader perspective on which the meaning of his life was founded. The well-lived life is not just about the success or otherwise of our actions; not just about whether we have enjoyed our lives or not. It involves determining principles for living that connect the self with the world, the internal with the external and the emotional with the political. Only by making such connections is the sense of the meaningful life possible.

At this point a rather different approach might be taken to the cultivation of well-being in the classroom. Rather than focus on analysing one's emotions, activities that encourage a connection with the wider world and the development of interests seems a better way of building that elusive sense of well-being. Developing an enquiring mind, cultivating habits of thought and practice that encourage the questioning of what lies outside the self, may enable a better sense of well-being than directing the gaze solely inward. Reflecting on the self is important in order that we understand ourselves and our actions better. But this is only adequate when balanced with a corresponding attention to the world outside the self. Aristotle's understanding of the fulfilling life recognised this need for balance as an activity of the soul, and only by cultivating this might we find a richer sense of well-being.

## Conclusion: education for life and through life

The tendency to look to science for solutions to today's problems can overlook the historical wisdom found in the attempts of philosophers and religious thinkers to grapple with the complex and often messy reality of being human. We can easily find ourselves seduced by the claim that science can solve all our problems. Philosophers and religious thinkers have been more pragmatic, suggesting that there are some things in human life that cannot be eradicated in the way that we might wish: and I have drawn attention to loss as one of life's inevitable pains. But I have also wanted to consider philosophical sources that take the reality of loss as the starting point for reflection on the meaning of one's life. The solutions offered are not just about cultivating inner peace of mind but about how to locate the self in the external world.

Taking seriously some of these philosophical and religious sources makes possible a shift from thinking about well-being as primarily located in *emotional* well-being to identifying well-being as that which emanates from the sense that one is living well. By making this shift, the emphasis moves from how to maximise feelings of happiness – by their very nature doomed to transience – to the prioritising of attitudes and actions that allow for the formation of the well-lived life. In this way, well-being is located alongside the practices that lead to the development of character.

This move from well-being to the well-lived life has wider implications for what is meant by 'education'. Increasingly, educational practice has been understood in terms that connects it to the development of the skills deemed necessary for living. The focus on attaining qualifications that fits students for the workplace has been part of this functionalist model. The focus on acquiring skills has also informed the way in which well-being strategies have developed, educational interventions addressing unhappiness through instilling a particular set of psychological skills in the child.

Neither account of the role of education is sufficient if attention is shifted to developing activities and forms of reflection that make for the well-lived life. If education is understood as a form of practice that enables the resources for the well-lived life, it can never be reduced to skills training. It has to be something more. The well-lived life takes time to establish; it is, moreover, never complete. The well-lived life is intimately connected to the development of character: something that takes time and which cannot be gained through short cuts or quick fixes.

Shifting attention from well-being to the well-lived life necessitates two things for education and educational practice.

The first relates explicitly to the curriculum offered in schools. At the outset, there needs to be a rich curriculum that offers opportunities for all to find subjects and disciplines that, through their exploration and practice, cultivate their sense of well-being. But it also means ensuring that there are spaces in the curriculum that allow for reflection on the nature of life and the meaning of a life. This need not mean adding anything radically new to the already packed school day. As the Department of Education notes, *all* National Curriculum subjects should provide 'opportunities to promote pupils' spiritual, moral, social and cultural development.' Significantly, the same statement highlights the 'explicit opportunities' for promoting pupils' development in religious education, and it is this subject which offers the possibility of opening up rather different discussions about how well-being might be understood and the strategies offered for its cultivation.[18] It is in this subject area, indeed, that children often get their first introduction to philosophical practices and themes, given that philosophy rarely forms an explicit part of the school curriculum. In claiming a particular role for Religious Education (RE) in the cultivation of 'spiritual, moral, social and cultural growth', the Department of Education's (DoE's) statement goes beyond supporting the teaching of this subject and offers the possibility of a broader challenge to the scientific models that have to date dominated the discussion of well-being. There are different ways of thinking about the things that promote well-being than neuroscience and psychology. Philosophical practices, religious traditions, stories and beliefs, all offer possibilities for exploring a variety of ways in which we might establish the sense of a meaningful life.[19] Well-being, read through this lens, gives way to the investigation of what makes for a well-lived life. And subjects like RE have a crucial role to play in exploring what such a life might involve.

A further point follows. If educational practice supports the development of richer ways of living, we must recognise that there are no short cuts to the art of living. This has implications for how we think about access to education throughout the lifespan.

If educational practices are understood as capable of providing resources and practices necessary for the well-lived life, then our educational institutions have a vital role in providing space for reflection and for what we might call spiritual or cultural enrichment *for all*. We might, with the German theologian Paul Tillich, call this spiritual or cultural enrichment 'the journey into depth.'[20] Tillich argues for the religious life as something which cultivates an engagement with the depths of experience. 'Entering into depth' involves questioning ourselves regarding the things that we do and value. Out of this questioning comes the possibility of new ways of being. Notably, he challenges the idea that the cultivation of such depth is something peculiarly connected to a particular class or profession or stage of life. Education is not to be reduced to something only for the middle class, the bookish or the young. As he puts it:

> Truth without the way to truth is dead … Look at the student who knows the content of the hundred most important books of world history, and yet whose spiritual life remains as shallow as it ever was, or perhaps becomes even more superficial. And then look at an uneducated worker who performs a mechanical task day by day, but who suddenly asks himself: 'What does it *mean*, that I do this work? What does it mean for my life? What *is* the meaning of my life?' Because he asks these questions, that man is on the way into depth, whereas the other man, the student of history, dwells on the surface among petrified bodies, brought out of the depth by some spiritual earthquake of the past. The simple worker may grasp the truth, even though he cannot answer his questions; the learned scholar may possess no truth, even though he knows all the truths of the past. (Tillich 1949, 61–2)

Tillich understands the enriched human life to involve grappling with these existential questions, and we might well ask about the role educational institutions can play in providing resources to help individuals respond to such questioning as and when it arises. For Tillich, it is through asking the kind of questions that this worker asks that better ways of living might be founded. This is a process that happens throughout life, not something that can be established once and for all in the formative years of formal education. If educational institutions are to support this kind of reflective thinking, it will be necessary to think again about how to promote access to such educational institutions for the members of the communities that surround them.

At this point, I become aware of my limitations when it comes to formulating policy. I am a philosopher of religion. To develop policies designed to address such concerns I need the help of colleagues in educational studies and social policy. I very much hope that there will be opportunities to do this work in the future. At this point, it is enough to have shown some of the limitations of the current well-being agenda and some of the ways in which a shift towards discussion of what makes for the well-lived life might prove helpful. The well-being agenda sought to address the problem of unhappiness in affluent societies. The so-called 'age of austerity' suggests a different context for the engagement with such discontent. As governments and populations struggle to find a way of moving beyond the affects of the global financial crisis, it seems likely that new forms of meaning will be needed that are not dependent upon the old consumerist solutions. Education in its richer iterations allows for different ways of finding meaning within the self and in the wider world. It is here that subjects seen as rather marginal to achieving economic growth – philosophy, theology and RE – might well come into their own, providing sources both for self reflection, but also for promoting forms of social engagement that create the basis for more fulfilling ways of living.

## Notes

1. I do not intend to give a comprehensive list here of the all the strategies put in place by the Labour government from 1997 to 2010, but that these strategies covered a wide range of areas can be evidenced from the following. The cross departmental programme 'Health, work and wellbeing: caring for our future' (2008) encompassed the Department of Work and Pensions, the Department of Health, the Health and Safety Executive, the Scottish Executive and the Welsh Assembly government. Under the 'Every Child Matters' umbrella, 'Healthy lives, better futures: the strategy for children and young people's health' (2009) emphasised the promotion of the emotional well-being and the mental health of children. Indications are that the Conservative-Liberal Democrat Coalition intends to continue to address issues of well-being, education secretary Michael Gove commenting that teachers needed not just academic expertise but also emotional intelligence (19 November 2010).
2. According to the Arts Council of Great Britain, the creative economy in fact grew faster than any other sector between 1997 and 2006, accounting for two million jobs and £16.6 billion of exports in 2007 ('Why the Arts Matter', 2010).
3. For critical reflections on this move see Richardson and Uebel (2007). For the key exposition of this position, see Ayer (1936).
4. We should note that some philosophers have rejected publishing in academic journals in philosophy in favour of engaging more directly with public concerns that might be illuminated by philosophical argument and method. See, for example, Baggini (2009), Warburton (2009) and de Botton (2000).
5. Broadly speaking, Anglo-American philosophy of religion has emphasised the application of reason to key topics in religion, while the 'continental' approach has attempted to incorporate desire, the emotions and the unconscious into the discussion of religion through a plethora of sources: literary, artistic, psychoanalytic and philosophical. For a useful account of the differences between 'Anglo-American' and 'Continental' philosophy of religion, see Jantzen (1996).
6. For examples of themes that seem divorced from the ordinary concerns of human life and the traditional religious attempts to respond to these, consider a recent edition of the leading journal in the area of philosophy of religion, *Religious Studies* 46: 4 December 2010. Articles include: 'Objections to Social Trinitarianism'; 'Composition Models of the Incarnation'; 'Sceptical Theism and Divine Lies' and 'Moral Omnipotence and Moral Perfection'.
7. See for example, Carlisle, Carter, and Whistler (2011) and Anderson (2010).
8. This is not an altogether original suggestion: a recent AHRC/ESRC-funded project 'Promoting Greater Wellbeing: Interacting the Happiness Hypothesis and Religion', brought together theologians and economists to discuss and develop policies which reflected the belief that theology could contribute much to the debate. See Atherton, Graham, and Steedman (2011).
9. For an excellent account of the Hellenistic schools and their approach to well-being, see Nussbaum (1994).
10. See, for example, Seneca (1997) for exercises designed to develop a reflective attitude.
11. For discussion of Seneca's political career, see Griffin (1992).
12. Wilkinson and Pickett challenge the idea that such a society could not be achieved: 'the evidence shows that even small decreases in inequality, already a reality in some rich market democracies, make a very important difference to the quality of life'. (2009, 271)
13. Feminist philosophers have made significant contributions to this rethinking of the individual. Both Jantzen (1998) and Battersby (1998) emphasise the realities of birth for an understanding of the individual as always located in community. The individual is not 'thrown into the world' as the existentialist philosopher Martin Heidegger famously claimed; we are always born between the legs of a woman and thus enter immediately into community, regardless of whether that community is an adequate or inadequate one.
14. Similar moves are also suggested by the British psychoanalyst D.W. Winnicott and the French analyst Jacques Lacan. For reflections on the similarities between these perspectives, see Green (2005).
15. See, for example, the Stoic philosopher and Roman Emperor Marcus Aurelius' reflections on the processes of the universe: 'Constantly think of the Universe as one

living creature, embracing one being and one soul; how all is absorbed into the one consciousness of this living creature; how it compasses all things with a single purpose, and how all things work together to cause all that comes to pass, and their wonderful web and texture' (*Meditations* Book IV, 40). The effect of such reflections, as Hadot (1995) notes is to develop a form of 'spiritual exercise' for cultivating a particular kind of perspective on the life that one is living.

16. This form of reflective detachment is cultivated in classical forms of analysis. Understood in this way, the goal of analysis is the 'introjection' of the analyst. The analyst and a more objective engagement with one's emotions are internalised, thus enabling the client to become an analyst to the self.

17. Responsible for the Sutherland Report (1999) that brought about free long-term care for the elderly in Scotland, there is a clear connection between Sutherland's personal ethical commitments and political and social actions.

18. http://www.education.gov.uk/schools/teachingandlearning/curriculum/a00199700/spiritual-and-moral (this statement was updated on 28 November 2011).

19. I am grateful to Stephen Pett for his suggestion of the possibilities inherent in this DoE statement.

20. Tillich's most accessible writings on depth and its promotion are found in his sermons *The Shaking of the Foundations* (1949). Avoiding the technical philosophical language of his volumes on systematic theology, this collection offers thought-provoking reflections on how to live richer and fuller lives.

# References

Anderson, Pamela, ed. 2010. *New topics in feminist philosophy of religion*. London: Springer.

Aristotle. 2002. *Nicomachean ethics*. Trans. Sarah Broadie and Christopher Rowe. Oxford: OUP.

Atherton, John, Elaine Graham, and Ian Steedman, eds. 2011. *The practices of wellbeing: Political economy, religion and wellbeing*. London: Routledge.

Ayer, A.J. 1936. *Language, truth and logic* (2007). London: Penguin.

Baggini, Julian. 2009. *Should you judge this book by its cover?* London: Granta.

Battersby, Christine. 1998. *The phenomenal woman*. Cambridge: Polity Press.

Boethius. 1969. *The consolation of philosophy*. Harmondsworth: Penguin.

Breuer, Joseph, and Sigmund Freud. 1893–1895. *Studies in Hysteria*. Trans. and ed. James Strachey. London: Hogarth Press, 1955.

Carlisle, Joseph, James C. Carter, and Daniel Whistler, eds. 2011. *Moral powers, fragile beliefs: Essays in moral and religious philosophy*. London: Continuum.

de Botton, Alain. 2000. *The consolation of philosophy*. Harmondsworth: Penguin.

Dienstag, Joshua Foa. 2006. *Pessimism: Philosophy, ethic, spirit*. Princeton, NJ: Princeton University Press.

Ecclestone, Kathryn, and Dennis Hayes. 2009. *The dangerous rise of therapeutic education*. London: Routledge.

Freud, Sigmund. 1930. *Civilisation and its discontents*. Trans. and ed. James Strachey. London: Hogarth Press, 1964, Standard Edition. vol. 21, 57–145.

Freud, Sigmund. 1937. *Analysis terminable and interminable*. Trans. and ed. James Strachey. London: Hogarth Press, 1964, Standard Edition, vol. 23, 209–253.

Green, André. 2005. *Play and reflection in Donald Winnicott's writings*. London: Karnac.

Griffin, Miriam. 1992. *Seneca: A philosopher in politics*. Oxford: Clarendon Press.

Hadot, Pierre. 1995. *Philosophy as a way of life*. Oxford: Blackwell.

Horwitz, Allan V., and Jerome C. Wakefield. 2007. *The loss of sadness: How psychiatry transformed normal sorrow into depressive disorder*. Oxford: OUP.

Jantzen, Grace. 1996. What's the difference? Knowledge and gender in (post)modern philosophy of religion. *Religious Studies* 32: 431–48.

Jantzen, Grace. 1998. *Becoming divine: Towards a feminist philosophy of religion*. Manchester, NH: Manchester University Press.

Johnston, Mark. 2009. *Saving God: Religion after idolatry*. Princeton, NJ: Princeton University Press.

Kristeva, Julia. 1988. *In the beginning was love: Psychoanalysis and faith*. New York, NY: Columbia.

Layard, Richard. 2005. *Happiness: Lessons from a new science*. London: Penguin.

Le Doeuff, Michèle. 2007. *Hipparchia's choice: An essay concerning women, philosophy, etc.* New York, NY: Columbia University Press.

Mill, John Stuart. 1871. Utilitarianism. In *Utilitarianism and other essays* (1987), ed. John Stuart Mill and Bentham Jeremy, 272–338. Harmondsworth: Penguin.

Nussbaum, Martha. 1994. *The therapy of desire: Theory and practice in hellenistic ethics*. Princeton, NJ: Princeton University Press.

Richard, Layard. 2005. *Happiness: Lessons from a new science*. Harmondsworth: Penguin.

Richardson, Alan, and Thomas Uebel, eds. 2007. *The Cambridge companion to logical empiricism*. Cambridge: CUP.

Schopenhauer, Arthur. 1966. *The world as will and representation*. New York, NY: Dover.

Seneca, Lucius Annaeus. 1969. *Letters from a stoic*. Trans. Robin Campbell. Harmondsworth: Penguin.

Seneca, Lucius Annaeus. 1997. *Dialogues and letters*. Trans. C.D.N. Costa. Harmondsworth: Penguin.

Soelle, Dorothee. 1975. *Suffering*. London: DLT.

Sutherland, Stewart R. 1969. What happens after death? *Scottish Journal of Theology* 22: 404–18.

Tillich, Paul. 1949. *The shaking of the foundations* (1962). Harmondsworth: Pelican.

Warburton, Nigel. 2009. *Free speech: A very short introduction*. Oxford: OUP.

Wilkinson, Richard, and Kate Pickett. 2009. *The spirit level: Why equality is better for everyone*. Harmondsworth: Penguin.

Williams, Bernard. 2005. *In the beginning was the deed*. Princeton, NJ: Princeton University Press.

Wolff, Jonathan. 2011. *Ethics and public policy*. London: Routledge.

# Index

academic achievement: focus on 43, 44; 'gap' in 46–9
Action for Happiness 1, 2, 58, 83
Advaita Vedanta 60
aesthetics 106–7
aggression: increases in 32, 84; reduction of 13, 15
All-Party Parliamentary Group on Scientific Research in Learning and Education 2
All-Party Parliamentary Group on Well-being in the Classroom: report (2007) 90
Allen, Graham 11–12
alphabet teaching 105
American Psychiatric Association 32, 34, 85
analysis: classical forms of 129
anger 57, 70, 85, 88, 123
anti-social behaviour 84, 90
anxiety 84, 85
Aristotle 70–1, 72, 74, 79, 100, 125; concept of *eudaimonia* 56, 60, 119; influence of 67–8
*arta* 61
arts: education in 101, 106–7, 111; state funding for 118
*atman* 60
Aurelius, Marcus 128–9
autonomy: as aspect of well-being 55; of pupil 64

Bain, Alexander 108–9
Bantock, Geoffrey 106–7
Bar-On, Reuven 42
Beck, Ulrich 30
Beckett, Samuel 83
Behavioural Insights Team ('Nudge Unit') 82, 90
behavioural problems *see* conduct disorders
behavioural psychology 4, 81–2, 117
behavioural science: determinism of 93, 94; political interest in 82–3, 89–91; utilitarian aspect of 92
behavioural training 89

behaviours: adapting 92; changing social attitudes to 34; targeted 13
Bell, Andrew 104
Benn, Melissa 76
Bentham, Jeremy 102, 103, 108, 110
Benzaquen, Adriana 38–9
Berkowitz, Marvin W. 49
Best, David 101, 106–7
Best Evidence Encyclopaedia 12
Biber, Edward 103, 105–6
Bible 57, 59, 60
Bier, Mindy C. 49
Birmingham and Midland Institute 106
birth rate: decline in 31
Blueprints for Violence Prevention 12, 15
Boethius 123
Boler, Megan 101
Bowlby, John 37
Bradshaw, Jonathan 10–11
Brahman 60
brain assessments 89
brain gym 28
Bray, Charles 105
British Child and Adolescent Mental Health Survey (1999) 32
British Cohort Study (1970) 32, 33
*British Quarterly Review* 102
Brook, David 91
Browne Review (2010) 118
Bruce Castle School, Tottenham 102
Buddhism, Theravada 60
bullying 71; reduction of 14, 18
bureaucrats: Marx on 92
Byrne, Liam 88
Bywater, Tracey 7–26

Cabinet Office *see* Behavioural Insights Team
Cameron, David 1–2, 81
Canadian Public Health Agency 19
capabilities, discourse of 3, 88–9, 91, 94
capitalism 30, 83, 108
caring for others 8, 58, 82
Cartmel, Fred 29

# INDEX

CASEL *see* Collaborative for Academic, Social and Emotional Learning
CASEL SELect Programs 46
CEP *see* Character Education Partnership
'Changing the subject?' (seminar series) 3
character discourse 43, 82, 87–90, 91, 93–4, 126
Character Education Partnership (CEP) 43
charity 61, 109
child guidance clinics 35–6
childcare 8
childhood, crisis of 2, 4, 27–40; historical perspective 28, 29–31, 35–6, 38–9; measurement and diagnosis of 31–9; quality of evidence for 29; romantic ideal of childhood 31; social science accounts of 29; therapeutic interventions 28 children: disadvantaged 7, 8; disaffection of 73, 78, 79; dominant model of staged development of 38; evaluations of 10; influenced by popular psychology 37; interviews 33–4; long-term effects of conduct disorders 84–5; mental illness 7, 84
Children's Act (2004) 10
*Childen's Charter* (film) 31
Children's Society 2, 31
Children's Workforce Development Council Commissioning Toolkit 12, 19
choice architecture 90, 91
*Chrestomathia* (Bentham and Mill) 102
Christianity 58, 60, 105, 108, 118
chronosystem 47, 48
Church of England 104
Cigman, Ruth 4, 65, 67–80
circle time 28, 86
citizenship 82, 87
Clack, Beverley 115–30
Claxton, Guy 56, 73, 75, 77, 79
Coalition government (2010– ) 1–3, 11, 81–2, 87, 128; and religious education 54
Cobbe, Frances Power 101
Cochrane Collaboration 12
cognitive behavioural therapy 28, 86, 91, 117
Cohen, J. 49
cohort studies 30–1, 32
Coleman, J. 54, 55
Collaborative for Academic, Social and Emotional Learning (CASEL) 4, 8, 12, 20, 41, 42; changes to 43; five skill areas 42, 44, 46; 2003 study 46
Collishaw, S. 32
community 121
Compayré, Gabriel 106
Comprehensive Spending Review 118
conduct disorders 8, 84–5, 86; gathering data on 32–3; targeted programmes for 13, 14–15; *see also* psychosocial disorders

Conduct Problems Prevention Research Group 42
conflict resolution 9, 13
Consortium on the School-Based Promotion of Social Competence 42
control, sense of 60
Cornum, Rhonda 81
Cottingham, John 56
courage 105
Coventry, England 105
crime 8, 85
Croesus, King 59
Csikszentmihalyi, Mihaly 56, 78
curriculum: Aristotle's influence on 68; capabilities 3; chrestomathic 102–3; including reflection on meaning of life 126–7; rigid and non-integrative 47; 'of the self' 100; traditional 3, 11, 73; *see also* religious education

death 60, 85, 120, 122, 123
decentralisation 11
decision-making 42, 44
DEMOS 91
Department for Children, Schools and Families (DCSF; *2007–2010*) 2–3, 10
Department for Education (DfE; *formed 2010*) 2–3, 54
Department for Education and Skills (DfES; *2001–2007*): Research Report (2003) 10
Department of Education (DoE): 1997 statement 126
depression 29, 74, 78, 84, 85
depth of experience 127
detachment 61, 124
determinism 93, 94–5
Dewey, John 72
*dharma* 61
Diagnostic and Statistical Manual (APA) 32, 34–5, 85
diagnostic criteria 85
Dickens, Charles: as advocate of emotional education 100, 106; *Hard Times* and Thomas Gradgrind character 90, 99, 101–2, 103, 106, 109, 110
Diener, Ed 55
Dienstag, Joshua Foa 121
disaffection 73, 78, 79
discipline, public school 88
disciplines 77, 78, 79
Dixon, Thomas 85, 90, 99–113
drama 106, 107
Dunkelblau, Edward 43
Dunn, Judy 31–2
Durkheim, Émile 30
Durlak, J.A. 12, 19, 48–9
duty 61, 102, 104

# INDEX

*Early intervention: The next steps* (Allen report) 11–12
Early Years Foundation Stage 8
Ecclestone, Kathryn 1–5, 54, 81–98, 100, 117
ECM *see* Every Child Matters
ecological systems theory: defined 47; research 47–8
Economic and Social Research Council 3
economics 83, 90; crisis 127; *see also* socio-economic factors
education: conviction of value of 79; enables well-lived life 126; 'from which nothing follows' (Whitehead) 75; humanistic 77; purpose of 72–6, 78; right to 46–7; that transcends the classroom 115–16; urban 45, 46–7, 48; *see also* schools
*Education, Health and Behaviour* (Isle of Wight study) 32–3, 36
Edwardian period 89, 93
Eid, Michael 55
Elementary Education Act (1870) 87, 101, 108
Elias, Maurice J. 41–52
'emotional': early use of term 106
'emotional inoculation' 84
emotional intelligence 3, 41–52; Goleman on 41–2, 100, 108; skill areas 42
emotional metrics 110
emotions: appropriate response to 70, 71–2; cultivation of 74; dangers of scientific approach to 110–11; 18th century concern with 100, 104; 'hardwired' nature of 119; inward-looking 120; link with aesthetics 106–7; 'negative' *vs.* 'positive' 57, 67, 68; as new secular category 108; 19th century concern with 100–1, 103–9; relationship with intellect 111; role of 41; transitory nature of 119; 20th century concern with 101, 108, 109; *see also* well-being, emotional
empathy 13, 15, 42, 57, 82, 88, 89
empiricism 36–7, 38
empowerment 44
enhancement agenda 67–80; complexity of 72; *vs.* knowledge agenda 73–7, 78
entrepreneurship 94
epigenetic code 89
equality 1; *see also* inequality
Erricker, Clive 58
*eudaimonia* 56, 59–60, 119
eugenics 89
European Union: child well-being rankings 27
Every Child Matters (ECM) 1, 10, 68, 128
evil: William James on 69

facts 99, 101, 103, 109, 110
faith communities 58, 62
families: extended 47; fluidity of 28; influence of 9, 48; policies concerning 8; religious emphasis on 59; role of 108; smaller 31; *see also* parents
Families and Schools Together (FAST) 15, 17, 19, 22
Family Links Nurturing Programme, The 15, 18, 19
FAST *see* Families and Schools Together
feminism 100, 118, 128
Fetzer Institute 43
Field, Frank 8
Finland 14, 86
flow 56, 78
free market model 118
free schools 3
Freud, Sigmund 36, 123
Furedi, Frank 93–4
Furlong, Andy 29

Gager, P.J. 45
generalities, risks of 72
genetic factors 83–4
Giddens, Anthony 30
global assessment tests 110
Goleman, Daniel 41–2, 100, 108
*Good Childhood, A* (Layard and Dunn) 31–2
Gove, Michael 76, 128
Gradgrind, Thomas 90, 99, 101–2, 103, 106, 109, 110
Gray, Gay 10
Greenfield, Susan 2, 90
Grimmitt, Michael 58, 61, 62–3, 65
Grist, Matt 88, 89
guides, instructional 85

Haberman, M. 46
Hadot, Pierre 120, 124
happiness: appropriateness as educational aim 53; Aristotle on 56, 60, 119; Boethius on 123; defining 116; doctrine of detachment from 61; elitist attitude to 119; genetic and trait-based factors 83–4; hedonic views of 55, 56, 57, 59; as integral component of education 65; Layard on 56, 58, 63, 83, 116, 121; link with caring and morality 58; mapping 56; Mill on 92–3; 19th century concern with 100; philosophical and religious ideas of 58, 59–61; philosophical *vs.* psychological views of 54–5, 56, 64; relationship with well-being 55–7, 116; 'science of' 28; utilitarianism and 102; William James on 69–70
*Hard Times see* Gradgrind, Thomas
Haybron, Daniel M. 56, 64

## INDEX

Hayes, Dennis 117
Haynes, N.M. 48
Hazelwood School, Edgbaston 102
Herodotus 59–60
Hertfordshire local authority 84, 85
Hick, John 64
higher education: free market model 118
Hill, Thomas Wright 102
Hinduism 60–1
Hodgson, William B. 109
Holyoake, George J. 109
Horwitz, Allan V. 122
human development model 58, 62–3, 64–5
humanities 4, 74, 117–8
hyperactivity 32, 84

ideas, inert 75–6
Illinois, University of 20
implementation integrity 45
Incredible Years (IY) series 14–15, 16–17, 21,
    22; Dinosaur Programme 13, 14
individual: in community 121; focus on
    responsibility of 120; transcending 124–5
individualism 31
inequality 83, 91, 120
Infant School Society 104
Infant School system 100, 104–6
injustice 70, 123
Institute of Economic Affairs 83
Institute of Psychiatry 84
International Classification of Disease 32, 36
interventions: arguments for 83–5; 'asset-
    based' 84; complex 19–20; cost-
    effectiveness 21; desirability of 53; evidence
    base for 89–90; incoherence of 86–7; long-
    term effects unknown 87; principles of 45–
    6; process evaluation 20–1; rise of 86–7;
    role of 3, 4, 8, 28–9; science-based 81–2
interviewing: as methodology 30–1, 33–4, 36,
    37
Ireland 15, 21
Islam 61
Isle of Wight 32–3, 36

Jäggerstätter, Franz 124–5
James, Henry 69
James, Oliver 84
James, William 68–70, 72
Jesus Christ 60
Jewish tradition 57, 59, 60
Job 57, 59
Johnston, Mark 122
*Journal of Child Psychology and Psychiatry*
    32
justice: as Biblical theme 59, 60; social 1, 57;
    *see also* injustice

*kama* 61
Kames, Henry Home 100, 104, 108
*karma* 60
Kehily, Mary 27
*KiVa* 14, 17, 19
knowledge: intrinsic value of 76, 77, 78; as
    life-enriching 78, 79; useful *vs.* useless 73;
    *vs.* well-being 68, 73–7
Kozol, J. 47
Kristeva, Julia 122
Kynaston, David 30

Labour government 1, 2–3, 10, 11, 86, 90,
    116, 117, 128
'Lancasterian' system 102, 103
Layard, Richard: and Action for Happiness
    2, 58, 83; on caring for others 58; as
    government advisor 2, 116; on happiness
    56, 58, 63, 83, 116, 121; on science 93, 117,
    121; views on Mill 64, 119; *A Good
    Childhood* (with Judy Dunn) 31–2;
    *Happiness: Lessons from a New Science*
    116
Lexmond, Jan 88, 89
life: balanced 94; enriched by knowledge 77;
    humanistic enrichment of 78; learning
    about 75; meaning of 119, 124–5, 126, 127;
    precarious nature of 121, 123; seen as
    threatening 93; well-lived 115, 121–5
life skills 71, 77, 91, 92, 94
lifestyle choices 82
literature, access to 106
London School of Economics 2
longitudinal studies 36
Lopez, Shane J. 57
loss 122, 123, 125
love 104–5, 122
luck 60
Lyubomirsky, Sonja 58

McDonald, Gus 81
McMahon, Darrin M. 55, 60
Macquarie Bank 81
macrosystems 47, 48
Marmontel, Jean-François 107
Marx, Karl 30, 92
Masterpasqua, F. 46–7
mastery, acquiring 79, 117
materialism 27, 28, 38, 83
mathematics, achievement in 47–8
M'Choakumchild, Mr 101, 102
meaning, sense of 55, 59, 63–4, 65, 123–5,
    127
measurement 2, 31–9, 63, 94, 110; of
    character capabilities 89; dangers of 92;
    utilitarianism and 102
media 30, 37

# INDEX

Medical Research Council, UK 19–20
medicalisation 85
medication 37, 38
mental health: of adolescents 31–2
mental hygiene movement 35, 101
mental illness: blurring of professional and popular perceptions of 85–6; children with 7, 84; defining and classifying 34, 35–7; diagnosis 85; preventing through interventions 84, 117; question of 'cure' for 123; statistics 84
microsystems 47, 48
Mihalic, Sharon 12
Mill, James 102–3, 107
Mill, John Stuart 75, 76, 89, 100, 101, 106–7, 111, 119; background and education 102–3; on emotion and aesthetics 106, 107; mental breakdown 74, 92, 107; utilitarianism 64; warning about striving for happiness 92–3; and Wordsworth and poetry 74, 76, 77, 78, 79–80, 107; *Autobiography* 103, 107; 'Reform in Education' 103, 105–6
Mills, C. Wright 3–4, 91–2, 94
Moceri, Dominic C. 41–52
modernity 30
*moksha* 60–1
monitorial system 102, 103
moral character 43
moral panics 35
moral philosophy 104, 109–10
moral values 2, 58
morality: Christian 105; confusion of psychology with 93–4; replacement with new categories 108; Wilderspin's system and 105
mothers: interviews with 33; loss of 122; responsibility for emotional education 104, 108, 109
Mulgan, Geoff 1, 71, 72, 73, 75, 77, 78
music 47, 76, 102, 106, 107
Myers, Kevin 27–40

Nagel, Tom 92
National Assessment of Educational Progress 46
National Association of Teachers of RE 54
National Child Development Study (NCDS) 32
National Curriculum Handbook for Teachers in England 68
National Education League 109
National Health Service (NHS) 21, 35–6
National Institute for Health and Clinical Excellence (NICE) 7–8, 20, 55
National Longitudinal Survey of Youth (NLSY79) 48

National School of Character (NSOC) award 43
National Schools 103, 104, 105
National Strategies 10, 11
NCDS *see* National Child Development Study
NEF *see* New Economics Forum
Neimark, Jill 57
Netherlands 13
Nettle, Daniel 56
neuroscience 41, 89, 117; affective 100, 110; popular 108
New Economics Forum (NEF) 2
New Jersey 45
Newcastle Report (1861) 103
NHS *see* National Health Service
NICE *see* National Institute for Health and Clinical Excellence
nihilism 79
nineteenth century 85, 87, 89, 93, 100–9
NLSY79 *see* National Longitudinal Survey of Youth
No Child Left Behind 47, 48, 49–50
Northern Ireland 13
Norway 14, 18
nostalgia 30, 31, 37
NSOC *see* National School of Character
nudge techniques 82, 90, 91
Nudge Unit *see* Behavioural Insights Team
Nuffield Foundation 84

Office for National Statistics 2, 32
Olweus Program 14, 15, 18
optimism 68, 69–70, 91; learned 83; Schopenhauer on 123
organizational systems 47, 48
Orr, Amy J. 48
*Oxford Review of Education* 54

Palmer, Sue 28
Panel Study of Income Dynamics 48
parenting: negative *vs.* positive 9; programmes 14–15, 17, 18, 19
parents: influenced by popular psychology 37; interviews with 33; materialism of 27; and questionnaire methodology 32–3; *see also* mothers
Parents Nurturing Programme 15
PATHS *see* Promoting Alternative Thinking Strategies
patriarchalism 101
Payton, John 12, 19
peer influences 9, 21
Penn Resiliency Programme 55, 56, 71–2, 86
performance character 43
Personal and Thinking Skills programme 86
pessimism 94, 121, 123–4

135

# INDEX

Peters, Richard 75, 76, 78, 79
Pett, Stephen 53–66
pharmaceutical companies 37
philosophy 67–8, 73–6, 77, 79, 92, 100, 115–30; Anglo-American *vs.* Continental 128; Greek 59–60, 119–20, 124; influence on policy 116; invisibility in contemporary debate 117–19; moral 68, 104; and relativism 77; and religion 55, 56, 64, 118; as science 118; 'well-lived life' concept 115, 121–7; Wittgenstein on 77; *see also* Aristotle; Mill, John Stuart
Pickett, Kate 120–1
PISA *see* Programme for International Student Assessment
playgrounds 104
Plowden Report (1967) 108
policy: behavioural science and 89–91; influence of positive psychology on 83, 100; philosophers' influence on 116; UK 1–3, 10–12
politics: interest in behavioural science 82–3, 89–91, 94; lack of will concerning inequality 120–1
positive psychology: antecedents of 35; Aristotle and 68, 70–1; and character development 87–8, 91; as 'emotional inoculation' 84; evidence-based 78; influence on policy 83, 100; Penn Resiliency Programme and 71–2; and religious education 55, 57, 58, 59, 63; William James and 68–70
Post, Stephen 57
post-traumatic stress disorder (PTSD) 84, 85
poverty 46–7, 48, 49
pride 70, 71
problem solving 42
professional development 19
professionalisation 118
Programme for International Student Assessment (PISA) 48
Promoting Alternative Thinking Strategies (PATHS) 13, 15, 16, 22, 46, 55, 56, 59
psychiatry 33–4, 35–6, 85, 122
psychoanalysis 36, 38, 85, 86, 91, 108, 122, 123, 128
psychology: behavioural 4, 81–2, 117; confused with morality 93–4; distinction from religion 54; early science of 108; evolutionary 100; experimental 37, 53; fashions in 85; 'new' 35; popular 34, 37, 90; social 37; view of happiness 55, 56, 64; *see also* positive psychology
psychosocial disorders 29, 32, 33; empirical methods in identification of 36–7; increasing diagnosis and subdivisions of

34–5, 37; medicalisation of 37, 38; *see also* conduct disorders
PTSD *see* post-traumatic stress disorder
public schools 88
purpose, sense of 55, 59, 64, 65, 123

Qualifications and Curriculum Authority (QCA): levels of attainment for RE 57
*Quarterly Review* 100
questionnaires, use of 32–3, 34, 36, 37

racial factors 46–8, 49
RAEs see Research Assessment Exercises
randomised control trials (RCT) 13, 14, 15, 16, 22, 36, 110
RE *see* religious education
reading skills 48
reason 101–2, 104
reflective thinking 86, 127
reincarnation 60, 61
relationship skills 42, 44
religion: Eastern 60–1; philosophy of 118; strategies for dealing with suffering 122; Tillich on 127; transcendence from the self 124; *see also* Christianity
religious education (RE) 4, 53–66; absence in well-being debate 57; ancient wisdom and virtues 57; contribution to well-being of pupils 64–5; cuts in 54; distinguishing features of various traditions 59–61; genericist approach to 62; human development model 58, 62–3, 64–5; linked with emotional education 109; and moral values 58; 19th century 108, 109; nominalist approach to 61–2; pedagogies of 61; place in curriculum 54, 61–3, 123, 126; positive psychology and 55, 57, 58, 59, 63; relationship with pupils' life worlds 63; and sense of meaning 55, 59, 63–4, 65; skills required for study of 57
*Religious Studies* 128
research: easier access to 11; US 3, 10
Research Assessment Exercises (RAEs) 118
Research Excellence Framework 118
*Research Papers in Education* 3
resilience 2, 12, 68, 71–2; Hertfordshire programme 84, 85; Penn programme 55, 56, 71–2, 86; 'toolkits' 89; US army programme 81, 83, 84, 90
riots 2
Roberts, Yvonne 71–2, 73, 75, 77
role play 13, 14, 107
Rose, Jim 100, 107
Rose Review (2009) 108
rote learning 101, 103–4, 105
Rousseau, Jean-Jacques 100
Royal Society of Arts (RSA) 3, 90, 91

# INDEX

Rutter, Michael 32–4, 36–7
Rutter scales 32–3, 35

sadness *see* unhappiness
Safeguarding Vulnerable Adults Act (2006) 85
Salovey, Peter 42
*samsara* 60
Savage, Mike 30, 31, 35
Save The Children 15, 27
schools: and character education 43; choice of programmes 3, 11; classroom environments 44; defining core values 43–4; desirability of intervention by 53; free 3; as organizational systems 47; public 88; purpose of 72–6, 78; role in fostering well-being 4, 7–8, 9; SEL programmes 12–19, 22; success in 44; underachievement 9; vulnerability studies in 85–6; *see also* state schools
Schools and Early Years Nurturing Programme 15
Schopenhauer, Arthur 123, 124
science: 'advocacy' 94; and character development 88, 89, 91, 93–4; dangers of relying on 110–11, 117–18; and emotional 'fitness' 90; emphasis on empiricism 36–7, 38; of happiness 28; and intervention strategies 81–2; linked with secular education 109; philosophy as 118; positivist 118; as solver of all problems 122, 125; and vulnerability 93; *see also* neuroscience
scientism 122
SEAL *see* Social and Emotional Aspects of Learning Strategy
SECD *see* social-emotional and character development
secondary data analysis 35
secularism 108–9
SEL *see* social and emotional learning
Seldon, Anthony 63, 68, 88
self: inward focus 120, 124, 125; language of 37; looking beyond 124; neo-liberal idea of 120
self-awareness 42, 44, 91
self-esteem 15, 71, 84
self-help 84, 85, 86, 91, 108
self-management 42, 44
Seligman, Martin E.P. 56, 57, 68, 83
Seneca 115, 120
Sennett, Richard 30
Shakespeare, William 75, 76, 77, 78, 79
*shalom* 59
Sharp, Peter 84
Sharples, Jonathan 7–26
Sheffield, England 14
Shriver, Lionel 67

skills: focus on 126; life 71, 77, 91, 92, 94; relationship 42, 44; targeted 13
Smith, Richard 64
Smith, Roger 36–7
Snyder, Charles R. 57
Social and Emotional Aspects of Learning Strategy (SEAL) 1, 2, 10, 22, 55, 56, 71, 72, 86, 88, 100; secondary school version 11
social and emotional learning (SEL) 3, 7–26; application to the achievement gap 46–7; and character education 43; conditions needed for 45; cost effectiveness 21; defining 7–8, 42–4; ecological influences 47–8; effectiveness 12; Goleman and 41–2; implementation of programmes 45–6; importance of effectiveness and fidelity of programmes 19–20, 22, 45; influences on well-being 9; link with school and life success 44; multi-modal programmes 13, 14–15, 16, 17, 18, 19, 22; process evaluation 20–1; research into influences on learning 48–50; search for evidence-based programmes 12–13; six sustainability factors 20; skill areas 42; targeted school-based programmes 12, 13, 14, 17; ten implementation steps 20; UK-available programmes 13, 14, 15, 16–18, 21–2; UK policy context 10–12; universal school-based programmes 12, 13–14, 16, 17, 18
social awareness 42
social change 29–30, 38
social-emotional and character development (SECD) 44, 45, 46, 48, 49–50
social justice 1, 57
social sciences 29–31, 91–4; interviewing techniques and cohort studies 30–1, 33–4, 36, 37; use of questionnaires 32–3, 34, 36, 37
socio-economic factors 7, 44, 46–8, 53, 83, 120
sociological imagination 3–4, 94
Socrates 119
Soelle, Dorothee 122
Solon 59–60
Spencer, Herbert 100, 103–4, 106, 108
Spock, Benjamin 37
staff training 50
state schools: funding 118; opposition to 108; as secular institutions 109
state intervention 53; *see also* policy
Stoics 119–20, 124
Strayhorn, T.L. 47–8
Strengths and Difficulties Questionnaire 14, 21
stress 84
success 44

# INDEX

suffering 60, 83, 93, 120, 122, 123, 125
Suissa, J. 54, 63–4, 65
SureStart 1
survey data: use of 35
Sutherland, Stewart R. 124–5
Swedenborgianism 104

Tallis, Raymond 89
Taylor, Matthew 90
Teacher Classroom Management Programme 15
teachers: importance of conviction by 79; problems of engaging children 78; and questionnaire methodology 33; student perception of 48; training 50; Whitehead on 78
Teece, G. 63, 64
testing, academic 47, 71, 75, 76, 78, 79
therapeutic ethos 28, 53, 82, 85, 91, 93, 94, 117
think-tanks 2, 3, 30, 91
third grade students (US) 48
Third Way ideology 1
Tickell, Clare 8
Tillich, Paul 127
Timberlake, J.M. 48
time trends, measuring 35
'Time trends in adolescent mental health' (Collishaw et al.) 32
Together4All 13
touchstones 44
trait-based factors 83–4
transcendence 57, 124–5
truth 127
Tupper, John Lucas 100–1, 106
Tyndall, John 109

unconscious 90, 91
unhappiness: ability to allow 94; appropriateness of 123; inevitability of 123; pathologised 122
UNICEF (United Nations Children's Fund) 2, 10–11, 27
United Kingdom: parenting programmes 15; policy 1–3, 10–12; SEL programmes 13, 14, 15, 16–18, 21–2, 46; well-being rankings 10–11, 27
United States of America: achievement gap 46–7; army resilience programme 81, 83, 84, 90; character education 43; mental-hygiene movement 101; performance in PISA tests 48; SEL programmes 3, 10, 13, 14, 15, 21, 41–52; see also Collaborative for Academic, Social and Emotional Learning
urban education 45, 46–7, 48
Urwin, Cathy 38
utilitarianism 64, 67, 92, 101, 102–3, 106

value, educational: conviction of 79
value, theory of 55, 56
values: affirmation of 49; vs. capabilities 88; core 43–4; education's relationship with 63–4; relative nature of 77
Vernon, Mark 56
Victorian period 85, 87, 89, 93, 100–2, 103–4, 105, 106, 107–9
virtues: Aristotle on 60; perceived traits 88; religious 57, 60
Vivekananda, Swami 61
vulnerability: accepting 122; categorising 85–6; deterministic view of 93, 94–5; potentiality for 94

Wakefield, Jerome C. 122
Waldstein, Charles 106
Wales 13, 15, 22
wealth 48, 83; Hindu attitude to 61
Weare, Katherine 10
Weber, Carl Maria von 107
Weber, Max 30
well-being, emotional: blurring between political and public assessments of 82; blurring between professional and popular assessments of 85; classifying 55; crisis of 1, 2, 82, 84; critiquing 119–20; defining 54–5; embraces multiple constructs 82; goal of 1–2; historical concern with 100–1; individual responsibilty for 120; vs. knowledge 68, 73–7; mapping 56; reductionist view of 87; relationship with happiness 55–7, 116; UNICEF report on 10–11; see also emotions; happiness
well-lived life 115, 121–7
Wellington College, Berkshire 55–7, 88
Westminster Review 99
White, John 73–4, 75, 77, 79
Whitehead, A.N. 65, 75–6, 78
WHO see World Health Organization
Wilderspin, Samuel 101, 104–6, 108
Wilkinson, Richard 120–1
Williams, Bernard 116
Wittgenstein, Ludwig 77
Wolff, Jonathan 116
wonder 102, 104
Wordsworth, William 74, 78, 79–80, 107
World Health Organization (WHO) 2, 32, 83
Wright, Andrew 58, 61–2

Young Foundation 1, 2, 71–2, 81
youth development programmes 46

Zins, Joseph E. 44

www.routledge.com/9780415693530

## Related titles from Routledge

# The Sociology of Disability and Inclusive Education

A Tribute to Len Barton

**Edited by Madeleine Arnot**

Len Barton's intellectual and practical contribution to the sociology of disability and education is well-known and highly significant. This collection addresses the challenge that the social model of disability has presented to dominant medicalised concepts, categories and practices, and their power to define the identity and the lives of others. Expert scholars explore a wide range of topics, including difference as a field of political struggle; the relationship of disability studies, disabled people and their struggle for inclusion; radical activism: organic intellectuals and the disability movement; discrimination, exclusion and effective change; inclusive education; the 'politics of hope', resilience and transformative actions; and universal pedagogy, human rights and citizenship debates.

This book was originally published as a special issue of the *British Journal of Sociology of Education*.

February 2012: 246 x 174: 160pp
Hb: 978-0-415-69353-0
**£85 / $145**

For more information and to order a copy visit
www.routledge.com/9780415693530

Available from all good bookshops

## The case of *Jeanne Dielman*

The film depicts three days in the life of a middle-aged woman living in a flat in Brussels with her son. She is a widow and supplements her income by prostituting herself at home every afternoon between 5 and 5:30pm. She follows a strict domestic routine that could go on forever if it wasn't for unexpectedly burning the potatoes on the kitchen stove at the end of day two. Entering the flat and finding her in the kitchen, the boy remarks, *'maman tu es toute décoiffée'*. She replies, *'j'ai trop laissé cuire les pommes de terre'*. What seems to be a minor incident turns out to be a major disruption in a reassuring sea of everydayness. Her implacable and yet at the same time comforting routine having been disrupted, she is unhinged and on the third day she kills her client in the bedroom.

The film lasts three hours and twenty minutes and comprises a series of long continuous scenes, often lasting three to four minutes, where actions are taking place in real time. But instead of inducing boredom, this 'gradually increases our attention to their construction and its significance' (Bergstrom, 1977, p.116).

Gilles Deleuze, who assigned some crucial function to the depiction of the everyday in films,[19] commenting on *Jeanne Dielman*, stated that 'Chantal Akerman wants to show "gestures in their fullness"' (Deleuze, 1989, p.196). Indeed the cinematic everyday situation is a key component of the Deleuzian concept of the 'time-image' that emerged principally with the Italian neo-realist movement at the end of WWII, in particular with *Umberto D* (Vittorio De Sica, 1952), a film of relevance to *Jeanne Dielman,* the two having often been studied side by side (Margulies, 1996, p.8), particularly given the importance of the kitchen scenes.[20]

But crucially here, Deleuze suggests that the everyday in films is a necessary state, to contrast with potential disturbances, and that the more banal the situation is, the greater the potential to introduce the brutal and the nightmarish.[21] This argument applies to *Jeanne Dielman* where the potatoes incident brings about a brutal murder. Deleuze further opposes the everyday to limit-situations (extreme situations): 'In fact, the most banal or everyday situations release accumulated 'dead forces' equal to the life force of a limit-situation'[22] (Deleuze, 1989, p.7). Deleuze hints here at the duality, and complementarity, between everyday situations and 'limit-situations' – murder in the case of *Jeanne Dielman* – the latter having to be understood as action situations, in contrast with periods of idleness that only make sense in relation to former dramatic situations or events. What is suggested here is that everydayness is not shown on the screen for itself, but rather as a primer or context to limit situations. This is very germane to my argument in Chapter 3 regarding the close and necessary relationship between the everyday and disruptions. Given the relentlessness of the everyday over nearly 3 hours, the murder provides indeed both the spectators and *Jeanne Dielman* with the necessary release of accumulated 'dead forces'.

## Jeanne Dielman's cinematography

Most striking is the cinematography, essentially composed of straight-on long shots, explained by Akerman in the following terms:

> it was the only way to shoot that scene and to shoot that film to avoid cutting the woman into a hundred pieces, to avoid cutting the action in a hundred places, to look carefully and to be respectful. The framing was meant to respect the space, her, and her gestures within it [...] We didn't have a lot of choice about where to put the camera because I didn't want angle shots. I wanted them all to be straight, as much as possible.
>
> *(Bergstrom, 1977, p.119)*

As a result, Delphine Seyrig, who plays Jeanne Dielman, is always bang in the middle of the frame, with the camera either facing her or at the side. Over three days the camera is sited in the same positions in the kitchen, the corridor, the bedroom, the bathroom and the dining room, weaving over time a careful network of daily gestures. *Jeanne Dielman* is a film that gives a lot of space to space – the camera often lingers for a few seconds after a character has left a space, the sort of spaces one never normally pays attention to: the corridor, the kitchen, the dining room, and in this case, spaces of no architectural significance or merit, drab spaces that are as anonymous and unnoticed as Delphine Seyrig's gestures when she peels her potatoes.

> I give space to things which were never, almost never, shown in that way, like the daily gestures of a woman. They are the lowest in the hierarchy of film images. A kiss or a car crash come higher, and I don't think that's an accident. It's because these are women's gestures that they count for so little. That's one reason I think it's a feminist film. But more than the content, it's because of the style. If you choose to show a woman's gestures so precisely, it's because you love them.
>
> *(Bergstrom, 1977, p.118)*

**FIGURE 4.5** *Jeanne Dielman* (Chantal Akerman, 1974) – kitchen planimetric shots

Over three days the actions and tasks performed by Jeanne are like a carefully catalogued study in domestic everydayness. It remarkably matches Perec's own analysis of the various functions performed in an apartment on a daily basis:

> I don't know, and don't want to know, where functionality begins or ends. It seems to me, in any case, that in the ideal dividing-up of today's apartments functionality functions in accordance with a procedure that is unequivocal, sequential and nycthemeral. The activities of the day correspond to slices of time, and to each slice of time there corresponds one room of the apartment. The following model is hardly a caricature.
>
> *(Perec, 2008, p.28)*

Perec proceeds to list a generic flat's functionality in relation to the different rooms, from morning to evening. In the table below I have matched Jeanne's actions to Perec's list for the first part of the day.

| Perec's list [until 10:30am only] | JD's list of actions until around 10:30am |
|---|---|
| 7:00 The mother gets up and goes to get breakfast in the kitchen | Jeanne wakes up, goes to the bathroom |
| 7:15 The child gets up and goes into the bathroom | the son is asleep – she puts the gas heater on in the room – she prepares his clothes – goes to the kitchen, puts the kettle on and polishes his shoes |
| 7:30 The father gets up and goes into the bathroom | she prepares the coffee – she wakes him up |
| 7:45 The father and the child have their breakfast in the kitchen | the son is having breakfast [she is getting dressed, ellipsed] |
| 8:00 The child takes his coat from the entrance hall and goes off to school | [the son gets dressed, ellipsed] the son has his coat on – she adjusts his scarf – he asks for extra pocket money – she kisses him – he goes out |
| 8:15 The father takes his coat from the entrance-hall and goes off to his office | |
| 8:30 The mother performs her toilet in the bathroom | |

| 8:45 | The mother takes the vacuum cleaner from the broom closet and does the housework (she then goes through all the rooms of the apartment but I forbear from listing them) | Jeanne tidies up the sitting room, her bedroom and does the breakfast dishes |
| 9:30 | The mother fetches her shopping basket from the kitchen and her coat from the entrance hall and goes to do the shopping | she grabs some money to go out – first to the post office – then she does the shopping |
| 10:30 | The mother returns from shopping and puts her coat back in the entrance-hall | Jeanne comes back, puts the shopping on the kitchen table, takes her coat off, puts away the shopping and makes a note of her shopping on the kitchen table |

But for the missing father in *Jeanne Dielman*, the comparison shows a remarkable correspondence. Perec's is a list and *Jeanne Dielman* is a visual list, a moving-image visualization of a daily routine.

The flat's dreariness could be described as an 'espace quelconque', as in 'any old space' as opposed to the Deleuzian sense of any-space-whatever. The studio-reconstructed flat is oozing in carefully staged gloominess and, for a film shot in 1975, it is untouched by the advent of modernism. There is no TV, only the radio, emphasizing the 'stuck in the past' lifestyle. The layout is simple and yet the rooms are like distinct cells, disconnected by moments of darkness as, at night, *Jeanne Dielman* is systematically switching off and on the light as she leaves and enters a room. It is a form of compartmentalized living with no open plan, no vista.[23] Day in and day out, Jeanne and her son connect from one 'cell' to another, the perfect visualization of Perec's 'Vivre, c'est passer d'un espace à un autre, en essayant le plus possible de ne pas se cogner' [To live is to move from one space to another, whilst trying your best not to bump yourself] (Perec, 1974).

The only sign of contemporariness is the flickering bluish glow emanating from the street signs at night and reflecting in the dining-cum-sitting-room. The flat has some passing resemblance to the depiction of the 'old'-style mode of living in Richter's *Die Neue Wohnung* (1930). In particular the dining-cum-sitting-room has the sort of furnishing and decoration seen in the drawing room flat shown at the beginning of *Die Neue Wohnung* and where 'the decorative furniture known as *vertiko*, which was popular at the end of the nineteenth century onwards and featured a space on top for all sorts of bric-a-brac, is the focus of ridicule' (Janser et al., 2001, p.45). Similar bric-a-brac features prominently in *Jeanne Dielman*, displayed in a glass cabinet situated in the dining room part, and shot face on, with its central mullion invariably in the middle of the frame. And in a similar scene to *Die Neue Wohnung*, we see *Jeanne Dielman*, on day three, dusting the china dolls and pots in the glass

FIGURE 4.6 Similarities between *Jeanne Dielman* (Chantal Akerman, 1974) and *Die Neue Wohnung* (Hans Richter, 1930)

cabinet (see Figure 4.6). However, the meaning is different: Richter aimed to ridicule, while Akerman wished to redeem everyday gestures, which participate in the poignancy of the slowly unfolding drama.

The space of the flat, built in the studio, is not neutral, it has been designed to fully participate and accompany the drama. Interestingly, in 'The Idea of the Home' Douglas hints at the active role of space over events:

> [...] we should focus on the home as an organization of space over time. This reveals a distinctive characteristic of the idea of home. Each kind of building has a distinctive capacity for memory or anticipation. Memory institutionalized is capable of anticipating future events.
>
> *(Douglas, 1991, p.294)*

In that sense, Akerman may have had the intuition that the flat itself, in all its dreariness, already contained the unfolding drama. But if the flat is painstakingly unmodern, the cinematography is, I would argue, thoroughly 'modern'. Each space is meticulously framed by Babette Mangolte, always from the same camera height. There is great attention to symmetry in the frame. There is a very strict orthogonal method of filming, with no diagonal shots. Across cuts, the camera shifts position by 90 degrees, each time facing a wall straight on. So in the dining-cum-sitting-room, the largest space in the flat, we see all four walls in 90-degree rotation.

For a smaller space such as the kitchen we only have two points of view at right angles from each other, from the door looking in and from the side wall looking towards the sink and the kitchen hob. As a result the views become a cross between an elevation and a sectional cut. This cinematographic 'purism' in all its systematicity, and orthogonality[24] anticipates the cinematography of later film-makers such as Wes Anderson in *The Grand Budapest*

## 80  Everydayness and cinema

**FIGURE 4.7** *Jeanne Dielman* (Chantal Akerman, 1974) – dining room planimetric shots

*Hotel* (2014). In that sense Akerman proposes a novel approach to filming a domestic architectural space that can be construed as 'modern' as it breaks away from former continuity editing models – with no point-of-view shots, no shot and reverse shots.

Intriguingly, the kitchen scenes are studied and portrayed in such a systematic way that they constitute a textbook 'cinematic kitchen use of everydayness', if this existed. However, what does exist and relates to it, are a number of architectural volumes, such as the Neufert, that provide 'architects and designers with a concise source of core information needed to form a framework for the detailed planning of any building project' (Neufert et al., 2000, p.1). And we can arrive at a striking comparison between the *Jeanne Dielman* kitchen scenes and a sample from Neufert's Architects' data prototypical kitchen layouts (Neufert et al., 2000, p.251).

The flat, in all its unfashionable commonness, participates in the description of very ordinary lives, lived by millions. The tedium of the everyday routine is unravelling almost in real time and its 'perfect depiction of the horror of the everyday world – a world predominantly conducted behind closed doors, and rarely projected large on the big screen – is spellbinding' (Chamarette, 2013). A domestic routine is everyone's safety net and we can all identify with that. Akerman asks us to confront the everydayness, which we would normally never question or reflect on. Even the upset in the routine – we can all be partly temporarily disturbed by having performed certain acts in a different order, although clearly not to the point of committing a murder. *Jeanne Dielman* illustrates perfectly Douglas's analysis of the home and the role of the mother:

> The very regularity of home's processes is both inexorable and absurd [...] those committed to the idea of home exert continual vigilance in its behalf [...] The vigilance focuses upon common presence at fixed points in the day, the week, the year, on elaborate coordination of movements [...] The persons who devote vigilance to the maintenance of the home apparently believe that they personally have a lot to lose if it were to collapse.
> 
> *(Douglas, 1991, p.287)*

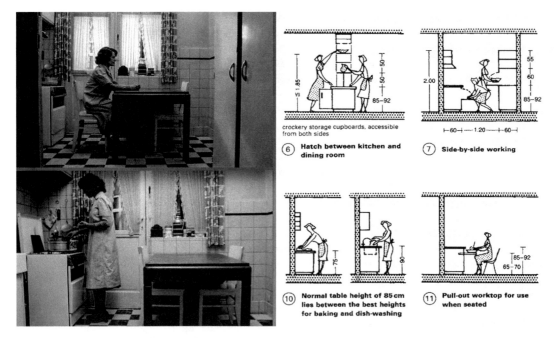

FIGURE 4.8 *Jeanne Dielman* (left) (Chantal Akerman, 1974) versus *Neufert's Architects' Data* (right © Courtesy of Neufert-Stiftung, Germany)

And indeed the disruption in Jeanne's routine leads to her world collapsing.

But more pertinently for architects, *Jeanne Dielman* shows a spatial practice of everydayness, a universal domesticity. In fact the hyperrealism[25] of *Jeanne Dielman* is such that it veers towards surrealism in the sense that the repetition is such that it gradually induces a sense of de-familiarization – a technique advocated by Perec – and akin to Aragon in the *Paysan de Paris* (Aragon, 2004) – and in which the ordinary becomes extraordinary. It is a film which makes us reflect on our own everydayness, it uncovers this reality that we try so hard to ignore, it fully participates in uncovering the Perecquian notion of the *infra-ordinaire*.

## Notes

1 It won 'le prix Jean Vigo' in 1974.
2 His engagement with film dates back to the 1950s at a time when he was a most avid cinemagoer and had started to write articles and film reviews. He much admired Eisenstein's *La Ligne Générale*, which he saw in 1959 (Bellos, 1993, p.216). In fact he was so impressed by the film that he suggested to his group of friends to name their up-and-coming literary review 'La Ligne Générale' after the film.
3 'Il m'importe peu que ces questions soient, ici, fragmentaires, à peine indicatives d'une méthode, tout au plus d'un projet. Il m'importe beaucoup qu'elles semblent triviales et futiles: c'est précisément ce qui les rend tout aussi, sinon plus, essentielles que tant d'autres au travers desquelles nous avons vainement tenté de capter notre vérité' (Perec, 1989, p.13).

**82** Everydayness and cinema

4 An FR3 1975 television series for which Perec was hired to write and read the commentary over amateur films shot with the popular 'Pathé-Baby' camera (de Bary, 2006, p.73).

5 According to Lefebvre, leisure activities have a special status as a critique of everyday life: 'And yet, be he an author or not, the man of our times carries out in his own way, spontaneously, the critique of his everyday life. And this critique of the everyday plays an integral part in the everyday: it is achieved in and by leisure activities' (Lefebvre, 2014, p.51).

6 I am referring here to his literary description as of course, since he is commenting over the images, the relationship between the different 'actors' would have been made clear.

7 This aspect has been discussed at length elsewhere and there is no need for me to revisit it here. Suffice it to remind readers of the influence exercised by Lukács (Wuillème, 2004) and the discussion regarding issues of realism and *Les Lieux* in particular (de Bary, 2005; Montfrans, 1999). Perec, commenting in an interview on *La Tentative de description de quelques lieux parisiens*, further qualifies his position: '...j'ai commencé à suivre cette relation avec l'autobiographie, j'ai écrit des morceaux d'autobiographie qui étaient sans cesse déviés. Ce n'était pas: «J'ai pensé telle et telle chose», mais l'envie d'écrire une histoire de mes vêtements ou de mes chats! ou des récits de rêve. [...] Pour moi, c'est cela le véritable réalisme: s'appuyer sur une description de la réalité débarrassée de toutes présomptions' (de Bary, 2005, p.482). For more information on Perec's early position on realism, and his link to Lukács, his paper at the Warwick conference is essential reading: « Pouvoirs et limites du romancier français contemporain », 5 May 1967, Warwick University (Wuillème, 2004).

8 Perec stated that 'Le roman, les livres sont une forme qui doit nécessairement être informé par le travail cinématographique...dans *La vie mode d'emploi* par exemple je sais qu'il y a un phénomène d'écriture qui est un peu analogue à celui du travelling ; c'est a dire qu'on s'approche et qu'on décrit des objets et de temps en temps on s'approche en gros plan d'un des objets...on le décrit plus abondamment, on rentre dedans...ça c'est quelque chose qui vient, je crois que ça vient d'une sensibilité cinématographique qui est très forte à notre époque' (INA, 8 April 1979).

9 'Je fais le constat-hypothèse que le film est déjà dans l'écriture, au travail d'iconisation et j'en viens au seuil d'une écriture-cinéma. N'est-ce pas que l'écriture-cinéma, par la pluralité des codes dont elle se construit, au-delà du dessin, de la gravure, du tableau, par ses images-mouvements ou ses images-temps est un lieu de transcodage, surcodage, de déconstruction-reconstruction, tel que Perec en montrait l'usage révolutionnaire, par l'imagination de tant de mode d'emplois de combinaisons calculées?' (Peytard, 1997, p.37).

10 An even bigger challenge was, on the one hand, how to handle a text that uses the second person singular '*tu*' [you], a most unusual literary form found only in some passages of Kafka and a handful of other writers and, on the other, what images to shoot without falling into the trap of a simple illustrative or literal adaptation. For example: 'Tu ne revois pas tes amis. Tu n'ouvres pas ta porte. Tu ne descends pas chercher ton courrier. Tu ne rends pas les livres que tu as empruntés à la bibliothèque de l'institut pédagogique. Tu n'écris pas à tes parents' (Perec, 2007, p.11). In addition, a third layer of complexity was introduced, a music track; as recalled by Queysanne 'l'idée du triple récit, c'est-à-dire celle d'un décalage entre le texte et l'image, en y ajoutant un travail sur le son et la musique. L'intervention de Philippe Drogoz et Eugénie Kuffer, qui s'étaient appelés "Ensemble 010", sur la musique de la bande-son fut très précieuse car, en faisant intervenir les bruits de façon musicale et non narrative, ils allaient dans le même sens que nous' (Perec, 2007, p.48).

11 A sestina is a poem with six stanzas of six lines and a final triplet, all stanzas having the same six words at the line ends in six different sequences.

12 *Métro-boulot-dodo*, meaning to commute (by métro), to work, and to sleep – is an expression that became popular in the 1960s and that describes the daily grind of the Parisians.

13 While the voice-over goes 'le temps passe, mais tu ne sais jamais l'heure. Il est dix heures, ou peut-être onze, il est tard, il est tôt, le jour naît, la nuit tombe, les bruits ne cessent jamais tout à fait, le temps ne s'arrête jamais totalement, même s'il n'est plus qu'une minuscule brèche dans le mur du silence, murmure ralenti, oublié du goutte à goutte, presque confondu avec les battements de ton coeur'

(Perec, 2007, p.15), constituting a poignant comment on time, time measured in the daily gestures of the everyday, circadian rhythms computing the time passing.

14 'J'aime rester étendu sur mon lit et regarder le plafond d'un oeil placide. J'y consacrerais volontiers l'essentiel de mon temps (et principalement de mes matinées) si des occupations réputées plus urgentes (…) ne m'en empêchaient si souvent. J'aime les plafonds, j'aime les moulures et les rosaces : elles me tiennent souvent lieu de muse et l'enchevêtrement des fioritures de stuc me renvoie sans peine à ces autres labyrinthes que tissent les fantasmes, les idées et les mots' (Perec, 1974, p.36).

15 Both Perec and Akerman are of Polish Jewish descent, lost parents in Auschwitz, and have explored their Jewish identity through their work.

16 She moved to New York in 1970.

17 My translation from the French: 'I write: I inhabit my sheet of paper, I occupy it, I travel across it. I call upon *blanks, spaces* […] Space starts just like that, with words only, signs drawn across a white page. To describe space; to name it, to trace it […]'.

18 My translation from the French: 'I like my bed. I like to stretch out on my bed and to gaze at the ceiling with a tranquil eye […] I like ceilings, I like mouldings and ceiling roses. They often serve me as a muse'.

19 'In everyday banality, the action-image and even the movement-image tend to disappear in favour of pure optical situations, but these reveal connections of a new type, which are no longer sensory-motor and which bring the emancipated senses into direct relation with time and thought. This is the very special extension of the opsign: to make time and thought perceptible, to make them visible and of sound' (Deleuze, 1989, pp.17–18).

20 'And in *Umberto D*, De Sica constructs the famous sequence quoted as an example by Bazin: the young maid going into the kitchen in the morning, making a series of mechanical, weary gestures, cleaning a bit, driving the ants away from a water fountain, picking up the coffee grinder, stretching out her foot to close the door with her toe. And her eyes meet her pregnant woman's belly, and it is as though all the misery in the world were going to be born. This is how, in an ordinary or everyday situation in the course of a series of gestures, which are insignificant but all the more obedient to simple sensory-motor schemata, what has suddenly been brought about in *pure optical situation* to which the little maid has no response or reaction. The eyes, the belly, that is what an encounter is … of course, encounters can take very different forms, even achieving the exceptional, but they follow the same formula' (Deleuze, 1989, p.1). In other words, the everyday in all its banality makes the maid's situation all the more poignant, a feeling conveyed through a purely visual situation without recourse to the movement-image or action-image in Deleuzian terms. The everyday gestures of the maid are part of her daily routine and participate in establishing an atmosphere of domesticity of which Umberto, sitting in a corner of the kitchen, is part. Even the way she breaks the news to Umberto, in a very matter of fact way, triggers Umberto to blurt out 'Goodness, how can you say it like that', to which she responds 'how do you want me to say it', before carrying on with her domestic tasks. The kitchen scene lasts for around three and a half minutes, and we need this length of time for the everyday to set in and to absorb the drama of the pregnancy announcement. The unrelenting daily routines anticipates her life ahead, there will be no escape as noted by Deleuze.

21 '[…] if everyday banality is so important, it is because, being subject to sensory-motor schemata which are automatic and pre-established, it is all the more liable, on the least disturbance of equilibrium between stimulus and response (as in the scene with the little maid in *Umberto D*), suddenly to free itself from the laws of this schema and reveal itself in a visual and sound nakedness, crudeness and brutality which make it unbearable, giving it the pace of a dream or a nightmare' (Deleuze, 1989, p.3).

22 Deleuze goes on '(thus, in De Sica's *Umberto D*, the sequence where the old man examines himself and thinks he has fever). In addition, the idle periods in Antonioni do not merely show the banalities of daily life. They reap the consequences or the effect of a remarkable event which is reported only through itself without being explained (the break-up of a couple, the sudden disappearance of a woman …)' (Deleuze, 1989, p.7).

**84** Everydayness and cinema

23 I recall an experiment in 2008 with some of my Masters students when I asked them to make a plan of the flat – it proved in fact difficult for them to get their heads around the layout – possibly because it was a studio set – and the results were very mixed, despite having watched the film for over three hours!

24 It may also remind us of some of the principles of modernism, found in Le Corbusier's writings such as 'Le Poème de l'angle droit' (Corbusier, 2012). The camera framing generates the space in the same way as, for Le Corbusier, 'the plan is the generator' [of space] (Le Corbusier and Etchells, 1986, p.180).

25 Akerman's work 'gains its force from its hyperrealist understanding of the lack of distinction between image and reality' (Margulies, 1996, p.10), blurring the line between realism and its representation, in particular through the long scenes shot in real time.

## References

Aragon, L. (2004) *Le Paysan de Paris*. Paris: Gallimard.

Bellos, D. (1993) *Georges Perec: a life in words / David Bellos*. London: Harvill.

Bergstrom, J. (1977) Jeanne Dielman, 23 Quai du Commerce, 1080 Bruxelles. *Camera Obscura*. 1 (2 2), 115–121.

Chamarette, J. (2013) Jeanne Dielman, 23, Quai du Commerce, 1080 Bruxelles. *Zodiac*. (78). [online]. Available from: http://sensesofcinema.com/2013/cteq/jeanne-dielman-23-quai-du-commerce-1080-bruxelles/ (Accessed 10 September 2016).

Corbusier, L. (2012) *Le Corbusier: Poem of the Right Angle (Le Poeme De L'Angle Droit): Le poème de l'angle droit*. Ostfildern: Hatje Cantz.

de Bary, C. (2005) Le réel contraint. *Poétique*. 144 (4), 481.

de Bary, C. (2006) *Le Cinématographe*. Cahiers Georges Perec. Vol. 9. Bordeaux: Le Castor Astral.

Deleuze, G. (1989) *Cinema 2: the time image*. London: Athlone.

Douglas, M. (1991) The Idea of a Home: A Kind of Space. *Social Research*. 58 (1), 287–307.

Ina.fr, I. N. de l'Audiovisuel- (n.d.) *Georges Perec et Alain Corneau à propos du film 'Série noire'* [online]. Available from: www.ina.fr/video/I00005540 (Accessed 21 June 2016).

James, A. S. (2009) *Constraining chance: Georges Perec and the Oulipo*. Avant-garde and modernism studies. Evanston, Ill.: Northwestern University Press.

Janser, A. et al. (2001) *Hans Richter: new living: architecture, film, space*. Baden, Switzerland: Lars Müller.

Le Corbusier & Etchells, F. (1986) *Towards a new architecture*. New York: Dover.

Lefebvre, H. (2014) *Critique of everyday life*. The three-volume text. London: Verso.

Margulies, I. (1996) *Nothing happens: Chantal Akerman's hyperrealist everyday*. Durham: Duke University Press.

Montfrans, M. van (1999) *Georges Perec : la contrainte du réel*. Amsterdam: Rodopi.

Neufert, E. et al. (2000) *Architects' data*. 3rd ed./rev. by Bousmaha Baiche and Nicholas Walliman. Oxford: Blackwell Science Publishers.

Perec, G. (1967) *Un homme qui dort*. Paris: Denoël.

Perec, G. (1974) *Espèces d'espaces*. Espace critique. Paris: Galilée.

Perec, G. (1978) *La vie mode d'emploi*. POL. Paris: Hachette.

Perec, G. (1989) *L'infra-ordinaire*. La librairie du XXe siècle. Paris: Seuil.

Perec, G. (2007) *Un homme qui dort – Texte intégral inédit du film*. La vie est belle éditions.

Perec, G. (2008) *Species of Spaces and Other Pieces (Penguin Classics)*. Penguin Classics.

Peytard, J. (1997) 'De l'écriture-calligramme à l'écriture-cinéma: le cas Perec', in *Le Cabinet d'amateurs – Revue d'études perecquiennes*. Presses universitaires du Mirail-Toulouse.

Wuillème, T. (2004) Perec et Lukàcs : quelle littérature pour de sombres temps ? *Mouvements*. 33–34 (3), 178.

# 5

# RHYTHMANALYSIS

Rhythmanalysis, a new science that is in the process of being constituted, studies these highly complex processes. It may be that it will complement or supplant psychoanalysis. It situates itself at the juxtaposition of the physical, the physiological and the social, at the heart of daily life.

*(Lefebvre, 2014, p.802)*

But in deciding the relative distances of the various objects, he has discovered rhythms, rhythms apparent to the eye and clear in their relations with one another. And these rhythms are at the very root of human activities. They resound in man by an organic inevitability [...]

*(Le Corbusier, 1986, p.72)*

## Defining Rhythmanalysis

The notion of Rhythmanalysis is first mentioned in Volume 2 of Lefebvre's *Critique* but is only formulated as a potential new science in Volume 3. Subsequently Lefebvre indicated in an interview in 1982 (Lefebvre, 2014, p.879) that he was planning to pursue this line of inquiry with a work on rhythms, revolving around the concept of 'rhythmanalysis'. The project was realized only after his death, with the publication by Catherine Regulier of *Elements de rythmanalyse. Introduction à la connaissance des rhythmes* (Lefebvre, 1992), and the book first appeared in English in 2004. It can be construed as the last volume of *Critique*. Lefebvre further defines Rhythmanalysis as follows:

The rhythmanalytical study [...] integrates itself into that of everyday life. It even deepens certain aspects of it. Everyday life is modeled on abstract, quantitative time, the time of watches and clocks [...] everyday life remains shot through and traversed by great cosmic and vital rhythms: day and night, the months and the seasons, and still more precisely biological rhythms. In the everyday, this results in the perpetual interaction of these rhythms with repetitive processes linked to homogeneous time.

*(Lefebvre, 2004, p.73)*

Rhythmanalysis[1] is a way of understanding time and space through the study of the cyclical and the linear, and how they exert a reciprocal action, further defining the cyclical as dictated by the cosmic rhythms, but also including body and biological rhythms, while the linear is the repetitive everyday.[2] The cyclical cosmic rhythms are the 'given', part of nature, while the everyday is different for everybody. In effect it is a way of making the study of everyday life more comprehensive by acknowledging the cosmic rhythms. But it is also the attempt to get us to think about space and time differently, and to think about them together. Lefebvre conceives the analysis of rhythms as a way of complementing his work on *The Production of Space* with *Critique,* but it is also an extension of his work on cities and the urban.

In order to enlighten his readers, Lefebvre proposes a couple of rhythmanalytical case studies, both concerned with the urban environment: *Seen from the Window*[3] and *Attempt at the Rhythmanalysis of Mediterranean Cities.* At the heart of the project is the human body, acting as 'métronome' of the rhythmanalysis – the body being itself constituted of complex internal biological rhythms – and yet Lefebvre is keen to distinguish it from a phenomenological approach.[4] However, Lefebvre warns that

The rhythmanalytical project applied to the urban can seem disparate, because it appeals to, in order to bring together, notions and aspects that analysis too often keeps separate: time and space [...] it can seem abstract, because it appeals to very general concepts.

*(Lefebvre, 2004, p.100)*

But its abstractness, and its appeal to general concepts, is here an attraction and a cue for expanding the rhythmanalytical concept to film analysis – and all the more so as Lefebvre specifically proposed a new approach to the space and time relationship, which is of course at the very heart of cinema. Not unlike Lefebvre leaning out of the window of his Parisian flat to grasp the fleeting city rhythms, we will be gazing into the cinema screen as our window onto the world.

### The case of *Jeanne Dielman*

Let us restart with *Jeanne Dielman*, which was studied together with Perec[5] in the previous section. What could constitute the cyclical and the linear in this case? And how could it help us grasp better the phenomena of everyday life in film? First we must consider the activities that take place over the three days.

The film reveals an astonishing regularity in the everyday pattern on three consecutive weekdays – and we can only speculate that a different pattern would take place at weekends. The vast majority of the activities are part of what Lefebvre would term the linear pattern of everyday life. Set activities are always taking place in the same spaces – they always eat dinner at the same time, sitting on the same chair – and ditto for breakfast. It shows the interrelation of space and time in the understanding of everyday life. The everyday establishes itself, creating hourly demands, and repetitive organization – the underlying rhythms – and

> all rhythms imply the relation of a time to a space, a localised time [...] a temporalised space. Rhythm is always linked to such and such a place, to its place, be that the heart, the fluttering of the eyelids, the movement in a street or the tempo of a waltz. This does not prevent it from being a time, which is to say an aspect of a movement or of a becoming.
>
> *(Lefebvre, 2004, p.89)*

The rhythmanalyst, Lefebvre tells us, has to observe a crowd in a square attentively to discern patterns of rhythms in the apparent disorder. In the case of *Jeanne Dielman*, the task is made easier by the ability to play a scene or scenes over and over again – compared to a live observation in a city piazza – but still we must be attentive so as not to let our senses be dulled by the apparent humdrumness of the scenes. The broad patterns of rhythms are all the same, but each one is slightly different from every other one. The rhythms in Day 2 and especially Day 3 accelerate – through the process of space–time ellipsis.

What we notice is what's different from the baseline. On Day 2, having had to go out again to buy some more potatoes in the afternoon, Jeanne checks the letterbox as if it was the morning – although this time she doesn't open it – but nearly does. On Day 3 she gets up an hour too early and finds the post office closed. This is also the scene when she goes to the café but finds her usual table already occupied. Her daily routine has been disturbed and 'We are only conscious of most of our rhythms when we begin to suffer from some irregularity' (Lefebvre, 2004, p.77). In *Jeanne Dielman* the rhythms of Jeanne's activities belong essentially to what Lefebvre refers to as the 'basic functions – eating, sleeping etc. – in standardized daily life' as opposed to the 'so-called higher functions (reading, writing, judging and appreciating, conceiving, managing, etc.), and their programmed distribution in time' (Lefebvre, 2014, p.759). As such, they are the linear everyday life. However, the cosmic and the cyclical are present in the clearly indicated day and night patterns – taking place over three days[6] – and would be accounted for and measured differently compared to the linear rhythms.

We should also briefly reflect on the sexual acts in *Jeanne Dielman* in relation to rhythmanalysis. If it was sex between partners, it would be a straightforward 'moment' that Lefebvre defines as follows:

> the 'moment' is *the attempt to achieve total realization of a possibility.* [...] it exhausts itself in the act of being lived. [...] the moment is born of the everyday and within the everyday [...] everyday life is the native soil in which the moment germinates and takes root.
>
> *(Lefebvre, 2014, p.651)*

and to be more precise 'among moments, we may include love, play, rest, knowledge, etc.'[7] In that sense, making love is a 'moment' in the everyday life pattern – but at the same time distinct from it. However, the act of prostitution makes it different, as sex becomes a commodity. In the post-1968 era, Lefebvre felt obliged to state that

> the critique of everyday life in no way excluded sexuality, but it did not accept its vulgarization[8] [...] The underlying project, doubtless incompletely formulated but inherent in the approach, involved the permeation of the sexual into everydayness, but not as commodity.
>
> *(Lefebvre, 2014, p.751)*

Essentially for Jeanne Dielman it is part of her 'work' pattern – taking place every afternoon – while for the client it is a 'moment' – hence the need to construe it as an asymmetrical pattern.

### Exhibition

Our next and main rhythmanalysis case study is Joanna Hogg's *Exhibition* (2013). It seems a fitting combination with *Jeanne Dielman* since Hogg co-curated over two years a major retrospective of the work of Akerman, a film-maker she greatly admires.[9] Both films are also very clearly structured around days passing by – three in the case of *Jeanne Dielman* – and ten for *Exhibition*. However, the two homes are very different. One is a flat while the other is a detached house, but most crucially, with *Exhibition* we have the unravelling of everyday life in a modernist house that was built in 1969 in the well-to-do London area around Kensington Gardens. We therefore have to first ask the question as to the influence of modernism on everyday life. Does a modernist space influence our perception of daily life? How different is it from the drab apartment in *Jeanne Dielman*, and does this matter? Lefebvre had much to say about the issue of modernity – including modernism and post-modernism within an architectural context[10] – but suffice to remember here that for him 'The everyday is covered by a surface: that of modernity [...] Modernity and everydayness constitute a deep structure that a critical analysis can work to uncover' (Lefebvre and Levich, 1987, pp.10–11) and to a certain extent this section contributes to revealing those links.

According to Philip Morton Shand, modernism is a 'scenario for human drama'[11] (Shand, 1934, p.9), a comment on modernism that I am only too happy to adopt here, as architecture in general is indeed a vessel for human drama – in real life but also in cinema, as all films take place in spaces that are deliberately accentuated and dramatized. In *Exhibition* the powerful presence of the house induces actions and reactions, it is both a commentary on modernism and on everyday life in a modern house. The house gets a credit at the end of the film by acknowledging the architect, James Melvin, it is clearly the third character in the film,[12] and together with the central characters, D (Viv Albertine) and H (Liam Gillick), they constitute an unusual *ménage à trois*.

The film is the encounter of two worlds: the modernist world and the film world. The Melvin house is the container in which the drama takes place, but the architecture itself, through its modernist vision, already creates its own fiction and vision. Stanford Anderson argues convincingly that to reduce modernism to functionalism is erroneous and that it constructed a fiction out of function. Commenting on Le Corbusier's Villa Savoye, Anderson posits that the spirit of L'Esprit Nouveau is present not only in the spatial ingenuity but also in the celebrated photographs exemplifying a new way of life, 'a vision of certain eternal goods: the loaf of

FIGURE 5.1 The Melvin house © François Penz

bread, the can of milk, the bottle of wine, light and air, access to the earth and the sky, physical health' (Anderson, 1987, p.24). Anderson further suggests that

> To the extent that the Villa Savoye permits that we live according to that vision, it does something more. It 'makes a world' that does not determine, but does allow us to live and think differently than if it did not exist. If this fiction can only exist, precariously, in the Villa Savoye, it may indeed be 'merely' a fiction, as valuable to us as other great stories. If its vision or principles can be generalized, we may have a literal grasp on a world that could not have been ours without the originating fiction.
>
> *(Anderson, 1987, p.29)*

This is a poignant comment in relation to *Exhibition*, as the Melvin house, the third character, is directly inspired by Le Corbusier's vision, as pointed out by John Partridge, who detects in his appraisal 'a spatial attitude that seems to hark back to early Corbusian days of the modern movement' (Partridge, 1971, p.90). It is also as if Partridge had anticipated Hogg's film as he refers to 'the house as a stage set coming alive at night'. In other words, the Melvin house as it stands is already embodying its own fiction.

*Exhibition* therefore presents us with a 'double fiction', that of the Melvin house onto which Hogg was able to project her own vision for a human drama. She creates a carefully constructed 'film world' that, as defined by Yacavone, is 'a complex object-experiences with both symbolic/ cognitive and affective dimensions' (Yacavone, 2009, p.83). And as spectators we are invited to be immersed into this 'world' and to believe in it, but to do so requires careful consideration, as expressed by David Lynch:

> once you start down a road to make a film you enter a certain world. And certain things can happen in that world, and certain things can't…so you begin to know these rules for your world, and you've got to be true to those rules.
>
> *(Yacavone, 2015, p.vi)*

Part of the rules invoked by Lynch are, in the case of *Exhibition,* about carefully constructing and elaborating the rhythms of everyday life – they become the skeleton on which the drama can be fleshed out.

> Film can bring something to our explicit attention within the framed image, and within the represented and fictional reality of a work, that would not normally be selected (i.e. noticed, emphasized, or otherwise accorded special importance) in everyday life experience.
>
> *(Yacavone, 2015, p.93)*

And in this case, what comes through explicitly is the steady pulse of everyday life gently unfolding in the fiction of the Melvin house. Rhythms become an important part in creating *Exhibition*'s world – an atmosphere is gradually established over the first two days in the sense formulated by Cronenberg, 'Each movie generates its own little biosphere and has its own little ecology and its climate, and you're attuned to that more than anything else' (Cronenberg, 2009). In this biosphere that carries its own rules, within which D and H evolve, seemingly nothing much happens at first. But this is precisely the point; Hogg establishes from the outset a crucial characteristic into which we, the spectators ease ourselves, we are entering a world, the world of *Exhibition*.

Day 1 and Day 2 are the equivalent of a prolonged establishing shot of the everyday – they establish the baseline against which all future actions will be gauged. Crucial to our rhythmanalysis study is Hogg's insistence on marking the start and the end of each day (see Figure 5.2). The clear morning-to-night structure constitutes the main cyclical pattern over the ten days. We identified a similar pattern in *Jeanne Dielman*, but the cosmic rhythm of daily life is more insistent and visible in *Exhibition* due to its prolonged exposure over a much longer time span. Contrary to *Jeanne Dielman*, where events occur over three consecutive days, the unravelling of the days in *Exhibition* is not consecutive and the time ellipsis is uncertain, but we can assume, judging by the vegetation, that it spans a summer season.

Within the cyclical patterning of the dawn to dusk structure, the linear everyday rhythm is situated in space and time. Over the course of the film we can observe repetitive actions taking place in rooms at pretty much fixed times – reinforced by similar camera set-ups, recurring shots with similar angles; D at her desk, H in his office, the view of the bed, the skyline in the morning, views of the kitchen, shots of the staircase. This contributes to establishing the film's biosphere; it anchors and creates the baseline and its tempo. And within this beat, the rhythm of everyday life evolves and subtly varies from day to day. During the course of Day 1, D and H have lunch, D is seen working in her study, at night H reads to D in bed. Day 2 starts as a bright day and they go to the park; at night the only sign of food is when D is seen cleaning the kitchen, and the last scene of Day 2 is D in bed recording herself while H is asleep. D and

**FIGURE 5.2** *Exhibition* (Joanna Hogg, 2013): Start and end of Day 2

H being artists essentially working from home, their everyday life is a far cry from the *métro-boulot-dodo* schema that shaped Lefebvre's *Critique* – although as mentioned before, it is starting from everyday life that genuine creations are achieved (Lefebvre, 2014, p.338).

So far nothing much has happened, but on Day 3 the arrival of the estate agents touring the house is the key dramatic disruption of D and H's everyday life rhythm. In *Jeanne Dielman* the disruption was the burning of the potatoes that unsettled her. This initial disruption of the everyday was the trigger for an exceptional disruption of the quotidian, a murder, exemplifying 'the age-old conflict between the everyday and tragedy' (Lefebvre, 2014, p.652). In *Exhibition*, we have a disruption, the sale of the house, that is, going back to the distinction between the ordinary and the everyday, well within the boundaries of the ordinary, although it is clearly not an everyday occurrence.

The cosmic part of the rhythmanalysis is essentially marked by the visibility of the night and day pattern, but D and H's sexual activities are also part of the cyclical, as discussed earlier with *Jeanne Dielman* – suffice it here to remind ourselves that it is part of what Lefebvre calls 'moments' that are 'born of the everyday and within the everyday' (Lefebvre, 2014, p.645). The only extra complexity introduced in *Exhibition* is that D and H have asynchronous sexual patterns. This is brought to our attention on Day 5, with a failed attempt by H to seduce a reluctant D in their bedroom during the daytime, while later that night D is clearly sexually aroused while H sleeps. Only on Day 9 will they make love on the couch downstairs, the night before the house-leaving party. There are also other small disruptions of the everyday, such as H leaving for a day and a night and the argument with the man who parked on their drive, but the key trigger from which all dramatic actions will ensue is the house being sold.

**FIGURE 5.3** *Exhibition* (Joanna Hogg, 2013): the visit of the estate agents

Out of the first five days, we could easily fashion an idealized day (Figures 5.2 and 5.4), a fiction of a modernist vision – a homage to *L'Esprit Nouveau*: it would start with a bright morning [start of Day 2], breakfast would follow [Day 4], H would be working in his study [Day 3], while D settles in hers [Day 1]. A light lunch would be had [Day 1] followed by a promenade in the park [Day 2]. D would settle with a yoga session [Day 1] while H fiddles with the boiler [Day 4]. Friends would come for dinner [Day 3] before D and H retire to bed, reading a book [end of Day 1]. An unadventurous account of everyday life, a fictional reconstruction of a fiction, the repurposing of cinematic metadata, the sort of exercise that Christian Marclay[13] has familiarized us with. It would constitute an idealized tranche of rhythmanalysis, where both the cyclical and the linear patterns are in evidence.

The potential sale of the house creates an interesting dynamic between the couple. H is pretty convinced that this is a good thing, and argues at breakfast on Day 3 that 'we can do something, we can build something, there are possibilities, we should do it while we can [...] we can do what we want'. To which D remains silent, shot head-on, a planimetric camera set up that pins her against the wall, indicating a no-escape situation.

D is living in a state of uncertainty, but as Lefebvre argues, not a bad place to find oneself: 'Uncertainty is not without its charm or interest; it can never last long. It maintains ambiguity, keeping what is possible in a state of possibility' (Lefebvre, 2014, p.40). He concludes that: 'To put it more clearly or more abstractly, ambiguity is a category of everyday life, and perhaps an essential category. It never exhausts its reality; from the ambiguity of consciousness and situations spring forth actions, events, results, without warning'. Ambiguity and uncertainty

**FIGURE 5.4** *Exhibition* (Joanna Hogg, 2013): D 'pinned' against the wall

**94** Everydayness and cinema

being a category of everyday life – not quite on the same level as a disruption – they are more a state of mind. But they are related and, in D's case, it is the disruption caused by the prospect of the sale of the house that causes the uncertainty.

But there is also another form of ambiguity that we should consider, that of spatial ambiguity in *Exhibition*. In 'the production of daily life [...] which includes the production of everyday space and time' (Lefebvre, 2014, p.806), what happens when some of the spaces are hidden? And I am referring here to all the unshown parts of the filmic rendition of the Melvin house, the missing bits, the parts of the house edited out – both inside and outside, of which there are quite a few: part of the top floor is 'missing', the swimming pool is absent (apart from an overhead shot of D floating in a context-less pool), and the house façades are kept to a few glimpses. How do we mentally reconstruct a house from parts standing for a whole, a form of synecdoche puzzle? And might it affect our viewing? Perhaps it does not matter and may after all be only a typical architect's concern, but I would propose that this constitutes a form of 'spatial ambiguity of consciousness' – paraphrasing Lefebvre – another category in the production of everyday space and time, and one that may unwittingly influence our perception of the Melvin house.

Related to this concept is Perec's idea of *un espace sans fonction*, the space without function that he defines as follows:

> I have several times tried to think of an apartment in which there would be a useless room, absolutely and intentionally useless. It wouldn't be a junkroom, it wouldn't be an extra bedroom, or a corridor, or a cubby-hole, or a corner. It would be a functionless space. It would serve for nothing, relate to nothing.[14]
>
> *(Perec, 2008, p.33)*

In filmic terms, *un espace sans fonction* [a space without function] could be interpreted as a space edited out – a space that might have been used but wasn't, for whatever reason, a space that had a real function in real life but which had been discarded and edited out by the film-maker – as are some of the spaces mentioned above in the Melvin house. Since Perec never quite cracked what it could be in practice, this could be one way of answering his quest. *L'espace sans fonction* can be construed as an absent filmic space, an expression of spatial blindness, but one that may well unconsciously weigh on our spatial perception.[15]

'Spaces are produced by narrating them. The everyday evolves in spaces that are conceivable only through narration. Only narration can transmit the quality of the everyday', posits Fischer-Nebmaier (Fischer-Nebmaier, 2015, p.33). In *Exhibition*, spaces are gently unfolded by the film's narration as the body travels from room to room, linking places and stitching them together. As 3D spaces become represented on the 2D screen, they become a form of origami in reverse.[16] *Exhibition* is a film that leaves plenty of space to space. Examples abound

**FIGURE 5.5** *Exhibition* (Joanna Hogg, 2013): empty space

right from the very start of the film: as D exits the frame, the camera lingers on the empty windowsill where she was lying before, cutting to the empty spiral staircase that had been waiting for D's descent and then again left to its own devices for a second or two. Highlighting the permanence of the space versus the insubstantiality of its inhabitation, it points to rhythms, to on/off patterns of occupations.

Places are pregnant with expectations, waiting to be filled, or as Lefebvre puts it: 'Every space is already in place before the appearance in it of actors' (Lefebvre, 1991, p.57). And when we exit, they carry on, spaces have a life of their own. That view which the camera lingers on in the opening shot (Figure 5.5) goes on to exist. Spaces are occupied sporadically in our everyday life, but they also imply an architecture that endures and survives us and will always be there to serve future generations. This is the ultimate cosmic cycle. The on/off rhythms allow Hogg to play at the edges of the continuity-editing tradition, which is respected but somewhat delayed in this mode of operation. Often, a space yet to be filled follows an emptied one. 'Ce qui est beau au cinéma, ce sont les raccords, c'est par les joints que pénètre la poésie' postulated Bresson [The cuts are where the magic of cinema resides, where poetry penetrates between the cracks] (Bresson, 1983). And it is in the crack between two adjacent frames that the invisible body is travelling, in the in-betweenness. Hogg's film starts to make us understand what Godard meant when Belmondo in *Pierrot Le Fou* (1965) says, 'Not to describe people's lives anymore, but just life – life itself. What lies in between people: space, sound, and colour'.[17] We get the sense in *Exhibition* that life in the Melvin house is always present, even when it is not visible.

FIGURE 5.6 *Exhibition* (Joanna Hogg, 2013): the free plan

Till puts forward the concept of 'thick time' that encompasses the past, present and future: 'Everyday time is thus thick time, a temporal space that critically gathers the past and also projects the future' (Till, 2009, p.98). In thick time, the everyday, subject to constant repetitions and cycles, is made of countless repetitive practices that harness everyday time, as a form of temporal space that evokes the past and anticipates the future. And for Till, you will find the idea of thick time or lived time, 'in the streets, [...] in the everyday. You will find the best understanding of lived time in your own, human, experience of it' (Till, 2009, p.96). You can also find 'thick time' in Hogg's film. It is replete with stratigraphic times; it conveys Le Corbusier's ideals that go back to the 1920s, the five points, in particular, are there.

For 'the eyes that can see', this would be the past. It says something about the present, in particular it demonstrates the absorption of a modernist space within an everyday context in the twenty-first century, and it is anticipating a future – the house being potentially sold.[18] It amounts to a 'filmic thick time' that comprises a series of narrative layers that comprise the ghosts of Le Corbusier and James Melvin, as well as Hogg's own memories of the house inhabited by the Melvin family, whom she knew well. All are permeating the film. A 'filmic thick time' encompasses the haunting from the past to not only inform the dialogues of the present, but also to enlighten the future. In that sense the concept of 'filmic thick time' allows for a departure from the museification of the modern movement. The value of *Exhibition* is also to show that modernism is alive and well, as lived and practised in everyday spaces. Bodily practices and the everyday – the everyday and the 'habitus' – demystify modernism and reconcile 'high' and 'low' architecture, Architecture and architecture. Consideration of everyday life in the Melvin house may serve as a critical political construct representing an attempt to suggest an architecture resistant to this commodification/consumption paradigm – as it becomes 'lived architecture'.

## Notes

1 In a footnote Lefebvre acknowledges that he borrowed the term *rythmanalyse* from Gaston Bachelard (Lefebvre, 2014, p.874).

2 He also adds another element, 'la mesure' or the tempo, the beat, although this remained an underdeveloped notion and will not be used here.

3 Lefebvre takes his own window in Paris – on rue Rambuteau in front of the Pompidou Centre – as a site of observation of the rhythms of the city: 'He who walks down the street, over there, is immersed in the multiplicity of noises, murmurs, rhythms [...] By contrast, from the window, the noises distinguish themselves, the flows separate out, rhythms respond to one another [...] In order to grasp the rhythms, a bit of time, a sort of meditation on time, the city, people, is required. Other, less lively, slower rhythms superimpose themselves on this inexorable rhythm, which hardly dies down at night: children leaving for school, some very noisy, even piercing screams of morning recognition [...] Then towards half past nine it's the arrival of the shoppers, followed shortly by the tourists, in accordance, with exceptions (storms or advertising promotions), with a timetable that is almost always the same; the flows and conglomerations succeed one another: they get fatter or thinner but always agglomerate at the corners in order subsequently to clear a path, tangle and disentangle themselves amongst the cars. These last rhythms (schoolchildren, shoppers, tourists) would be more cyclical, of large and simple intervals, at the heart of livelier, alternating rhythms, at brief intervals, cars, regulars, employees, bistro clients. The interaction of diverse, repetitive and different rhythms animates, as one says, the street and the neighbourhood. The linear, which is to say, in short, succession, consists of journeys to and fro: it combines with the cyclical, the movements of long intervals. The cyclical is social organization manifesting itself. The linear is the daily grind, the routine, therefore the perpetual, made up of chance and encounters' (Lefebvre, 2004, pp.28–30).

4 'A philosopher could ask here: "Are you not simply embarking on a description of horizons, phenomenology from your window, from the standpoint of an all-too-conscious ego, a phenomenology stretching up to the ends of the road, as far as the Intelligibles: the Bank, the Forum, the Hotel de Ville, the embankments, Paris, etc.?" Yes, and yet no! This vaguely existential (a slightly heavy technical term) phenomenology (ditto) of which you speak, and of which you accuse these pages, passes over that which quite rightly connects space, time and the energies that unfold here and there – namely rhythms. It would be no more than a more or less well used tool. In other words, a discourse that ordains these horizons as existence, as being. Now the study of rhythms covers an immense area: from the most natural (physiological, biological) to the most sophisticated. The analysis consists in understanding that which comes to it from nature and that which is acquired, conventional, even sophisticated, by trying to isolate particular rhythms. It is a difficult type of analysis, one for which there are possible ethical, which is to say practical, implications. In other words, knowledge of the lived would modify, metamorphose, the lived without knowing it. Here we find, approached in a different way, but the same, the thought of metamorphosis' (Lefebvre, 2004, p.18).

5 It has to be noted that Perec also contributed to rhythmanalysis with typical Oulipian logic by re-imagining the functions of an apartment's rooms in relation to activities based 'no longer on circadian, but on heptadian rhythms. This would give us apartments of seven rooms, known respectively as the Mondayery, Tuesdayery, Wednesdayery, Thursdayery, Fridayery, Saturdayery, and Sundayery' (Perec, 2008, p.32). Perec added that 'A habitat based on a circa-annual rhythm exists among a few of the "happy few" who are sufficiently well endowed with residences to be able to attempt to reconcile their sense of values, their liking for travel, climatic conditions and cultural imperatives. They are to be found, for example, in Mexico in January, in Switzerland in February, in Venice in March, in Marrakesh in

**98** Everydayness and cinema

April, in Paris in May, in Cyprus in June, in Bayreuth in July, in the Dordogne in August, in Scotland in September, in Rome in October, on the Cote d'Azur in November, and in London in December'. Not short of spatial imagination – and humour – he also imagined 'an apartment whose layout was based on the functioning of the senses. We can imagine well enough what a gustatorium might be, or an auditory, but one might wonder what a seeery might look like, or a smellery or a feelery' (Perec, 2008, p.31).

6 'Cyclical repetition is easily understood if one considers days and nights – hours and months – the seasons and years. And tides! The cyclical is generally of cosmic origin; it is not measured in the same way as the linear' (Lefebvre, 2004, p.90).

7 We cannot draw up a complete list of them, because there is nothing to prevent the invention of new moments.

8 'The years following 1968 witnessed a renewal of daily life by sex and sexuality, which proved illusory and rapidly lapsed into vulgarity' (Lefebvre, 2014, p.751).

9 'Over two years, *A Nos Amours* (curators Adam Roberts and Joanna Hogg) have presented the most exhaustive retrospective ever given of the filmmaker and artist Chantal Akerman's film and video works: more than 40 films in 25 screenings. Many of the films were translated and subtitled for English-speaking audiences for the first time anywhere. The director herself attended a number of screenings to answer questions and meet audiences'. See: https://www.ica.org.uk/whats-on/seasons/nos-amours-chantal-akerman-retrospective.

10 Venturi and Scott Brown, by rejecting the modernist ideal in favour of the ordinary and the everyday, have been seen as 'inventing' post-modernism…and in the process raised the issue of whether the everyday is part of modernity or not. Is everyday life modern or post-modern? Or neither? Interestingly, by the early 1980s Lefebvre was well aware of the post-modern movement but sceptical: 'Today, another question is on the agenda: the end of modernity. This was noisily proclaimed as the 1980s approached [...] It was unquestionably in architecture that the announcement caused the greatest stir. Common to technology, art, social practice and everyday life, the architectural is a domain that should not be underestimated or regarded as subsidiary. Developments in architecture always have a symptomatic significance initially, and a causal one subsequently. The Venice Biennale of 1980 was devoted to postmodernity in architecture – a slogan launched in the USA two or three years earlier. In what, according to its promoters, did it consist? In a return to monuments, a neo-monumentalism freed from the grip and imprint of political power, whereas monuments were, historically, expressions, tools and sites of the reigning powers. One ought (argued Ricardo Bofill) to go so far as to invert symbols'. He then concluded that 'the alternative – modernity or postmodernity – was a false' hypothesis and that in the '…meanwhile, daily life goes on' (Lefebvre, 2014, pp.719–720).

11 Philip Morton Shand, an eccentric architecture buff and wine merchant, wrote a series of articles all entitled 'Scenario for human drama' that appeared in *The Architectural Review* in 1934–35. His articles are some of the most readable accounts of the rise of modern architecture at the time – much admired by Reyner Banham – but beyond the title he never explains or refers to the scenario for human drama.

12 There are very few films that credit houses or buildings – Lovell House.

13 See, for example, *The Clock* (2010), which is a 24-hour film with clock scenes from fiction films, corresponding to the real time of the day.

14 'J'ai plusieurs fois essayé de penser à un appartement dans lequel il y aurait une pièce inutile, absolument et délibérément inutile. Ça n'aurait pas été un débarras, ça n'aurait pas été une chambre supplémentaire, ni un couloir, ni un cagibi, ni un recoin. Ç'aurait été un espace sans fonction. Ça n'aurait servi à rien, ça n'aurait renvoyé à rien' (Perec, 1974, pp.66–67).

15 For example the swimming pool in *Exhibition* is an extraordinary space that we only see in 'plan' when D floats in it – as we don't see the edge of it, it stands for the infinite pool as Lewis Carroll's map of the ocean.

16 In the sense that origami starts as a 2D sheet to become a 3D shape – while film represent 3D spaces onto a two-dimensional screen space.

17 'Ne plus décrire la vie des gens, mais seulement la vie, la vie toute seule, ce qu'il y a entre les gens… L'espace, le son et les couleurs' Godard – Belmondo's dialogue in *Pierrot le Fou*.

18 This is in fact what happened: the house was sold – The *Daily Mail* online published photographs of the house on 20 February 2015 with the following headlines: 'Would you spend £8m on this? Brutalist three-bedroom central London is offered for sale for huge sum because it has two car spaces (plus a swimming pool and sauna)'. www.dailymail.co.uk/news/article-2961535/Brutalist-three-bedroom-central-London-home-offered-sale-8MILLION-two-parking-spaces-plus-swimming-pool-sauna.html

## References

Anderson, S. (1987) The fiction of function. *Assemblage*. (2), 19–31.

Bresson, R. (1983) *Le Figaro*. 16 May.

Cronenberg, D. (2009) *David Cronenberg Interview* [online]. Available from: www.contactmusic.com/interview/cronenberg (Accessed 12 September 2016).

Fischer-Nebmaier, W. (2015) 'Space, Narration, and the Everyday', in Wladimir Fischer-Nebmaier et al. (eds) *Narrating the city: histories, space, and the everyday*. Space and place; v. 15. New York: Berghahn Books.

Le Corbusier (1986) *Towards a new architecture*. New York: Dover.

Lefebvre, H. (2014) *Critique of everyday life*. The three-volume text. London: Verso.

Lefebvre, H. (1992) *Eléments de rythmanalyse: introduction à la connaissance des rythmes*. Collection explorations et découvertes en terres humaines. René. Lourau (ed.). Paris: Editions Syllepse.

Lefebvre, H. (2004) *Rhythmanalysis: space, time and everyday life*. Athlone contemporary European thinkers. London: Continuum.

Lefebvre, H. (1991) *The production of space*. Oxford: Basil Blackwell.

Lefebvre, H. & Levich, C. (1987) The everyday and everydayness. *Yale French Studies*. (73), 7–11.

Partridge, J. (1971) 8 Houses through one pair of eyes. *The Architectural Review*. (August), 89–93.

Perec, G. (1974) *Espèces d'espaces*. Espace critique. Paris: Galilée.

Perec, G. (2008) *Species of Spaces and other pieces*. Penguin Classics.

Shand, P. M. (1934) Scenario for a human drama. *The Architectural Review*. LXXVI (75), 9–16.

Till, J. (2009) *Architecture depends*. Cambridge, Mass. London: MIT Press.

Yacavone, D. (2009) Towards a theory of film worlds. *Film-Philosophy*. 12 (2).

Yacavone, D. (2015) *Film worlds: a philosophical aesthetics of cinema*. New York: Columbia University Press.

# 6

# CINEMATIC TYPOLOGIES OF EVERYDAY LIFE AND ARCHITECTURE

The typology is made up of prototypes [...] some films are more central to a given prototype than others. The types can further be combined in many different ways [...]

*(Grodal, 1997, p.6)*

To raise the question of typology in architecture is to raise a question of the nature of the architectural work itself. [...] This in turn requires the establishment of a theory, whose first question must be, what kind of object is a work of architecture? This question ultimately has to return to the concept of type.

*(Moneo, 1978, p.23)*

## The case for cinematic typologies of everyday life and architecture

*Kitchen Stories* (Hamer, 2003) could be read as a metaphor for what I am trying to achieve with this book. Set in the 1950s, it is the story of Swedish efficiency researchers coming to Norway for a study of Norwegian men, with a view to optimizing the use of their kitchens. Folke Nilsson (Tomas Norström) is assigned to study the habits of Isak Bjørvik (Joachim Calmeyer). By the rules of the research institute, Folke has to sit in what looks like a tennis umpire's chair in the corner of Isak's kitchen – and from there observe him. Isak pretty much stops using his kitchen and in turn observes Folke through a hole in the ceiling.

And by studying films closely as we have done in previous chapters, we too are in the umpire's chair observing Isak, D & H, Jeanne Dielman and many others, in their natural everyday environment.[1] By doing so we can turn cinematic scenes into data and compile statistics out of drama for the purpose of analysing the everyday. In other words, I am suggesting the exploitation of the content of film for a purpose it was not intended for, as we can't leave cinema to be mere entertainment, it contains far too precious archival material of all sorts to

Cinematic typologies of everyday life and architecture **101**

**FIGURE 6.1** Observing the observed in *Kitchen Stories* (Bent Hamer, 2003)

leave it at that. It involves considering film with renewed interest and new eyes, we 'have to become pure, look and observe…what? Everyday life and first and foremost the lives of others'[2] (Lefebvre, 1961, p.352).

Each film mentioned and studied so far has served this very purpose of furnishing us with an analysis of everyday life within a spatial and architectural context. According to Laura Mulvey, there are three modes of looking associated with film,[3] but here we are only interested in the first two forms of observations. The camera has recorded and observed scenes, and in turn we have observed the observed. Film provides us with a comprehensive architectural user's manual of lived space. That's part of the value of fiction films: they are instructions for living, we learn by example. They provide an accelerated education in lived and practised situations – they are a form of practice of everyday life. The framing of the human form in its architectural surroundings is central to the anthropomorphic nature of film – and here lies its attraction.

Our observations on the cinematic everyday constitute a form of taxonomy[4] – we have observed the observed – it is an empirical way of proceeding based on closely scrutinizing film material (Bailey, 1994, p.6). But out of this taxonomic approach can we explore the formulation of a cinematic typology of everyday life and architecture? I use the term typology here in a conceptual sense in contrast to the taxonomy mentioned earlier, which is empirical.[5] The history and theory of architecture is not short of attempts at formulating typologies, most famously with the work of Jean-Nicolas-Louis Durand and his *Précis* (Durand, 1823), a typological systematization of architectural knowledge whereby architectural 'types' emerged through a 'process of reducing a complex of formal variants to a common root form' (Madrazo, 1994, p.18). This tradition lasted well into the twentieth century, motivated by the fact that

> classification in architecture, beyond historical description and scientific analysis, lies in the hope that out of an ordering of the variety of buildings of the past will come theoretical principles, which may be applied in designing new buildings, of new forms, to answer new programmes and new circumstances.
>
> *(Steadman, 1979, p.29)*

Indeed, typologies have been construed as a way of supplementing traditional intuitive methods of design, favoured by the modernists, providing tools of analysis and classification, to help designers not to 'fall back on previous examples for the solution of new problems' (Colquhoun, 1969, p.71).

What I am suggesting here is that it might be possible to observe and classify cinematic activities of everyday life with a view to creating a typology of inhabited, lived-in and practised architectural forms. However, such a typology could hardly be organized as Durand's *Précis* – essentially a classification according to building shapes – as everyday life cannot be systematized in relation to building shapes alone, although this may have a bearing, as it is a far more elusive and multi-dimensional notion. We have to invent and explore categories and types according to activities, functions, circadian cycles, rhythms, and many other variables. However, a typology of everyday life has never been proposed by Lefebvre and others, let alone a cinematic one, although Lefebvre does briefly evoke systems of representations of the everyday in the form of a typology based on empirical case studies.[6] The idea of a cinematic typology of everyday life and architecture can therefore only provide an initial framework, a context from within which designers might operate, or find inspiration. It is not a tool for providing ready-made solutions to a given problem. It will not fulfil Steadman's, but might contribute to new programmes and new circumstances.

While there are no such precedent studies to refer to, we can point to works that present some similarities. For example, on the architecture side, *Fundamental Concepts of Architecture: The Vocabulary of Spatial Situations* is a compendium that 'contains no scientific definitions and does not offer the kind of information normally found in reference books; instead, the reader is invited to examine architecture from an experiential perspective' (Janson and Tigges, 2014, p.6). It constitutes a new phenomenological approach to architectural vocabulary and

> although the terms 'roof', 'base' and 'wall' do appear in this volume, the individual concepts do not refer primarily to constructive contexts [...] the concrete architectural

phenomenon is foremost; description concentrates on the situative contents of the respective term in close connection with concrete structural-spatial form.

*(Janson and Tigges, 2014, p.6)*

And although there is no reference to film as such, the idea of interpreting architecture as a series of situations experienced through movement and active participation (Janson and Tigges, 2014, p.285) is germane to my own take in construing the experience of everyday life in buildings through cinema – and is also a useful model for the next section, the architectonic of cinema.

In a previous section on 'the disruption of the everyday', I made the point that we need the establishment of an everyday as a necessary baseline from which dramatic events will emerge. The scene in *Pulp Fiction* where Butch (Bruce Willis) is making toast while Vincent (John Travolta) is reading on the loo could hardly be more mundane, but it's the confluence of the two that is lethal to Vincent, as he gets shot down by Butch as he comes out of the toilet. And key to this scene is the toast jumping off the rack, triggering Butch into a cause-and-effect reflex action. Who could have thought that toasters could be so deadly?

Drama emerged out of the native soil of two everyday routines, and it's the contrasting dull bits that make the scene interesting; in that sense I am here nuancing Hitchcock's quip, 'Drama is life with the dull bits taken out' (Page and Thomas, 2011, p.58). Of course cinema is about drama, but the dull bits are the necessary 'glue' that keeps the film going. The point here is that the formation of cinematic typologies of everyday life and architecture necessarily involve a focus on the baseline, the routine and the mundane, with which we have already established that film is replete, allowing us to potentially construct valuable catalogues of lived and practised spaces.

Architectural typologies are also a form of baseline – they necessarily flatten and are blunt instruments. By analogy, they too keep the dull bits in and take the drama out. We know, for example, that Durand

> consciously modified some of the plans to make them appear more regular and geometric than they actually were [...] It can be asserted that what Durand was intending with the simplification and regularization of the drawings was to use the individual buildings to illustrate some generic principles of architecture. This is the reason he found it necessary to eliminate individual or accidental traits by subjecting the representations of buildings to a process of regularization.
>
> *(Madrazo, 1994, p.13)*

**FIGURE 6.2** Toast shooting scene in *Pulp Fiction* (Quentin Tarantino, 1994)

Durand subjected buildings to a process of adjustment in order for them to fit the typological mould. Similarly, the creation of cinematic typologies of everyday life and architecture implies a degree of simplification.

## A cinematic typology according to rhythmanalysis

There are so few books that contain the words 'cinema and everyday space' in their title, that *Cinema, Gender, and Everyday Space: Comedy, Italian Style* (Fullwood, 2015) is of interest here. It is a form of cataloguing of everyday cinematic spaces, albeit of a very confined type, of comedies produced in Italy from 1958 to 1970, as explained by the author:

> In this book, I look at spaces that I have termed 'everyday' spaces: the beach, the nightclub, the office, the car, and the kitchen. I use the term 'everyday' primarily to signal scale. Rather than the larger, macro spaces of continent, nation, region, or city, I am concerned with the smaller-scale spaces of everyday experiences. The spaces I discuss are those which occur most frequently across the breadth of Comedy, Italian Style.[7]
>
> *(Fullwood, 2015, p.6)*

The book can be interpreted as a form of cinematic typology of everyday life,[8] and for example, the chapter devoted to the 'modern' kitchen, a symbol of the evolution of Italian domestic space in the 1960s, echoes some of my own studies in *Dielman* and *Exhibition*. Fullwood's study also resonates with Moran's book *Queuing for Beginners: The Story of Daily Life from Breakfast to Bedtime* (Moran, 2008) – this time an everyday life account, told from a cultural studies perspective, of a typical British day, from breakfast to bedtime, a form of city symphony partly inspired by Perec's notion of the infra-ordinary.[9] Both books point towards possible ways of organizing typologically the cinematic metadata of the everyday according to spaces and function. Borrowing from Moran's dawn-to-dusk structure, Fullwood's study could, at a push, be re-organized in that way – the beach, the nightclub, the office, the car, and the kitchen – becoming 'kitchen, car, office, beach and finally nightclub'.

This points to a typology that would contain elements of Lefebvre's rhythmanalysis – the passage of time over a day, or a succession of days, which is the cosmic element, while the everyday goes on in a linear fashion day after day – with the two types of repetition, the cyclical and the linear being indissociable (Lefebvre, 1992). So for the sake of our study, some films could be re-organized as a single day – taken from various situations and moments, as I demonstrated with *Exhibition*, re-constituting and creating a 'model' day made out of several days. But of course not all films would lend themselves to this re-purposing, and we can create typical days out of several films. Using, for example, Tarantino's films, we could imagine having breakfast in a Los Angeles diner with Mr Blonde and co. (*Reservoir Dogs,*

1992), watching daytime TV on the couch with Melanie and Louis in a Hermosa Beach condominium (*Jackie Brown*, 1997), next we could have a burger with Jackie Brown in the Del Amo Fashion Center mall, and round off the day by joining Mia and Vincent at Jack Rabbit Slim's restaurant (*Pulp Fiction*, 1994). And this all within the city of Los Angeles.

We could of course mix films and film-makers, and in a globalized world there might be some interest in creating 'study days' across time zones and cultures, for which Jarmusch's *Night on Earth* (1991) has already shown the way. The film comprises five sections, each concerning a taxi journey, taking place in five different cities: Los Angeles, New York, Paris, Rome and Helsinki. The five taxi journeys are slices of everyday life[10] in five countries across the globe that all start with a 90-second montage of the city – from the sunny early morning in Los Angeles to the small hours in snow-covered Helsinki. The five sections as a whole constitute a unique form of rhythmanalysis as they mix both the everyday taxi rides and the cosmic passage of life on Earth, from day to night.

## Cinematic typologies according to housing types

### *The oneiric house*

This clears the ground for further investigations. We started with typologies that involved rhythmanalysis, and there are many other possible forms that we need to explore. Let's restart with the home, so vividly evoked by Bachelard, and where everyday life flourishes. There are many different types of homes, but as pointed out by Lefebvre, the Bachelardian ideal is almost gone: 'the magic place of childhood, the home as womb and shell, with its loft and its cellar full of dreams' and has been replaced by 'dwellings'.[11] And yet Bachelard's ideal home is cinematically revived and studied in the *Spaces of the cinematic home*[12] (Andrews et al., 2016), a book that proposes an investigation, which 'comprises fourteen chapters which chart its structure from cellar to garret, as well as extending beyond the interior to consider the garden and the land as an extension of the house' (Andrews et al., 2016, p.13).

Other studies of the cinematic detached house comprise Rawlinson's thesis,[13] the oneiric house mainly concentrating on Hitchcock (*Psycho, The Birds*) and Tarkovsky (*The Sacrifice, Nostalghia*), thus recreating a fictional house made of many cinematic parts, vividly expressed in Figure 6.3.

For any one of those images in Figure 6.3 we could think of many other films. It is a picture of the fundamental idea of the home rather than of a house type – for a 'home is not the same as a house [...] Does a home need to be anything built at all, any fabric? I think not' (Rykwert, 1991, p.51) – it is a home made of dreams, illusions, nightmares and memories. It is about

FIGURE 6.3 The oneiric house © Martha Rawlinson

what the idea of home may mean to any one of us, irrespective of whether we live in a terraced house, a bungalow or a tower block. Yet the construction of a dream home is not so straightforward, as it involves choices:

If I were the architect of an oneiric house, I should hesitate between a three-story house and one with four. A three-story house, which is the simplest as regards essential height, has a cellar, a ground floor and an attic; while a four-story house puts a floor between the ground floor and the attic. One floor more, and our dreams become blurred. In the oneiric house, topo-analysis only knows how to count to three or four.

*(Bachelard, 1964, p.25)*

Whatever the number of floors, there is certainly a place for such an imaginary home or homes, and there is a need to study how such emotionally charged images act as a revelator of the nature of the dwelling they represent. In terms of typology, it belongs to a cinematic typology of the imagination within which everyday life unravels in a fictional architecture, where each cell is a mind space. It is a house without a façade – not unlike Doisneau's image of *Les Locataires* (1962). It is the cinematic equivalent of Saul Steinberg's drawing that inspired Perec's *Life, a User's Manual* (La Vie mode d'emploi): 'I imagine a Parisian apartment building whose façade has been removed'.[14] Cinema affords the creation of multiple oneiric houses within which everyday life can be infinitely composed and recomposed.

But if we consider housing typologies, the detached house, complete with garden, cellar and attic, represents a relatively small percentage of the housing stock, 17.4 per cent in England (Department for Communities and Local Government, 2010, p.9).[15] Moran argues that

Bachelard's insistence that this dream house is a cultural universal, [...] belongs to a very particular political economy. His house has 'space around it', its ultimate embodiment being the thatched cottage or hermit's hut first encountered as a distant glimmer of light on a dark night [...] This clearly excludes certain sorts of house, such as the urban terrace or the high-rise flat, which have a much more visible relationship with a collectively experienced everyday life.

*(Moran, 2004, p.624)*

### A cinematic typology of terraced and semi-detached houses

This points to a broadening of our cinematic typology of everyday life according to a range of housing types. Moran's study focused on 'three of the most common types of housing in contemporary Britain, which are all based on a serial repetition and collectivity which is often denied: urban terraces, high-rise flats and suburban housing estates'. In particular, he accurately captures the significance of the image of the terraced house:

The monolithic sameness of the terraced house has become part of the iconography of the everyday in contemporary Britain. A good example is the opening titles of the popular

British soap opera, *Coronation Street*, with its panning shots of parallel terraced streets and back alleys, and its final homing in on the eponymous, soot-stained terraced street with a pub and corner shop at either end. Ever since the terraces were built, photographers and filmmakers have exploited the capacity for panoramic immensity in the long, repetitive rows.

*(Moran, 2004, p.609)*

Indeed, British films abound with images of terraced houses, not surprisingly, since they represent nearly 30 per cent of the housing stock,[16] and perhaps most prominently in the so-called 'Kitchen Sink' films where everyday life unfolds in ordinary, often run-down, terraced-house settings. For Battersea alone, the subject of a large research project,[17] *Poor Cow* (Loach, 1967), *This is My Street* (Hayers, 1964), *Up the Junction* (Collinson, 1967), *The Optimists of Nine Elms* (Simmons, 1973), *Brannigan* (Hickox, 1975), *Cosh Boy* (1953), *Melody* (1971), *Mix Me a Person* (1964), *Villain* (1971), and many more, all have prominent scenes in and around Victorian terraced houses. And many of the terraced houses seen in *This is My Street*, *Poor Cow* and *Up the Junction* did not survive the slum clearances of the 1960s. There lies a landscape of memory of post-war British housing developments, a form of *Lieux de mémoire* (sites of memory) after Pierre Nora (Nora, 1989).

**FIGURE 6.4** Terraced houses in *This is My Street* (Sidney Hayers, 1964)

Cinematic typologies of everyday life and architecture **109**

However, if terraced houses have been generously represented on the silver screen, that is not the case for semi-detached houses, which is curious as they represent a sizeable 26 per cent of the English housing stock (Department for Communities and Local Government, 2010, p.9). 'Symbol of middle-class aspiration, conservatism and compromised individualism, the semi-detached house is England's modern domestic type par excellence' (Wilkinson, 2015, p.2) and has come to be symbolic of the English suburbs. Graham Greene wrote about the semi-detached that 'these houses represented something worse than the meanness of poverty, the meanness of the spirit' (Greene, 2001, p.40). George Orwell and others were not much kinder,[18] and this 'bad press' may account for the semi's lack of screen appeal. The 'meanness' is quite evident in *Family Life* (Ken Loach, 1971) where a suburban semi-detached, complete with Crittall windows, is the ideal life setting for the dull and conservative parents of Janice (Sandy Ratcliff), set in their ways and their ordinary lives, and who will be gradually pushing their daughter to the edge of sanity. Mike Leigh's *Bleak Moments* (1971) and *Abigail's Party* (1977), both staged in semi-detached homes, didn't help the cause, and nor did *Billy Liar* (John Schlesinger, 1963) where great care was taken to

> ensure that the interiors supported the feeling of hollow social progress [...] The semi-detached house was designed to suggest the assuredness of Fisher senior (Wilfred Pickles), a self-employed TV engineer, who exemplified the emergent lower middle class. The somewhat garish dwelling [...] was designed as an ugly pre-war 'desirable residence', the living room of which was furnished with ghastly chainstore furniture – uncut mocquette suite, plaster ornaments, half-moon hearth rug, flashy cocktail cabinet, tiled fireplace.
>
> *(Ede, 2010, pp.109–110)*

We should also mention *All The Way Up* (James MacTaggart, 1970) with Warren Mitchell, a comedy based on David Turner's aptly named play *Semi-Detached* (1962), but overall there is a distinct paucity of examples. In other words, the cinematic incarnation of the semi-detached has come to be shorthand for a mild dystopian suburban environment, 'ugly desirable', yet home to nearly a third of the UK population.

But it is not just about the memories of past architecture. Film contains precious social mores and everyday gestures that have been folded away and preserved in the celluloid. For example, *This is My Street* is awash with moments of ordinariness that we can't fail to notice, partly because of the contrast with our own contemporary life: it's Margery's mother repeatedly sweeping the pavement in front of the house, it's the old neighbour reading the papers sitting on a chair in the street; it's the kids freely roaming the streets; it's the back gardens with all the washing lines; it's the tea and meal rituals, the scenes in the pubs and dance halls; it's the house keys on a string that everybody pulls out of the letter box to open the front door – to name just a few. In *Poor Cow*, as Joy moves across various abodes to suit the vagaries of her unpredictable

**FIGURE 6.5** Semi-detached houses in *All the Way Up* (James MacTaggart, 1970)

social condition, we are treated to a whole typology of dwellings, including scenes of everyday life in a Victorian tenement when she finds refuge with her aunt Emma while Dave, her boyfriend, is in prison. We see her living in cramped quarters, a shared water-tap on the landing and a tin bath before the fire, complete with communal courtyard scenes where little Jonny, her son, plays.

This is not about revelling in some kind of kitchen-sink-drama nostalgia[19] but rather a way to nuance, inform, and complement any history of housing with lived and practised 'data' of everyday life, for example as a companion to architecture of the post-war period in Britain (see for example: Bullock, 2002 and Wall, 2013) or cultural or sociological studies pertaining to the same period, like Moran (2004)), or as a commentary alongside Penny Woolcock's documentary of slum clearance, *Out of the Rubble* (BFI, 2016). Carrying on with the terraced house, a cinematic typology of everyday life according to that particular housing type would need to include what Moran calls 'the refurbished terrace', and here a good example would be the London home of Tom (Jim Broadbent) and Gerri (Ruth Sheen) in *Another Year* (Leigh, 2010), a rather substantial specimen complete with conservatory and large garden. Many examples would need to be added, across several decades, to constitute a longitudinal cinematic archaeology[20] of everyday life in British terraced houses. Semi-detached houses,[21] tower blocks and flats can all be included in creating such a typology. This would constitute a new typology, charting the evolution of ordinary life over time, according to housing types.

## Everyday environment versus everyday life

However, a number of other forms of potential cinematic typologies of everyday life and architecture have emerged in the course of this research. They are worth noting, but first we should clarify the issue of everyday environment and everyday life, for there are differences worth highlighting. We have seen in an earlier chapter that when it came to discussing the everyday, the Farrell review of *Architecture and the Built Environment* (2014) was essentially devoted to the improvement of the everyday environment by 'making the ordinary better', while there was scant reference to everyday life. So, is there a confusion between everyday life and everyday environment? Aren't they the same? There is, of course, a considerable overlap between the two, but they are markedly different as one is the container of the other, for 'Architecture is inescapably concrete and it forms the fabric and the setting of everyday life' (Upton, 2002, p.707), while for Lefebvre 'The production of daily life [...] includes the production of everyday space and time'[23] (Lefebvre, 2014, p.806).

We must therefore make a distinction in our analysis – or at least be aware of the differences – in order to work with both notions. There are films that portray both everyday environment and everyday life. Typically the kitchen-sink films mentioned above – everyday life in terraced houses – would squarely fit into this category. Venturing to France, *Amélie* (Jeunet, 2001) similarly presents us with a rather ordinary life: she works as a waitress in a café and lives in an ordinary one-bedroom flat in Montmartre. Most, if not all, of Mike Leigh's films also depict ordinary lives in ordinary settings (Watson, 2004) – a key characteristic of the so-called film realism tradition. The same applies to the cinema of the Dardenne brothers 'in which the material world offers up images and moments of everyday life that both drive and exceed the narrative in whose service they have been photographed' (Mosley, 2012, p.3). The Dardennes' films have even been construed as

> indirectly expressing the ideas of Henri Lefebvre and the Situationists after him: on everyday life and city spaces; on the relations between work and money; and on the loss of a fundamental social bond in the phenomenon of alienated labour.
>
> *(Mosley, 2012, p.19)*

We must also cite Jacques Tati, whose 'film-making innovation was to turn everyday life into an art form' (Bellos, 1999), an approach equally praised by Toubiana:

Tati has filmed something essential in the course of the 20th century: he filmed the countryside, the everyday life in the countryside (*Jour de fête*), then he filmed 'la vie pavillonnaire' (*Mon Oncle*) [...] he especially filmed and captured in an ultra-sensitive manner, not unlike a genial seismographe, the passage from the countryside to the city, this epic migration of man and objects from an ancient world towards the modern world.[24]

(*Makeieff et al., 2009, p.7*)

In other words, over 20 years, from *Jour de Fête* (1947) to *Playtime* (1967), Tati has charted just about the entire spectrum of French everyday life within its fast-evolving quotidian environment.

It would also be hard not to mention Eric Rohmer who, as suggested by Cavell, is one of the great proponents of the everyday: 'Rohmer's great subject is the miraculousness of the everyday' (Cavell, 2005, p.419). Indeed, Rohmer was able 'to magic the wondrous out of the quotidian' [faire surgir le merveilleux à l'intérieur du quotidien] (de Baecque and Herpe, 2016, p.335), both from within everyday life but also through working with the most banal and ordinary everyday environment:

It is clear that it was not only out of thriftiness that Rohmer moved into already existing settings, in the provinces, in the suburbs of Paris, and in Paris itself [...] More than ever, he decided to conceal himself in the fabric of everyday life, as trivial and banal as possible, with its tasteless wallpapers, the gray drabness of mass transit, and the special meals people grant themselves because it's Sunday.[25]

(*de Baecque and Herpe, 2016, p.453*)

Rohmer's cinema is pure everyday life deployed within very ordinary settings. Jean-Luc Godard is in the same league, stating:

All my films have been reports on the state of the nation; they are newsreel documents, treated in a personal manner perhaps, but in terms of contemporary actuality [...] During the course of the film – in its discourse, its discontinuous course, that is – I want to include everything, sport, politics, even groceries.

(*Godard, 1972, p.239*)

And unsurprisingly he has been the object of everyday studies – see for example *Reinventing the everyday in the age of spectacle: Jean-Luc Godard's artistic and political response to modernity in his early works* (Süner, 2015). Following in the French New Wave's footsteps, Jim Jarmusch has also been continuously exploring aspects of everydayness in just about all his films. He does it most systematically in *Paterson* (Jim Jarmusch, 2016), an invitation

Cinematic typologies of everyday life and architecture **113**

**FIGURE 6.6** Paterson with his dog in front of his house in *Paterson* (Jim Jarmusch, 2016)

to partake, through the characters of Paterson (Adam Driver) and his wife, in a celebration of daily patterns over seven days, mixing rhythmanalysis and the poetics of everyday life, a form of mindfulness at play. In a different category, but equally precious for its high content of everydayness, is *The Strange Little Cat* (Ramon Zürcher, 2013), a slow-paced study of everyday life in a Berlin flat over a single day, a clear homage to *Jeanne Dielman*.

But we must leave the masters of everyday life and the everyday environment and explore the champions of the non-everyday life within the everyday environment – and by non-everyday life, I mean here films that contain so much drama that it would be hard to classify them as a cinema of everyday life. The way Hitchcock explains how suspense functions, as already explored in Chapter 3, throws some light on the balance between drama and the everyday – essentially making the point that ordinary situations are the necessary foundations from which to build up the suspense. So for example, *Rear Window* (1953) could, at the start, be interpreted as an everyday life study of a New York Greenwich Village courtyard. It is a cinema of observation, of an intensive observation – a form of cinematic laboratory of everydayness. And this enclosed system could tick on forever, but of course it gradually turns to drama as Jeff (James Stewart) starts to take a keen interest in the couple in front of his windows.

So, to clarify, what I call films of everyday life and everyday environment are movies where there might be some elements of drama, but it remains well within the confines of ordinary life, to come back to this distinction between ordinary and everyday. Hogg's cinema would typically fall within this category, as the sale of the house in *Exhibition* is completely within the ordinary range – but the murders in Hitchcock films are not. Tarantino's films are hardly about everyday lives, but that doesn't stop Jules and Vincent from having very mundane conversations – for example the often-quoted dialogue about 'royal with cheese'[26] which takes place while on their way to a double killing. But the environment in Tarantino's films is very ordinary, more often than not shot on location – for example, South Bay in Los Angeles for *Jackie Brown*. Exceptional circumstances are tamed by incredibly humdrum dialogues[27] and banal settings – like the suburban house at the start of *Kill Bill 1* – we are even treated to an unusual overhead plan shot of the kitchen and dining room while the voice-over informs us of the characters' past relationship.[28]

So the next possible permutation, out of four, are films of everyday life taking place in non-everyday environment. For this purpose I interpret non-everyday environment to be what Foucault calls heterotopia, i.e. other spaces, *Des espaces autres,* and defined thus:

> Because these places are absolutely different from all the sites that they reflect and speak about, I shall call them, by way of contrast to utopias, heterotopias [...] As for the heterotopias as such, how can they be described? What meaning do they have? We might imagine a sort of systematic description [...] of these different spaces, of these other places. As a sort of simultaneously mythic and real contestation of the space in which we live, this description could be called heterotopology.[29]
>
> *(Foucault, 1986)*

**FIGURE 6.7** *Jackie Brown* (Quentin Tarantino, 1997): a non-everyday life in an everyday environment

As part of such 'other spaces', Foucault identifies, amongst others, the museum, the library, prisons, cemeteries, retirement homes – amongst others – all spaces that are in effect outside of our daily routine. However, within each of those institutions, there are people for whom going to work in a hospital or a museum is part of their everyday life, although for the majority of people it would be a rarely visited institution. I do not make a distinction between architecture – with a small 'a' – and Architecture with a capital 'A'. Everyday life unravels in both in just the same way – as Upton concedes: 'The idea of the everyday forces us to acknowledge that Architecture is part of architecture, that designers are a part of the everyday world, not explorers from a more civilized society or detached doers for clients and to cities' (Upton, 2002, p.711). In that sense, Foucault's concept of heterotopia is relevant to the environment part, but much less to everyday life. For example, *Museum Hours* (Jem Cohen, 2012) is an excellent study of everydayness in a museum environment, the life of a museum attendant, Johann (Bobby Sommer), in the Kunsthistorisches Museum in Vienna. The world constructed by Cohen constitutes a remarkable example of everyday life within a heterotopia.[30] And given that the narrative of *Museum Hours* is well within the norms of ordinariness, it fully qualifies under the banner of a movie of everyday life that takes place in a non-everyday environment.

As for films of non-everyday life taking place in non-everyday environments, most prison films and war movies, for example, would qualify. They provide examples of exceptional events taking place in heterotopic spaces. In that sense they are probably less relevant for this study that concentrates on the everyday. However, it is worth mentioning that some films, such

**FIGURE 6.8** *Museum Hours* (Jem Cohen, 2012): everyday life in a non-everyday environment

as *Bringing Out the Dead* (Scorsese, 1999) may prove extremely useful in gaining a fast-track insight into the workings of an accident and emergency (A&E) department. Following the life of an ambulance driver (Nicolas Cage), it gives us access to complex situations, with the hospital architecture being a container of human drama, acting as an amplifier to dense emotional states. Stars glamorize the most banal of settings, Peter von Bagh in *Helsinki, Forever* (2008) tells us, and conversely stars, and actors in general, can make the grandest of settings and the most heterotopic of spaces seem ordinary. In *Museum Hours*, the Kunsthistorisches Museum becomes an ordinary setting by habituation as we, the spectator, repeatedly have access to it from the point of view of Johann, a museum attendant – as opposed to being a very occasional visitor for whom the museum environment is indeed alien and outside our daily routine. Through a process of banalization, heterotopic spaces in film become more approachable, understandable and habitable, it is one of the great values of fiction.

In this chapter we have already identified a number of potential cinematic typologies of everyday life and architecture according to circadian and linear rhythms, spaces of imagination (oneiric house) and dwelling types. Finally, we have also considered the four possible permutations between everyday life and everyday environment, non-everyday life and everyday environment, everyday life and non-everyday environment, and as non-everyday life and non-everyday environment.

Several more typologies come to mind and are briefly listed below, awaiting further exploration. Some films provide us with rare opportunities for a **longitudinal study of everyday life and everyday environment**. Filmed over a period of nearly 12 years, *Boyhood* (Richard Linklater, 2013) charts the everyday life of a not-untypical American family, concentrating on Mason (Ellar Coltrane), his elder sister Samantha (Lorelei Linklater) and his estranged parents, Olivia (Patricia Arquete) and Mason Senior (Ethan Hawke). It is not only a longitudinal study of everyday life representative of a certain American way of life at the start of the twenty-first century, but it also offers a rich sampling of everyday environment, dwelling types, school environments, neighbourhoods etc. Along the same vein, *The Tree of Life* (Malick, USA, 2011), provides a rapid longitudinal study of children growing up in 1950s small-town America.

In a very different register, *Divine Intervention* (Suleiman, 2002) is representative of a particular type of everyday, **the politics of the everyday**. Situated in Nazareth, it is a fine observation of everyday neighbourhood scenes that builds an atmosphere of claustrophobia, a place of no hope, where people are depressed and behave almost mechanically, entering and exiting frames in very matter-of-fact ways. An almost silent film in parts, it is a subtle interpretation of how the Palestinian–Israeli conflict affects people in their daily lives and everyday situations. By contrast *The Girl Chewing Gum* (John Smith, 1976) is a rare example of **the everyday as fiction**. It consists almost entirely of a single continuous shot of Stamford Road in Dalston Junction, East London, where a voice-over appears to direct the passers-by. This approach turns the ordinary everyday spaces and everyday lives into a work of fiction by a simple directorial artifice. Smith anticipates the numerous efforts at considering **the everyday as an art form,** as for example explored by Eric Hattan, at the FRAC (Fonds Régional d'Art Contemporain), Marseille in April 2014. Hattan's *habiter l'inhabituel* exhibition is a play on words on Perec's *interroger l'habituel,* and challenged visitors' sense of observation as shown in Plate 3. This brief additional list of cinematic typologies of everyday life is by no means exhaustive, and no doubt readers will be able to think of many others.

## Notes

1 Aside from *Kitchen Stories*, we could also add the example of *Chevalier* (Tsangari, 2016) as a mode of filmic self-observation – six men aboard a yacht compete to determine who will be the 'best in general' and in the process observe each other closely, studiously making notes of their colleagues' everyday activities, from sleeping to walking – a form of endotic study that Perec would have approved of.
2 My translation from the French: 'se constituer en pur regard [...] regardez avec clairvoyance (quoi? La vie quotidienne, et d'abord celle des autres) [...] Le regard, comme fait pratique et social, comme organe sensoriel important [...] on devient regard pur, et clair, et clairvoyance : voyant et voyeur. D'une extériorité par rapport à ce qui intéresse les gens de la vie quotidienne, on tire force et intérêt' (Lefebvre, 1961, p.352).
3 'There are three different looks associated with cinema: that of the camera as it records the pro-filmic event, that of the audience as it watches the final product, and that of the characters at each other within the screen illusion [...] This complex interaction of looks is specific to film' (Mulvey, 1975, pp.17–18).
4 According to Bailey, 'we will reserve the term taxonomy for a classification of empirical entities. The basic difference, then, is that a typology is conceptual while a taxonomy is empirical' (Bailey, 1994, p.6).
5 This is a loose distinction, a taxonomy being very similar to a typology, and in some cases I will use the two terms interchangeably – but undoubtedly the term typology is much more prevalent in architecture.
6 'Nous découvrons plutôt des systèmes, très relatifs et assez fragiles malgré leur ténacité, de *représentations*, qui assure à la quotidienneté quelque chose de stable. (ces considérations analytiques correspondent à des faits empiriques constatables, à des cas et des situations qui peuvent se classer et donner lieu à une typologie)'. (Lefebvre, 1961, pp.65–66).
7 Fullwood goes on to add: 'It is no coincidence that they were all also iconic spaces of everyday life associated with the economic miracle, which were being heavily mediated in other spheres as well. The fact that the comedies represent the "beach" as a routine part of characters' lives, a holiday space perhaps more readily associated with a break from the everyday, gives a sense of the kind of consumerist lifestyle the genre represents. They are also spaces that take on particular gendered inflections across the genre. While the leisure spaces of beaches and nightclubs and the domestic space of the kitchen are particularly associated with femininity, the spaces of the office and the car are the primary sites that the genre uses in its construction of masculinity' (Fullwood, 2015, p.6).
8 Interestingly, in her book Fullwood does not refer to Lefebvre's theory of everyday life but instead focuses on *Production of Space* (Lefebvre, 1991).
9 'This book is also about the "infra-ordinary" – the unremarkable and unremarked upon aspects of our lives. I should begin by warning you that, if you profess an interest in this overlooked research area (which to a certain extent you have already done by picking up this book), you will probably need to develop a thick skin. Some people may accuse you of trying to rediscover what a certain strain of English pragmatism likes to call "the bleeding obvious". I am often asked, with benevolent

bemusement, why I study such obscure topics as the symbolism of the lunch break, the history of crossing the road or the politics of sitting on sofas' (Moran, 2008, p.3).

10 For a comprehensive analysis of *Night on Earth*, consult Andrew Otway's chapter, as he makes interesting connections between urban wayfinding and that of everyday life, arguing that 'the very act of taking a taxi ride, which can also involve wayfinding, are both practices of everyday life' (Otway, 2012, p.173).

11 The home 'confronted with functional housing, constructed according to technological dictates, inhabited by users in homogeneous, shattered space, it sinks and fades into the past. With this rupture – that is the substitution of functional housing for "dwellings", of buildings for edifices and monuments – what are known as modern town planning and architecture abandoned the historic town' (Lefebvre, 2014).

12 This is one of the very few studies of the spaces of the cinematic home, with an excellent summary introduction to the topic, and although it doesn't focus on the everyday, some of the chapters, for example on the kitchen, the stairs and the dining room, are very relevant to my study.

13 See Martha Rawlinson's third-year dissertation *The House that Image Built: Cinema's Phenomenology of the Home* (2012) that I supervised – deposited in the Faculty of Architecture and History of Art Library, University of Cambridge.

14 'This project has more than one source. One is a drawing by Saul Steinberg that appeared in *The Art of Living* (London, Hamish Hamilton, 1952) and shows a rooming-house (you can tell it's a rooming-house because next to the door there is a notice bearing the words No Vacancy) part of the façade of which has been removed, allowing you to see the interior of some twenty-three rooms (I say 'some' because you can also see through into some of the back rooms). The mere inventory – and it could never be exhaustive – of the items of furniture and the actions represented has something truly vertiginous about it' (Perec, 2008, pp.40–41).

15 It's difficult to tell if the cinematic portrayal of detached houses is over-represented, but in *Spaces of the cinematic home*, the chapters on the basement and the attic refer primarily to US film examples – unsurprising as the proportion of detached dwellings, with basement and attic, is much higher in America than in Europe.

16 The vast majority of the terraced houses were built in Victorian times: 'One in five (21%) dwellings were built before 1919 although three quarters of these older dwellings have been subject to at least some major alterations since they were built and 43% have had extensions or loft conversions added' (Department for Communities and Local Government, 2010, p.13). This situation regarding the age of the housing stock is well captured in *The Dilapidated Dwelling* (Patrick Keiller, 2000).

17 See the AHRC research project entitled Cinematic Geographies of Battersea: www.cam.ac.uk/research/features/cinematic-geographies-of-battersea

18 In *Coming up for air*, George Orwell wrote: 'You know how these streets fester all over the inner-outer suburbs. Always the same long, long rows of little semi-detached houses – the numbers in Ellesmere Road run to 212 and ours is 191 – as much alike as council houses and generally uglier. The stucco front, the creosoted gate, the privet hedge, the green front door, The Laurels, The Myrtles, The Hawthorns, Mon Abri, Mon Repos, Belle Vue. At perhaps one house in fifty some anti-social type who'll probably end in the workhouse has painted his front door blue instead of green' (Orwell, 2001, p.9). Manfred Mann's lyrics in 'Semi Detached Suburban Mr. James' (1966) didn't bring much hope for suburban man either:

> 'Do you think you will be happy, giving up your friends
> For your semi-detached suburban Mr. James [...]
> So you think you will be happy, taking doggie for a walk
> With your semi-detached suburban Mr. James.'

19 That would be the opposite of the 'Downtonising' tendency (from the ITV series *Downton Abbey*, 2010–2015) 'To Downtonise the past is to rid a book or film or TV drama of the things that some in the audience might dislike about the present – black people, uppity proles, uppity Poles, women who

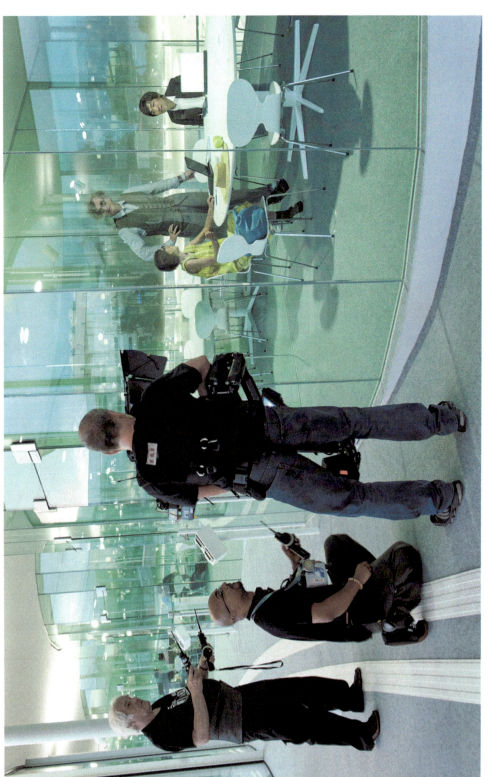

PLATE 1 Wim Wenders talking to Sanaa Architects – a production still from *If Buildings Could Talk* © 2010 Neue Road Movies, photograph by Donata Wenders. The crew while shooting listed from left to right: Stereographer Alain Derobe – 1st Assistant Camera Thierry Pouffary – DoP Jörg Widmer – Architect Ryue Nishizawa – Director Wim Wenders – Architect Kazuyo Sejima.

**PLATE 2** Performing domestic tasks in *Home* (Ursula Meier, 2009)

**PLATE 3** *Habiter l'inhabituel*, exhibition by Eric Hattan (2014). An extra line of columns has been inserted in the exhibition hall and is revealed by the presence of a jacket underneath one of the columns (© François Penz)

**PLATE 4** The Elements of Architecture Venice Biennale 2014: windows (© Fondazione La Biennale di Venezia – Archivio Storico delle Arti Contemporanee. Photo by Francesco Galli)

**PLATE 5** The right to light in *L'Homme d'à coté* (Gastón Duprat and Mariano Cohn, 2009)

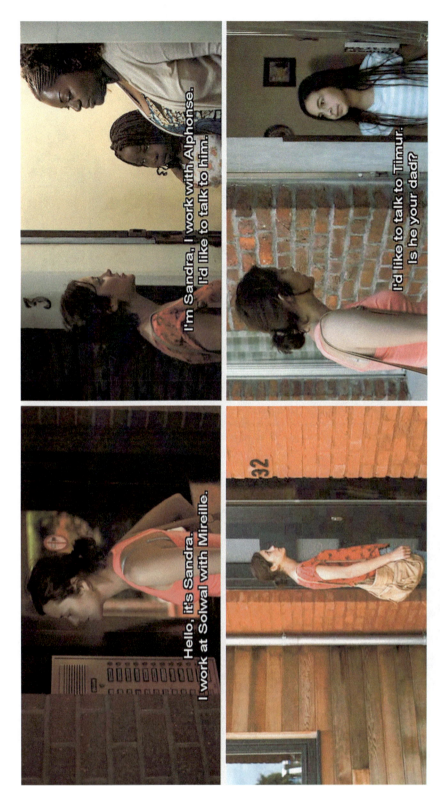

PLATE 6 *Two Days One Night*: the doors of hope and expectations (Dardenne brothers, 2014)

**PLATE 7** Shorthand for architecture in *Drive* (Nicolas Winding Refn, 2011)

**PLATE 7** continued

Cinematic typologies of everyday life and architecture **119**

don't know their place, kids who have exchanged their right to graze their knees outdoors for the right to contract carpal tunnel syndrome indoors. The tendency to reverse backwards into the future is a particularly British phenomenon [...] Britain is obsessed with a past that never existed' (Jeffries, 2016).

20 This builds on a process dubbed 'cinematic urban archaeology' developed for the Battersea AHRC project (Penz et al., 2017) and whereby we excavated the successive cinematic strata accumulated over the urban fabric of Battersea, making visible the emergence of the modern city and its subsequent transformations since the year 1895. It is an approach that charts the changes in the urban fabric, but it is also about human behaviour and social practices and conditions – and it is suggested here that this form of longitudinal study can be extended to the practice of everyday life by housing types over time, across the twentieth century for example.

21 There is no doubt that the remarkable *The Tina Trilogy* by Penny Woolcock would provide a rich terrain for a study of everyday life taking place in the semi-detached housing estates in Leeds.

22 Beyond British examples – it could be envisioned to create such typological studies by country, France, Italy, Germany, USA, Japan etc. come to mind.

23 For Lefebvre, the everyday environment is in part the equivalent of the social space – in the physical sense 'there exist social time or social time scales which are distinct from biological, physiological and physical time scales. There is a social space which is distinct from geometric, biological, geographic and economic space. Everyday space differs from geometric space in that it has four dimensions, which are in a two-by-two opposition: "right/left–high/low"'. Everyday space is therefore lived space. Lefebvre also adds: 'Similarly, everyday time has four dimensions which differ from dimensions as mathematicians and physicists would define them, namely the accomplished, the foreseen, the uncertain and the unforeseeable (or again: the past, the present, the short-term future and the long-term future)' (Lefebvre, 2014, p.525). For Lefebvre, everyday life, the topic that had engaged his attention for so long, became reinterpreted against the background of a changing production of space post-1968, with the publication in 1974 of *La production de l'espace*, published in English in 1991 (Lefebvre, 1991) but he doesn't refer to the everyday environment, and never clearly defines the relationship between the everyday environment and everyday life, except in a few instances: 'The specific spatial competence and performance of every society member can only be evaluated empirically. "Modern" spatial practice might thus be defined – to take an extreme but significant case – by the daily life of a tenant in a government-subsidized high-rise housing project' (Lefebvre, 1991, p.38).

24 My own translation from the French 'Tati a filmé quelque chose d'essentiel au cours du 20eme siècle: il a filmé la campagne, la vie à la campagne (période *Jour de fête*), puis il a filmé la vie pavillonnaire (*Mon Oncle*), [l'aspiration au confort petit-bourgeois de l'après-guerre et la découverte du formica], et il a surtout filmé et capté de manière ultrasensible, tel un sismographe de génie, le passage de la campagne à la ville, cette grande transhumance des hommes et des objets, d'un monde ancien vers un monde moderne' (Makeieff et al., 2009, p.7).

25 'Ce n'est pas seulement par économie que le cinéaste investit des décors déjà existants, en province, en banlieue parisienne ou à Paris [...] Plus que jamais, il a décidé de se cacher dans le tissu du quotidien, aussi trivial et banal que possible. Avec ses papiers peints de mauvais goût, avec la grisaille des transports en commun et les menus plaisirs qu'on s'accorde parce que c'est dimanche'.

26 The French equivalent of a McDonald's 'quarter pounder' burger.

27 As when Mr Wolf (Harvey Keitel), in the process of helping to clean the mess in Jules and Vincent's car from having blown out Marvin's brain, asks in the bedroom, 'are you an oak man, Jimmy?'

28 'This Pasadena homemaker's name is Jeanne Bell. Her husband is Dr. Lawrence Bell. But back when we were acquainted, four years ago, her name was Vernita Green. Her code name was copper head… mine was black mamba'.

29 'Ces lieux, parce qu'ils sont absolument autres que tous les emplacements qu'ils reflètent et dont ils parlent, je les appellerai, par opposition aux utopies, les hétérotopies [...] Quant aux hétérotopies

proprement dites, comment pourrait-on les décrire, quel sens ont-elles ? On pourrait supposer [...] une sorte de description systématique [...] de ces espaces différents, ces autres lieux, une espèce de contestation à la fois mythique et réelle de l'espace où nous vivons; cette description pourrait s'appeler l'hétérotopologie'

30 At the risk of binary thinking, the opposite of heterotopia, i.e. the spaces of our daily life, would result in 'homotopia'.


## References

Andrews, E. et al. (2016) *Spaces of the cinematic home behind the screen door*. Routledge advances in film studies; 34. New York: Routledge.

Bachelard, G. (1964) *The poetics of space*. Boston: Toronto: Beacon Press; Saunders Ltd.

Bailey, K. (1994) *Typologies and Taxonomies*. SAGE Publications, Inc.

Bellos, D. (1999) *Jacques Tati: his life and art*. London: Harvill.

Bullock, N. (2002) *Building the post-war world: modern architecture and reconstruction in Britain*. London: Routledge.

Cavell, S. (2005) *Cities of words: pedagogical letters on a register of the moral life*. Harvard University Press.

Colquhoun, A. (1969) Typology and Design Method. *Perspecta*. 1271–1274.

de Baecque, A. and Herpe, N. (2016) *Éric Rohmer, A Biography*. Berlin, Boston: De Gruyter.

Department for Communities and Local Government (2010) *English housing survey: housing stock report 2008*. London: Department for Communities and Local Government Publications.

Durand, J.-N.-L. (1823) *Précis des leçons d'architecture données à l'Ecole royale polytechnique*. [Nouvelle édition]. Paris: Chez L'Auteur.

Ede, L. N. (2010) *British film design: a history*. Cinema and society series. London: I.B. Tauris.

Foucault, M. (1986) Of Other Spaces. *Diacritics*. 16 (1), 22–27.

Fullwood, N. (2015) *Cinema, gender, and everyday space: comedy, Italian style*. First edition. New York, NY: Palgrave Macmillan.

Godard, J.-L. (1972) *Godard on Godard: critical writings*. Cinema two series. Jean Narboni and Tom Milne (eds). London: Secker and Warburg.

Greene, G. (2001) *A gun for sale: an entertainment*. New edition. London: Vintage Classics.

Grodal, T. (1997) *Moving pictures: a new theory of film genres, feelings and cognition*. Oxford: Clarendon Press.

Janson, A. and Tigges, F. (2014) *Fundamental concepts of architecture: the vocabulary of spatial situations*. Basel/Berlin/Boston: Birkhäuser.

Jeffries, S. (2016) Backwards to the future: how Britain's nostalgia industry is thriving. *The Guardian*. 25 July [online]. Available from: www.theguardian.com/film/2016/jul/25/backwards-to-the-future-how-britains-nostalgia-industry-is-thriving (Accessed 25 July 2016).

Lefebvre, H. (1961) *Critique de la vie quotidienne – Vol. 2 – Fondements d'une sociologie de la quotidienneté*. Le 'Sens de la marche.' Paris: L'Arche.

Lefebvre, H. (1991) *The production of space*. Oxford: Basil Blackwell.

Lefebvre, H. (1992) *Eléments de rythmanalyse: introduction à la connaissance des rythmes*. Collection explorations et découvertes en terres humaines. René Lourau (ed.). Paris: Editions Syllepse.

Lefebvre, H. (2014) *Critique of everyday life*. The three-volume text. London: Verso.

Madrazo, L. (1994) Durand and the Science of Architecture. *Journal of Architectural Education*. 48 (1), 12–24.

Makeieff, M. et al. (2009) *Jacques Tati: deux temps, trois mouvements*. Paris: Naïve: Cinémathèque française.

Moneo, R. (1978) On Typology. *Oppositions*. (13), 23–45.

Moran, J. (2004) Housing, memory and everyday life in contemporary Britain. *Cultural Studies*. 18 (4), 607–627.

Moran, J. (2008) *Queuing for beginners: the story of daily life from breakfast to bedtime*. London: Profile Books.

Mosley, P. (2012) *The cinema of the Dardenne brothers [electronic resource]: Responsible Realism*. Directors' Cuts. New York: Columbia University Press.

Mulvey, L. (1975) Visual Pleasure and Narrative Cinema. *Screen*. 16 (3), 6–18.

Nora, P. (1989) Between Memory and History: Les Lieux de Mémoire. *Representations*. [Online] (26), 7–24.

Orwell, G. (2001) *Coming up for air*. New edition. London: Penguin Classics.

Otway, A. (2012) Night on earth, urban wayfinding and everyday life, in François Penz and Andong Lu (eds.) *Urban cinematics: understanding urban phenomena through the moving image*. Intellect. pp.167–178.

Page, R. and Thomas, B. (2011) Google-Books-ID: ep9f2vR5BYIC. *New narratives: stories and storytelling in the digital age*. University of Nebraska Press.

Penz, F. et al. (2017) 'Cinematic Urban Archaeology: the Battersea case', in François Penz and Richard Koeck (eds) *Cinematic Urban Geographies*. New York: Palgrave Macmillan.

Perec, G. (2008) *Species of Spaces and Other Pieces (Penguin Classics)*. Penguin Classics.

Rykwert, J. (1991) House and home. *Social Research*. 51–62.

Steadman, P. (1979) *The evolution of designs: biological analogy in architecture and the applied arts*. Cambridge urban and architectural studies; 5. Cambridge: Cambridge University Press.

Süner, A. (2015) Reinventing the everyday in the age of spectacle: Jean-Luc Godard's artistic and political response to modernity in his early works. *Studies in French Cinema*. 15 (2), 123–137.

Upton, D. (2002) Architecture in Everyday Life. *New Literary History*. [Online] 33 (4), 707–723.

Wall, C. (2013) *An architecture of parts: architects, building workers and industrialization in Britain 1940–1970*. Routledge research in architecture. Routledge.

Watson, G. (2004) *The cinema of Mike Leigh: a sense of the real*. London: Wallflower Press.

Wilkinson, T. (2015) Typology: the semi-detached house. *Architectural Review*. [online]. Available from: www.architectural-review.com/archive/typology/typology-the-semi-detached-house/8685582. fullarticle (Accessed 31 July 2016).

**PART 3**

# An architectonic of cinema

# 7

# INTRODUCTION TO AN ARCHITECTONIC OF CINEMA

> If anything is described by an architectural plan, it is the nature of human relationships, since the elements whose trace it records – walls, doors, windows and stairs – are employed first to divide and then selectively reunite inhabited space. But what is generally absent in even the most elaborately illustrated building is the way human figures will occupy it.
>
> *(Robin Evans 1997, p.56)*

My interpretation of Neufert meets *Jeanne Dielman* at the end of Chapter 4 recalls early attempts at standardization centred around the kitchen – famously in the example of the Frankfurter Küche [the Frankfurt Kitchen] in the 1920s, where intriguingly the use of films proved a crucial part of the process (Bullock, 1984). In 1927 the city of Frankfurt commissioned three short films by the Frankfurt film-maker and photographer Paul Wolff. The sequences on the use of the minimal multifunctional spaces in one of the films, *Die Frankfurter Küche*, are reminiscent of the motion studies in Frank B. Gilbreth's book *Primer of Scientific Management* (Gilbreth, 1912). The architect Margarete Schütte-Lihotzky was inspired by this book when designing the Frankfurter Küche, and while Gilbreth recommended the use of films to improve the efficiency of industrial production, she used the film to prove the efficiency of the kitchen that had already been improved according to the 'principles of scientific management of the home' (Janser et al., 2001, p.38).

The use of film to improve efficiency in the kitchen was furthered by Frank B. Gilbreth's wife, Lillian Gilbreth,[1] as in '1926 she began to carry out her own sophisticated motion study experiments on household tasks such as making a bed, setting a table, washing dishes, and baking' (Graham, 1999, pp.651–652). By observing the observed, Lillian Gilbreth was a precursor of the use of film, doing with documentaries what I have come to advocate for fiction films, i.e. turning cinematic scenes into data and compiling statistics out of drama. Slightly later, Ernst Neufert's Bauentwurfslehre (Architect's data) played a central role in normalizing the use of architectural standards – but without the use of film. First published in 1936, this book remains a first port of call for most designers who rely on the metric system; it is still listed as a bestseller in architecture books and has been through numerous revised editions (Vossoughian, 2014, p.36). As is evident in the kitchen example with *Jeanne Dielman*, Neufert's breakthrough was not only in the idea of architectural standardization but also in the graphic style of presentation, inspired by the new typography, which would be key to its success.[2] Over the years there have been other architectural standards on offer, such as the *Metric Handbook* (Adler, 1999), and I would argue that the latest offering, in a long line of architectural standardization efforts, is the Rem Koolhaas exhibition and publication of the *Elements of Architecture* (Koolhaas et al., 2014), exhibited at the Venice Biennale in 2014.[3]

The publication of the *Elements of Architecture* comprises 15 volumes that include the floor, the wall, the ceiling, the roof, the door, the window, the façade, the balcony, the corridor, the fireplace, the toilet, the stair, the escalator, the elevator and the ramp. Koolhaas identified them as recurrent and fundamental elements of architecture and that

> the number of these elements remains stubbornly the same. The fact that elements change independently according to different cycles and economies, and for different reasons, turns building into a collage of smoothness and bricolage – a complexity revealed in its full extent only by looking under a microscope at its constituent parts – the elements.[4]
>
> *(Caution and Koolhaas, 2014, p.193)*

What Koolhaas hoped for with this publication and exhibition was to bring about a 'modernisation of the core of architecture and architectural thinking itself'.[5] The attraction of Koolhaas's approach in relation to this book is that it focuses on the humble elements – doors, windows etc. – that make the fabric of architecture. To come back to the discussion on the nature of everyday architecture, it is architecture with a small 'a'. It is not the grand gesture, the iconic or the 'star architect'. It is an examination of what passes unnoticed in our everyday life – floors, walls, toilets, stairs etc.

Following from that, my main hypothesis is that an architectonic of cinema has the capacity to extend our understanding of our everyday environment, and cinema is replete with examples, as most films are architectonic in the sense that they invariably include doors, windows etc. with a few exceptions such as landscape films. Joanna Hogg's *Exhibition* (2013), studied in a previous chapter, is a very good example, as it explicitly visualizes all the key architectonic elements in the Melvin house. But as we will see, some movies are more architectonic than others, it is a matter of degree. An architectonic of cinema is concerned with the key building elements that pertain to architecture, but more modestly, compared to Koolhaas, I will be

FIGURE 7.1 The Elements of Architecture Venice Biennale 2014: doors (© Fondazione La Biennale di Venezia – Archivio Storico delle Arti Contemporanee. Photo by Francesco Galli)

concentrating on three elements rather than 15: windows, doors and stairs – but with remarks on corridors, walls and even corners. My aim is to show how their many functions are 'cinematically practised and revealed'. It will essentially throw new light on building elements that are often taken for granted. Benjamin had already noted that 'Architecture has always represented the prototype of a work of art the reception of which is consummated by a collectivity in a state of distraction' (Benjamin, 1999, p.232), but hinting that cinema had the capacity to reveal overlooked architectural elements

> By close-ups of the things around us, by focusing on hidden details of familiar objects, by exploring commonplace milieus under the ingenious guidance of the camera, the film, on the one hand, extends our comprehension of the necessities which rule our lives.
> *(Benjamin, 1999, p.229)*

In other words, my approach could be perceived as complementing Koolhaas's *Elements of Architecture* (and vice versa). The overlap is also evident in two instances: films are occasionally mentioned in the publications,[6] and at the Biennale in 2014 there was a screen projection made of hundreds of clips selected from different fiction films featuring elements of architecture.[7]

**128** An architectonic of cinema

But it is difficult to discuss an 'architectonic of cinema' without briefly going back to the idea of 'tectonic' in architecture, which can be defined very simply as 'the art of joining'. And an architecture that 'wears its tectonic on its sleeve' makes construction details explicit and does not aim to hide, on the contrary.

Frampton further elaborates:

> The full tectonic potential of any building stems from its capacity to articulate both the poetic and the cognitive aspects of its substance [...]. Thus the tectonic stands in opposition to the current tendency to deprecate detailing in favor of the overall image.
>
> *(Frampton, 1996, p.26)*

This issue has been keenly debated amongst architectural theoreticians of architecture, but at stake is an architecture of image versus a tectonic architecture that reveals. To give an example, Frank Gehry's architecture is generally regarded as tectonically obscure, as the art of joining has disappeared in favour of a sculptural and imagistic approach.[8] In that sense, to rethink architecture focusing on basic elements of architecture, door, windows, stairs etc, as Koolhaas proposed, constitutes a tectonic approach.

A historically significant example that reveals the tectonic nature of architecture is Le Corbusier's Villa Savoye sequence in Pierre Chenal's *Architectures d'Aujourd'hui* (1931). This cinematic sequence is the translation of Le Corbusier's Five Points – pilotis, garden roof, free plan, ribbon window and free façade – elaborated in 1927 (Oechslin and Wang, 1987, p.86). The five points are part of Le Corbusier's fundamental vocabulary of architecture, in itself a form of tectonic, and the Villa Savoye sequence is an illustrated reading of Le Corbusier's text where the camera underlines the five points one by one. At some point the camera pans over the windows of the free façade and then glides vertically over a column on the ground floor to situate us inside the villa.

**FIGURE 7.2** *Architectures d'Aujourd'hui* (Pierre Chenal, 1931): the Villa Savoye's façade

The film stresses one by one the five points; it is the transformation of Le Corbusier's writings, mediated by the screen language – see also Penz, 2013. Another example is Charles and Ray Eames's film *House After Five Years of Living* (1955). The film, composed entirely of photographic stills, explicitly shows the passage between a world of architectural tectonics details – the steel frame, the use of the transparent panels, the windows, the stairs – to an embodied poetic approach that transcends the techniques that the Eameses clearly aimed to elicit. Through the use of light, shadows and reflections, the film reconciles on the screen the art and the science, the poetic and the technique, succeeding in striking a balance between the two.

Beyond those clear historical examples, we should also note that Michael Tawa's writing on film and architecture is germane to my approach, as is evident in the reference to tectonics in his introduction:[9]

> The main purpose of this book is to help inform and enrich the spatial and tectonic dimensions of architectural design. The intent is to discern within cinema those qualities, conditions and techniques that might be useful for design strategies, tactics and practices.
>
> *(Tawa, 2010, p.1)*[10]

**FIGURE 7.3** *House after Five Years of Living* (Charles and Ray Eames, 1955): tectonic elements

## 130 An architectonic of cinema

Overall, Koolhaas's *Elements of Architecture*, as well as Tawa's approach, are all a very useful basis for my way of thinking. It is an approach that has also been occasionally touched upon in film studies, for example in Elsaesser and Hagener's chapters focusing on 'Cinema as window and frame and Cinema as door – screen and threshold' (Elsaesser and Hagener, 2010).[11]

I will be extending the approach of Chenal/Le Corbusier and the Eameses to fiction films. Exploiting the value of fiction films in relation to everyday life in Part 2 proved very fruitful and a similar approach will be used, but for single architectural elements. Instead of regarding the architectural elements as passive nouns – doors, windows, corridors – they will be viewed in the active role of verbs and actions that embodies affects and carries emotions. As rightly remarked by Pallasmaa, 'The act of passing through a door is an authentic architectural experience, not the door itself. Looking through the window is an authentic architectural experience, not the window itself as a visual unit' (Pallasmaa, 2000, p.8). The hypothesis that film can help us to go from a strict architectonic approach to an embodied and poetic architectonic vision will be tested in the next four chapters. To enrich our understanding of the elements of architecture with affect and lived experience is an attempt to address Robin Evans' remark on the absence of the way human figures occupy 'even the most elaborately illustrated buildings'.

## Notes

1 In an interview, Gilbreth described her research process as follows: 'First, a motion picture is made of the individual at work. The picture is taken to a laboratory and studied at leisure. Then a chart is drawn up to show every stage of the process. From this chart it can be seen whether or not some of these processes may not be cut out altogether' (Graham, 1999, pp.651–652).

2 'Individual drawings are numbered sequentially in the interest of guiding the reader's eye, as well as assuring narrative coherence. Words are interspersed with pictorial signs in order to reduce sentence lengths and hence also accelerate the transmission of meaning. Illustrations resemble comic book-style caricatures, probably to make reading less taxing. Plans and elevations are of uniform dimensions (though not necessarily at uniform scale), which facilitates comparative analysis. Column widths are short, which minimizes eye movement. Graphic conventions (for drawings and page layouts both) are kept constant, assuring consistency. Human figures are included in many of the drawings to communicate scale and proportion. The drawings are all monochromatic, thus easing the reading of line weights. The entire text appears in a sans serif font, which, according to the prevailing wisdom of the time, was supposed to improve legibility' (Vossoughian, 2014, p.42).

3 And not surprisingly, Koolhaas refers to Neufert in his opening statement (this text was inscribed on the façade of the central pavilion of the Elements of Architecture at the Giardini in Venice in 2014): 'Architecture is a profession trained to put things together, not to take them apart. But no architect in their right mind would dare to write today an "Elements of Architecture" that intended to describe both what the components of architecture are and how they should be put together [...] Architects now have dropped proportion in favor of dimension. Neufert is our pedantic Vitruvius, with his Bauentwurfslehre, published in Nazi Germany in 1936, now gone global' – and Koolhaas goes on to add: 'That impulse, once so strong and confident in all cultures that gods, deities, rulers, emperors, popes, and princes were addressed for thousands of years in grandiose dedications by the confident

Introduction to an architectonic of cinema **131**

authors of architectural treatises has been weakening gradually over the last few centuries and is now extinct. Le Corbusier's dedication 'à l'autorité' in his La Ville Radieuse (1935) was perhaps the last one, and saddled him with the lifelong accusation of authoritarianism'.

4 Koolhaas adds: 'In this exhibition – and in its catalogue – we examine micro-narratives revealed by focusing on the scale of the fragment: *Elements of Architecture* looks at the fundamentals of our buildings, used by any architect, anywhere, anytime. We do not uncover a single, unified history of architecture, but the multiple histories, origins, contaminations, similarities and differences of these very ancient elements and how they evolved into their current versions through technological advances, regulatory requirements, and new digital regimes'.

5 'My obsession with *Elements* is to assert that elements such as the elevator or the escalator have never really been incorporated into either the ideology or the theory of architecture', he says. 'Now, with new digital intersections, digital hybrids, digital combinations, the risk is that architecture is simply incapable of thinking of its entire repertoire'. See online www.dezeen.com/2014/06/06/rem-koolhaas-elements-of-architecture-exhibition-movie-venice-biennale-2014/

6 For example in the volume on Doors, the idea of the 'farcical door' is illustrated by an image from *A Night at the Opera* (Marx Brothers, 1935) – showing how 'the door is the ultimate comic element of architecture, building up and foiling expectations, and facilitating frantic passages on and off stage' (Koolhaas et al., 2014, p.520).

7 This compilation, which was only available during the Biennale, was the work of Davide Rapp, who writes '*Elements* [the title of the compilation] is a film about space, a film as a set of spaces. It incorporates scenes from different movie genres, merging the clips one into the other in a continuous flow of images, sounds, and actions. A movie montage is an editing technique in which shots are composed in a fast-paced fashion that compresses time and conveys a lot of information in a relatively short period. The simple act of juxtaposing separate shots of corridors, stairs, or facades evokes connections that cannot be found in a single shot. The various spaces of fiction exist simultaneously in a continuous dynamic. *Elements* is a film without any plot, story, or characters. Architecture in movies appears frequently as a background of the action and it can be represented in many ways: top views, one-point perspectives, frontal planes, long takes, and close-ups. The framing highlights the proportions and the geometries of the elements, while the presence, or the absence of sounds, noises, and scores unveils their prerogatives and materialities. Elements asks the viewer to focus on the fifteen elements through the fast transitions between the clips, revealing contrasts and affinities, lines and shapes, recurring patterns and motives, movements and rhythms. In this framework each scene, cut out from the original movies, gets a new meaning and unveils the close and ambivalent connections between cinema and architecture' (Caution and Koolhaas, 2014, p.201).

8 'This brings up the difficult question of the limits of sculpture versus architecture: where does structural expressivity lie between sculpture on the one hand and architecture on the other? How can one demonstrate this difference by example, or, more precisely, how can one demonstrate the limits of the sculptural versus the tectonic within architecture? For me this is a point at which one may discriminate between Frank Gehry and Enric Miralles, say. In almost all of Miralles's work the tectonic element is closely integrated with the sculptural. In Gehry's case, apart from his very early work, there's no interest whatsoever in the tectonic. He's only interested in plasticity, and whatever makes it stand up will do – he couldn't care less. That's very evident in Bilbao' (Frampton et al., 2003, p.51).

9 Tawa's book specifically refers to tectonics in its title: *Agencies of the Frame: Tectonic Strategies in Cinema and Architecture* (Tawa, 2010).

10 Tawa adds: 'I come to a film, or more often to a scene or sequence in that film, with a view to developing its usefulness for the architectural design process. Even then, the scope is limited to tectonic and formal concerns of spatial organisation, volumetric composition, tempo and duration, materiality, spatial experience and the phenomenological condition of architecture – in short, to a concern for the way the film has been "made" and constructed' (Tawa, 2010, p.20).

11 A window in cinema 'keeps the spectator visually at arm's length while nonetheless drawing him/her in emotionally, by deploying window and frame as mutually regulating conceptual metaphors for looking at a separated reality that nonetheless exists for our benefit' adding that doors 'by contrast, deal with the different ways the spectator enters into this world, physically as well as metaphorically' (Elsaesser and Hagener, 2010, p.37).

## References

Adler, D. (1999) *Metric handbook: planning and design data*. Second edition. Oxford; Boston: Architectural Press.

Benjamin, W. (1999) 'The work of art in the age of mechanical reproduction', in *Illuminations*. Pimlico. pp. 211–244.

Bullock, N. (1984) First the kitchen – then the façade. *AA Files*. (6), 58–67.

Caution, L. and Koolhaas, R. (2014) *Fundamentals: 14th international architecture exhibition – La Biennale Di Venezia*. First edition. Venice: Marsilio Editori Spa.

Elsaesser, T. and Hagener, M. (2010) *Film theory: an introduction through the senses*. London: Routledge.

Frampton, K. (1996) *Studies in tectonic culture: the poetics of construction in nineteenth- and twentieth-century architecture*. John Cava (ed.). Cambridge, Mass: MIT Press.

Frampton, K. et al. (2003) A Conversation with Kenneth Frampton. *October*. 10635–58.

Gilbreth, F. B. (1912) *Primer of scientific management*. London: Constable.

Graham, L. D. (1999) Domesticating efficiency: Lillian Gilbreth's scientific management of homemakers, 1924–1930. *Signs: Journal of Women in Culture and Society*. 24 (3), 633–675.

Janser, A. et al. (2001) *Hans Richter: new living: architecture, film, space*. Baden, Switzerland: Lars Müller.

Koolhaas, R. et al. (2014) *Elements of architecture*. Venice: Marsilio Editori Spa.

Oechslin, W. and Wang, W. (1987) Les Cinq Points d'une Architecture Nouvelle. *Assemblage*. (4), 82.

Pallasmaa, J. (2000) From Frame to Framing. *Oz*. 22 (1) [online]. Available from: http://newprairiepress.org/oz/vol22/iss1/2 (Accessed 26 September 2016).

Penz, F. (2013) 'L'ombre de l'Acropole – La Villa Savoye construite par le cinéma', in Roberta Amirante et al. (eds) *L'invention d'un architecte. Le voyage en Orient de Le Corbusier*. Paris: La Fondation Le Corbusier. pp.407–413.

Tawa, M. (2010) *Agencies of the frame: tectonic strategies in cinema and architecture*. Newcastle: Cambridge Scholars.

Vossoughian, N. (2014) Standardization Reconsidered: Normierung in and after Ernst Neufert's Bauentwurfslehre (1936). *Grey Room*. 54 (Winter 2014), 34–55.

# 8

# WINDOWS

The window offers views that are more than spectacles; mentally prolonged spaces. In such a way that the implication in the spectacle entails the explication of this spectacle. Familiarity preserves it; it disappears and is reborn, with the everydayness of both the inside and the outside world.

*(Lefebvre, 2004, p.33)*

Je crois que notre fonction c'est d'ouvrir des fenêtres [...] dans ce travail d'ouverture de fenêtre qu'est le notre, il faut choisir les paysages que nous montrerons [...] Ce serait merveilleux de pouvoir ouvrir des fenêtres sur des paysages absolument inattendus, inconnus, invraisemblables, mais ça, c'est très difficile. L'homme est un animal d'habitudes [...] Alors il faut des fenêtres et ces fenêtres vont dévoiler, vont faire dire aux gens: tiens mais c'est vrai.

*Jean Renoir*[1] *(Reboul, 1995, pp.129–130)*

## Introduction

Let us start with Perec's *Un homme qui dort*, which was studied in a previous chapter for its relentless portrayal of the everyday in the life of a young Parisian student. The main space in the film is the young man's bedroom, an attic *chambre de bonne*, a very cramped space. Most relevant here is the dormer window leading onto the roof, and how it is handled. Given the barely five-square-metre bedroom, the window is a godsend, a breathing and recreational space, without which life in such a constrained space would be even more miserable.[2]

Over many varied sequences the film shows the modes of practising the window and the activities that it affords. The dormer window isn't just a means for ventilation and lighting, but

**FIGURE 8.1** *Un homme qui dort* (Bernard Queysanne, 1974): practising the dormer window

provides a perch on the inside for reading and eating a sandwich, a seating space on the outside for smoking and reflecting, a place for looking out during the day or looking in at night. The full gamut of using a dormer window is explored (see Figure 8.1). But the overall impression is one of freedom, that it affords a space outside, a bowl of oxygen, an extension of a room, a place for the mind to expand, a liberty associated with exploring an outdoor roof space, probably something that he does without permission, making it even more delicious, a world yet untouched by health and safety regulations. However small an aperture, it expands one's horizon precisely because it is possible to step outside. And inside it is the focus of one's gaze. 'A roof', Bachelard reminds us, 'tells its *raison d'être* right away: it gives mankind shelter from the rain and sun he fears […] We "understand" the slant of a roof. Even a dreamer dreams rationally; for him, a pointed roof averts rain clouds' (Bachelard, 1964, p.18). And although Perec's young man's dream state turns to nightmare, his everyday practice of the attic dormer window elicits the potency of Bachelard's oneiric attraction to the attic space.

As a spectator we can't fail to notice the window in *Un homme qui dort*. However, we may or we may not notice the basin or the broken mirror. Similarly in my analysis of *Jeanne Dielman*, the flat's windows are regularly seen and used. But they do not play any particular role in the slowly unfolding drama, they are thoroughly unmemorable and yet essential to the practice of everydayness. We know from Bazin's study of the décor of Jean Gabin's room in Carné's *Le Jour se Lève* (1939) that viewers have a very selective memory. Bazin carried out a series of surveys following screenings of *Le Jour se Lève*, and found that people forgot around 30 per cent of the furniture from Gabin's bedroom, including some large pieces of furniture such as a chest of drawers with a marble top, the sink and the bedside table (Bazin, 1998, p.87). Bazin offered a simple explanation: spectators hadn't noticed those items because there was no reason to, they had no dramatic function in the film. He added that 'Le cinéma doit traiter le décor en acteur du drame' [Cinema must treat the décor as an actor in the drama] if it is to be noticed. But when it comes to the world of architecture, Bernard Tschumi suggested, over an image of a woman pushing a man out of a window, that 'To really appreciate architecture, you may even need to commit a murder' (Tschumi, 2012, p.46).[3] No doubt Tschumi's rather extreme suggestion would go some way to getting that window noticed.

Cinema, on the other hand, regularly uses windows to dramatic effect – this is what I would call the **cinematographic window,** the window that lets itself be penetrated by the camera, which unwittingly lets the camera in. We see it at the beginning of *Rear Window* (Hitchcock, 1953), where the roving camera sweeps across the courtyard before penetrating James Stewart's flat through the window while he is asleep in his wheelchair. Hitchcock does it again at the start of *Psycho* (1960) as the camera zooms onto the hotel window and penetrates the intimacy of the couple. It is at its most spectacular again at the start of de Scola's *A Giornata Particulare* (1977), where the camera climbs daringly along the inner façade of the Palazzo Federici in Rome before sliding through the open window into Antonietta's (Sophia Loren) kitchen, following her throughout the flat. In *Le Plaisir* (Ophüls, 1952), less spectacular but equally compelling is the camera movement outside the house of the local brothel, peering delicately at each window at night, leering at the women entertaining the locals, and as noted by Ropars 'Ophüls déjà, dans *Le Plaisir,* redessinait ainsi l'espace avec le temps [...] avec les mouvements libres de sa caméra, calqués sur les hésitations de son propre regard' [In *Le Plaisir*, Ophüls was already redesigning space with time [...] its free camera movements closely translating his own hesitations] (Ropars-Wuilleumier, 1970, p.230).

The daring of such cinematographic moves reached its pinnacle with *I am Cuba* (Mikhail Kalatozov, 1964), in the scene where the camera gets inside a cigar factory, entering from one

**FIGURE 8.2** The voyeuristic window in *Le Plaisir* (Max Ophüls, 1952)

window and exiting through another at the other side of the building, in one uninterrupted sequence shot. An adjunct to the cinematographic window is the **mythical cinematographic window,** such as the penultimate scene in Antonioni's *The Passenger* (1975) or the pan in Renoir's *Le Crime de Monsieur Lange* (1936). All have required extraordinary technical feats and have become celebrated cinematic window scenes. In the category of **spectacular cinematographic window,** who could forget the scene in *The Hudsucker Proxy* (Coen Brothers, 1994) where Waring Hudsucker commits suicide by jumping through the window of a skyscraper? Not that one would remember that particular window and what it looked like in detail, but the idea that one could 'fly' through a window makes us think of a glazed opening in a different way.

Much more subtle is Béla Tarr's exploration of the **liminal condition** between the two states on either side of a window: the indoor and the outdoor, as remarked by Rancière,

> *Le personnage typique de Béla Tarr, c'est désormais l'homme à la fenêtre, l'homme qui regarde les choses venir vers lui. Et les regarder, c'est se laisser envahir par elles, se soustraire au trajet normal qui convertit les sollicitations du dehors en impulsions pour agir.* [Béla Tarr's typical character is nowadays the man at the window, the man who observes things coming towards him. And to watch them is to allow them to invade him, to refrain from the normal course of action which transforms outside forces into an impetus to act.]
>
> *(Rancière, 2011, p.37)*

Béla Tarr is particularly fond of showing the motivated gaze of an observer looking out or in – as if feeling the distance between two situations. In an interview, Béla Tarr confessed to

> liking to see the inside and the outside within the same shot – we feel better the space and the distance between the two scenes – you are inside you feel as if you are outside – you are outside you feel you are inside.[4]

The two spaces conjoin and fuse, as in the opening shot of *Damnation* (1988).[5]

Tarr explores here the passage between two states, and as the camera reverses it is as if the bleak outdoors was penetrating inside through the window and into the body of the man gazing out. We have gone from an unmotivated camera movement to a subjective point of view. The mesmerizing bleakness of this scene anticipates the rest of the film. The slow backward camera movement that lasts four minutes is the opposite of the seven minutes of the penultimate shot in Antonioni's *The Passenger*, where the camera slowly leaves Locke's room in a forward movement and escapes cowardly through the window, leaving him to his fate.[6] In *Damnation* we are joining Karrer's fate (Miklós Székely B.). Fittingly, both camera moves explore the threshold condition in reverse directions corresponding to a beginning and an

**FIGURE 8.3** The man at the window in *Damnation* (Béla Tarr, 1988)

ending – in *Damnation* it is the opening scene and the world is 'penetrating' us, while in *The Passenger* we are leaving the scene. Bachelard commented:

> Outside and inside are both intimate – they are always ready to be reversed, to exchange their hostility. If there exists a border-line surface between such an inside and outside, this surface is painful on both sides […] In this drama of intimate geometry, where should one live?
>
> *(Bachelard, 1964, pp.217–218)*

## Renoir and windows

Many film-makers conceive windows as a form of escape, in particular Jean Renoir who, as Douchet noted, has a poetic vision: 'la fenêtre a pour mission naturelle d'ouvrir sur le paysage, vers le dehors, et finalement d'ouvrir au monde […] La fenêtre invite à un mouvement mental' (Douchet, 1997, p.111). Douchet proceeds to quote what he justly regards as the most famous example in Renoir's cinema, *Une Partie de Campagne* (1936) 'au moment où les deux jeunes canotiers ouvrent les volets de l'auberge dans laquelle ils déjeunent et que soudain apparaissent, comme dans un tableau impressionniste, les femmes à la balançoire'

(Douchet, 1997, p.112). It is an extraordinarily evocative shot. The sudden appearance of the women on the swing is a projection of desires and dreams; those two men from the countryside haven't just opened a window, but expanded their horizon onto a new life, a new dream, a means to escape their everyday reality – in this case the prospect of seducing women from a different world, from a different class, a window of possibilities, a window of opportunity.

The notion of a 'window onto the world' brings us naturally to consider Alberti's often quoted and misquoted aphorism on the subject. Friedberg reminds us that 'Alberti's 1435 metaphor for the painting (pictura) as an "open window" (*aperta finestra*) remains a pivotal trope in debates about the origins, practices, and traditions of perspective, debates that continue to pose key questions about visual representation itself' (Friedberg, 2006, p.26). But Friedberg makes a crucial distinction between Alberti's window as a painting device versus windows in a building:

> Alberti's metaphoric 'window' was a framing device for the geometrics of his perspective formula. While it implied a fixed position for the viewer of single-point perspective, it did not assume or imply that the 'subject to be painted' should be the exact view of what one would see out of an architectural window onto the natural world, as in a 'window on the world'.
>
> (Friedberg, 2006, p.32)

This is a poignant consideration for Renoir's window scene mentioned above, in *La Partie de Campagne*. The shutters opening in *La Partie de Campagne* are also a tribute from the world of cinema to impressionism – a tribute from Jean Renoir to his father Auguste Renoir. It marks the passage from one mode of representation to another. In that sense this scene is both cinema and painting together, architecture and the representation of the world outside the window. It

**FIGURE 8.4** The window of opportunities: *La Partie de Campagne* (Jean Renoir, 1936)

can be construed as a rare example of the reconciliation, in one single scene, of Alberti's window as *pictura* with his architectural concept of the 'open window' *aperta finestra*.

Douchet further elaborates on the issue of depth of field:

> Cette dialectique du près et du loin, si fine qu'on ne la remarque qu'en y prêtant la plus grande attention tant ses effets sont gommés, caractérise à mes yeux le secret de la mise en scène de Renoir. Elle a, en revanche, une conséquence dont la visibilité n'échappe à personne : *la profondeur de champ* [...] et pourtant elle découle du mouvement d'ouverture de la fenêtre [...] Dès lors, la profondeur de champ exige son élargissement. Le monde est un. Affirmation que Renoir ne cesse de répéter dans ses écrits, ses interviews, et surtout qu'il ne cesse de filmer. La vision fermée par le cadre de la fenêtre limite le champ mais elle n'arrête pas le monde.
>
> *(Douchet, 1997, p.113)*

The world is one, affirms Renoir, meaning that from the position of the spectator on the inside of the window, we are reconciled with the outdoor contained within the frame, thanks to the use of a great depth of field, one of Renoir's trademarks. Douchet ventures further and suggests that for Renoir the world extends way beyond the window frame and that 'le off renoirien couvre toute l'étendue du monde. Il submerge la caméra' [for Renoir, the off-screen extends to the rest of the world – it transcends the camera]. Renoir uses the off-screen camera or *hors champs* to good effect through sound in particular, but he had a remarkable intuition in suggesting that our vision and imagination go way beyond the visible, the edge of the window frame.

Decades later this same type of preoccupation has been the subject of research amongst cognitive psychologists.[7] Science eventually vindicated Renoir's intuition that 'the world is one' by demonstrating that when we look at a window, in real life or in films, we know that there is a world beyond the frame, a world that we can imagine quite accurately.

## The architect's viewpoint: Perret and Le Corbusier

But we must return once more to Douchet's analysis of the role of the window in Renoir's films:

> *Etant donné la force symbolique que Renoir attribue à cet élément usuel, il convient d'examiner d'un peu plus près cette figure. Repensons donc son dessin. Il s'agit généralement, dans l'architecture française, d'un rectangle plus haut que large, constitué de deux parallèles reliées entre elles à chacune de leurs extrémités par deux verticales plus longues. Cette proportion n'est pourtant pas fixe. En changeant de proportion, la fenêtre change de nom mais pas de fonction. Au départ elle est une découpe, un espace d'ouverture dans un mur fermé qui draine la vision et la dirige vers l'espace du monde. Elle est comme*

*un canal par lequel s'échappe l'imaginaire, l'appétit de vivre, le besoin d'exister. Renoir rêve la fenêtre à l'inverse de la définition qu'en donne le dictionnaire. Ce dernier dit : 'Ouverture faite dans un mur, une paroi, pour laisser pénétrer l'air et la lumière.' Renoir rectifie et filme une 'ouverture … pour répondre à l'appel d'air, pour s'évader vers la lumière'.* [Given the symbolic force that Renoir attributes to this ordinary element, it is necessary to examine it a little more closely. Let us therefore reconsider his reasoning. In French architecture, it is generally a rectangle taller than wide, consisting of two parallel lines connected at each end by two longer verticals. However, this proportion is not fixed. By changing the proportion, the window may be named differently, but its function remains the same. Initially it is a cutout, an opening in a blank wall that channels the vision and directs it towards the outside world. It is like a channel through which escapes the imaginary, the appetite for life, the need to exist. The way Renoir dreams of windows, turns on its head the dictionary's definition. The latter states: 'Opening made in a wall in order to let the air and the light penetrate'. On the contrary, Renoir films an 'opening … to respond to the call for air, to escape towards the light'.

*(Douchet, 1997, pp.111–112)*

Douchet touches here on a number of key points relevant to this section. He challenges, through Renoir, a very basic architectural definition of what a window is, and goes on to propose his own rather poetic definition as a 'channel of our dreams', while Renoir's own quote reaffirms this idea of freedom and escape towards the light. But Palladio was clear in his definition of what a window should achieve:

Make sure when making windows that they do not let in too much or too little light and that they are not more spread out or closer together than necessary. One should therefore take great care over the size of the rooms which will receive light from them because it is obvious that a larger room needs much more light to make it luminous and bright than a small one; and if the windows are made smaller and less numerous than necessary they will be made gloomy; and if they are made too large the rooms are practically uninhabitable because, since cold and hot air can get in they will be extremely hot or cold depending on the seasons of the year.

*(Palladio, 1997, p.60)*

Jacques Tati would certainly have approved of this definition, and *Playtime* (1967) could be read as an illustration of Palladio's principle that too much glazing can only lead to puzzlement, ambiguity and confusion.

In general, architects have longed debated what a window was. For example, Le Corbusier reported that 'Loos told me one day: A cultivated man does not look out of the window; his window is a ground glass; it is there only to let the light in, not to let the gaze pass through' (Colomina, 1992, p.74). Loos was clearly advocating a rather introverted interior with no Renoirien means of visual escape. And according to Colomina: 'Whereas Loos' window had split sight from light, Le Corbusier's splits breathing from these two forms of light. 'A window is to give light, not to ventilate! To ventilate we use machines; it is mechanics, it is physics' (Colomina, 1992, p.121). But the real debate amongst architects was that between Perret and Le Corbusier about the window's shape, which Douchet conceives as being of an oblong configuration 'd'un rectangle plus haut que large'. Colomina evokes the debate between both architects in the following terms:

> Perret maintained that the vertical window, *la porte fenêtre*, 'reproduces an impression of complete space' because it permits a view of the street, the garden, and the sky, while the horizontal window, *la fenêtre en longueur*, diminishes 'one's perception and correct appreciation of the landscape'. She adds that 'What the horizontal window cuts from the cone of vision is the strip of the sky and the strip of the foreground that sustains the illusion of perspectival depth. Perret's *porte fenêtre* corresponds to the space of perspective. Le Corbusier's *fenêtre en longueur* to the space of photography.
>
> *(Colomina, 1992, p.112)*

Of La Villa Savoye (1929), Le Corbusier said 'The house is a box in the air, pierced all around, without interruption, by a *fenêtre en longueur*' (Colomina, 1992, p.114). Le Corbusier had long anticipated the role of film as an effective means of communication and made his intentions perfectly clear in *Architectures d'Aujourd'hui* (Pierre Chenal, 1931).[8] The section featuring La Villa Savoye starts with an establishing shot of the 'box in the air' followed by a continuous camera movement, panning over the *fenêtres en longueur*. The windows are again prominent in the interior shot, a pan from left to right, seemingly traversing the glass to briefly hover above the outside garden, before cutting to the base of the ramp. The camera movements and the cuts aren't motivated by movements or actions. There are no characters except for a woman climbing the ramp at some point. The space is the main and only character and it has been suggested that in itself it contains its own drama, functioning as a film: 'This kind of spatial system has been called cinematic because of the sense of an unfolding suspense, rendered palpable as previously withheld but anticipated spaces come into view and into availability for use' (Tawa, 2010, p.119), thus echoing Colomina's remark, 'The house is no more than a series of views choreographed by the visitor, the way a filmmaker effects the montage of a film' (Colomina, 1992, p.114). In that sense the scene of La Villa Savoye in *Architectures d'Aujourd'hui* constitutes a film of the film, a form of *mise en abyme*, where the sweeping of the camera over the *fenêtres en longueur* further reminds us of the unwinding of celluloid film frames.[9]

**142** An architectonic of cinema

## The case of *la porte fenêtre* and *la fenêtre en longueur* in film

Intriguingly, the battle of the windows between Le Corbusier and Perret would be given a new twist thanks to two films – *L'homme d'à coté* (Gastón Duprat and Mariano Cohn, 2009) and *38 Témoins* (Lucas Belvaux, 2012). Both are fiction films staged in buildings designed by the two architects; *L'homme d'à coté* is staged in a Le Corbusier villa in Argentina, while *38 Témoins* takes place in a block of flats designed by Perret in Le Havre – and in both cases a key component of the film revolves around windows. Unwittingly, the film-makers have allowed the conversation between *la porte fenêtre* and *la fenêtre en longueur* to last well into the twenty-first century.

*L'homme d'à coté* is, as far as I know, the only fiction film staged in a building by Le Corbusier. It takes place in the only house built by Le Corbusier in South America, La Maison Curutchet in La Plata, Argentina (Lapunzina, 1997). The house itself has an interesting history and is not a typical villa on the model of La Villa Savoye, as it is situated on an urban site, shoehorned by 'three existing party walls, a ready available box, which Le Corbusier filled with a masterful display of his architectural elements and principles, as well as with the whole drama of his spatial poetry' (Lapunzina, 1995, p.131). In the film the house is occupied by Leonardo (Rafael Spregelburd) and his family. He is an internationally renowned designer who works from home and so does his wife, a yoga teacher – and except for the fact that they have a daughter, the set-up is very reminiscent of Hogg's *Exhibition*, artists/creatives spending most of their time in a modernist house. This makes La Maison Curutchet one of the main protagonists of the film and central to the plot. The film starts with Leonardo being woken up one morning by heavy hammering sounds. In search of the noise source, he walks around the house, taking the viewers on a comprehensive tour of the house, a cinematic architectural promenade. As Leonardo goes down the ramp we can fully appreciate the various levels of transparency of the house, produced by the columns, the brise-soleils and the *fenêtre en longueur* – providing a complex play of light and shade. The noise comes from the wall of a neighbour who wants to pierce a window in a blank wall, to Leonardo's horror, as it overlooks one of La Maison Curutchet's internal courtyards and living quarters.

*L'homme d'à coté* is the tale of the need for sunlight through a window, and it becomes a battleground between the two neighbours. Leonardo, who lives in a house replete with *fenêtres en longueur*, in line with Le Corbusier's principles, is unmoved by Victor's (Daniel Araoz) request. There ensues between Victor and Leonardo a series of amusing dialogues as to the nature of windows. Victor does not seem to understand Leonardo's objection and attempts to explain that he 'needs of a little the sunlight that he [Leonardo] has too much of'. Indeed, Le Corbusier had to deploy some impressive brise-soleil to counteract the effect of the sun. It turns out that it is as much a battle of social classes as for the right to light, as the sophisticated bourgeois-bohemian Leonardo is having to negotiate with Victor, a larger-than-life, plain-speaking, working-class, secondhand car salesman. *L'homme d'à coté* makes a valuable contribution to the debate on windows – *fenêtres en longueur* – while also being a good introduction to the nature of windows in terms of the right to light and sunlight – as well as its implications within a social, societal and architectural context through a lived experience.

Turning to *38 Témoins*, Perret's *portes fenêtres* are equally central to the plot. The film takes place in an area of celebrated apartment blocks built by Perret in 1946 as part of the reconstruction of Le Havre. Situated in the rue de Paris, the flats are part of a vast ensemble of the post-WWII reconstructed city and are now a UNESCO heritage site. Perret's project used a concrete system 'poteau dalle' that expresses the structure, and the flats are stilted on a series of striking colonnades that often feature in fiction films, symbolizing the quintessential modernist city (Etienne-Steiner, 1999). Essentially, the plot revolves around the fact that a woman has been murdered one night in the street and that there are potentially 38 witnesses according to the layout of the flats and the positions of *les portes fenêtres*. But nobody wants to come forward as a witness. The windows remain 'silent witnesses'.

Only *les portes fenêtres* know the truth. The film creates a claustrophobic atmosphere with too many windows and too much light, something that Palladio had warned about. People live furtive lives with their curtains drawn. Paradoxically, with so much fenestration, the characters are gasping for air. Of course the witnesses have not only heard the woman screaming but could, from their windows, have a full view of the street. *38 Témoins* is another classic case of modern architecture associated with dystopia in films, and an invaluable companion to *L'homme d'à coté* in the discussion regarding Perret and Le Corbusier over the right fenestration for modern architecture. *L'homme d'à coté* raises the issue of the right to light, while *38 Témoins* grapples with the right to see – and not tell. And both make valuable contributions to the nature of windows of the type that is not easily grasped or aired in any architectural compendium – from 'elements of architecture' they have become 'elements for living'.

**FIGURE 8.5** A world of *portes fenêtres* in *38 Témoins* (Lucas Belvaux, 2012)

**144** An architectonic of cinema

In the debate over the window ratio, film-makers never interfered or took sides. They simply used the windows that best served the film's narrative. Cinematic windows are never in it for themselves, but for what they stand for in dramatic terms.

## The case of *L'Eclisse* (Antonioni, 1962)

Renoir rejects the idea of showing an unexpected landscape through a window, in favour of the familiar, arguing that framing the familiar will make viewers notice and ask questions (see Renoir's quote at the start of this chapter). In the opening scene of *L'Eclisse* (1962), taking place in Riccardo's flat, Vittoria (Monica Vitti), opens the sitting-room curtain to reveal the EUR water tower. It's early morning and they have been up all night arguing. The grey mushroom-shaped water tower looming over a bare and liminal suburban landscape has an eerie quality that adds to the unnerving atmosphere surrounding the end of their relationship. Although this would have been a familiar site to people living in the EUR,[10] this landscape would have been verging on the unexpected for many spectators. The window through which Vittoria contemplates the water tower is a ribbon-type window favoured by Le Corbusier. This isn't surprising, given that the EUR is a twentieth-century modernist development. Vittoria's own flat is also situated in the EUR residential district and during the course of the film she regularly visits her mother and her newly acquired boyfriend, Piero (Alain Delon), who both live and work in the heart of Rome, in the medieval part of the city. Vittoria goes back and forth between the old and the new districts and in the process is frequently looking out of windows – there are at least ten such sequences. *L'Eclisse* could therefore be conceived as a tale of two

**FIGURE 8.6** *L'Eclisse* (Michelangelo Antonioni, 1962): Vittoria lost in window space

windows – *les fenêtres en longueur* versus *les portes fenêtres*. Antonioni is not taking sides for either Perret or Le Corbusier, and Vittoria's gaze is invariably lost in space, irrespective of the shape of the window.

However, there is one particular occurrence that in my view holds the clue to her window gazing. At 25 minutes into the film, the camera is situated in the street outside Vittoria's block of flats, and only the ground-floor entrance is illuminated. Suddenly, in the dark façade two windows are lit above the entrance. Vittoria has just come home, has opened the flat's door and has switched on a corridor light. From the same fixed camera position, we follow her silhouette progressing in the flat from the larger window on the left to a smaller one on the right. Across a cut, the camera zooms to a black part of the façade. Then a light is switched on and for a couple of seconds we see an open window with a poster at the back. The poster is a drawing of a woman looking towards a window. The frame – and the window – is empty for a few seconds, a rather typical occurrence in Antonioni's films, leaving plenty of space to space where 'le cinéma antonionien n'a cessé de dessiner et de décliner une architecture ou une topologie du vide' [Antonioni's cinema never ceased to design and enumerate an architecture or topographical vacuum] (Moure, 2001, p.14). Then Vittoria enters the frame from the left and leans forward to deposit a package lower down. She turns her back to the camera to exit the frame on the left again. Across a cut we find her inside her brightly-lit sitting room.

The significance of the scene resides in the poster at the back of the room. It is just about possible to make out the text situated at the bottom: *Il Disegno Francese, da Fouquet a Toulouse-Lautrec*. It is the poster of the exhibition that took place in Rome at the Palazzo di Venezia between December 1959 and February 1960. The woman on the poster is easily identifiable as a pencil drawing by Paul Signac entitled 'Étude pour un dimanche : femme debout de dos devant une fenêtre' [known in English as 'Study for "Sunday": Woman at the

**FIGURE 8.7** *L'Eclisse* (Michelangelo Antonioni, 1962): poster by Signac in the background

Window', 1888–89]. The original drawing is 24 cm × 16 cm and has clearly been blown up to poster size – as a result, she and Vittoria are of comparable size. Signac's 'Woman at the Window' turns her back to Vittoria.

They could be construed as a sort of mirror image of each other. It is hard to tell what Signac's woman is doing. Her right arm is raised against the glass, she doesn't seem to be engaged in any particular activity apart from looking outside. She could be contemplating a landscape, a street, a garden, we simply do not know, as all we can see is a white/grey blur. She might have been there for a while, daydreaming. I hypothesize here that Vittoria emulates Signac's 'Woman at the Window'. Indeed, throughout the film, Vittoria is herself mysteriously looking out of windows. **The contemplative window, the dreamy window, the window as escape**, are all contained in Signac's drawing and throughout the film. From the first scene in Riccardo's flat, when Vittoria opens the curtains and looks out onto the water tower, she simply stays there. She later looks out of the window again, standing in the middle of the room. She stops talking to Riccardo, simply gazes out. Later, when she is at her flat, she goes towards the window, looking up, gazing out. These are unmotivated gazes outside any action, outside a fiction.

But *L'Eclisse* reveals more conventional moments of window practices; for example when Vittoria's neighbour Anita comes to visit, another neighbour, Marta, calls on the phone and invites them to her apartment nearby. For a while we see them pursuing their telephone dialogue, as well as having visual contact, waving at each other from their respective illuminated windows in the night. This is an example of a **window as communication** and a far cry from

**FIGURE 8.8** A typology of windows and affects in *L'Eclisse* (Michelangelo Antonioni, 1962)

**FIGURE 8.9** *L'Eclisse* (Michelangelo Antonioni, 1962): window across the courtyard

those pure dream moments evoked earlier. There are **windows that hide**, as when Riccardo calls Vittoria from the street outside her flat at night. Standing in the dark, she can see him but he can't see her. She does the same when Piero comes by, but this time she shows up at the window and engages with him. And there are **windows that separate and unite** at the same time – as when Vittoria and Piero kiss across the glass pane of the French window in Piero's office. Vittoria is outside on the balcony side, and Piero on the inside. They performed a similar scene in Piero's flat, kissing across a glass-doored cabinet, and Vittoria never seems happier than when embracing through a glass pane.[11]

There are **windows that interrogate**, as in the scene when Vittoria first visits Piero's parents' flat. First the camera stands in front of a half-open window, which frames an open window across a courtyard. The intense sunlight illuminates the wall, turning the window into a black hole. As often in Antonioni's films, for a second or two we are left with a space of expectation, two windows facing each other, pregnant with anticipation. Then a woman appears in the window across the courtyard (see Figure 8.9) – she stands by the window's edge in full sunlight, looking towards the camera. She is wearing a short-sleeved dress and rests her left hand on the window. She is middle-aged, buxom, with her brown hair in a bun. It is a vision of a painting, framed not unlike an Antonello da Messina portrait on a black background. Vittoria gazes at her from behind the glass of the half-open window. Two windows and two women are facing each other: two lives, two destinies. No acknowledgment, no nodding, no smile, pure gazing for about two seconds, in total silence. Then the woman is reabsorbed by the black hole as she slides backwards, still holding Vittoria's gaze. Her footsteps break the stillness. One can't help wondering, who was she? Did she know Piero's parents? What was she thinking when looking at Vittoria? The whole scene lasts no more than six seconds; the window returns to its black-hole status, Vittoria moves on and the Aristotelian equilibrium is restored.

This is one of the more poignant window moments in *L'Eclisse*, a celebration of an ephemeral moment of everydayness that sums up Antonioni's take on the notion of realism: 'J'éprouve le besoin d'exprimer la réalité dans des termes qui ne sont pas tout à fait réalistes' – I feel the need to express reality in terms that are not completely realistic (Antonioni, 2008, p.293). *L'Eclisse*, like all his films, breaks in and out of a conventional narrative flow, slowed down by empty spaces that 'appear to multiply while at the same time fragmenting' (l'espace semble se multiplier en se morcelant) (Ropars-Wuilleumier, 1970, p.79).

Vittoria is disconnected from the world – those are pure moments of idleness – and Deleuze argues that those moments of idleness disconnected from the movement-image are key to the elaboration of the time-image:

> Antonioni's art will continue to evolve in two directions: an astonishing development of the idle periods of everyday banality; then, starting with *The Eclipse*, a treatment of limit-situations which pushes them to the point of dehumanized landscapes, of emptied spaces that might be seen as having absorbed characters and actions, retaining only a geophysical description, an abstract inventory of them.
>
> *(Deleuze, 1989, p.5)*[12]

Along similar lines, Ropars remarks that in Antonioni's films

> l'espace immédiatement perçu enferme l'image cinématographique dans l'éternel présent qui caractérise une présentation dramatique; aussi faut-il, pour que le temps devienne perceptible dans sa réalité sensible, estomper la présence de cet espace; à quoi s'est efforcé tout le cinéma moderne, jusqu'à atteindre un pouvoir d'abstraction. [The immediately perceived space encloses the cinematographic image in the eternal present that characterizes a dramatic presentation. It is therefore necessary to erase the presence of space in order for time to become perceptible in a discernible reality. This is what modern cinema has endeavoured to do, until it reaches a power of abstraction.]
>
> *(Ropars-Wuilleumier, 1970, p.228)*

And by modern cinema, we should understand the Deleuzian concept of time-image. Ropars pursues that in *L'Eclisse*, Antonioni manages to use 'l'espace pour exprimer le temps, parvient à exprimer l'espace sans supprimer le temps, même si celui-ci n'apparaît qu'en creux et comme un manque' [space to express time, manages to express space without suppressing time, even if it only appears in negative as a lack] (Ropars-Wuilleumier, 1970, p.89). Ropars suggests here that space takes over to the detriment of time. But space is not 'in it for itself' but as a series of signs, indicators of alienation. From the deserted and incomplete streets of the EUR to the large pillar of the borsa that splits Vittoria and Piero, all the spaces in the film anticipate the doomed relationship. Vittoria is its agent of destruction, living in a world situated 'à la frontière d'une mort spirituelle, toute l'existence du film est dans ce passage à la mort, dans la naissance mouvementée de l'arrêt du mouvement' (Ropars-Wuilleumier, 1970, p.89). And all of Vittoria's contemplative gazing through windows is part of this process.

Ropars further suggests that

> le temps se réduit à une succession extérieure d'incidents, qui demeurent impuissants à susciter dans l'âme de Vittoria une résurrection. Le temps n'a plus de prise sur elle, comme elle n'a plus de prise sur les êtres, équivalents des choses, qui peu à peu les remplacent au lieu de les exprimer. [time is reduced to an external succession of incidents, which remain incapable of arousing a resurrection in Vittoria's soul. Time has no hold over her, and she too no longer has a hold on other beings, equivalents of things, which little by little replace them instead of expressing them.]
>
> *(Ropars-Wuilleumier, 1970, p.85)*

I have already suggested that Vittoria, in view of her love of clouds, shares some characteristics with Baudelaire's *l'étranger* (see endnote 11). I will also venture that she has some passing resemblance to Perec's young man in *Un homme qui dort*. He too stands outside time and he too is lost in the world,[13] his only salvation residing in incessant loitering in the city. Vittoria is not *un homme qui dort* but *une femme qui rêve*!

Deleuze referred to *L'Eclisse*'s 'idle periods of everyday banality', and I have already demonstrated that there are equally interesting 'idle periods of everyday banality' in *Un homme qui dort* in Chapter 4. It is useful here to come back to the notion that everydayness as an architectonic of cinema is aiming to uncover and reveal in films what isn't normally noticed in cinema, precisely because it is banal. The spaces and windows in *L'Eclisse* are very common and very banal – but the way they are used and practised makes them particularly interesting to study.

Along similar lines, Tawa mobilized the tectonics of cinema and architecture 'for reading, producing, mapping and implementing new configurations of thought, figures of speech, states of being, gestures, trajectories, geometries, strategies, tactics, techniques and technologies' (Tawa, 2010, p.14). In doing so Tawa proposes 'to work at the very materiality of architecture in an elemental and substantial way. It is to work with, to work and *put to work* all the themes, tropes and components of architecture-static and dynamic geometric order;' adding that

> There is a rarely explored and interminable resource for foundational inquiry and radical tectonic investigation into these architectural fundaments, in this basic tectonic lexicon

**150** An architectonic of cinema

> – for example, that the door *reveals*; that passage under the lintel is a sublime and liminal *experience*; that the window is an eye to the wind; that door and death are cognate figures; that the scotia harbours an articulating darkness.
>
> *(Tawa, 2010, pp.117–118)*

As an illustration to his approach, Tawa analyses *L'Avventura* (Antonioni, 1960), the scene at the beginning of the film where Claudia (Monica Vitti) waits outside while her friend Anna (Lea Massari) is having a private moment, reconnecting with her boyfriend, Sandro (Gabriele Ferzetti).

It is a scene revolving around a window that visually links Claudia, standing outside, with Anna and Sandro inside, on the first floor.

> Sandro is embracing his fiancée Anna, while her close friend Claudia waits for them in the town square. Claudia is framed looking up at the apartment through a partially opened window in the corner of the screen. The geometry and spatial dynamics of the scene are critical. Through the window, the horizon is occluded by thick trees so that the room, while clearly a private domestic realm or interiority, also reads as an exterior which extends the civic square. The way Antonioni frames the scene, inside and outside exchange their normal status: the public realm becomes a subset of the private, while the private world of the couple becomes exposed to an outside that is normally occluded.
>
> *(Tawa, 2010, p.272)*[14]

**FIGURE 8.10** Window onto the street in *L'Avventura* (Michelangelo Antonioni, 1960)

Clearly this is a key scene and Antonioni is deftly using the window frame and the depth of field.[15] Claudia, filmed with great depth of field in the square below, is effectively situated in-between the couple. This window scene already anticipates events to come.

But Tawa seizes here the opportunity to highlight some of the possibilities offered by cinema:

> Antonioni's use of space has evident implications for tectonic practice in architecture. The disposition of several geometric systems, overlaid by multiple dynamic trajectories, develops potential energies and tensional interactions within a spatial field. These can be used to create specific relationships between spaces of different kinds, to stabilise and amplify their connections or to unsettle and destabilise them.
>
> *(Tawa, 2010, p.273)*[16]

Tawa hints at how an architectonic of cinema might open numerous possibilities to which I will return in the last chapter of the book.

Aldo Rossi had already noted that

> in architecture every window is the window both of the artist and of anybody at all, the window children write about in letters: 'Tell me what you see from your window'. In reality, a window is an aperture like any other, which perhaps opens out on a simple native village; or it is simply any opening from which one can lean out. Moreover, the window, like the coffin, presents an incredible history. Of course, from the point of view of construction, the window and the coffin resemble one another; and the window and coffin, like the palace, like everything else, anticipate events which have already happened, somewhere, here or some other place.
>
> *(Rossi, 1981, p.45)*

Rossi also talks of 'old photographs' that grow on him 'like a sentiment, which over time accumulated many things'. He is inspired by melancholic images that he collects, such as the one of a window opening onto a balcony, a palm tree and the sea (Rossi, 1981, p.63). For Rossi, buildings are containers of past and future events; they are full of narrative possibilities; some of them have already been explored in the movies; the spaces contained between buildings, walls, doors and windows, have for Rossi in-built capacity for a wide range of scenarios, and windows have 'seen it all'. Similarly, an architectonic of cinema should be a guide to future events – as architecture is always about anticipating the future...even when restoring the past. In that sense *L'Eclisse* opens new horizons as to what the practice of a window might be, and it could be construed as the cinematographic equivalent to Delaunay's project, *Les Fenêtres simultanées sur la ville* (1912), a continuous exploration of the window. Delaunay's project inspired Guillaume Apollinaire to compose a poem appropriately named *Les Fenêtres*, of which an extract is below:

[...]

Tu soulèveras le rideau

Et maintenant voilà que s'ouvre la fenêtre

[...]

La fenêtre s'ouvre comme une orange

Le beau fruit de la lumière.

*(Apollinaire, 1918, p.18)*[17]

The last verse is a tribute to Delaunay, for whom colour was the 'fruit' of light. And in the poem, *la fenêtre* opens onto a world imagined by Apollinaire. The poet attempts here to match with words what Delaunay was doing with colours. An architectonic of cinema has to somehow translate, interpret and render, in and with design, what Antonioni, and other film-makers, are doing with moving images. It's the confrontation of two art forms, the assimilation and overlap from one to another, and vice versa.

## Notes

1 My translation from the French: 'I believe that our duty is to open windows [...] in this job of window opening that is ours, we must choose which landscape to show [...] it would be wonderful to be able to open windows on totally unexpected, unknown and unbelievable landscapes, but it's very difficult, Man is a creature of habits [...] and so we have to open windows and those windows will reveal, and people will say: but of course...' (Reboul, 1995, pp.129–130).

2 In the book, the room is described in one paragraph: 'Ta chambre est le centre du monde. Cet antre, ce galetas en soupente qui garde à jamais ton odeur, ce lit où tu te glisses seul, cette étagère, ce linoléum, ce plafond dont tu as compté cent mille fois les fissures, les écailles, les taches, les reliefs, ce lavabo si petit qu'il ressemble à un meuble de poupées, cette bassine, cette fenêtre, ce papier dont tu connais chaque fleur, ces journaux que tu as lus et relus, que tu liras et reliras encore, cette glace fêlée qui n'a jamais réfléchi que ton visage morcelé en trois portions de surfaces inégales, ces livres rangés : ainsi commence et finit ton royaume' (Perec, 1967, pp.49–50).

3 Adding that 'Architecture is defined by the actions it witnesses as much as by the enclosure of its walls. Murder in the Street differs from the Murder in the Cathedral in the same way as love in the street differs from the Street of Love'.

4 "The Turin Horse" : Détail – Béla Tarr, éléments de: Bertrand Loutte et Tom Weichenhain (Arte, 10 February 2011).

5 'Une longue ligne de pylônes sous un ciel gris. On n'en voit ni le départ ni l'arrivée. Des bennes y circulent. [...] la pure image d'un espace et d'un temps uniformes. Quelque chose pourtant se passe : tandis que les bennes avancent sans fin, la caméra, elle, a commencé à reculer. Une bande verticale noire apparaît : l'encadrement d'une fenêtre. Puis une masse noire obstrue l'écran. [...]un homme est là, derrière la fenêtre, immobile [...] le long chapelet uniforme sous le ciel gris, c'est ce qu'il voit de sa fenêtre. Ce plan-séquence qui ouvre *Damnation*, c'est comme la signature du style de Béla Tarr' (Rancière, 2011, p.31).

6 In this shot we are rejoining a world of ordinariness where an old man is sitting against a wall, a learner driver in a Fiat 500 is circling around the piazza and a woman passes by running – gradually everydayness is taking over as the drama unfolds.

7 Julian Hochberg, according to Intraub, 'describes a situation in which the camera sweeps across a scene. If it sweeps to the right, layout shifts across the screen toward the left and disappears beyond the left-hand edge. Yet, he points out, 'in most situations there is a compelling perception of space, in which an extent has been traversed and about which the viewer has a clear visual knowledge. That extent is larger than the screen and exists nowhere but in the mind of the viewer' (Intraub, 2007, p.454). 'The viewer's representation beyond the screen is palpable—creating the sense of continuous, complex spaces that in reality do not exist (e.g., interiors of starships, old western towns)'. Intraub carried on this research on boundary extension and showed conclusively that 'similar to aperture viewing and cinematic communication, scene representation essentially "ignores" the spurious boundaries of a given view. Whether exploring the world through vision or touch, we sample it only a part at a time and yet experience a coherent representation of a continuous world' (Intraub, 2007, p.464).

8 *Architectures d'Aujourd'hui* is part of a trilogy together with *Bâtir* and *Trois Chantiers*. All three were a collaboration between film-maker Pierre Chenal and Le Corbusier. It constitutes Le Corbusier's first and most tangible foray into film-making. While scholars have tended to concentrate on Le Corbusier, not much was known about Pierre Chenal. In 2006, I published a paper that examined Pierre Chenal's early cinematic career and went on to consider the origin of Le Corbusier's interest and attitude to Cinema before examining the nature of their collaboration. Following an analysis of both *Bâtir* and *Architectures d'Aujourd'hui*, I suggested that while *Bâtir* was undeniably directed and edited by Chenal, it appeared as though *Architectures d'Aujourd'hui* was very much under Le Corbusier's influence (Penz, 2006).

9 Strangely, Le Corbusier never seems to have made a rapprochement between the *fenêtres en longueur* with the cinema screen ratio, which over the twentieth century became more and more like the ribbon window shape.

10 EUR in Rome was originally chosen by Mussolini in the 1930s as the site for the 1942 World's Fair – the letters EUR standing for Esposizione Universale Roma – to celebrate 20 years of Fascism. EUR is now a residential and business district in Rome.

11 Another moment Vittoria becomes excited and joyous is when she is looking through the cockpit of the plane taking them to Verona. She points excitedly towards the clouds. Vittoria is like *l'étranger* [the stranger] in Baudelaire's *Le Spleen de Paris*: 'Eh ! qu'aimes-tu donc, extraordinaire étranger ? – J'aime les nuages...les nuages qui passent...là-bas...là-bas...les merveilleux nuages !' (Baudelaire, 2016, p.6). She is *l'étranger*, a stranger to life who only likes clouds. And no wonder Delon felt also like a stranger when finding himself in the EUR.

12 Adding, referring to the dehumanized landscapes of the EUR district: '[...] a purely optical or sound situation becomes established in what we might call "any-space-whatever", whether disconnected, or emptied (we find the passage from one to the other in *The Eclipse*, where the disconnected bits of space lived by the heroine – stock exchange, Africa, air terminal – are reunited at the end in an empty space, which blends into the white surface)' (Deleuze, 1989, p.5).

13 As is obvious from the voice-over: 'Dans le silence de ta chambre, le temps ne pénètre plus, il est alentour, bain permanent, obsédant, faussé, un peu suspect : le temps passe, mais tu ne sais jamais l'heure. Il est dix heures, ou peut-être onze, il est tard, il est tôt, le jour naît, la nuit tombe, les bruits ne cessent jamais tout à fait, le temps ne s'arrête jamais totalement, même s'il n'est plus qu'une minuscule brèche dans le mur du silence, murmure ralenti, oublié du goutte à goutte, presque confondu avec les battements de ton cœur'.

14 Tawa goes on to state that 'The scene is clearly an assemblage of spatial geometries and tensions, calibrated to the psychological tensions of the narrative and mobilised for dramatic ends. The agency of the assemblage drives the general themes of contempt and recklessness characterising the individuals' relationships with each other and their environment. Spatial order and dynamics are manipulated to convey states of psychological and subjective crisis, together with their moral and ethical implications.

They condense the chronological temporality and dynamics of the narrative into a single a-chronic spatial figure which stands-in for the entire film' (Tawa, 2010, p.273).

15 This shot could be conceived as an homage to Gregg Toland's cinematography in Welles's *Citizen Kane* (1941) that first attracted attention for its use of deep-focus shots.

16 Adding 'They can stretch and dilate relationships, converting them from tenuous static associations into lines of deterritorialisation and flight. They can reinforce the dominance of a spatial system or produce fractures, modulations and variations within it. They can convey certain relationships between interior spaces, between interior and exterior spaces, between private and public domains, between the various zones of a building or environment or between components and materials of a building's technical assembly. There are also implications for a consideration of architectural space not in terms of distinctive form or aesthetic value, but in terms of the dynamic interactions that are mapped out, registered and promoted in the character of its fabric and the programmatic opportunities it affords' (Tawa, 2010, p.273).

17 My translation from the French:
'You will lift the curtain
And now here is the window opening
The window opens like an orange [...]
The beautiful fruit of light'

## References

Antonioni, M. (2008) *The Architecture of Vision Writings and Interviews on Cinema*. Chicago University Press.

Apollinaire, G. (1918) *Guillaume Apollinaire calligrammes poèmes de la paix et de la guerre (1913–1916)*. Mercure de France.

Bachelard, G. (1964) *The poetics of space*. Boston: Toronto: Beacon Press; Saunders Ltd.

Baudelaire, C. (2016) *Le Spleen de Paris*. CreateSpace Independent Publishing Platform.

Bazin, A. (1998) 'Marcel Carné – Le Jour se Lève', in Jean Narboni (ed.) *Le Cinéma Français de la Libération à la Nouvelle Vague 1945–1958*. Paris: Cahiers du Cinéma. pp. 76–113.

Colomina, B. (1992) *Sexuality & space*. Princeton papers on architecture; 1. Jennifer Bloomer (ed.). New York: Princeton Architectural Press.

Deleuze, G. (1989) *Cinema 2: the time image*. London: Athlone.

Douchet, J. (1997) Les fenêtres de chez Renoir. *Les éditions P.O.L.* (24), 111–118.

Etienne-Steiner, C. (1999) *Le Havre : Auguste Perret et la reconstruction*. Rouen: L'Inventaire.

Friedberg, A. (2006) *The virtual window: from Alberti to Microsoft*. Cambridge, Mass.: MIT Press.

Intraub, H. (2007) 'Scene Perception – The World Through a Window', in Mary A. Peterson et al. (eds) *In the Mind's Eye: Julian Hochberg on the perception of pictures, films, and the world*. OUP USA. pp.454–466.

Lapunzina, A. (1995) '*The Urban Canvas: Urbanity and Painting in Maison Curutchet*', in 1995 Lisbon: pp. 130–136.

Lapunzina, A. (1997) *Le Corbusier's Maison Curutchet*. New York: Princeton Architectural Press.

Lefebvre, H. (2004) *Rhythmanalysis: space, time and everyday life*. Athlone contemporary European thinkers. London: Continuum.

Moure, J. (2001) *Michelangelo Antonioni : cinéaste de l'évidement*. Champs visuels. Paris: L'Harmattan.

Palladio, A. (1997) *The four books on architecture / Andrea Palladio; translated by Robert Tavernor and Richard Schofield*. Cambridge, Mass.: MIT Press.

Penz, F. (2006) 'Notes and Observations Regarding Pierre Chenal and Le Corbusier's Collaboration on Architectures d'Aujourd'hui (1930–31)', in Belkıs Uluoglu et al. (eds) *Design and cinema: form follows film*. Newcastle, UK: Cambridge Scholars Press. pp. 149–167.

Perec, G. (1967) *Un homme qui dort*. Paris: Denoël.

Rancière, J. (2011) *Béla Tarr: le temps d'après*. Actualité critique 6. Paris: Capricci.

Reboul, Y. (ed.) (1995) *Maupassant multiple : actes du colloque de Toulouse, 13–15 décembre 1993*. Les Cahiers de Littératures. Toulouse: Presses universitaires du Mirail.

Ropars-Wuilleumier, M. C. R. (1970) *L'Écran de la mémoire : essai de lecture cinématographique*. Éditions du Seuil.

Rossi, A. (1981) *A scientific autobiography / postscript by Vincent Scully*. Oppositions books. Cambridge, Mass.: MIT Press.

Tawa, M. (2010) *Agencies of the frame: tectonic strategies in cinema and architecture*. Newcastle: Cambridge Scholars.

Tschumi, B. (2012) *Architecture concepts: red is not a color*. New York: Rizzoli.

# 9

## DOORS

I am from the 'Man Comes Through a Door How?' school of dramaturgy. Suppose a man comes into a room, just walks in. Another chap is there. Then the small talk. 'How are you?' 'I'm fine.' That sort of thing. The second man says to the new arrival, 'Please put the doorknob back,' and we see that throughout the small talk the visitor had the doorknob in his hand. First we laugh, then we begin to wonder why the man was so distracted that he didn't notice he'd taken the doorknob with him. And we're into our scene.

*Alfred Hitchcock (Freeman, 1985, p.49)*

It is pleasurable to press a door handle shining from the thousands of hands that have entered the door before us; the clean shimmer of ageless wear has turned into an image of welcome and hospitality. The door handle is the handshake of the building. The tactile sense connects us with time and tradition: through impressions of touch we shake the hands of countless generations.

*(Pallasmaa, 2007, p.56)*

Referring to Hitchcock's films and his penchant for focusing on architectural details, Jacobs coins the expression '**door-knob cinema**'[1] (Jacobs, 2007, p.28), which would not have particularly embarrassed Hitchcock, given his fondness for door-knob anecdotes. There are indeed plenty of 'door-knob' scenes in classical cinema, almost invariably associated with suspense. Suffice here to mention the scene in *Rebecca* (Hitchcock, 1940), when the young Mrs de Winter (Joan Fontaine) approaches by the stairs the bedroom of her husband's late wife, hesitates, looks behind her and in front; the camera proceeds to zoom first on the 'castle-size' bedroom door, then cut to a close-up of the door-knob, where her hand is seen sliding onto and turning the knob slowly. At the next cut the camera is in the bedroom, her shadow being projected into the room. Hitchcock could have made the 'door-knob' moment last longer. Indeed, it is reported in the door section of the *Elements of Architecture* that 'the apparently simple task of opening a door involves a sequence of at least 20 instantaneous sub-decisions and calculations, each with implications for ergonomics and safety' (Koolhaas et al., 2014, p.509).[2] Bruce Block's own analysis of breaking down the filming of a hand opening a door is more modestly whittled down to seven sub-events (although that doesn't involve closing the door): (1) The hand reaches for the doorknob (2) The hand grasps the knob (3) The hand turns the knob (4) The door latch moves (5) The door begins to open (6) The hand releases the knob (7) The door completely opens (Block, 2007, p.211).

Doors involve relatively complex mechanisms and modes of operation to which we have typically become blind in our everyday life – operating them in a state of near-anaesthesia. And although they are far less dangerous than stairs, as we'll see in the next section, it pays to approach them with some caution, as there are 300,000 door-related accidents per year in the US alone (Koolhaas et al., 2014, p.509). Film has, of course, exploited the accident potential of doors, and we only have to remind ourselves of the slapstick scenes in *The Rink* (Chaplin, 1916), and the chaos that ensues as Chaplin slaloms through the 'in' and 'out' doors of the kitchen restaurant in an attempt to escape the head waiter. Naturally, films are replete with doors, and so is real life. In fact, we physically interact more with doors than with any other architectural elements – apart from floors. There are the doors of our homes, the doors of our

**FIGURE 9.1** Tor struggling through doors in *Ed Wood* (Tim Burton, 1994)

workplaces and offices, public places and public transport. Our everyday life is crammed with doors of different shapes and sizes, that we push and pull hundreds of times a week without ever thinking about it. But if we were to put our minds to it, we might remember doors better than windows because we practise them so much. Often, the way cinema engages with doors reveals characteristics and potential that we would normally overlook, and brings a new take on this humble architectural element. To quote just a few examples, in *Prénom Carmen* (Godard, 1983), lovers interact with each other by flinging doors and windows open and shut in an empty flat. In *Ed Wood* (Tim Burton, 1994), Tor (George Steele) is so large and clumsy that he nearly brings the whole set down by knocking on the side of a door frame.

In *Dogville* (Lars von Trier, 2003), the town houses consist of white outlines painted onto a sound stage, and when Chuck (Stellan Skarsgård) enters his house, the absence of a door is made up by realistic opening and closing entrance sounds. And towards the end of *Amélie* (Jeunet, 2001), when Nino (Mathieu Kassovitz) comes up to Amélie's flat, they are both tensely listening on the other side of the same door – as put by Simmel *'the door represents […] how separating and connecting are only two sides of precisely the same act'* (Simmel, 1997, p.65).

Unsurprisingly, few fiction films,[3] to my knowledge, have doors as the main subject – except for one, *Les convoyeurs attendent* (Benoît Mariage, 1999). Given our focus, it is difficult to not at least mention it. In a bid to enter *The Guinness Book of Records*, Roger (Benoît Poelvoorde) trains his son to open and close a door 40,000 times in 24 hours. There ensues a series of humorous scenes where the door is decontextualized, either on a stage or in the middle of a garden. As the door is repeatedly opened and closed in quick succession, the repetitive actions induce in the viewer a process of defamiliarization – a key surrealist strategy. We may start to

**FIGURE 9.2** Doors that unite and separate in *Amélie* (Jean-Pierre Jeunet, 2001)

**FIGURE 9.3** Doors as mental state in *Spellbound* (Alfred Hitchcock, 1945)

ponder the nature of doors as in, what is a door? Or why doors? What about the ergonomics of the door? And so on.

In movies, doors are not just physical doors but passages into worlds of fantasy: 'You unlock this door with the key of imagination' says the narrator of *The Twilight Zone* (Rod Sterling, 1959), and as Dorothy (Judy Garland) opens the door in *The Wizard of Oz* (Victor Fleming, 1939) a world in sepia turns to colour. Doors can convey mental states; in *Spellbound* (Hitchcock, 1945), when Constance Petersen (Ingrid Bergman) and Anthony Edwardes (Gregory Peck) kiss for the first time, Hitchcock uses the dissolve to a symbolic shot of multiple doors opening, a reference to Bergman's psychological and sexual awakening.

There are also multiple film versions of Lewis Carroll's *Alice in Wonderland* – complete with rabbit holes and door scenes. All have become famous and have contributed to shaping our collective imagination about doors in a metaphysical sense. But in a physical sense, the nature of doors has evolved markedly over the centuries

> … a traditional element once invested with physical heft and iconography has turned into a dematerialized zone, a gradual transition between conditions registered by ephemeral technologies (biometric detectors, body scanners) rather than physical barriers. The transformation took place concurrently with a transformation in society: whereas

isolation was once the desired condition, our professed aspirations now are for movement, flow, transparency, accessibility – while maintaining the utmost security…a paradox that the door is charged with resolving…

*(Koolhaas et al., 2014)*

Both in film and as architectural elements, the nature and use of doors varies tremendously and keeps evolving, thus providing a rich interplay for our investigation.

Unlike doors, windows, which we studied in the last chapter, do not imply a movement; a gaze, yes, but very few characters actually go through windows, apart from the likes of Waring Hudsucker, or if it is a *porte-fenêtre*, which combines both door and window qualities. Doors, on the other hand, imply a movement through them. In film terms, doors are more likely to be linked to the Deleuzian notion of the movement-image than the time-image associated with windows. We only have to consider the chase between Bodhi (Patrick Swayze) and Utah (Keanu Reeves) through a row of houses in *Point Break* (Kathryn Bigelow, 1991) to realize what an obstacle doors are to smooth running. Doors tend to lead somewhere, they are an entrance or an exit, usually a combination of both. Compared to windows, doors appear to have proved less attractive to poets and writers in general, apart from Musset,[4] but Simmel makes the following point in comparing windows with doors:

> the teleological emotion with respect to the window is directed almost exclusively from inside to outside: it is there for looking out, not for looking in. It creates the connection between the inner and the outer chronically and continually, as it were, by virtue of its transparency; but the one-sided direction in which this connection runs […] gives to the window only a part of the deeper and more fundamental significance of the door.
>
> *(Simmel, 1997, p.66)*

With the concept of 'the **door, a spatial tool with a variable topology**' – (*La porte, outil d'un espace à topologie variable*), Abraham Moles goes further than Simmel and assigns to doors important functions as they regulate time and space and are a mode of spatio-temporal appropriation, part of Moles's psychosociology of space approach.[5] 'The invention of the term "variable topological spaces", a scholarly term to designate the idea of the door, complements the concept of the appropriation of space by the wall. The door, or movable wall changes the topology of the accessible and the inaccessible, which changes from one moment to the other the idea of inside and outside' (Moles and Rohmer, 1998, pp.61–62).[6]

Moles construes the door as an architectural element with movement built into it. 'La paroi mobile' has also a built-in variable geometry – it can or should be opened or closed, according to Musset; it is a permanent invitation to experience movement. The door as a 'paroi mobile à topologie variable' is most in evidence in a sequence from a short movie, *Traces* (Ches Hardy,

**FIGURE 9.4** Revolving door in *Traces* (Ches Hardy et al, 2008)

2008), that features one of the two revolving doors leading into the lecture room of the extension designed by Sandy Wilson at Scroope Terrace (Department of Architecture, Cambridge University). It is a door that most users would have long stopped paying attention to. And yet the film reveals the extraordinary within the ordinary – it is as if a chunk of wall was slowly starting to revolve around a central axis under its own steam – the perfect illustration of Moles's concept.

Another example of a 'paroi mobile', this time in a fiction film, includes a scene in *L'Avventura* (Antonioni, 1960), when Claudia, waiting for Anna, stands at the threshold of Sandro's flat, first peering through the open door before slowly and hesitantly closing it – in the process the camera (and the viewer), situated inside the corridor, experience the whole gamut of light, from bright to shades of grey to darkness.

Moles also introduces another element, that of exploring spatio-temporal passages:

> **the door is a time-dependent system** – 'note main door closes at 4pm' indicates various institutions [...] It introduces a new dimension of space, it necessarily offers a space–time experience. There will be appropriation of this space–time dimension only to the extent that we have a cognitive perception of this space–time topology, that is to say regarding the opening and closing of the variable geometric spaces on offer the doors that separate or join areas of space, constitute elements of a labyrinth, both in terms of space and time:

the opening hours of the doors [...] the knowledge of the city, is the knowledge of this space–time maze, wherein the open spaces vary from one moment to another according to certain rules known to the locals: banks close at 4pm [...] and it is this knowledge that gives us a space–time mastery, which brings us the notion of spatial appropriation.

*(Moles and Rohmer, 1998, p.12)*

In *Helsinki, Forever* (Peter von Bagh, 2008), the narrator, commenting over images of characters running across the city, through doors and passages, asks the question 'What are the corridors and passages in Helsinki?'[7] Moles makes the point that local knowledge is paramount in order to be able to navigate the labyrinths of the city – in a world controlled by time-dependent door systems, a homegrown cognitive perception of the space–time topology can be a life-saver. This is manifest in *Drive* (Nicolas Winding Refn, 2011), where the driver's (Ryan Gosling) unparalleled knowledge of the routes and passages of downtown Los Angeles is at the heart of the film:

you give me a time and a place, I give you a five-minute window. Anything happens in that five minutes and I'm yours. No matter what. Anything happens a minute either side of that and you're on your own. Do you understand?

*(the driver – aka Ryan Gosling in* Drive*, 2011)*

Similarly in *Birdman* (Alejandro G. Iñárritu, 2014), the scene where Riggan (Michael Keaton) accidentally locks himself outside the theatre's fire door, forcing him to walk back in his

**FIGURE 9.5** Riggan stuck in a door in *Birdman* (Alejandro G. Iñárritu, 2014)

underwear through Times Square to re-enter the theatre by the main door – also explores the hazardous labyrinthine nature of our cities.

Noël Burch, this time adopting a film theory standpoint, explored the different spatial-temporal permutations between two diegetic spaces separated by a door and explains it as follows:

> If shot A shows someone coming up to a door, putting his hand on the doorknob, turning it, then starting to open the door, shot B, perhaps taken from the other side of the door, can pick up the action at the precise point where the previous shot left off and show the rest of the action as it would have 'actually' occurred, with the person coming through the door and so on. This action could even conceivably be filmed by two cameras simultaneously, resulting in two shots that, taken together, are an absolute continuity of action seen from two different angles. To obtain as complete a continuity in the edited film, all we would have to do is cut the tail of shot A into the head of shot B on the editing table.
>
> *(Burch, 1981, p.5)*

In this example, the absolute continuity of action referred to implies an almost real-time cut across the door. We can think of numerous film scenes that illustrate Burch's point, for example in *The Servant* (Losey, 1963), the first time Barrett (Dirk Bogarde) enters Tony's house (James Fox), the back-to-back shots between outdoor and indoor create a sense of a real-time continuity of action.

Burch[8] subsequently proposes that there are altogether three ways of relating two consecutive shots, shot A and shot B in terms of space: first, the cut between two shots pertaining to the space with elements of visual continuity across the cut. In other words, we move across the same space as in *The Servant* example. Second, there is the case where there is no visual continuity across the cut but we are likely to be within the same flat/house or a similar type of space. And finally, there could be no visual continuity across the cut and we are in a completely

**FIGURE 9.6** The door as a cut: *The Servant* (Joseph Losey, 1963)

FIGURE 9.7 Doors linking time and space across the city in *Ed Wood* (Tim Burton, 1994)

different type of space. In other words, a door can act **as an accelerator and condenser of space–time** situations, such as in the scene in *Ed Wood* (Tim Burton, 1994) when Ed Wood (Johnny Depp) watches Bela Lugosi (Martin Landau) closing his front door and almost simultaneously opens his own front door, some time after that and several miles away – a form of time travel across two doors.

So if a **door is often identified with a cut** in films, what is the implication for 'real-life' situations? Do we experience going through doors as an experience akin to a cut? Perec, during a visit to a Frank Lloyd Wright house, implies that he experienced a form of real-life dissolve between indoor and outdoor:

It's hard obviously to imagine a house which doesn't have a door. I saw one one day, several years ago, in Lansing, Michigan. lt had been built by Frank Lloyd Wright. You began by following a gently winding path to the left of which there rose up, very gradually, with an extreme nonchalance even, a slight declivity that was oblique to start with but which slowly approached the vertical. Bit by bit, as if by chance, without thinking, without your having any right at any given moment to declare that you had remarked anything like a transition, an interruption, a passage, a break in continuity, the path became stony [...] Then there appeared something like an open-work roof that was practically indissociable from the vegetation that had invaded it. In actual fact, it was already too late to know whether you were indoors or out.

*(Perec, 2008, p.37)*

If a door is a spatio-temporal tool in the architectural panoply, it implies that we not only experience a spatial passage between two rooms, but that we must also be cognitively aware of the time dimension and its implication (after Moles). Otherwise we will be in the same position as noted by Perec – unaware of the threshold between indoor and outdoor, having the strange experience of a dissolve. Perec's experience, Moles's unconventional approach and Burch's taxonomy start to build a profile of what a door might be in terms of an architectonic of cinema, opening new avenues.

But let us pursue our investigation, restarting with Jean Renoir. Douchet remarked that for Renoir a door wasn't

*une porte à la Lubitsch, instrument de surprises, de hasards et d'imprévus. Pas une porte à la Hitchcock dont il faut dangereusement chercher la clé, ou à la Lang, derrière laquelle se cachent de lourds secrets. Non, la porte, chez Renoir, ne demande qu'à s'ouvrir et, surtout, qu'à livrer passage. C'est pour cette fonction circulatoire qu'elle l'intéresse fondamentalement [...] la porte, fondamentalement, ferme, mais qu'il préfère l'utiliser pour les entrées, pour faire entrer [...] Puisque le mouvement de la vie ne s'arrête jamais chez Renoir, la porte figure la nécessité du passage, nécessité d'un changement permanent. Elle illustre par son dessin et sa fonction une pensée générale, un imaginaire cosmique qui sous-tend la mise-en-scène du cinéaste.* [A Lubitsch-type door, an instrument of surprises, hazards and unforeseen events. Not a Hitchcock door to which one must dangerously seek the key, or a Lang door, behind which hang heavy secrets. No, in Renoir, doors only ask to be opened and, above all, to give way. He is fundamentally interested in this circulatory function [...] the door basically closes, but he much prefers to use it for entries, to allow entry ... Since the movement of life never stops with Renoir, the door symbolizes the necessity of passage, the necessity of a permanent change. By design and function, the door

**166** An architectonic of cinema

illustrates a general philosophy, a cosmic imaginary that underlies Renoir's mise-en-scène.]

*(Douchet, 1997, p.111)*

Douchet mentions Lubitsch, renowned for his playfulness with doors,[9] and he could have also mentioned Keaton and Chaplin, already mentioned, as doors always played an important role in silent cinema.[10]

For Renoir a **door is an instrument of passage**, not just for circulating from A to B, but it has also a more metaphorical dimension: it symbolizes the vitality of life and its constant changes. But interestingly, Douchet notes that Renoir uses a door mainly as an entrance. Of course, in practice we must be using a door in both directions, so that it is as much an exit as it is an entrance. A one-way door is most unusual. My own rapid recollections of movies confirm this impression – a door in the movies is mainly for entering a space. It is the way into the main space where often the action will take place. Pursuing the example of *The Servant*, the outdoors is the street on which the house is situated. The street has no particular dramatic function except for grounding it in London. The vast majority of the action takes place in Tony's house, and we therefore see many more entrances than exits. But exits can be very dramatic and memorable, as in *Gone with the Wind* (Victor Fleming, 1939) when, towards the end of the film, Rhett (Clark Gable) leaves Tara. He opens the door to a landscape shrouded in fog and utters 'Frankly, my dear, I don't give a damn' in response to Scarlett O'Hara's (Vivien Leigh) tearful question: 'Where shall I go? What shall I do?'

Privileging the entrance, as Renoir does in his films, is also reflected in the architectural vocabulary – we refer to the entrance hall and not the exit hall; the same applies in French, which refers to 'un hall d'entrée' as opposed to 'un sortoir'. Bachelard further comforts us in the understanding of a door as an entrance,

> For the door is an entire cosmos of the half-open. In fact, it is one of its primal images, the very origin of a daydream that accumulates desires and temptations: the temptation to open up the ultimate depths of being, and the desire to conquer all reticent beings […] Is there one of us who hasn't in his memories a Bluebeard chamber that should not have been opened, even half-way?
>
> *(Bachelard, 1964, pp.222–224)*

The door is a temptress; it lures us into opening it, to discover an unknown. Many films use the 'Bluebeard temptation syndrome' to good effect, as for example in *Rebecca* (Hitchcock, 1940), mentioned earlier.

In the process of being opened, the **door acts as a revelator**. In *The Servant*, Tony, who has become infatuated with Vera, goes upstairs at night, knocking on her door from the half

**FIGURE 9.8** The 'Bluebeard' door in *Rebecca* (Alfred Hitchcock, 1940)

landing. She peers through the door, then closes it again. As Tony goes down the stairs to wait for her, she reopens the door, this time wide open, revealing Barrett smoking a cigarette in her bed while reading the paper. Since we had so far assumed that he was Vera's brother, the door reveals the true nature of their relationship. In this case, the door doesn't assume a circulatory function and presents us with a different form of spatio-temporal attribute. Vera exits, but not over a cut, as the camera stays in the same position throughout the scene. And yet the fact that the door is thrown wide open to reveal Barrett is a good illustration of Moles's idea of the variable-geometry mobile partition 'la paroi mobile à géométrie variable'. There is a second scene in *The Servant* that demonstrates the door as a revelator. Tony and his girlfriend come back unexpectedly at night to find Tony's bedroom lit, occupied by Vera and Barrett who are unaware of their early return. Tony creeps up the stairs. His bedroom door is ajar, producing a play of light and shadow on the staircase wall. At some point, Barrett, made aware of some noise in the house, ventures onto the first floor landing by throwing open the bedroom door. His projected shadow reveals unequivocally his nudity. Tony looks up at Barrett, who takes a puff of smoke leaning on the banister. We never see Barrett, only his shadow. Tony, stunned, is unable to react and hangs on to the banister. The earlier door revelation of the true nature of Vera and Barrett's relationship was for the eyes of the spectators only. This time it is for

**168** An architectonic of cinema

**FIGURE 9.9** The door that reveals in *The Servant* (Joseph Losey, 1963)

Tony's benefit. And for the second time the 'truth revelator' is a door being thrown wide open – but the second time it is an indirect revelation, through a play of light and shadows… vindicating Bachelard's remark 'And what of all the doors of mere curiosity, that have tempted us […] for an unknown that is not even imagined!' (Bachelard, 1964, p.224).

But a door is also a threshold that divides two zones, two worlds. In Antonioni's films we often see characters 'inhabiting' the **threshold** between outside and inside. It is Vittoria in *L'Eclisse*, leaning against the wall at the café door in Verona airport, neither in nor out, looking at the barmaid. It is Claudia in *L'Avventura* at the threshold of Sandro's flat, as previously mentioned, hesitantly closing the door. Typical time-image moments made even more awkward because of the nature of the threshold as the viewer expects an action-movement from a door opening. The inherent sensory motricity built into the door wills the character to enter – but Vittoria remains propping up the door. She has been stripped of motor capacities on all sides, and this makes her see and hear what is no longer subject to the rules of a response or an action, she records rather than reacts (Deleuze, 1989, p.3). On the nature of doors, Zumthor asks 'Maybe you know a tall slim door that makes everyone who comes through look great?' (Zumthor, 2006, p.51). In the case of Monica Vitti standing on thresholds, the reverse applies – she glamorizes those very ordinary doors, we not only notice them, it is she who makes them look great. Bachelard has much to say about the relationship between inside and outside:[11] 'The opposition of outside and inside ceases to have as coefficient its geometrical evidence […] Inside and outside are not abandoned to their geometrical opposition' (Bachelard,

**FIGURE 9.10** Inhabiting the threshold in *L'Eclisse* (Michelangelo Antonioni, 1962)

1964, p.230). Indeed, by inhabiting the threshold, Vittoria makes obvious the potential of inhabiting a threshold – the door is not just a passive element of architecture or an active verb as suggested by Pallasmaa;[12] it is also a space that can be colonized.

But we must return to Béla Tarr, the film-maker of the threshold, if there is such a thing, and already encountered in the windows chapter. In his films the dialectics of the threshold, of the inside and outside, offer countless diversified nuances and permutations. There is a scene in *Damnation* (1988) where Karrer attempts to enter the home of the nightclub singer (Vali Kerekes). She is inside her flat, the door ajar but secured by a chain as he stands just outside, on the threshold. We, the spectators, are situated on Karrer's side – an over-his-shoulder shot. He occasionally tries to push in, but the chain resists. The door, **the threshold, is the contested space**. It is an intimate scene that gains its power from being acted out on either side of the door. She emerges out of a black background; her arm above her head holding onto the side of the door and the chain across her neck attractively frames her face. They stand very close to each other and although he is occasionally trying to muscle in, she is not frightened; she tells him that she loves him, as well as to go away, before slamming the door shut. Given the spatial configuration in this intimate scene, the inside and outside appear to waver at times, we are both inside and outside, experiencing a 'sudden doubt as to the certainty of inside and the distinctness of outside […] in this ambiguous space, the mind has lost its geometrical homeland and the spirit is drifting' (Bachelard, 1964, p.218). There is also much wavering and hesitation in the scene between Mary (Lesley Manville) knocking on the door of Tom and Ruth's home, with Ronnie

(David Bradley), Tom's brother, unsure whether to let her in, in *Another Year* (Mike Leigh, 2010).

A variation on the 'threshold as contested space' is **the door of rejection** deployed by the Dardenne brothers in *Two Days One Night* (2014). As often with the Dardenne brothers, the plot is deceptively simple. Sandra (Marion Cotillard), wife and mother of two, has had to take time off from work after a nervous breakdown. She works for a solar panel company and while she was away her colleagues managed to cover for her by working slightly longer hours. Subsequently the management proposes a €1,000 bonus to all staff if they agree to make Sandra redundant. Sandra's fate is resting in the hands of her 16 colleagues and she decides to visit each of them over the course of a weekend (hence the title) in an attempt to keep her job – this would mean that the majority of her co-workers would have to forego their bonus. There is a crucial vote to be staged on the Monday morning, and Sandra is racing against time to contact them all. In the course of the film she goes from one house to another, from one block of flats to another. Like most of the Dardenne films it is shot in Seraing, an industrial town near Liège, and is a rapid portrayal of everyday working-class environment, from the centre to the periphery. Every encounter entails Sandra knocking at a door, ringing a doorbell or speaking into an intercom.

*Two Days One Night* could be interpreted as a film about doors, the nature of doors, although no doubt this is not what the Dardenne brothers had in mind. She visits 12 of her colleagues and every encounter is different. And tellingly, none of her co-workers ever invite her in; all the conversation always take place on doorsteps, entrance halls or through intercoms. The pattern is always the same: Sandra arrives at a door, mustering enough courage to ring or knock, and as such it is the perfect illustration of Janson and Tigges's analysis:

> A particularly complex situation is opened up by the door of a private house or an apartment by virtue of the manifold modulations of invitation or defence, of orientation, communication and control. Before a stranger's door, the individual – who stands either outside or in a kind of transition space, on a doormat, entrance grating, beneath a porch or in a protective door niche – signals his or her desire to enter by knocking or ringing a bell. The visitor is then perhaps observed or interviewed, through a crack in the door, window, a spy hole, or an intercom system, before the door is opened hesitantly and distrustfully, or flung open joyfully.
>
> *(Janson and Tigges, 2014, p.93)*

All 12 doors are different – wooden, part-glass part-metal or just plain and unmemorable – and none are joyfully flung open; rather it is a variation on the same theme of reluctance, rejection and sadness: 'I am not voting against you but I really need my bonus', is the most common reply. It is also a study in what we do when we are waiting for an answer after having

FIGURE 9.11 Opening onto a private world in *Two Days One Night* (Dardenne brothers, 2014)

rung a bell or knocked on a door. Sandra looks at the door with some intensity as if she has never looked at a door before – but she doesn't notice the door – she is gazing through it, willing it to open. So before it is a door of rejection, it is a **door of expectation and hope**.

She might start to look to the side or upstairs, as we all do in such situations. If it takes too long she may give signs of slight annoyance. And every situation is different – sometimes a child answers the door, or a wife with a small baby – some doors were opened wider than others and most would keep an arm or a hand on the door frame as if to block or to prevent further intrusion. The camera invariably stays outside the homes, but we briefly peer into the interiors; doors are mediators between two worlds: the public and social stage and the intimacy of domesticity. *Two Days One Night* provides a unique taxonomy of door situations, from expectation to rejection, and varied insights into how we behave in front of doors and inhabit thresholds.

For Perec, a **door is first and foremost a protection** from the outside:

> We protect ourselves, we barricade ourselves in. Doors stop and separate. The door breaks space in two, splits it, prevents osmosis, imposes a partition. On one side, me and my place, the private, the domestic [...] on the other side, other people, the world, the public, politics. You can't simply let yourself slide from one into the other, can't pass from one to the other, neither in one direction nor in the other. You have to have the password, have to cross the threshold, have to show your credentials, have to communicate, just as the prisoner communicates with the world outside.
>
> *(Perec, 2008, p.37)*

**FIGURE 9.12** 'Honey, I'm home' in *The Shining* (Stanley Kubrick, 1980)

But in films the notion of protection from doors is often challenged. In *The Shining* (Stanley Kubrick, 1980), Perec's principles don't apply as Jack (Jack Nicholson) is forcibly breaking down his wife's hotel room door with an axe – and for Anton Chigurh (Javier Bardem) in *No Country for Old Men* (Cohen brothers, 2007), closed doors offer little protection for his trademark captive bolt pistol.

Moving on with our investigation, David Trotter and Louis Seguin propose yet another level of understanding of the nature of doors by commenting on the spatial organization of Renoir's *Le Crime de Monsieur Lange* (1936). The film is set in a 'door-rich' complex labyrinthine type of space. Trotter uses the notion of 'deep and shallow' spaces – after Hillier and Hanson[13] – in order to make sense of the spatial organization between the interior and exterior of a building:

> a 'deep' space within a building attainable only by passage through other spaces, and thereby adapted for its owner's exclusive use, as sanctuary or shrine; and the 'shallow' spaces (neutral, inclusive, open-ended) through which the visitor must pass in order to attain it.
>
> *(Trotter, 2013, p.184)*

He further argues that

> The film makes an exact distinction between deep and shallow spaces [...] When Batala arrives in the morning [...] Two lengthy high-angle panning shots, one from each end of the shop, conduct him in leisurely fashion across semi public shallow space to the door

of his office [...] When Valentine in turn leaves, we look in the opposite direction, from deep space, out through the open door down the length of the composing shop's activity and casual friendliness, into shallow space.

*(Trotter, 2013, pp.193–194)*

What Trotter's analysis suggests is that doors are the key to the passage from shallow and deep spaces, from private to public spaces. Seguin, on the other hand, gives the following account:

*Le Crime de Monsieur Lange* begins with the establishment of a double assemblage, specifically, by opening two doors. The first, before the arrival of the Delage driven by Henri Guisol (Meunier's son), is the door of the sordid 'Café-Hôtel de la Frontière' where René Lefèvre (Amédée Ange) and Florelle (Valentine Cardès) will rest and spend the night before crossing the Belgian border. The door even repeats itself three times: first a barrier, then the door of the house, finally the bedroom door, as if to push deeper the narrative inside the drama.

*(Seguin, 1999, p.49)*[14]

Seguin's remark about the film being a series *d'emboîtement* evokes scenes organized as a series of layers, reminiscent of Russian dolls. This is in effect quite close to Trotter's own use of the notion of the **deep and shallow spaces**, those passages are controlled by doors, the passages from one zone to another. Both invoke an analysis of filmic space that lends itself to imagining a plan of the set and, as Trotter also noted,

So complex was the set of *Le Crime de Monsieur Lange*, built in its entirety in the studios at Billancourt, and so clearly integral to the film's dramatic effect, that André Bazin felt moved to include a diagram in his discussion of the rigor of the camera movements that expose it to view.

*(Trotter, 2013, p.194)*

Trotter, Seguin and Bazin have (re)discovered the importance of the architectural plan for spatial film analysis. Robin Evans had long understood its importance in relation to other art forms – paintings and literature in particular – and on this subject recommended to

Take the portrayal of human figures and take house plans from a given time and place: look at them together as evidence of a way of life, and the coupling between everyday conduct and architectural organisation may become more lucid.

*(Evans, 1997, p.57)*[15]

## An architectonic of cinema

This is what we have done here – we have looked closely at the human figure in relation to its architectural interaction with the unassuming door. Films give us an insight into how doors are used in everyday situations – it makes us notice their multiple usage – something of which we have often become unaware in our everyday practice. The door, this most anodyne element of the architectural vocabulary, looked at through the camera lens, with the help of others, allows for different modes of assemblage, hopefully opening new horizons, pointing towards new aptitudes, capacity and potential.

We evoked the so-called door-knob cinema with Hitchcock, the variable topology door and the door as a time-dependent system with Moles, the door as a cut with Burch and the door as accelerator of space–time. For Renoir, the door is an instrument of passage: it is also a revelator, a threshold and a contested space. We should also remember the door of rejection, the door of expectation and hope, the doors of deep and shallow spaces and, of course, the door as protection. This constitutes a short attempt at revealing the door's cinematic architectonic potential, many more examples would spring to mind, but 'if one were to give an account of all the doors one has closed and opened, of all the doors one would like to re-open, one would have to tell the story of one's entire life' (Bachelard, 1994, p.224).

## Notes

1 This is in relation to Bazin's derogatory mention of 'la mise-en-scène genre bouton de porte' in an article on Italian neo-realism (Bazin, 1985, p.282).
2 This is typical of a Hierarchical Task Analysis (HTA), which is a core ergonomics approach.
3 In this context it is worth mentioning *The London Story* (Sally Potter, 1986), a short fiction film involving a woman (Jacky Lansley) who recruits a cabinet minister (Arthur Fincham) and a cabinet doorman (George Antoni) in a plot to expose governmental wrongdoings. The film features a curious scene where the doorman repeatedly practises the art of opening doors – not as straightforward as one may think! He is also interviewed and gives this account:
Doorman: '*When I left school I was 15 – I went to straight to work for a hotel opening doors there – I got very good references and moved on to other doors which led to the position I am in now*'.
Interviewer: '*What is your current position?*'
Doorman: '*I am often required to open doors for members of the cabinet*'.
Interviewer: '*Do you have access to all the important doors?*'
Doorman: 'More or less...'
Interviewer: '*What do you think of the people you are letting in and out?*'...
Doorman: '*I just open the doors...I am not paid to have an opinion...*'
Interviewer: '*Do you have any hobbies?*'
Doorman: '*...Well yes...door opening...*'
4 The title of a play by Alfred de Musset, published in 1845, *Une porte doit être ouverte ou fermée* (Musset, 1904) – a door must be opened or closed.
5 Moles was 'un exceptionnel passeur transdisciplinaire' (Devèze, 2004, p.189) and a broad thinker who considered space as 'une denrée consommée par l'homme pour l'ensemble de ses actes' (Moles and Rohmer, 1998, p.82). His studies on the 'consumption' of space led him to create an interdisciplinary field involving aspects of psychology and sociology but also architecture, urbanism, geography and phenomenology as well as structuralism. 'Héritier de Bachelard dont il avait suivi l'enseignement, Moles reprend à son compte les thèmes classiques de la poétique de l'espace

(l'opposition dedans/dehors, la porte, etc.). L'un et l'autre analysent la dualité fondatrice de l'approche phénoménologique –poétique, opposant l'homme raisonnable à l'être de l'expérience immédiate. L'analyse poétique suppose la mise entre parenthèses de la rationalité, l'abandonnant provisoirement aux géomètres, pour cerner les composantes les plus sensibles' (Moles and Rohmer, 1998, p.12).

6 The original French quote: 'La porte, outil d'un espace à topologie variable : Le mur accompagne l'évolution humaine depuis la paroi de la caverne ou le rempart de la hutte. L'invention d'espaces à topologie variable, terme savant pour désigner l'idée de porte, vient compléter la notion d'appropriation de l'espace par la paroi. La porte, paroi mobile qui change la topologie de l'accessible et de l'inaccessible, qui modifie d'un instant à l'autre l'idée de dedans et de dehors, la porte, comme nous le rappelle à la fois l'électronique (gating) et la poésie (Musset) est un système dépendant du temps. « Nos portes ferment à 18 heures », dit le magasin ou le bureau. Elle introduit une nouvelle dimension de l'espace, elle propose nécessairement l'expérience d'un espace-temps. Il n'y aura appropriation de l'espace-temps que dans la mesure où l'homme a une perception cognitive de la topologie de cet espace-temps, c'est-à-dire de l'ouverture ou de la fermeture des espaces géométriques qui lui sont offerts. Ainsi les portes qui séparent ou joignent des domaines de l'espace, constituent les éléments d'un labyrinthe, à la fois dans l'espace : les domaines, à la fois dans le temps : les heures où l'on peut s'y trouver. Si celles-ci sont régulières et connaissables, elles créent un jeu de contraintes objectivables. La connaissance de la ville, c'est la connaissance de ce labyrinthe spatio-temporel, dans lequel les espaces ouverts varient d'un moment à un autre selon certaines règles connues de l'habitant : les banques ferment à 16 heures. Les espaces que je puis explorer et où je peux agir, ceux qui me sont ouverts ou qui me sont fermés, varient à un rythme, sinon régulier, tout au moins connaissable, et c'est cette connaissance qui me donne la maîtrise de l'espace-temps qui m'est offert, qui m'apporte par là l'idée d'une appropriation'.

7 We can all think of examples in our own city – the Cambridge University library offers a good example: 'the open stack shelves doors will close at 6.45pm but the reading room will remain open until 7pm – the main doors of the library will close at 7.15pm' – regularly announced on the library tannoy system gradually restricts the movement of readers. Also, each Cambridge College will have its own way of controlling access: 'main gates will be shut after 11pm but the small gate on the west side will remain open until midnight' and around midnight there will be a rush for the little gate!

8 Pursuing his analysis of time and space, Burch arrives at 15 basic possible permutations (five for time and three for space) for moving from one space to another. Burch also acknowledges that there could be 'an infinite number of permutations, determined not only by the extent of the time ellipsis or reversal but also, and more importantly, by another parameter that is capable of undergoing an almost infinite number of variations too: the changes in camera angle and camera–subject distance (not to mention deliberate discrepancies in eye-line angles or matching trajectories, which are less easy to control but almost as important)' [p.12]. He concludes that 'although camera movements, entrances into and exits from frame, composition, and so on can all function as devices aiding in the organization of the film object, I feel that the shot transition will remain the basic element in the infinitely more complex structures of the future' [p.12] adding that his study is the basis for a 'truly consistent relationship between a film's spatial and temporal articulations and its narrative content, formal structure determining narrative structure as much as vice versa. It also implies giving as important a place to the viewer's disorientation as to his orientation. And these are but two of the possible multiple dialectics that will form the very substance of the cinema of the future, a cinema in which découpage in the limited sense of breaking down a narrative into scenes will no longer be meaningful to the real film-maker and découpage as defined here will cease to be experimental and purely theoretical and come into its own in actual film practice' [p.15]. While Burch's study was essentially carried out from a purely theoretical viewpoint, his typology can more widely contribute to the vast enterprise of digital editing and movie-making tools informed by the history and theory of film-making, something he alludes to when referring to 'the cinema of the future', and an interest shared by many others, such as cognitive psychologist Julian Hochberg: 'Today moving pictures raise questions that must concern

**176** An architectonic of cinema

cognitive psychologists and neurophysiologists and some of the answers to those questions should help the computer scientists who work at automating movie making' (Peterson et al., 2007, p.396).

9 A good example would be *Ninotchka* (Ernst Lubitsch, 1939), the corridor scene where maids and butlers go back and forth through a door from which we can only hear and gather what's happening inside – a scene entirely from the point of view of a door.

10 Chaplin's *The Pilgrim* (1923) is a fine representative of that tradition, with wonderful slapstick door scenes.

11 'First of all, it must be noted that the two terms "outside" and "inside" pose problems of metaphysical anthropology that are not symmetrical. To make inside concrete and outside vast is the first task, the first problem, it would seem, of an anthropology of the imagination. But between concrete and vast, the opposition is not a true one. At the slightest touch, asymmetry appears' (Bachelard, 1964, p.215).

12 'The act of passing through a door is an authentic architectural experience, not the door itself' (Pallasmaa, 2000, p.8).

13 Trotter takes here an original approach by extending Hillier and Hanson's 'The social logic of space', a new theory of space, to film analysis (Hillier and Hanson, 1984).

14 My translation from the French: '*Le Crime de Monsieur Lange* commence par la mise en place d'un double emboîtement, plus précisément, par l'ouverture de deux portes. La première, avant l'arrivée de la Delage conduite par Henri Guisol (le fils Meunier), est la porte du sordide *Café-Hôtel de la Frontière* où René Lefèvre (Amédée Ange) et Florelle (Valentine Cardès) vont se reposer et passer la nuit avant de passer la frontière belge. La porte se répète même trois fois : d'abord une barrière, puis la porte de la maison, enfin la porte de la chambre, comme pour mieux enfoncer le récit dans son drame' (Seguin, 1999, p.49).

15 On the subject of doors – to which he devotes a whole section in his essay – Evans notes that 'In sixteenth-century Italy a convenient room had many doors; in nineteenth-century England a convenient room had but one. The change was important not only because it necessitated a rearrangement of the entire house, but also because it radically recast the pattern of domestic life' (Evans, 1997, p.64).

## References

Bachelard, G. (1964) *The poetics of space*. Boston: Toronto: Beacon Press; Saunders Ltd.

Bazin, A. (1985) *Qu'est-ce que le cinéma?* Paris: Cerf.

Block, B. A. (2007) *The visual story: creating the structure of film, television, and visual media.* Amsterdam; Boston: Focal Press.

Burch, N. (1981) *Theory of film practice*. Princeton, N.J.: Princeton University Press.

Deleuze, G. (1989) *Cinema 2: the time image*. London: Athlone.

Devèze, J. (2004) Abraham Moles, un exceptionnel passeur transdisciplinaire. *Hermès, La Revue.* (2), 188–200.

Douchet, J. (1997) Les fenêtres de chez Renoir. *les éditions P.O.L.* (24), 111–118.

Evans, R. (1997) *Translations from drawing to building and other essays.* AA documents 2. London: Architectural Association.

Freeman, D. (1985) *The last days of Alfred Hitchcock: a memoir featuring the screenplay of 'Alfred Hitchcock's The short night'.* London: Pavilion.

Hillier, B. and Hanson, J. (1984) *The social logic of space*. Cambridge: Cambridge University Press.

Jacobs, S. (2007) *The wrong house: the architecture of Alfred Hitchcock*. Rotterdam: 010 Publishers.

Janson, A. and Tigges, F. (2014) *Fundamental concepts of architecture: the vocabulary of spatial situations.* Basel/Berlin/Boston: Birkhäuser.

Koolhaas, R. et al. (2014) *Elements of architecture*. Venice: Marsilio Editori Spa.

Moles, A. and Rohmer, E. (1998) *Psychosociologie de l'Espace*. Victor Schwach (ed.). Paris: Editions L'Harmattan.

Musset, A. de (1904) *Fantasio ; Il faut qu'une porte soit ouverte ou fermée*. Blackie's little French classics. W. F. P. Prior (ed.). London: Blackie & Son, Limited.

Pallasmaa, J. (2000) From Frame to Framing. *Oz.* 22 (1), [online]. Available from: http://newprairiepress.org/oz/vol22/iss1/2 (Accessed 26 September 2016).

Pallasmaa, J. (2007) *The eyes of the skin: architecture and the senses*. Chichester: Wiley-Academy.

Perec, G. (2008) *Species of Spaces and Other Pieces (Penguin Classics)*. Penguin Classics.

Peterson, M. A. et al. (2007) *In the Mind's Eye: Julian Hochberg on the perception of pictures, films, and the world*. OUP USA.

Seguin, L. (1999) *L'espace du cinéma: hors-champ, hors-d'œuvre, hors-jeu*. Ombres/Cinéma. Toulouse: Ombres.

Simmel, G. (1997) 'Bridge and door', in Neil Leach (ed.) *Rethinking architecture: a reader in cultural theory*. London: Routledge. pp. 63–67.

Trotter, D. (2013) *Literature in the first media age: Britain between the wars*. Cambridge, Massachusetts; London: Harvard University Press.

Zumthor, P. (2006) *Atmospheres: Architectural Environments – Surrounding Objects*. Birkhäuser GmbH.

# 10

## STAIRS

### The invention of cinematic scalalogy

We don't think enough about staircases. Nothing was more beautiful in old houses than the staircases. Nothing is uglier, colder, more hostile, meaner, in today's apartment buildings. We should learn to live more on staircases. But how?

*(Perec, 2008, p.38)*

l'escalier excède la fonction qui lui est ordinairement assignée : non réductible à un lieu de passage, il pourrait être le lieu du passage, c'est-à-dire du changement [...] De quels étranges pouvoirs l'escalier est-il détenteur ? De quelle nature sont les relations qu'il entretient avec l'espace ? L'univers troublant des gravures de Piranèse soulève la remise en question complète de la fonction articulatrice de l'escalier.[1]

*(Decobert, 2012, p.16)*

...so let's talk stairs and be guided first by Friedrich Mielke, who has spent a lifetime studying them.[2] He proposes that

Scalalogy is the science of the interactions between humans and stairs, between foot and step. Since no one could possibly climb a stair without having contact with its steps, an interdependency is created, between the claims made by the living, and the reflection of such claims by the material.

*(Koolhaas et al., 2014, p.1241)*

Cinematic scalalogy, if such a thing exists, could therefore be interpreted as the art of observing the interactions between humans and stairs through the medium of film. Mielke proposes a broad classification of German stairs and identifies three types: spiral, winding and straight – to which he also adds an exterior 'free' stair (Koolhaas et al., 2014, p.1300).

Interestingly, Lydie Decobert, a 'Hitchcockian scalalogist', also proposes three types of cinematic staircases, broadly equivalent to Mielke's, but based on *Number Seventeen* (Hitchcock, 1932)

> On peut répertorier dans ce film trois types d'escaliers très différents qui revêtiront par la suite de multiples aspects : les escaliers à retours, en vis et droit [...] L'escalier à retours, avec son étagement en voles tournantes, ses paliers, sa rampe sinueuse jouxtant des balustres ouvragés, est ici le plus emprunté (comme il le sera dans la majorité des films) ; l'escalier en vis enroulé autour d'un noyau, par son exiguïté et son retrait implique le secret : quatre ans plus tard un escalier similaire conduit au message caché dans la boite de chocolats de *Secret Agent*. Quant à l'escalier droit, rigide et monumental, imposant, voire écrasant, il sera la structure idéale dans des films comme *Spellbound*, *Strangers on a Train*, ou *I Confess*. [In this film we can list three very different types of staircase that will eventually take on multiple aspects: dog-leg, spiral and straight stairs [...] The dog-leg staircase with its turning steps, its half-landings, its sinuous handrail adjoining the crafted balustrade, is here the most used (as it will be in the majority of films). The spiral staircase, by its narrowness and its discretion, implies a secret: four years later a similar staircase leads to the message hidden in *Secret Agent*'s box of chocolates. As for the straight staircase, rigid and monumental, imposing, even crushingly so, it will be the ideal structure in films like *Spellbound*, *Strangers on a Train*, or *I Confess*.]
>
> *(Decobert, 2008, p.18)*

So what might designers learn from a cinematic architectonic approach to scalalogy? What can we gain from Decobert and others? Certainly there have been some efforts and studies focusing on staircases in film, mainly coming from film studies – for example Eleanor Andrews, in the *Spaces of the Cinematic Home*, has a chapter on the staircase that sets out 'to discern, whether there is any consistency in meanings of the upward and downward movement via the staircase in film, and seeks to discover what these might be' (Andrews et al., 2016, p.137). In the process Andrews does a close analysis of the stair scenes in *The Servant* (Joseph Losey, 1963) – where staircases occupy no less than a quarter of the film's duration, as noted by Tobe in her careful study of Losey's film, from an architectural point of view (Tobe, 2007). But the majority of the writing on stairs in film concentrates on Hitchcock (Jacobs, 2007; and also Brill, 1983), which is not surprising as Douchet notes that

> *Le cinéaste au monde qui accorde le plus d'importance à l'escalier est sans conteste Hitchcock. Je ne connais pas de film de Hitchcock sans une utilisation extrêmement féconde*

*de l'escalier, au sens où la plupart de ses escaliers réservent de la part de son créateur une invention à chaque fois renouvelée et toujours étonnante.* [Hitchcock is the film-maker who attaches the most importance to the staircase. I do not know of a Hitchcock film without an extremely fertile use of the staircase, in the sense that most staircases provide him with an endless source of invention, always renewed and always astonishing.]

*(Douchet, 2000, p.40)*

Indeed, Hitchcock's mastery and attention to detail were second to none.[3]

Pallasmaa would not disagree, as he too has carefully considered Hitchcock's stairs,[4] but as an architect he notes that 'Besides the door, the stair is the element of architecture which is encountered most concretely and directly with the body' (Pallasmaa, 2007, p.32). This never more so than in *Exhibition* when D is hugging the top of the spiral staircase (Figure 10.1) – an unusual image, and one that reminds us of how little we are in direct physical contact with our architectural surroundings as furniture and objects act as mediators.

Our feet, mainly the soles of our shoes, are our main point of contact with buildings, apart from our hands in relation to openings, without forgetting stair ramps and handrails, which are an essential component of stairs. In fact, details of handrails, complete with hands clasping them, are often included in architectural chapters on stairs (see Figure 10.2). But paradoxically, the image of a hand grasping a handrail in film, especially in close-up, usually implies that all health and safety regulations are about to be violated. It signals the build-up of suspense and

**FIGURE 10.1** D hugging the staircase in *Exhibition* (Joanna Hogg, 2013)

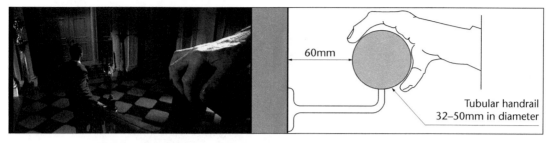

**FIGURE 10.2** Handrails in *Night of the Demon* (Jacques Tourneur, 1957) [left] – and technical detail in Campbell et al., 2014, p.252

that the hand invariably belongs to a villain. It is extraordinary how, on the surface, similar visual conventions of an architectural element can have a totally different meaning.

## The dangerous stairs

This points to the built-in element of danger associated with stairs – abundantly documented in film but also in architectural treatises. So are stairs dangerous? Probably more than we think, as according to Templer

> Using stairs involves risks that are greater than walking on the level because the consequences of a fall are likely to be more serious. Using a stair, however, should be no more dangerous than running, driving, riding a bicycle, or playing football. Nevertheless, we learn quite early to use stairs with appropriate caution. Most of us know that stairs are more dangerous than level floors, but this does not dissuade us from using them. One might conclude that stairs are somewhat dangerous but not to an unacceptable degree, and certainly not to the extent that we might consider avoiding them completely [...] The U. S. Consumer Product Safety Commission (1987) estimates that in 1986, 1,464,224 people were treated in hospital emergency rooms, and 6,200 died, after being injured as a result of falls on floors, landings, stairs, and ramps in the home, where more than half of all falls occur.
>
> *(Templer, 1992, p.4)*

Unsurprisingly, the majority of deaths are amongst the elderly, although the unmarried aged 40–49, a category also prone to alcohol consumption and substance abuse, are over-represented (Templer, 1992, p.5).

But if real-life stairs are potentially hazardous, what about their cinematic incarnation? It would depend greatly on the film-maker. Deaths attributable to falls – including stairs – account for 10 per cent of the death toll in Hitchcock films, while being shot accounts for 33 per cent (Frost

**182** An architectonic of cinema

FIGURE 10.3 Detective Arbogast falling backwards down a straight staircase in *Psycho* (Alfred Hitchcock, 1960)

and Vasiliev, 2013). Most famously imprinted in our collective imagination is the death of the detective Arbogast (Martin Balsam) in *Psycho* (1960). As Arbogast enters the house

> he looks up the stairs. This exchange creates the Hitchcockian tension between the subject's look and the stairs themselves, or rather the void on the top of the stairs returning the gaze, emanating some kind of a weird unfathomable threat. The camera then provides a kind of a geometrically clear God's point of view shot image of the entire scene.
> 
> *(Fiennes, 2006)*

At the point of the overhead shot, Arbogast cautiously reaches the top of the stairs, still holding his hat in his right hand, when Mother suddenly appears from a room on the right of the landing; she slashes his face with a large knife, Arbogast falls backwards all the way down, followed by Mother, who stabs him repeatedly while on the floor.

## A typology of cinematic stairs

This is a classic backwards fall on a **straight stair**. Campbell had warned:

> Detailed studies have shown that most accidents happen on the top three steps […] The danger from long flights is that if an accident does occur it can be more serious […]

significantly more accidents happen on straight flights of stairs than spiral stairs, dog-leg stairs or those with winders, and more serious injuries also result.

*(Campbell et al., 2014, p.250)*

Clearly Hitchcock had done his homework. But help is at hand and 'the setting out of most staircases is not complicated, but does require some basic skills in geometry and arithmetic'. For instance, the opening pages of the *Elements on Stairs* are devoted to eliciting the ratio between the step height (riser) and the step width (tread) and may be summarized as follows:

François Blondel (1618–1686) is likely to have been the first to measure the human step and use it as a base for his formula, which is still being used today. He postulated that two steps (riser height = R) and one tread (tread depth = T), should together make the length of 65cm. Blondel's formula 2R + T = 65cm is also useful for stair research as a tool for comparing time-related and people-related idiosyncracies and deviations.

*(Koolhaas et al., 2014, p.1204)*

It would take another idiosyncratic Frenchman, Jacques Tati, to challenge Blondel's approach in a short film, *Cours du Soir par Jacques Tati* (Nicolas Rybowski, 1967), that demonstrates, in front of an attentive class, the art of hitting a stair nosing at a precise angle with the foot, so as to lose one's balance but in a controlled manner, i.e without falling. However, achieving the desired effect of losing one's balance is proving difficult for Tati's pupils and requires a more scientific approach calling on simple geometry and arithmetic as explained on the blackboard by Hilaire.[5]

Tati's demonstration is the perfect companion to Blondel's formula and stairs literature in general. It makes abundantly clear that on the one hand 'short flights are just as dangerous and

**FIGURE 10.4** Tati challenging Blondel's formula in *Cours du Soir par Jacques Tati* (Nicolas Rybowski, 1967)

very short flights (1–3 steps) are particularly so', and on the other that 'People tripping on the way up usually fall forwards and catch themselves' (Campbell et al., 2014, p.250).

Also intriguing and counterintuitive is the little-known fact that **spiral stairs** are in fact safer: 'when people do trip on spiral or dog-leg stairs they are more likely to be able to break their fall against the walls or the balustrade before they have fallen very far' (Campbell et al., 2014, p.250). Indeed, no falls or deaths occur on any of Godard's *Alphaville* (1966) spiral staircases, of which there are several.

In fact, the repeated and insistent use of spiral stairs is unique and particular to *Alphaville*. It forms a unique typology, which could be construed as the beginning of a 'stair museum', spiral ones to start with, a project dear to Mielke,[6] albeit a Malrucian *musée imaginaire*. The first one, in the dilapidated Red Star hotel, is more akin to a medieval spiral staircase and allows for an intimate scene, snugly wrapping around the bodies of Lemmy Caution (Eddie Constantine), disguised as Ivan Johnson, and former spy Henry Dickson (Akim Tamiroff). On the way up to his garret, Dickson wheezes, collapses and sits along the slow climb of his personal and tortuous stations of the cross. The old-fashioned staircase echoes Dickson's inability to adapt to the futuristic environment of Alphaville. The upward spiral brings him closer to heaven, as he dies shortly after that.

The second, third, fourth and fifth spiral staircases are variations on the theme of the modernist interpretation of stairs, associated with the dystopian atmosphere of the film. As such, spiral stairs participate in the creation of a broad motif and atmosphere of circularity, present in the signage of flashing neon discs, as well as in the dialogue: 'time', says Alpha 60, 'is an endless circle'. The circle has been interpreted as the ubiquitous symbol of Alphaville and associated with 'evil, the tyranny of the computer and the permanent technocratic present tense' (Darke, 2005, p.61). But the second stair in particular must retain our attention. It is a most elegant staircase situated in L'Institut de Sémantique Générale and, thanks to Raoul Coutard's sympathetic cinematography, we are treated to several ascents and descents in real

**FIGURE 10.5** Spiral staircases in *Alphaville* (Jean-Luc Godard, 1966)

**FIGURE 10.6** 'L'ai-je bien descendu?' in *Alphaville* (Jean-Luc Godard, 1966)

time, by Lemmy Caution and Natasha von Braun (Anna Karina). The image of Anna Karina coming down is endearing in two ways (Figure 10.6). It first confirms Mielke's statement that the spiral staircase is the best staircase in the world, for its comfort and safety (Koolhaas et al., 2014, p.1329), but also the way she descends it, with great poise and grace, we almost expect her to ask Lemmy Caution, watching her at the bottom of the stairs, 'L'ai-je bien descendu?' – 'did I descend it well?' This ultra famous French one-liner pronounced in 1933 by Cécile Sorel as she reached the foot of the grand stair of the Dorian du Casino de Paris, is something that all French people will at some point declaim while walking down a staircase – a peculiar form of popular culture turned collective memory and associated with stairs.

Our cinematic scalalogy demands that we also consider the winding and the straight stairs as identified by Decobert and Mielke. Let us restart with the straight stair, already evoked with *Psycho*, and identified as the most dangerous of all. In *The Shining* (Stanley Kubrick, 1980), everything is familiar to start with; but the everyday is the perfect cover from which the uncanny can germinate – familiar figures gradually return from repression. Jack's (Jack Nicholson) repressed violence and alcoholism are finally rising to the surface – and the setting, the grand staircase in the Overall Hotel, is the ideal setting for it. His wife Wendy (Shelley Duvall) is gradually walking backwards, managing to keep Jack at bay with a bat. On the way up we keep switching viewpoints between Jack and Wendy – and as we near the top of the stairs, more and more of the grand hall of the Overall Hotel is revealed. As we have established, stairs are intrinsically dangerous, but playing dangerous games on them becomes doubly dangerous. The scene becomes quite terrifying as Jack ascends close to her, baiting her repeatedly: 'I'm not gonna hurt you. I'm just gonna bash your brains in'. Not a scene one would expect in a public space, but as Pallasmaa remarks,

> Construction in our time has normalized emotions into the service of the social situations of life and has, at the same time, censored the extremes of the scale of human emotions: darkness and fear, dreams and reverie, elation and ecstasy. Suppressed emotions, however, seek their object and exposure. Anxiety and alienation, hardly hidden by surface rationalization, are often the emotional contents of today's everyday settings. The dimension of the heimlich hides its opposite, the unheimlich, always ready to enter the scene.
>
> *(Pallasmaa, 2007, p.35)*

Jack's emotional state worsens with every step, as if ascending the stair was gradually ramping up his anger. Normally the grand hall below would be filled with people milling around – and one wouldn't expect such a scene on a public staircase – but the cavernous hotel hall is eerily empty and the scene becomes an intimate scene of pure domestic violence despite the grand space around them. The promised terrifying violence rises to the level of the amazing spectacle that they are offering to no one, but as if played out to a crowd of thousands. The scene reaches its climax when Jack lunges forward to grab the bat and Wendy manages to hit him on the head. Jack tumbles backwards all the way down the stairs. Campbell, Templer and others had warned of the danger of straight stairs.

But they are nowhere more lethal than on the monumental Odessa steps in Eisenstein's *Battleship Potemkin* (1925), where the troops of Tsar Nicholas II relentlessly massacre the civilians as they advance from the top of the stairs towards the harbour. Lasting nearly ten minutes, this must count for the longest continuous cinematic stairs scene, and provides plenty of evidence to corroborate the statistics on the danger of straight stairs, as we see a great many people falling over as they hurry down the steps in an attempt to escape the advancing troops and reach the harbour. We know that there was a mutiny on the Battleship *Potemkin* in 1905, but we also know that the brutal repression did not take place on the steps, but in other parts of the city, including the harbour. This is fiction standing in for real events.[7]

Much has been written about this film that invented a new form of screen language: montage. But the key interest in relation to this section is that those steps are still with us today – and still serve their original purpose of linking Odessa, built on the plateau, with the harbour below. Those images have become part of our worldwide collective imagination, as the Odessa steps have become what Pierre Nora calls des *lieux de mémoires* – sites of memories (Nora, 1989). *Potemkin* is part of the immaterial fabric of the city – and Eisenstein's images are still there hovering above the steps, stuck to them like invisible glue. As Eisenstein rightly said, 'Absolute realism is by no means the correct form of perception' (Fabe, 2014, p.197). In other words verisimilitude is not what matters here, but the feeling about what it might have been like – a sentiment, an emotion. If one was trying to make a documentary, it would probably be just as subjective, while at the same time everybody would be able to point out all the

**FIGURE 10.7** The Odessa steps in *Battleship Potemkin* (Sergei Eisenstein, 1925)

inaccurate details. But in creating a fiction, the need for historical accuracy evaporates, and in this case it became even more real than the reality – and is still impacting on the city of Odessa today, as both a real landmark and a cinematic one have coincided over a fiction, now spatially rooted in those steps.

On the subject of straight stairs it would be difficult not to mention Keaton's *The Cameraman* – and his acrobatic descents of the three flights of stairs separating his bedroom from the communal telephone downstairs. This is an astonishing example of an 'animated staircase section' – and a far cry from his retired approach to another straight staircase, in Beckett's *Film* (1965), as his character 'O' is being 'camera-shy', a curiously architectonic film essay on the subject of *esse est percipi*, 'to be is to be perceived' (Deleuze, 1986, pp.66–67). As for **the winding staircase**, the so-called dog-leg stair and other variations, an essential component of our stair *musée imaginaire*, we can turn once again to Tati and the house where Hulot resides in *Mon Oncle* (1958). In one particular scene we witness him ascending the stairs towards his attic home, and while doing so, at every step of the way, we see part of his body being framed by a disparate range of windows and openings – clearly a metaphor for a human-scale

**188** An architectonic of cinema

architecture (Figure 10.8). It is a climb composed of many types of stairs, although they are in part hidden from view but fully visible to our mind's eye. We, as spectators, have a clear articulation of a building structure organized around staircases and being deployed in front of our eyes, in all its intricacies, levels and openings. It is an object lesson in a practised and lived *promenade architecturale*, a new interpretation of Le Corbusier's concept whereby each successive framing of Hulot's body by a window constitutes a form of cinematic montage, edited in the camera.

Tati creates something novel out of vernacular architecture, something cinematically modern out of a traditional building, making us notice and value our everyday environment, however banal. This would fall within the category of the everyday stairs or the staircase of our everyday life. Hulot would go up this staircase every day, probably more than once, and its oneiric value is also in the ascent, a sort of picturesque scenic climbing, culminating in the opening of the window and the play of light onto the canary singing. Lasting a minute, it is a real-time stair ascent shot as an elevation, a rarity in cinema. As a scene it is precious and contrasts with most staircase scenes in cinema, for example in Hitchcock's films, which have much more of a

**FIGURE 10.8** Hulot's climb in *Mon Oncle* (Jacques Tati, 1958)

dramatic value than an everyday one. A typology of stairs of the everyday is also visible in *Le Samourai* (1967) in a long scene where we follow Jeff Costello (Alain Delon) going up and down a variety of stairs in a number of Parisian and suburban locations. Over 1 minute and 40 seconds we have a quick succession of straight, dog-leg and winding staircases, a prime example for our *musée imaginaire* of stairs. But unlike the scene in *Mon Oncle*, these are not the stairs of Jeff Costello's everyday life and, although they are completely ordinary stairs encountered in any city, it is the sheer accumulation and diversity of stairs in one long scene – 1 minute and 40 seconds is long at the movies – that makes it remarkable. Jeff Costello is on his way to a dangerous meeting, his life on the line. The twisting, turning, descending and climbing are an expression of the turmoil in his life – a case of spatially organized narrative with the stairs as the perfect match for his mood – and the sheer length of the scene adds to the suspense.

## The stairs of our everyday

Film has also the capacity of making us revisit the stairs of our everyday life that are typically overlooked. I am thinking here of a short movie (1 minute 10 seconds), *Vertical Promenade* (Miguel Santa Clara, 2008), centring around a concrete staircase in the Scroope Terrace extension built by Colin 'Sandy' Wilson in 1959. It is a space that I use almost daily, and yet it was through the cinematography of the elasticized vertical promenade that I was able to fully appreciate the remarkable aesthetic of this staircase, in all its details. But one of the most arresting images of stairs of everyday life can be found in Fernand Léger's *Ballet Mécanique* (1924). In the course of this short film we see the image of a washerwoman (*laveuse de linge*) climbing a flight of outdoor stone stairs, straight stairs, with a laundry bag on her right shoulder. The scene would be banal and unnoticed if it wasn't for the fact that she never reaches the top of the stairs. She keeps climbing the same four steps and keeps going back to where she starts. The stairs scene comes back three times in quick succession – the first time the washerwoman goes up seven times, then ten times, and then five. Dudley Murphy, the cinematographer, argued that the scene expressed the futility of life because she never got to the top (Dixon, 2011, p.14–15). The fact that the washerwoman on the fourth step raises her left arm, as if to shrug, looking straight at the camera, smiling and talking as if to say 'well that's life, what can we do?', reinforces Murphy's point, but it also highlights the repetitive nature of her daily life, her daily grind. We can only imagine that those are the steps of her everyday life, that she would have been using day in, day out for most of her adult life. This is a poignant scene, stairs as an expression of the futility of life, stairs as resignation, the stairs that hurt and wear you out, stairs in an everyday life context, circa 1924.

Climbing stairs can indeed be hard work, and in *Kiss Me Deadly* (Robert Aldrich, 1955), we catch Mike Hammer climbing a seemingly infinitely long and straight public stairway, on the side of Bunker Hill in Los Angeles, to reach the aptly named Hillcrest Hotel. Out of breath, he

**FIGURE 10.9** *Ballet Mécanique* (Fernand Léger, 1924): the steps of everyday life

walks into the lobby and approaches the landlady, who is sorting the mail: 'A guy could get a heart attack walking up here'. She responds: 'Who invited you?' Hammer asks, 'Carmen Trivago, what room?' The landlady replies, 'Follow your ear'. And knowing that 'Climbing stairs takes on average seven times as much energy as walking on the flat' (Neufert et al., 2000, p.192), no wonder Hammer felt tired. I am not sure how accurate the Neuferts' assessment is, but modern digital technology and GPS tracking devices can now be used to account accurately for our daily use of stairs.[8]

## Stairs' directionality

As Diderot remarked, *l'esprit d'escalier*[9] – 'staircase wit' – the clever remark thought of too late as one goes down the stairs on the way home – implies that the downward trajectory aids the reflective thinking process: stairs as an aid to thinking. But how do we think about stairs when we think about them? Do we see ourselves climbing or descending them? In French we say 'emprunter un escalier' – meaning you 'borrow a stair', i.e. you don't own it, thus reinforcing its transitory nature; but in this expression it remains 'direction' neutral. Pallasmaa posits that 'The staircases of cinema reveal the innate asymmetry of the stair, rarely thought about by architects. Rising stairs end in Heaven, whereas descending stairs eventually lead down to the Underworld', adding that 'Stairs are most often photographed upwards from below, and consequently, an ascending person is seen from behind and a descending character from the front'[10] (Pallasmaa, 2007, p.32–33). But Douchet is quite categorical that, in Hitchcock's films, the asymmetry of the stair is revealed and that stairs are usually descended:

> Bien sûr qu'il y a des montées chez Hitchcock, mais l'essentiel est la descente. Elle est ce à quoi normalement la raison, la morale, la religion, la société, les bonnes moeurs, le côté victorien s'opposent : il ne faut pas se laisser aller. Or chez Hitchcock on a besoin de se laisser aller. La descente est chez lui à la fois refus, mais aussi abandon, et souvent,

lorsque la descente est assumée, qu'on accepte ce par quoi l'on est attiré, à ce moment-là la descente devient salut. C'est le sens de l'utilisation de l'escalier ou de la notion de descente dans *Notorious*. [Of course there are stairs being climbed in Hitchcock, but the majority are descended. The descent is what reason, morality, religion, society, Victorian values usually oppose: we must not let ourselves go. But in Hitchcock's films, we need to let go. The descent is at once a negation, but also an abandonment, and often, once the descent is consented, an acceptance by attraction, at that point it becomes a salvation. This is the meaning of the use of the staircase or the notion of the descent in *Notorious*.]
*(Douchet, 2000, p.40)*

If film-makers may by and large favour showing stairs being descended for added dramatic purposes, we often climb stairs in romantic scenes – in *This is My Street* (Sidney Hayers, 1964) when Margery (June Ritchie) and Harry (Ian Hendry) first kiss on a small, steep and narrow staircase in a Victorian terraced house. Much more disturbing is the violent love scene in *A History of Violence* (David Cronenberg, 2005) between Edie (Maria Bello) and Tom (Viggo Mortensen) on their way upstairs – without forgetting the celebrated scene, see Figure 10.10, when Rhett (Clark Gable) carries Scarlett (Vivien Leigh) up Tara's grand stairs in *Gone with the Wind* (Victor Fleming, 1939). And finally, it's hard not to mention a man ascending a

**FIGURE 10.10** Staircase scene in *Gone with the Wind* (Victor Fleming, 1939)

free-standing staircase in the middle of the woods in *Fahrenheit 451* (François Truffaut, 1966) – a striking and poetic moment, the pure expression of gratuitous stairs as an element of architecture!

I hypothesize here that architects tend to think of stairs as going up, simply because of the universal drawing convention that shows stairs in plan with an arrow pointing upwards, indicating the ascent. And unsurprisingly the staircase section of *The Vocabulary of Spatial Situations* only refers to climbing:

> The act of climbing a staircase, for example, can be transformed by a constructive arrangement according to dramaturgical considerations into a scenic experience, so that we follow our own movements through space like a performance [...] In a way that is analogous to the actions of an actor on a stage, which generate a second reality through the production of a play, the reality of the purely functional act of 'ascending stairs' [...] In architectural design, pure functionality is transformed into an experiential reality, one that thematizes the function itself. The function of level changes can be staged by an expressive gesture; a purely functional movement can be invested with a certain rhythm; the effort of ascending can be transformed into a dramatic sequence; perception and orientation are enriched by a characteristic atmosphere. Between the dark grotto below and the floating platform above in Balthasar Neumann's Bruchsal Staircase, I see myself climb directly from the extremes of the gloomy depths below into the bright expanse above.
>
> *(Janson and Tigges, 2014, p.273)*

Here Janson and Tigges appear to imbue the stair with the capacity to deliver a scenic experience as one climbs, which reminds us of Auguste Choisy's remarks (Choisy, 1899, pp.409–422) regarding the placement of buildings on the Acropolis to be appreciated by a mobile spectator on his way up to the Parthenon. The picturesque promenade is to be enjoyed climbing, and there is no mention of the descending return journey. Similarly, the ramp scene of La Villa Savoye in Chenal and Le Corbusier's film, *Architectures d'Aujourd'hui* (1931), only shows the woman ascending it (Penz, 2013). Likewise when Vesely describes the experience of the Würzburg residence ceremonial staircase, it is always on the way up:

> As we ascend to the first landing and turn, the staircase becomes part of the structure of the room [...] In the Würzburg residence we can recognize the presence of architectonics immediately in the tension between the ascending movement of the steps and the upper part of the hall.
>
> *(Vesely, 2006, p.93)*

But, once climbed, stairs have to be descended too. We are up and can only come down, there is a double dynamic specific to stairs that implies that '*l'escalier contient sa propre force de dépassement, invisible de prime abord* – stairs contain their own invading force, invisible at first.

*(Decobert, 2012, p.19)*

Poignantly, Philippe Garrel's *Le Révélateur* (1968) presents us with a rare staircase scene that contains the innate asymmetry and ambiguity of stairs by playing with our perception. A woman (Bernadette Lafont) is moving very slowly on straight stairs, holding the handrail with both hands. The conundrum for the spectator is that it is at first impossible to know whether she is going up or down. Most unusually, it could be either way. The revelation comes when her husband (Laurent Terzieff) is seen emerging out of the shadow at the top of the stairs. It suddenly makes sense: the woman is coming down the stairs and we are witnessing her descent through a low-angle shot. Complementing this scene is Marcel Marceau's short film where he communicates admirably through mime the climbing and descending of an imaginary stair – eliciting the marked differences involved in both directions through the bodily gestures (Ina.fr, 1959).

**FIGURE 10.11** The ambiguous stairs in *Le Révélateur* (Philippe Garrel, 1968)

**194** An architectonic of cinema

Bachelard, on the other hand, as the architect of the oneiric house,[11] was very clear in articulating the directionality of stairs in relation to the various spaces of the home:

> we always go down the one that leads to the cellar, and it is this going down that we remember, that characterizes its oneirism. But we go both up and down the stairway that leads to the bedchamber. It is more commonly used; we are familiar with it [...] Lastly, we always go up the attic stairs, which are steeper and more primitive. For they bear the mark of ascension to a more tranquil solitude. When I return to dream in the attics of yester-year, I never go down again.
> *(Bachelard, 1964, p.26)*

But Bachelard also warns that the cellar is 'foremost the dark entity of the house, the one that partakes of subterranean forces [...] becomes buried madness, walled-in tragedy'[12] (Bachelard, 1964, pp.18–20). Stories of criminal cellars leave indelible marks on our memory – and nowhere is this better expressed than in Hitchcock's *Psycho* (1960), where in the last scene, Lila Crane (Vera Miles) slowly descends the cellar stairs towards the horrific discovery of the mummified corpse of Mother.

Overall in cinema,

> the connotations vary according to the use and context of this setting within the narrative [...] Whatever may be found at the top or bottom of the staircase, whether it be familiar, anticipated, dreaded, or unknown, will dictate the tenor of the ascent or descent.
> *(Andrews et al., 2016, p.150)*

**FIGURE 10.12** Going down in *Psycho* (Alfred Hitchcock, 1960)

And the staircases of cinema, if studied carefully, may inform designers that a stair is not only a way to connect two levels within a building, but a way to understand that there is a field of relationships not always visible and obvious, but permanently available, something more complex and enigmatic (Vesely, 2006, p.77).[13] We have to keep re-imagining stairs as complex and active elements – as verbs as opposed to static elements – as architectural experience as opposed to passive nouns. The act of climbing a staircase is an authentic architectural encounter, not the staircase itself – and is transformed by events that take place – and as we see in films, stairs acquire different meanings according to situations – they become alive with action, they are a receptacle and conduit for human drama.

## Notes

1 My translation: 'The staircase exceeds the function usually assigned to it: not reducible to a passage, it could be the place of passage, that is to say of change [...] What strange powers do staircases possess? What is the nature of its relations with space? The eerie universe of Piranesi's engravings raises the fundamental articulating function of the staircase'.

2 The vast majority of the 'Elements' volume is devoted to Mielke's work.

3 http://boards.straightdope.com/sdmb/archive/index.php/t-334810.html 'Hitchcock was concerned with those little touches. I heard him speak and met him once. He was talking about the filming of *Psycho*, the scene where Martin Balsam (the detective) goes into the Bates house and up the stairs. He let Saul Bass (the wonderful title designer) direct that sequence for suspense, and Saul Bass shot Balsam's foot on the stair, hand on the rail, full body going up a stair, foot on the next stair, etc.

Hitch said he rejected the footage, because having so many cuts made Balsam appear to be guilty of something – he becomes an invader, an outsider. Hitchcock wanted Balsam to be innocent and the object of audience sympathy (and to investigate what the audience wants him to investigate). He reshot the sequence, leaving the camera static, and just watching Balsam go up the stairs...where, of course, Mother is waiting.

Interestingly enough, a few years after I heard him tell this anecdote, he made *Frenzy*. Towards the end, when Jon Finch has escaped from jail, has a steel bar in his hand, and is going up the stairs to murder the person who framed him...and it's shot in many cuts: hand on railing, foot on stair, hand carrying steel bar, etc. Finch is, in fact, an invader, an intruder; he (and the audience) think that he's going to do murder. So, Hitch paid attention to such details'.

4 'Why are Hitchcock's stairways invariably to the right from the entrance as seen by the viewer? Is it because the staircase stands for the heart of the house?' (Pallasmaa, 2007, p.33).

5 Hilaire: '...sachant qu'un homme fait de longueur de jambe environ 1 mètre et qu'il fait normalement un angle de 30 degrés lorsque qu'il se met à marcher, nous avons à calculer la longueur de son enjambée ou de sa foulée et nous voyons qu'elle est égale ici à la tangente, soit environ 60 centimètres... comme nous savons d'autre part que la distance du point A au point d'arrivée B, c'est à dire le contact pied-marche est égale à 1.80m, nous voyons assez simplement que le nombres de foulées nécessaires pour arriver à la marche est égale à 1.80 sur 60 centimètres, ça fait trois enjambées...'

6 Mielke devotes a page to the idea of a stair museum: 'my ideal stair museum consists of a central building like the Palazzo Valmarana in Vincenza with a multiple-combined spiral staircase' (Koolhaas et al., 2014, p.1273).

7 'The wonderful irony of *Potemkin*'s place in film history is that even though Eisenstein did not strive to create a mimetic illusion of reality, his film was nevertheless experienced as stunningly real. Jay Leyda in *Kino*, his history of Russian and Soviet film, writes that "One of the curious effects of the film has been to replace the facts of the Potemkin Mutiny with the film's artistic 'revision' of those

# 196 An architectonic of cinema

events, in all subsequent references, even by historians, to this episode." "Absolute realism," Eisenstein wrote, "is by no means the correct form of perception." His films teach us that a film can come across as even more authentic when a director departs from the conventions of realistic representation' (Fabe, 2014, p.36).

8 Having myself experimented with an activity watch that records stair climbing in my everyday life and environment, I was surprised to find an average daily count of 22 stair climbs – and almost double if I was to visit the University of Cambridge library – unsurprising with the architecture collection on its sixth floor!

9 'Sedaine, immobile et froid, me regarde et me dit : « Ah ! Monsieur Diderot, que vous êtes beau ! » Voilà l'observateur et l'homme de génie. Ce fait, je le racontais un jour à table, chez un homme que ses talents supérieurs destinaient à occuper la place la plus importante de l'État, chez M. Necker ; il y avait un assez grand nombre de gens de lettres, entre lesquels Marmontel, que j'aime et à qui je suis cher. Celui-ci me dit ironiquement : « Vous verrez que lorsque Voltaire se désole au simple récit d'un trait pathétique et que Sedaine garde son sang-froid à la vue d'un ami qui fond en larmes, c'est Voltaire qui est l'homme ordinaire et Sedaine l'homme de génie ! » Cette apostrophe me déconcerte et me réduit au silence, parce que l'homme sensible, comme moi, tout entier à ce qu'on lui objecte, perd la tête et ne se retrouve qu'au bas de l'escalier' (Diderot, 2000, p.28).

10 Pallasmaa goes on to add: 'Stairs photographed from above express vertigo, falling or panicked escape. The preference of showing staircases from below has its natural technical reasons – a stairway photographed from above seems to escape the picture – but this very fact reveals the psychological difference between ascending and descending movements. The staircase is the most important organ of the house. The stairs are responsible for the vertical circulation of the house in the same way that the heart keeps pumping blood up and down the body. The regular rhythm of the stairs echoes the beating of the heart and the rhythm of breathing.' [33]

11 'If I were the architect of an oneiric house, I should hesitate between a three-story house and one with four. A three-story house, which is the simplest as regards essential height, has a cellar, a ground floor and an attic; while a four-story house puts a floor between the ground floor and the attic. One floor more, and our dreams become blurred. In the oneiric house, topoanalysis only knows how to count to three or four' (Bachelard, 1964, p.25).

12 *La cave est alors de la folie enterrée, des drames murés.*

13 Vesely's full quote on stairs: 'Consider a staircase and its space, designed for efficient movement between two levels of a building. What is in one sense a pure object, intended to serve a clearly defined purpose, is at the same time a field of relationships – not always visible and obvious, but permanently available. These relationships are available in all our preliminary design decisions, including those about the staircase's general character and overall spatial arrangement. When we speak about the character of the staircase as being domestic or public, simple or monumental, we have in mind a quite precise relationship between the space, the light, the size and material of the staircase, and the movement that occurs on it. There is a striking contrast between the inexhaustible richness of possible interpretations and the limited number of plausible or optimal solutions. This limitation is even more puzzling in more complex designs such as those of residences, libraries, theaters, and concert halls. Most spatial situations show a remarkable level of identity that cannot be derived from simple characteristics alone; it is something more complex and enigmatic (Vesely, 2006, p.77).

## References

Andrews, E. et al. (2016) *Spaces of the cinematic home behind the screen door.* Routledge advances in film studies; 34. New York; Routledge.

Bachelard, G. (1964) *The poetics of space.* Boston: Toronto: Beacon Press; Saunders Ltd.

Brill, L. W. (1983) Hitchcock's *The Lodger. Literature/Film Quarterly.* 11 (4), 257–265.

Campbell, J. W. P. et al. (2014) *Staircases: history, repair and conservation*. London: Routledge.

Choisy, A. (1899) *Histoire de l'architecture*. Paris: Gauthier-Villars.

Darke, C. (2005) *Alphaville (Ciné-File French Film Guides)*. I.B. Tauris.

Decobert, L. (2008) *L'Escalier dans le cinéma d'Alfred Hitchcock : Une dynamique de l'effroi*. Paris: Editions L'Harmattan.

Decobert, L. (2012) *L'escalier ou les fuites de l'espace : Une structure plastique et musicale*. Paris: Harmattan.

Deleuze, G. (1986) *Cinema 1: The movement image*. Cinema / Gilles Deleuze; Vol. 1. London: Athlone Press.

Diderot, D. (2000) *Paradoxe sur le comédien*. Paris: Flammarion.

Dixon, B. (2011) *100 silent films*. BFI screen guides. London: BFI.

Douchet, J. (2000) 'L'escalier', in Jacques Aumont (ed.) *La mise en scène*. Arts et cinéma. 1re éd Bruxelles: De Boeck Université.

Fabe, M. (2014) *Closely watched films: an introduction to the art of narrative film technique*. 10th anniversary edition. Berkeley: University of California Press.

Frost, A. and Vasiliev, Z. (2013) The 39 stats: Alfred Hitchcock's obsessions in numbers. *The Guardian*. 12 August. [online]. Available from: https://www.theguardian.com/film/picture/2013/aug/12/alfred-hitchcock-film-statistics (Accessed 3 August 2016).

Ina.fr, I. N. de l'Audiovisuel (1959) *Le mime Marceau démonstration montée d'escalier* [online]. Available from: www.ina.fr/video/I16041869 (Accessed 4 September 2016).

Jacobs, S. (2007) *The wrong house: the architecture of Alfred Hitchcock*. Rotterdam: 010 Publishers.

Janson, A. and Tigges, F. (2014) *Fundamental concepts of architecture: the vocabulary of spatial situations*. Basel/Berlin/Boston: Birkhäuser.

Koolhaas, R. et al. (2014) *Elements of architecture*. Venice: Marsilio Editori Spa.

Neufert, E. et al. (2000) *Architects' data*. 3rd ed. Oxford: Blackwell Science Publishers.

Nora, P. (1989) Between Memory and History: Les Lieux de Mémoire. *Representations*. (26), 7–24.

Pallasmaa, J. (2007) *The architecture of image: existential space in cinema*. Helsinki: Rakennustieto.

Penz, F. (2013) 'L'ombre de l'Acropole – La Villa Savoye construite par le cinéma', in Roberta Amirante et al. (eds) *L'invention d'un architecte. Le voyage en Orient de Le Corbusier*. Paris: La Fondation Le Corbusier. pp. 407–413.

Perec, G. (2008) *Species of Spaces and Other Pieces (Penguin Classics)*. Penguin Classics.

Templer, J. (1992) *The staircase – History and theories – Studies of hazards, falls and safer design*. Cambridge, Mass.: MIT Press.

Tobe, R. (2007) Plato and Hegel stay home. *arq: Architectural Research Quarterly*. 11 (01), 53.

Vesely, D. (2006) *Architecture in the age of divided representation: the question of creativity in the shadow of production*. Cambridge, Mass: MIT Press.

# 11

## JOINING THE DOTS

> In the shops we come across innumerable works devoted to everyday acts: housework, cookery, dressing, sleep, sexuality, and so on. We can even buy 'encyclopaedias' that attempt to assemble these particular aspects. But what is missing in such works is the whole, the sequence. Everyday acts are repeated (reproduced) by dint of this sequence and what it involves.
>
> *(Lefebvre, 2014, p.678)*

Lefebvre provides us with our starting point for this section. We have so far concentrated on the isolated fundamental elements of the architecture of our everyday life and environment, namely windows, doors and stairs. But, to paraphrase Lefebvre, what is missing is the whole, the sequence that assembles the elements of architecture, and this is what film is particularly good at: assembling sequences that have windows, doors and stairs, amongst others – in other words, we need here to join the dots. This chapter is in two parts: the first considers specifically the position of stairs, the central spine of the house which entrances, landings, corridors and doors feed from and into. The second part is a case study of a sequence in Godard's *Le Mépris* (1963), where all the elements are thrown together in joining even more dots. And let us come back to Robin Evans's quote that opened Part 3 as he rightly remarks that 'If anything is described by an architectural plan, it is the nature of human relationships, since the elements whose trace it records – walls, doors, windows and stairs – are employed first to divide and then selectively reunite inhabited space' (Evans, 1997, p.56). Having selectively studied the elements in the previous sections, it is now time to reunite them.

The staircase, which controls all the vertical movements, is the most important organ of a block of flats:

**FIGURE 11.1** Inhabiting staircases in *Delicatessen* (Jean-Pierre Jeunet and Marc Caro, 1991)

> For all that passes, passes by the stairs, and all that comes, comes by the stairs: letters, announcements of births, marriages, and deaths, furniture brought in or taken out by removers, the doctor called in an emergency, the traveller returning from a long voyage. It's because of that that the staircase remains an anonymous, cold, and almost hostile place.
>
> *(Perec, 1996, p.3)*

However, communal staircases are not only a passing place but can also be places for interactions. A good example is the scene in *Delicatessen* (Jeunet and Caro, 1991) where Louison (Dominique Pinon) is making soap bubbles on the landing just outside his flat door – to entertain the two children sitting on the steps.

At the same time, Robert (Rufus) is observing the whole scene from the landing above, and so is Julie (Marie-Laure Dougnac) as she climbs the stairs. In just over a minute a staircase becomes a place of encounter for Louison and Julie (they have never met before), entertainment and observation (the neighbours above and below). The landing has temporarily been turned into a stage, with spectators watching from the wings, while the steps provide a natural seating arrangement (Figure 11.1). Stairs are not only about connecting levels, but can also be inhabited, have a social function, and be far from hostile, provide indeed an endless field of potential relationships, as remarked by Vesely (Vesely, 2006, p.77).

## The end of stairs?

But the poignant aspect of this scene is that it may well become a thing of the past; not so much because inhabiting staircases is an eccentric idea in breach of health and safety regulations, but because stairs themselves are gradually becoming obsolete. This is what Koolhaas has to say on the matter:

> The diktat of the fifteenth-century architectural theorist Leon Battista Alberti 'The fewer staircases that are in a house, and the less room they take up, the more convenient they are esteem'd' has proved to be a prophesy for the contemporary condition. The staircase is considered dangerous – safety requirements limit architects' ambitions – and is possibly endangered, only still in existence in order to fulfil the requirement of having an exit strategy, though the stair may be making something of a comeback as an aid to fitness.
>
> *(Caution and Koolhaas, 2014, p.275)*

Staircases have indeed become an endangered species and have been replaced by lifts and elevators, although they survive mainly as escape staircases.

Koolhaas's suggestion that stairs may make a 'comeback as an aid to fitness' was made plain by former New York Mayor, Michael Bloomberg, who in 2013 issued 'an executive order requiring city agencies to promote the use of stairs. The Center for Active Design, a new non-profit organization, hopes to increase visibility and access to at least one staircase in all new buildings in the city' (Koolhaas et al., 2014, p.1237). The promotional material showed a poster with 'burn calories, not electricity – walking up the stairs just two minutes a day helps prevent weight gain. It also helps the environment' (Koolhaas et al., 2014, p.1237). Clearly stairs are not going to disappear any time soon, but my own analysis, which is by no means exhaustive, shows that there are a lot fewer stair scenes in film, in particular in the more recent decades, especially in American movies. This would seem to tally with Koolhaas's observation – not entirely surprising since we know that film shows with some accuracy the visible side of a society and an epoch. In other words, if stairs are used less and less by a society, this would be reflected in films. Films record and communicate with unique immediacy how people in different cultures and cities live in domestic buildings and communal spaces. Therefore film is a faithful translator not only of the evolution of the fabric of the city but also of social changes.

This raises another important issue, that of cultural differences – indeed when it comes to stairs, I would hypothesize that while they are commonly represented in European cinema, their appearance in US movies seems to be dwindling as stairs – apart from the odd fire-escape scene[1] – are replaced by elevators. This is perhaps not surprising as American architecture is not particularly known for its stairs and staircases. The stair book in *Elements of Architecture* is almost entirely devoted to European examples – compiled by Friedrich Mielke – bar six pages, out of 308, devoted to US fire escapes and New York boutique stairs (Koolhaas et al., 2014, pp.1202–1508). As a result, some of the great cinematic stair scenes are European – Eisenstein's Odessa steps being the most famous of all – or by European film directors, Hitchcock in particular, who continued to exploit the in-built dramatic qualities of stairs throughout his Hollywood films (see the Stairs chapter). And some of the great stair scenes in American cinema are a product of imported European-style architecture – for example, the house in *Gone with the Wind*, Tara, is of Greek Revival style, typical of the antebellum houses of the nineteenth-century Southern United States. There are obvious exceptions, such as the celebrated stair scene in *Sunset Boulevard* (Billy Wilder, 1950) and numerous scenes in Spike Lee's *Do the Right Thing* (1989) taking place on the brownstone stoops of Brooklyn townhouses.

## The rise of the lift

So if stairs are gone or at least more sparse, what of lifts and elevators? Let us restart with a key scene in *Pulp Fiction* (Tarantino, 1994). We are driving along downtown Los Angeles with Vince and Jules.[2] They park the car and grab their guns. They walk along the street towards the entrance of what looks like a hacienda-style Hollywood block of flats, continuously talking. They cross the entrance hall towards the lift – an old-fashioned lift with a brownish metal door.

They get into the lift and carry on talking about foot massage[3] throughout the duration of the lift ride. So far the scene is in real time or near real time – as there are two cuts that correspond to the entrance door to the apartment block and the lift door. A third cut occurs when they come out of the lift, as the camera is situated in the corridor. The rest of the scene is in real time, shot in Steadycam in front of Jules and Vince. It lasts around three minutes, with continuous dialogue, up to the point when they are about to knock on the door of the flat they are looking for.

**FIGURE 11.2** The lift in *Pulp Fiction* (Quentin Tarantino, 1994)

## Corridors

The lift provides the crucial link that joins entrance, two doors and the upper-floor corridor. What is of particular interest here is the corridor scene – all the more so since it is an element of architecture that has not been alluded to so far. Evans make the point that 'The history of the corridor as a device for removing traffic from rooms has yet to be written' (Evans, 1997, p.70).[4] Indeed, the literature on corridors is still very sparse, almost non-existent, and the corridor volume in *Elements of Architecture* must be one of the very few books on the subject and sheds some welcome light on the topic. Film, on the other hand, has long celebrated corridors in all shapes and sizes – suffice to mention just two: Hulot in *Playtime* (Tati, 1967) patiently waiting for Giffard to go down an impossibly long and echoing corridor, and in *The Shining* (Kubrick, 1980), Danny's eerie tricycle ride along the desolate corridors of the Overlook Hotel.[5]

*Pulp Fiction* provides us with yet another classic corridor scene, and one that benefits from being read in conjunction with Steven Connor's essay on corridors – 'A love letter to an unloved place' (Connor, 2004). The scene is long, or is perceived as such due to the endless corridors and twisting and turning, a typical hostel architecture with endless doors leading off the corridor:

> Corridors are institutional, associated not with private homes, but with schools, hospitals, hotels, town halls, office buildings, police stations, radio stations and barracks. The fundamental unhomeliness of corridors is suggested by the fact that the rooms to which they give access are nearly always numbered, in a way that rooms in a private house, however massive, could never be.
>
> *(Connor, 2004)*

Indeed, Vince and Jules are looking for a particular door, identified by its number. They finally find the door, but they are a touch too early so they have to linger around, still pursuing the same endless conversation…

> corridors are retarders rather than accelerators of movement. In this lies much of their strangeness. Corridors are dilatory, displacing, and distempering. They are for dallying, lingering, hovering, and, most of all, for waiting. As one moves through or along a corridor, which in theory is there to provide quick and direct access to different locations on one floor of a building, the persons one meets in the corridor are usually waiting.
>
> *(Connor, 2004)*

The *Pulp Fiction* corridor is definitely a 'retarder' – it allows Vince and Jules to fully engage in their pseudo-philosophical conversation; it is an important scene in the build-up of their characters.

**FIGURE 11.3** The corridor as 'retarder' in *Pulp Fiction* (Quentin Tarantino, 1994)

They are not just brutal killers after all, and they can argue their points well. But above all the long scene is building the tension towards the killing scene which is to follow. It is a form of suspense as defined by Hitchcock. We know what's going to happen, and as spectators we are almost willing them to get on with the action, which is being delayed. When they reach the right door and walk away because it's too early, the camera does not follow them but remains static as if waiting for them in front of the marked door – the rest of the conversation is shown from a distance – 'corridors are places of dangerous irresolution, and uncertain purpose […] They are vectors, hesitations, zones of passage, architectural prepositions' (Connor, 2004).

But we must briefly mention here Godard's *Alphaville* (1966), a film that features at least two seminal corridor and elevator scenes – as well as many spiral staircases, as mentioned in the previous chapter. In the opening section of the film, Lemmy Caution's (Eddie Constantine) arrival at his hotel is shot as a single unedited sequence that depicts him walking through the hotel's revolving doors, checking in, riding a glass-door elevator, followed by a backward tracking shot along the many twisting and turning corridors where Lemmy is accompanied by Natasha, the seductress, to his hotel room. No mention of foot massage, but the ancestry of the *Pulp Fiction* scene is very clear. Of relevance here is the notion of non-place – after Augé[6] – which started to be used in film theory by Wollen in particular (Wollen, 2002) and was reprised in Drake for his analysis of *Alphaville* (Godard, 1966):

> *Alphaville* is almost entirely made up of architectural non-places: the city is a patchwork of transitional zones – corridors, staircases, offices, hotel rooms – liberally interspersed with their characteristic signage – arrows, numbers, neon.

Corridors are non-places, spaces of transit. But as Wollen notes, 'Architecture in film is never just itself' (Wollen, 2002, p.199) and in both scenes – *Alphaville* and *Pulp Fiction* – the never-ending corridors with their many twists and turns, their drab and repetitive nature, are a metaphor for the vicissitudes of the lives of Lemmy Caution and Jules and Vince. Jules and Vince are in a funnel and a tunnel; they are in it together, there is no choice, no dithering, they are killers joined at the hip on a mission. For Jules and Vince and Lemmy Caution, the corridor scene anticipates the tribulations ahead. Their troubled life is expressed by the tortuous paths of non-places, a prime example of a spatially organized narrative.

*Drive* (Nicolas Winding Refn, 2011) provides us with yet another level of resolution in our 'joining the dots' investigation. Three scenes in quick succession need to be briefly analyzed. All involve the same set-up, the basement car park, the lift, the corridor and the apartment doors. In scene 1, driver (Ryan Gosling) parks his car in the apartment block basement and first encounters Irene (Carey Mulligan) as she comes up the lift. The next shot is a reverse shot from driver's point of view, showing Irene walking to her car as the lift door slowly closes. This is followed by driver coming out of the lift in the corridor. He is next in his flat contemplating downtown Los Angeles from his window, in the dark. A major difference compared to the *Pulp Fiction* scene is how quickly he gets from the basement to his flat – just over 20 seconds, quite an ellipsis in time and space. His flat is reduced to a corridor – a lift – flat interior – and the car basement. The lift is the crucial link between the flat and the garage, but we never see the outside of the block of flats. It's an assembly of a kit of parts, typical of the way film-makers negotiate the passage between the city and the interiors. It is a visual shorthand for architecture in the city. Except for an unusual 'worm's-eye view' establishing shot of the building exterior, a similar assembly of shots can be seen in *Limits of Control* (Jim Jarmusch, 2009) when Lone Man (Isaach de Bankolé) first arrives at his apartment in the Torres Blancas tower, Madrid. And in this case, Jarmusch's cinematography lingers over the architectural details as he is a fan of the building – therefore Lone Man's journey to his flat takes a minute, three times longer than for driver.

In *Drive*'s second scene, Irene, carrying a laundry basket, joins driver in the lift – he asks for her floor, they exchange brief glances and smiles while the lift goes up. It cuts to the lift door opening as she comes out; he is following her in the corridor. They both open their front doors without a word and enter. The first scene established the apartment-block configuration and that Irene and driver passed each other in the basement. The second scene, lasting 40 seconds, places Irene and driver in the same lift space and establishes that they are neighbours, two doors from each other along the same corridor. In the third scene, Irene's car has broken down in the car park of the local supermarket – driver, who happens to be around, helps her. From the supermarket car park we cut to the lift and, in the next shot, Irene is opening her apartment front door, making way for driver, who carries her grocery bags. The longest part of this scene is in the lift, with her son staring at driver. In this third scene, the shorthand is getting shorter and there are fewer and fewer dots to join – the time–space ellipsis has squeezed out the basement and the corridor. The architecture gets reduced to the very minimum, simply because scenes 1 and 2 allow the viewers to orientate themselves.

But we needed this spatial and social priming to understand scene 3. Film cuts the dull bits from our environment and does without the parts that have already served their purpose – but isn't that what we ourselves do without noticing it, as we go about our everyday life? Perec taught us that the spaces of our everyday life are neither continuous nor homogeneous, and that we don't really know where and how it assembles itself, precisely because everydayness is not evidence but opacity: a form of blindness. Therefore, isn't this cinematic spatial and temporal shorthand a reflection of how we perceive our environment? Or might it be that film further influences us in this process?

The lift and the corridor carry on being crucial to the film, and key scenes take place in them. In this downtown Los Angeles apartment block they are places of encounters, some good, some bad, and with no stairs in sight, for all that passes, passes by the corridors and the lift, and all that comes, comes through the corridors and the lift. There is no escape. Connor rightly makes the point that

> It is surprising how often corridors are scenes of violence. It is very hard for makers of gangster films or thrillers to resist the temptation of shoot-outs in corridors. In how many films does the heroine flee down a corridor from her assailant, hair flying and strappy shoes clacking? How many times have we seen the shotgun barrel appear round the corner at the end of the corridor, turning it into a shooting range, turning it into the barrel of a gun?'
>
> *(Connor, 2004)*

But corridors are also 'lieux de parole et de rencontres' – they are non-places that don't belong to anybody in particular. Their semi-private, semi-public nature can be liberating and a fertile ground for communication[7] – as in the scene when Irene's husband Standard (Oscar Isaac), freshly out of prison, is able to meet driver, thanking him for having helped his wife – a potentially tense situation. Film-makers often recognize the mental ground of architectural impact more subtly than an architect (Pallasmaa, 2007, p.33), and film may help us to identify complex situations that would otherwise escape us.

But let us conclude this section with Aldo Rossi, who reflects on architecture, and corridors, as a matrix of possible scenarios for human drama:

> In the project there is a long, narrow corridor sealed off at either end by a glass door: the first opens onto a narrow street; the second, onto the lake from where the blue of the water and the sky enters the villa. Of course, whether a corridor or a room, it is inevitably a place in which someone will say sooner or later, 'Must we talk about all this?' or 'See how things have changed!' and other things that seem to be taken from some screenplay or drama. The long afternoons and the children's shouts and the time spent with the

**206** An architectonic of cinema

family also are inevitable, because the architect had foreseen that the continuity of the house depended on its corridor – and not just in terms of its plan.

*(Rossi, 2010, p.34)*

Rossi's analysis points to an approach that exploits the potential of the corridor in our everyday life and everyday environment. He hints at a narrative expressive space approach, whereby the film (screenplay) within the architecture can articulate the spatial quality of a space, that can be rediscovered as a place as opposed to a non-place. It is an invitation to explore a matrix of situations where space becomes the receptacle of future events and experience.

### An architectonic reading of Godard's apartment scene in *Le Mépris* (1966)

The second part of this chapter rounds up the architectonic of cinema through the architectural vocabulary at play in the apartment scene in Godard's *Le Mépris*. It is an opportunity to evoke other elements of architecture not mentioned in the previous chapters, namely walls, ceilings, corners and objects. The scene analysis acts as a vehicle for a summary discussion on the subject, which is by no means exhaustive. It is a way of bringing together the dialectics of the architectonic of cinema into one coherent scene, which has the length and density necessary to justify a thorough spatial examination. All the spaces and rooms in the flat are used, and there is a complete unity of time and space. The scene lasts 30 minutes, about a third of the film, and is shot in real time or near real time.

The flat scene is pivotal to the whole story in the film. It opens when Camille (Brigitte Bardot) and Paul (Michel Piccoli) enter the flat. They arrive in their apartment as a couple and leave it 'decoupled', as if the flat's front door had had some supernatural properties. Certainly the flat itself is central to their discussion; it quickly becomes a contested space. As it becomes more and more obvious to Paul that Camille may have ceased to love him, he implies that they would have to sell the flat: while he works on his script in the study, she asks 'what would you do if I stopped loving you?' Paul's answer 'I wouldn't do the script and we would sell the flat'. At this point she answers that she would prefer to keep the flat, but later on, in their last discussion in front of the window, she says 'sell the flat, see if I care'. So the flat itself as a piece of real estate is central to their argument, but Godard also uses it in a most interesting way to dramatically express the unfolding narrative.

### Objects

The flat is in an unfinished state, the assumption is that they have recently moved in. As soon as they enter, Camille pauses and blurts out 'When will you call your friends about the curtains…I've just about had it', adding 'Red velvet…it's that or nothing'. This scene sums up

Camille's state of mind, she probably resents having to live with doors waiting to be hung, propped up against the walls, and light bulbs popping out of walls.

But of course the state of the flat is a reflection of the state of their relationship. Of particular interest are the objects and the furniture that are contained and dotted in space. While they are not listed as part of 'elements of architecture', objects and furniture nevertheless play a key role in our spatial perception. De Certeau et al. poignantly remarked that

> A place inhabited by the same person for a certain duration draws a portrait that resembles this person based on objects (present or absent) and the habits that they imply. The game of exclusions and preferences, the arrangement of the furniture, the choice of materials, the range of forms and colors, the light sources, the reflection of a mirror, an open book, a newspaper lying around, a racquet, ashtrays, order and disorder, visible and invisible, harmony and discord, austerity or elegance, care or negligence, the reign of convention, a few exotic touches, and even more so the manner of organizing the available space, however cramped it may be, and distributing throughout the different daily functions (meals, dressing, receiving guests, cleaning, study, leisure, rest) – all of this already composes a 'life narrative' before the master of the house has said the slightest word.
>
> *(De Certeau, 1990, p.145)*

In this case the objects and furnishing openly confess Camille and Paul's 'life narrative' in the sense that they are faithful indicators of Godard's narrative intentions. In particular the absence[8] of anything personal, expresses the lack of intimacy and stands for the hollowness of their relationship. They have made no effort to personalize the spaces apart from a full-size

FIGURE 11.4 *Le Mépris* (Jean-Luc Godard, 1963): the unfinished flat

**FIGURE 11.5** The statue in *Le Mépris* (Jean-Luc Godard, 1963)

statue[9] in the sitting room – the sorry witness of their first fight, she seems to hang her head in shame (see Figure 11.5). Colours are also symbolic: white walls and primary colours, blue, red and yellow, and recur throughout the film from the opening credits onwards. They spend time together on the red couch (love) and their final fight takes places on the blue chairs (discord). There is also a strange and rather incoherent mix of furniture – a designer couch and armchairs, while the dining-room table and chairs look rather anonymous. It speaks for a state of confusion. However sparse, the objects and furniture are useful pointers in the panoply of the film-maker, fully expressing the narrative stance. They fully participate in the formation of the film world and the dramatic atmosphere.

Interestingly, the flat is a real place, as opposed to a studio, in what seems to be a relatively new neighbourhood somewhere in Rome. The style is modern and points to a recent construction. It is a large flat, which consists of a long sitting room with a dining room at one end and a few steps leading to what seems to be a terrace on the other side. There is a kitchen by the dining room and a corridor leading to a study, bathroom and bedroom, conceived as a separate unit as it has its own door and small lobby. Their bedroom is off the main corridor entrance with its own separate bathroom.[10] It has the appearance of what one would call a large and comfortable place.

## Walls

The first scene is a long sequence shot [1'51"] where the camera is situated by the entrance (see Figure 11.6). The camera pans and rotates, and in this first shot we get a 360-degree vision of the flat. It is a form of establishing shot. After that, viewers can orientate themselves. All the other zones, the deeper spaces, bedrooms and bathrooms, are hinted at. But crucially, what we note is that it is an architecture of walls and holes in walls. The upper horizon of the film frame

Joining the dots **209**

**FIGURE 11.6** Doors as gaps between walls in *Le Mépris* (Jean-Luc Godard, 1963)

is level with the upper part of the door frame. It shows that a door is not a door, it is a gap between two walls. The lack of a complete framing – as the upper part is cut on most doors – denies its status of what Lefebvre calls 'the door as an object' that frames itself and reverts to the status of hole in the wall.[11]

As a result, a large proportion of the image is made up of walls – and are walls important? Do we notice walls? Should we notice walls? Certainly this film sequence raises such questions. The gaps between walls become spatial discontinuities. It is the triumph of walls.

So one possibility would be to read this scene as a reflection on walls – at least we can start in this way to get a different angle on this scene. Titled *Walls Have Feelings* (2000), Katherine Shonfield's book is an obvious reference for this section, especially her excellent analysis of *Repulsion* (Polanski, 1965) and *Rosemary's Baby* (Polanski, 1968) that unusually mixes filmic considerations in parallel with extracts from building catalogues and technical specifications:

> In the course of the film [*Repulsion*], the surfaces of the flat start to crack, and can no longer hold back the outside. At its climax, the walls begin literally to smear the edge between Deneuve and themselves [...] In *Repulsion*, Carol's fears are concentrated on the questionable integrity of the walls of her flat. These walls – unsponsored by either the Royal Institute of Chartered Surveyors, or Architects – are nevertheless remarkable in that they explicitly demonstrate three types of constructional failure, attendant on contemporary changes in building practice in post-war London. Damp penetration, cracking of internal surfaces, and failure of mastic sealants all come under the microscopic eye of Carol's technical inspection.
>
> *(Shonfield, 2000, pp.55–56)*[12]

The cinematic walls in Polanski's world of the 1960s present, unusually, a menace to their occupiers. They no longer protect but aggress. There is no such threat in *Le Mépris*, no damp patches or cracks in sight. However, the walls fulfil a different narrative function that we'll interpret here through Moles's own take, which throws new light on how we might perceive the humble wall with the idea of a 'wall as condenser of distance'[13] (Moles and Rohmer, 1998, pp.58–59). In this case we should read that walls can also separate emotionally and become 'condensers of emotions'. In other words, a wall as a condenser of distance, implies that if two people are miles apart they do not hear or see each other – the same as if they are on each side of a common wall, hence the idea of 'condensing distances'. But in the case of Paul and Camille the walls and the gaps that consistently separate them, in isolated frames (Figure 11.7), have the same effect – it is as if they were miles apart, the walls having condensed their emotions towards a state of incommunicability.

As part of the state of being unfinished, the walls are also completely bare. A couple of paintings are propped on the floor, waiting to be hung. There is, however, one painting hanging on the wall behind Paul's desk, a theatrical print. We particularly notice it as the camera frames it on its own for a few seconds. It is hard to fathom what the meaning of this shot is, but certainly Perec has plenty to say on the nature of walls and their relationship to paintings:

> I put a picture up on a wall. Then I forget there is a wall. I no longer know what there is behind this wall, I no longer know there is a wall, I no longer know this wall is a wall, I no longer know what a wall is. I no longer know that in my apartment there are walls, and that if there weren't any walls, there would be no apartment.
>
> *(Perec, 2008, p.39)*[14]

**FIGURE 11.7** Walls as 'emotional condensers' in *Le Mépris* (Jean-Luc Godard, 1963)

FIGURE 11.8 The door with no middle in *Le Mépris* (Jean-Luc Godard, 1963)

Perhaps Godard is trying to answer Perec's plea that we shouldn't forget that there is a picture on the wall and that behind the picture there is the wall – a shot dedicated to combating our natural propensity not to notice our everyday environment.

As mentioned previously, the doors have lost their function. Not the front door and not the bathroom doors. But the others have. And yet one door is of particular interest. The door leading to the study. It is unfinished and the middle glass pane hasn't yet been mounted. As a result both Paul and Camille 'practise' that door either by turning its handle and opening it or by stepping across the missing glass portion in the middle. Their use of the door undermines its very purpose, but it also reconnects with a slapstick cinema tradition with which Godard was familiar.[15] The result is vaguely comic, but more importantly it makes us notice that particular door, questioning its function and validity.

Parts of the flat are simply not shown: parts of the kitchen, part of their bedroom. We only get a glimpse of the second bedroom when Camille skirts around the decorator's ladder, most of the second bathroom is unknown and finally Paul's study is shown only from one side. The outside world is nearly absent, or rather ignored, the windows have only one function in the film: to provide light, although we can occasionally get a glimpse of the views past the protagonists – but they have no narrative function as such. The other usual window functions, ventilation and view, are not practised, the couple having withdrawn into themselves. Ventilation is mentioned, but not shown, as Camille finds it difficult to sleep with the window open at night – she uses this as a pretext for sleeping on the sitting room couch. Paul doesn't glance once at a window (Camille briefly looks out from the sitting room window), but he does mention the outside world when he asks Camille if she has noticed the ugly building going up in front.

## Corners

Ceilings are part of what has been ignored or simply not there,[16] due to the style of framing that cuts across the top of the doors. But floors are well represented throughout the scene. Apart from the kitchen and the two bathrooms that are tiled, there is a wooden parquet floor throughout the flat, with the addition of a couple of white shaggy rugs in the sitting room. But of all the spaces in a house or a flat, corners are probably the most neglected and rarely figure in films – or rather corners are always present, by default, but have no narrative function, and a chapter on the architectonic of corners would no doubt be a very slim one. We must therefore be grateful to Godard for having shot a scene where Camille takes refuge in the corner of the bathroom, sitting on the toilet and having a cigarette. Literature on corners is equally sparse,[17] except of course for Bachelard who devotes a chapter to them, stating that

> The point of departure of my reflections is the following: every corner in a house, every angle in a room, every inch of secluded space in which we like to hide, or withdraw into ourselves, is a symbol of solitude for the imagination; that is to say, it is the germ of a room, or of a house [...] that most sordid of all havens, the corner, deserves to be examined.
>
> *(Bachelard, 1994, p.136)*

Of course, what most viewers would have noticed is Camille sitting on the toilet – not so much the corner. True, toilets tend to be in corners, partly because bathrooms are small by nature. Nevertheless, this is a corner scene of some narrative significance, since Camille is getting away from Paul who has just slapped her face in the sitting room. Adding insult to injury, he quipped 'why did I marry a 28-year-old typist?' Moving to a corner of a bathroom is indeed the most intimate part of a flat or a house and, however disreputable a refuge, to paraphrase Bachelard, it deserves our attention.[18]

A corner, adds Bachelard, is 'a sort of half-box, part walls, part door [...] An imaginary room rises up around our bodies, which think that they are well hidden when we take refuge in a corner'. Camille is hoping for some respite from the argument, the first of three. The narrative implication is that she probably feels cornered as 'it is not easy to efface the factors of place'. She is sitting, pensive, withdrawn into her corner, as the expression goes, and Paul appearing at the door of the bathroom and questioning her further 'why the thoughtful air?', is a clear invasion of her privacy. He is peering over the half-box wall of her corner 'construct'.

Finally, the last element of cinematic architectonic to mention is the stairs. In fact, this is the first and the last space we see in the scene, as it corresponds to entering and exiting the flat. But its reappearance in the final scene is of great dramatic importance as, following their third fight, it is on the staircase that Camille pronounces the words 'je te méprise', twice, 'I despise you'. The scene picks up on the hostility and coldness inherent to communal stairs. It is a form of

**FIGURE 11.9** Inhabiting corners in *Le Mépris* (Jean-Luc Godard, 1963)

**FIGURE 11.10** Camille going down the staircase in *Le Mépris* (Jean-Luc Godard, 1963)

abandonment and the stairs are an appropriate place for such a statement as it implies going down, running away, exiting the flat and the relationship.

This flat scene is visualizing a portion of everydayness, it is a full demonstration of how to use the space, as a near-complete panoply of activities is performed in a very short space of time. It is an ideal vehicle for studying some of the elements of architecture in a single scene – where each of them is linked to the next one, not as a single element, but as part of a continuous space where the whole amounts to contributing to the joining of the dots.

Over the course of Part 3 we have redefined the elements of architecture as an 'architectonic of cinema', not so much in terms of their physical construct but in terms of the way they are experienced. The aim was to demonstrate that an architectonic of cinema was made up of the elements of architecture plus affect and emotions. We considered here windows, doors and stairs and evoked corridors, lift, walls, corners and objects. Clearly this is a brief and partial analysis and by no means exhaustive. Each chapter is replete with cinematic examples and for every one of those, readers could think of many more. The hope is to have proposed a novel and complementary approach to our understanding of architectural elements.

## Notes

1 New York-based films in particular, as fire staircases often populate the sides of apartment block façades. Naturally cinema has occasionally exploited this dramatic potential: the practice of sleeping on fire escapes on a hot summer's night can be observed in Alfred Hitchcock's 1954 movie *Rear Window*; in *West Side Story* (Robert Wise and Jerome Robbins, 1961), Tony (Richard Beymer) serenades Maria (Natalie Wood), not from a balcony, but on a New York fire escape; in *Breakfast at Tiffany's* (Blake Edwards, 1961), Holly (Audrey Hepburn) and Paul (George Peppard) escape from the party via the fire escape; and more recently in *Frances Ha* (Noah Baumbach, 2012), Sophie (Mickey Sumner) and Frances (Greta Gerwig) bask in the outdoor splendour of their fire escape staircase.
2 This is the often-quoted conversation on naming hamburgers in the US versus France: 'quarter pounder with cheese, the metric system and le royal with cheese'.
3 The conversation is related to one of Marcellus' acolytes who gave his wife Mia a foot massage and ended up with a speech impediment, having been thrown from the fourth floor of his apartment block. Vince and Jules ponder over Marcellus' action and the severity of the punishment in relation to the foot massage. It is intense and bordering on the metaphysical.
4 Adding, 'From the little evidence I have so far managed to glean, it makes its first recorded appearance in England at Beaufort House, Chelsea, designed around 1597 by John Thorpe. While evidently still something of a curiosity, its power was beginning to be recognised, for on the plan was written "A long Entry through all". And as an Italianate architecture became established in England so, ironically enough, did the central corridor, while at the same time staircases began to be attached to the corridors and no longer terminated in rooms'.
5 There is a good analysis of this scene in the corridor volume in *Elements of Architecture* (Koolhaas et al., 2014, pp.998–1005).
6 We know from Augé that the concept of 'non-place' designates spaces associated with transport, transit, commerce, leisure (Augé, 1995, p.94) and that they are the real measure of our time potentially quantifiable by totalling all the air, rail and motorway routes, the mobile cabins called 'means of transport' (aircraft, trains and road vehicles) (Augé, 1995, p.79). For Augé, non-places are a product of supermodernity: 'If a place can be defined as relational, historical and concerned with identity, then a space which cannot be defined as relational, or historical, or concerned with identity will be a non-place. The hypothesis advanced here is that supermodernity produces non-places meaning spaces which are not themselves anthropological places and which, unlike Baudelairean modernity, do not integrate the earlier places: instead these are listed, classified, promoted to the status of "places of memory", and assigned to a circumscribed and specific position' (Augé, 1995, pp.77–78).
7 During a group supervision with my Year 2 students, one of them described the potential of corridors in a student hostel situation – she talked about 'corridor-time' when they all come out of their room for a chat, sitting down in the corridor: 'it's informal...two start chatting and a third one comes and says "are we having a corridor-time?" and starts knocking on all the doors...about 12 doors...and often as many as 10 students come out'.

8  Lefebvre sees in the absence of objects an important meaning: 'If objects form a system – something we can accept in the case of functional objects, such as utensils and furniture – its meaning is to be found not in what it declares, but in what it dissimulates, which extends from the tragic to the mode of production via the malaise of daily life. The production of daily life, which is opposed to daily life as oeuvre, thus includes the production of everyday space and time, as well as the objects that fill up the everyday, the mass of objects intended to fill time and space. This mass is likewise simultaneously homogeneous and fragmented, and hierarchically organized' (Lefebvre, 2014, p.806).

9  Ancient statues are present throughout the film, as if recalling the Homeric odyssey experienced by the couple.

10  For an accurate plan of the flat, see McGrath, 2016, p.96.

11  In Lefebvre's *Production of Space*, there is a chapter on Spatial architectonics where he asks us to consider a door: 'Is it simply an aperture in the wall? No. It is framed (in the broadest sense of the term). A door without a frame would fulfill one function and one function only, that of allowing passage. And it would fulfill that function poorly, for something would be missing. Function calls for something other, something more, something better than functionality alone. Its surround makes a door into an object' (Lefebvre, 1991, p.209). Original French quote: 'voici une porte. Trou dans le mur ? Non, elle s'encadre. Sans encadrement, la porte accomplirait une fonction : permettre le passage; elle l'accomplirait mal. Il lui manquerait quelque chose. La fonction veut quelque chose d'autre, de plus, de mieux, que le fonctionnel. L'encadrement fait de la porte un objet'.

12  Shonfield adds: 'Even more insidiously than in *Repulsion*, the apparently innocent walls have swallowed up Rosemary's physical and architectural integrity. She becomes the embodiment of her own violated interior: a zone without borders. There is no longer an edge between Rosemary and her witchy neighbours, and it is only a matter of time before she fulfills her own twisted version of the Madonna role: by bearing the Devil's own son' (Shonfield, 2000, p.56).

13  'le mur est une condensation de la distance dans la mesure où la distance affaiblit, réduit, élimine, interdit, sépare. Le mur matériel, à l'abri duquel s'est formé notre moi profond, est une accumulation d'atomes lourds dans un petit espace, milieu de propagation des impulsions sensorielles [...] L'atténuation des phénomènes physiques est, en d'autres termes, liée au nombre d'atomes du milieu intermédiaire : plus ceux-ci sont nombreux, plus faible est le phénomène ; plus il est « lointain » dans ses apparences de l'autre côté de la paroi ; le mur condense donc bien l'espace. La personne qui est située de l'autre côté de mon mur mitoyen est d'autant plus éloignée psychologiquement – savoir dans ses effets, et dans les témoignages de sa présence – que ce mur est plus épais, qu'il compte plus d'atomes au mètre cube'. Moles goes on to add: 'Le mur est l'expérience la plus concrète que l'homme ait de la paroi ; le mur est physiquement la synthèse des propriétés de la paroi, il en est aussi historiquement l'archétype et ce n'est qu'une réflexion fonctionnelle qui en dissocie les propriétés. Jusqu'à ce jour, la seule analyse psychologique qu'on ait faite du mur a été une psychanalyse de l'habituel : épais, lourd ou mince, humide ou chaud, opaque, pâle ou ensoleillé, le mur était un substrat de l'habitation que l'architecte dotait de perfectionnements au gré d'une technologie dévorante. Il a fallu la rigueur fonctionnaliste du Bauhaus pour saisir dans les faits, et imposer dans les réalisations, la possibilité de dissocier les fonctions du mur sous l'angle perceptif au lieu de les accepter comme un composé de propriétés solidaires, évoquées par exemple par Bachelard'.

14  Perec adds that 'The wall is no longer what delimits and defines the place where I live, that which separates it from the other places where other people live, it is nothing more than a support for the picture. But I also forget the picture, I no longer look at it, I no longer know how to look at it. I have put the picture on the wall so as to forget there was a wall, but in forgetting the wall, I forget the picture, too. There are pictures because there are walls. We have to be able to forget there are walls, and have found no better way to do that than pictures. Pictures efface walls. But walls kill pictures. So we need continually to be changing, either the wall or the picture, to be forever putting other pictures up on the walls, or else constantly moving the picture from one wall to another'.

15 See for example the flat scene in *Prénom Carmen* (Godard, 1983) where the two characters playfully hit each other with doors and window frames as a prelude to a love scene.

16 Ceilings are barely mentioned in Bachelard but mentioned in Moles as part of 'la cloture visuelle', pondering 'dans l'espace de l'appartement le problème du jeu dialectique entre le plafond comme Ersatz de ciel et le plafond comme Couverture' (Moles and Rohmer, 1998, p.73). But they are celebrated in Perec: 'I like ceilings, I like mouldings and ceiling roses. They often serve me instead of a Muse and the intricate embellishments in the plasterwork· put me readily in mind of those other labyrinths, woven from phantasms, ideas and words', adding scornfully, 'But people no longer pay any attention to ceilings. They are made dispiritingly rectilinear or, worse still, done up with so-called exposed beams' (Perec, 2008, p.18).

17 As for Perec, his own fondness for ceilings, walls, doors and stairs did not stretch to corners, except for this quote listed under Placid small thought no 1: 'Any cat-owner will rightly tell you that cats inhabit houses much better than people do. Even in the most dreadfully square spaces, they know how to find favourable corners' (Perec, 2008, p.24).

18 We shouldn't be too 'down' on corners as in everyday language they are also associated with expressions such as 'this is a nice corner of the world' which has a French equivalent 'c'est un joli coin', meaning 'this is a nice place'.


## References

Augé, M. (1995) *Non-places: introduction to an anthropology of supermodernity*. London: Verso.

Caution, L. and Koolhaas, R. (2014) *Fundamentals: 14th international architecture exhibition – La Biennale Di Venezia*. First edition. Venezia: Marsilio Editori Spa.

Connor, S. (2004) A 'love letter to an unloved place', broadcast in BBC Radio 3's *Nightwaves*, 22 June 2004.

De Certeau, M. (1990) *L'invention du quotidien*. Collection Folio/essais 146, 238. Nouv. éd. Paris: Gallimard.

Evans, R. (1997) *Translations from drawing to building and other essays*. AA documents 2. London: Architectural Association.

Koolhaas, R. et al. (2014) *Elements of architecture*. Venice: Marsilio Editori Spa.

Lefebvre, H. (1991) *The production of space*. Oxford: Basil Blackwell.

Lefebvre, H. (2014) *Critique of everyday life*. The three-volume text. London: Verso.

McGrath, B. (2016) 'Drawing time', in Karen A. Franck (ed.) *Architecture timed: designing with time in mind*. John Wiley & Sons. pp. 88–97.

Moles, A. and Rohmer, E. (1998) *Psychosociologie de l'Espace*. Victor Schwach (ed.). Paris: Editions L'Harmattan.

Pallasmaa, J. (2007) *The architecture of image: existential space in cinema*. Helsinki: Rakennustieto.

Perec, G. (1996) *Life a user's manual*. London: Panther.

Perec, G. (2008) *Species of Spaces and Other Pieces (Penguin Classics)*. Penguin Classics.

Rossi, A. (2010) *A scientific autobiography*. Cambridge, Mass: MIT Press.

Shonfield, K. (2000) *Walls have feelings: architecture, film and the city*. London: Routledge.

Vesely, D. (2006) *Architecture in the age of divided representation: the question of creativity in the shadow of production*. Cambridge, Mass: MIT Press.

Wollen, P. (2002) 'Architecture and film – places and non-places', in Peter Wollen (ed.) *Paris Hollywood: writings on film*. London: Verso. pp. 199–218.

# PART 4
# CINEMATIC AIDED DESIGN

# 12
# TOWARDS A CINEMATIC APPROACH TO EVERYDAY LIFE AND ARCHITECTURE

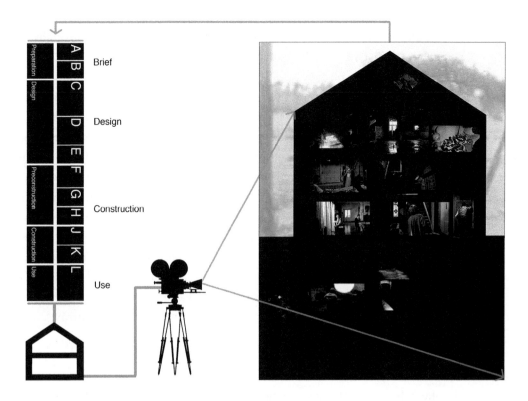

FIGURE 12.1 Closing the loop (house image by Martha Rawlinson)

The purpose of this concluding chapter is essentially to 'close the loop' opened up in the introduction (see Figure 12.1). Over decades, film-makers have used, expressed and characterized large portions of our built environment that constitute a formidable reservoir of post-occupancy studies. I referred to it as the most comprehensive lived-in building data in existence. While we could exploit this formidable archive in several different ways, one of the most promising avenues explored here is the uncovering of everyday life and how it relates to the built environment. The process of closing the loop implies eliciting potential avenues for the post-occupancy studies of everyday life in architecture. This book has modest design-orientated goals, as I am well aware of the pitfalls associated with an instrumental approach that could only lead to tautological considerations – as noted by Keiller.[1] The aim in this last section is therefore to show potential directions for the future, as opposed to guidelines or formulae.

The term Cinematic Aided Design is of course a play on words on Computer Aided Design (CAD). It implies an alternative to the current proliferation of CAD tools available to the design profession – or rather it is an approach that would complement it and be an attempt at a genuine aid to design. More accurately, it should be construed as injecting a form of cinematic intelligence at various stages of the design process. Images of cinema have shaped our collective imagination,[2] but there have been only very timid forays in the use of what I define as cinematic aided design (see Keiller's quote). Even the ubiquitous computer animated fly-throughs have not taken advantage of the last 120 years of screen language rhetoric.[3] In my view, CAD tools have failed creative architects, because they do not incorporate new artistic thinking, rooted in scenographic and cinematic practice, into architectural design, visualization and communication. And in a small way the Cinematic Aided Design approach is an attempt to address this lack.

Architecture straddles science and the humanities, and we need to inject some cinematic intelligence into architectural digital technology thinking if we are to maintain cultural diversity, individual creativity and human-centredness. And yet despite major advances in the design of virtual environments for 3D games and cinema, led by the need for human-centred, experience-based engagement, there has been no fundamental review of the principles on which Autocad, the dominant CAD software, is based since its release decades ago.[4] Lawson, Koolhaas and others have long raised concerns,[5] while *The Architectural Review* launched a campaign, with the concept of 'Notopia', denouncing the effect of the digital world on our built environment: 'The digital world is one of sensory deprivation: there is nothing to touch, taste or smell, a realm bereft of delight and intimacy of the most human kind' (Murray, 2016a), adding that

> by the end of the century our world will consist of isolated oases of glassy monuments surrounded by a limbo of shacks and beige constructions, and we will be unable to distinguish any one global city from another [...] its symptom (which one can observe without even leaving London) is that the edge of Mumbai will look like the beginning of Shenzhen, and the center of Singapore will look like downtown Dallas.
>
> *(Murray, 2016b)*

To a certain extent, cinema had anticipated this dystopic tendency; we only have to think of Tati's city in *Playtime* (1967), made of a seemingly infinite number of identical glazed urban blocks, cloned from the Esso office building erected at La Défense in 1963, itself inspired by the Lever House building by SOM (1952). And in *Her* (Spike Jonze, 2013), the city, a seamless collage of location shots from both Los Angeles and Shanghai, goes some way to affirm Murray's intuition.

However, we have to recognize that the CAD industry, BIM (Eastman, 2011) and parametricism (Schumacher, 2010), are here to stay and no doubt prosper. The thorny question of how architecture can overcome the hindrance to creative, diverse architecture represented by generic software, is somewhat linked to my own preoccupation, but I have no desire here to dwell any further on the shape of the digital future and its impact on buildings, only to note that there is much research and debate taking place, see for example: Cardoso Llach, 2015; Carpo, 2013; Spiller and Clear, 2014 to mention just a few.

My key concern remains that aspects of cinematics – centred on everyday life – can be combined with architectural culture and practice, to potentially catalyse a conceptual paradigm shift in architectural design process – or at the very least contribute to a new awareness. And to pursue this line of thinking we must turn briefly to Nicholas Negroponte, founder of the MIT media lab and one of the key pioneers of Computer Aided Design. He posits in *The Architecture Machine* (Negroponte, 1970, pp.46–47) that thanks to a simulation model

> a designer or a machine can observe the performance of an environment, a specific context. Someday, designers will be able to subject their projects to the simulations of an entire day or week or year of such events as use patterns and fast time changes in activity allocations.[6]

He further comments on a photographic record of a busy crossroads in a city: 'In this case the simulation is the real world, the best model but the most expensive. Similar displays will soon be manageable by computers' (Negroponte, 1970, p.46). Negroponte raises here a number of useful issues in relation to this chapter, and I interpret the moving-image camera as the 'machine' that can observe the performance of an everyday environment.

But the key question posed here is: in what way does a movie constitute a model of the world? Philip Steadman arrived at the same conclusion as Negroponte, by acknowledging 'the difficulty in experimenting with buildings in general [...] they are too big, too expensive, and it takes too long', hence the need for simulation in order to run 'the model faster than the world' (Steadman, 1975, p.33), and proposes a very useful definition of what a model is:

> The word 'model' is used here in the broadest sense, to mean any kind of representation, image or simulacrum of some object or phenomenon. In the present context the reference

is of course specifically to models or representations of buildings and other artefacts, and to models of the functional environments for which these buildings or designed objects are intended.

*(Steadman, 1975, p.29)[7]*

Mitchell also reminds us of the history of a general systematic framework for the comparative analysis of the forms of things that goes from Aristotle to Durand and beyond (Mitchell, 1975, p.53). Ultimately, computer models have gradually replaced hand calculations and the use of physical scale models in order to compare patterns of behaviour, for example, patterns of urban activities in the context of complex spatial environments, or to simulate human behaviour or daily routines (Steadman, 2016, p.294). Generally, models try first to replicate the existing patterns of the real-life environment and – following a phase of adjustment and calibration against the existing – can start to simulate the effects of changes from the exiting pattern in the near future (Steadman, 2016, p.295). All models of that type are about predicting the future.

So when Negroponte asserts that the real world is the 'best simulation model', we can construe that films, which do portray the 'real world'[8] (especially when shot on location), are modelling the world in the sense that they are a moving-image representation or a simulacrum. But the world they represent is only real in the sense that the streets and buildings are the existing ones, but the patterns of behaviour observed would have been directed by the film-maker. The modification of typical behavioural everyday routines can be observed in film when the baseline is disturbed, as discussed in a previous chapter. Such modifications constitute a form of modelling from the existing pattern, and we can further study systematic everyday behaviour patterns, for example according to building types as discussed in Chapter 6, with a view to establishing a general framework for the sake of comparative analysis.

The idea of films as model is clearly a loose, fuzzy and informal concept, although its potential has long been recognized:

> Stories, whether told orally, presented on the stage, read in a book, or seen in a film, are also simulations: ones that run on conscious minds. They were the very first artificially created simulations, designed long before computers were invented [...] All our visual experience is based on our models of the world, on simulations.
>
> *(Oatley, 2013, p.272)*

Film simulates and models everyday life worlds using spatially organized narratives. However, film does also present some unique and distinct features that are lacking in conventional models, namely the social, societal and human dimension, which is notoriously hard to compute. Sociologists such as Becker have argued that fiction films have often meant to 'analyze and comment on the societies they present, many times those in which they are made. Examples range from Gillo Pontecorvo's pseudo-documentary *The Battle of Algiers* (1966) to classic Hollywood fare like Elia Kazan's 1947 *Gentleman's Agreement*' (Becker, 2007, p.8). And historian Mark Ferro has claimed that 'As agents and products of history, films and the world of films stand in a complex relationship with the audience, with money and with the state, and this relationship is one of the axes of its history' (Ferro, 1983, p.358).

Film not only models the deep structure of everyday life in the form of architecturally expressed narratives, but can also reveal social practices where social relations are spatially organized. It is an approach that

> entails a critical analysis of the design process to ensure that the primacy of experience is not lost to the complexities or scale of the development; to failures of communication; to the imperatives of capital development, or to the lure of geometry as an end in itself.
>
> *(Dovey, 1993, p.267)*

In other words, we should resist the temptation to rely solely on the increasing availability of building and urban computer models that remain severely limited in their ability to comprehend the experiential, the social and the emotional dimensions of the lived and practised everyday spaces.

## Situations

I advocate here a human-centred approach in order to better understand the communicative nature of architecture interpreted through situations as represented in film. A cinematic approach to everyday life and architecture implies a focus on everyday environmental experiences and situations of people in the built environment. The notion of situations is therefore critical.

The previous chapters have dealt with the exploration of lived spaces – as well as elements of architecture – that constitutes a filmic description of a series of phenomena, referring to experiencing daily situations. In all of those cases, cinema takes from the building reality while at the same time transforming and reinterpreting even the most basic of architectural elements. It gives something back to the environment from which it has been taken, and questions fundamental notions that are often taken for granted. Hence the iterative loop, expressed in Figure 12.1, between the *house that cinema built* and the *house that the architect will build*. This cross-over is made possible because of the notion of lived experience and embodied cognition. Pallasmaa noted:

> Lived space is always a combination of external space and inner mental space, actuality and mental projection. In experiencing lived space, memory and dream, fear and desire,

value and meaning, fuse with the actual perception…The modes of experiencing architecture and cinema become identical in this mental space, which meanders without fixed boundaries.

*(Pallasmaa, 2001)*

This form of 'mental meandering' is crucial to our understanding of architectural situations elicited through film by its performative character. Vesely points out that

when we are looking at a photograph, a drawing, or a model of the same building [...] we are to some extent prisoners of an abstracted and mediated view. True, we can focus differently and see things precisely, but only with the help of our imagination as the main source of concreteness and embodiment. It is only in perceptual experience that we can freely and fully observe, explore, and move around the building.

*(Vesely, 2006, p.60)*

That is true of photography, drawings and physical models, but cinema affords a different experience much closer to the lived space as argued by Pallasmaa:

A film is viewed with the muscles and skin as much as by the eyes. Both architecture and cinema imply a kinesthetic way of experiencing space, and images stored in our memory are embodied and haptic as much as retinal pictures [...] Both art forms define frames of life situations of human interaction and horizon of understanding the world.

*(Pallasmaa, 2007, p.18)*

This is a commonly held phenomenological view of film that has been explored extensively – see for example: Trotter, 2008; Marks, 2000 and Sobchack, 1991 – amongst others.

Film provides us with a formidable array of interpretive human situations,[9] events and experiences of everyday life. The concept of situations is relevant here as 'We experience architecture in the form of situations [...] We experience a situation as architectural by virtue of the way in which it noticeably shapes the spatial conditions of our movements and activities' (Janson and Tigges, 2014, p.284). Lefebvre also referred to situations in relation to the everyday and the theory of 'moments' as he explored the relationship between the special ('la fête') and the ordinary ('la banalité') – a concept already explored in the chapter on rhythmanalysis. However, for Lefebvre, the moment creates situations, although they do not coincide, and while he acknowledges its spatial dimension, it is essentially a temporal concept:

Like time, the moment reorganizes surrounding space: affective space – a space inhabited by symbols which have been retained and changed into adopted themes (by love, by play, by knowledge, etc.). The space of the moment, like time, is closed off by constitutive decisions.

*(Lefebvre, 2014, p.647)*

In other words, moments in time create situations that get interwoven into the fabric of everyday life that change our spatial perception as our daily environment turns into an 'affective space'. But more useful here is Vesely's use of situations:

The best place to start is in the sphere of typical situations close to everyday existence. Because we always live somewhere, the situations most familiar to us are those related to the place of our dwelling [...] What gives such situations a very high degree of stability is their repetitive nature originating in the daily cycle of human life, which has its ultimate source in primary cosmic conditions and movements. It is on this level that the identity (sameness) of morning, of evening, and of the seasons is most conspicuously manifested.

*(Vesely, 2006, pp.376–377)*

From Vesely's point of view, the nature of situations is associated not only with daily human activities but also with the very nature of its settings and environment.[10] However, he also warns that 'the surprising degree of integrity in the character of well-established situations, preserved under changing conditions and in different places, resists full explanation'[11] (Vesely, 2006, p.382), partly because of the difficulty that we have of being objective when we are immersed within a situation. By way of exploring the 'character of well established situations' Vesely refers to the example of the French café as follows:

If we look closely at a concrete example – a French café, for instance – it is obvious that its essential nature is only partly revealed in its visible appearance; for the most part that essence is hidden in the field of references to the social and cultural life related to the place. Any attempt to understand its character, identity, or meaning and its spatial setting that uses conventional typologies, relying solely on appearance, is futile. Its representational, ontological structure can be grasped through a preunderstanding that is based on our familiarity with what is being studied and with the segment of world to which it belongs. Preunderstanding in this case is a layered experience of the world, acquired through our involvement in the events of everyday life. The identity of the French café is to a great extent defined by the café's institutional nature, rooted in the habits, customs, and rituals of French life. Its identity is formed in a long process during which the invisible aspects of culture and the way of life are embodied in the café's visible fabric, as if they were a language conveyed in written text. The visible 'text' of the café reveals certain common, deep characteristics, such as its location, its relation to the life of the street, its transparency of enclosure, a certain degree of theatricality (the need both to see the life of the outside world and to be seen in it, as if the café-goer were an actor), an ambiguity of inside and outside expressed not only in the transparency of enclosure but also in the café's typical furniture, and so on. These are only some of the characteristics that contribute to the identity and meaning of the French café as a culturally distinct typical situation.

*(Vesely, 2006, pp.77–79)*

This is a very useful example as this is where film can, I believe, help in eliciting such deep structures involving complex social, cultural, anthropological features amongst others – yet at the same time in a very banal and ordinary setting, a place that Lefebvre construes as 'an extra-familial and extra-professional meeting place […] a place where the regulars can find a certain luxury, if only on the surface; where they can speak freely […] where they play' (Lefebvre, 2014, p.63) – a place that can be associated with 'moments' as well as everyday banality.

Pursuing the same theme, the film-maker who comes to mind to reveal the identity of the French café as practised and lived space, is Eric Rohmer (Jean-Luc Godard would also be a contender). There isn't a film by Rohmer without one or even several café scenes, apart of course from his costume films. Perhaps this is not surprising as we know that, for most of his life, Rohmer used Parisian cafés for meetings, for writing and for observing situations that would later make their way into his films (de Baecque and Herpe, 2016). Three very different scenes come to mind. In the first one, *La Femme de l'Aviateur* (1981), Anne (Marie Rivière) and a girl friend enter a café-brasserie, Le Chaillot. They want to have a quick lunch and at first have to stand as no tables are free.

This quite long scene (six minutes) is shot on location. The crowded and noisy lunchtime café-brasserie is conveyed in all its detail: the hunt for a table, the difficulty in calling the

**FIGURE 12.2** Café scene in *The Aviator's Wife* (Eric Rohmer, 1981)

waitress, ordering the food, while at the same time eliciting the special intimacy that the two women enjoy despite, or rather because of, a busy café environment (translated by Rohmer's use of close-ups). The second film with several café scenes is *Les nuits de la pleine lune* (*Full Moon in Paris*, 1984). In the first scene of interest here, Octave (Fabrice Luchini) meets Louise (Pascale Ogier). They are old friends but Octave is in love with her, and throughout the film he is attempting to woo her without much success. It's a long scene, eight minutes, taking place in the afternoon, involving two characters essentially talking and flirting – but also visiting the basement bathroom and observing others around them.

The second scene shows a typical 'moment' outside their daily life, as they are both engaged in other relationships, that turns the anonymous, and almost empty, café environment into an affective and private space. The last scene captures yet another dimension; it takes place very early in the morning (it's still dark), and sees Louise entering a very small local café. She orders

**FIGURE 12.3** Café scene (1) in *Full Moon in Paris* (Eric Rohmer, 1984)

**FIGURE 12.4** Café scene (2) in *Full Moon in Paris* (Eric Rohmer, 1984)

a coffee and sits in a corner next to a man drawing (László Szabó). She reluctantly engages in a conversation with a stranger, as may happen in any public place, but warms to his story and his children's drawings. Again this is a long scene that speaks of the poetic of the café, the men standing at the bar, the conversation with a stranger.

Rohmer carefully exposes the strata of everyday life in a French café and allows us to experience this particular world in all its intimacy. As spectators we become involved in events and situations that would be otherwise inaccessible to us.

## Atmosphere

In search of the 'Magic of the Real', Zumthor too marvels at an everyday life scene in a café: 'Café at a students' hostel, a thirties picture by Baumgartner. Men just sitting around – and they're enjoying themselves too. And I ask myself: can I achieve that as an architect – an atmosphere like that, its intensity, its mood' (Zumthor, 2006, p.19). In his quest for atmosphere, Zumthor is marvelling at a photograph, but later he also refers to film: 'A place of great learning for me in this respect is the cinema. Of course the camera team and directors assemble sequences in the same way. I try that out in my buildings' (Zumthor, 2006, p.45). Architecture generates spatial atmospheres that are linked to the notion of situations: 'An atmosphere is the expressive force through which a situation that has been engendered by architecture seizes us in affective terms all at once and as a totality' (Janson and Tigges, 2014, p.26). It is a holistic measure that is hard to define, and yet it pervades a space and is haptically perceived: 'How do people design things with such a beautiful natural presence, things that move me every single time. One word for it is atmosphere. [...] the task of creating architectural atmosphere also comes down to craft and graft' (Zumthor, 2006, p.11).

Film helps us to attain something like fragments or moments of atmospheres, pertaining to everyday life situations.[12] The notion of atmosphere is 'skin deep', in the sense of tactile and haptic, which doesn't mean that it is shallow, but it is based on first impressions. The atmosphere of the situation is the tip of a very large iceberg, which lurks under the surface. Getting underneath the surface implies plunging into the political, the socio-economical, the anthropological, the historical and many more layers. The film stays at the surface, and yet it embodies some of the invisible deep strata of everyday life. It is interloping between the atmosphere and the situation.

The film-maker has constructed a world that we are invited to enter and share with other viewers in the same way we would enter a café, a home, a museum or a hospital. We can be fully immersed in its atmosphere and climate without necessarily grasping the essential nature of the situation, which is only partly revealed in its visible appearance, as argued by Vesely. But we get something extra: the affective dimension of film that often reveals hidden dimensions between the perceptual and the affect. In real life we experience space perceptually but not necessarily emotionally. But as the story unfolds in a film, the affective dimension derives from the people, the actors, who are carefully deployed in a spatially organized fashion. And, as shown in Chapter 2, film simplifies reality through spatial and emotional characterization. In real life our minds may wander, not notice, we may dream of an elsewhere, but in film our attention is being directed. Merleau-Ponty argues that our 'perceptual field is infinite and deployed across the horizon. And whatever object one may focus on, it always stands out from the completeness of the world'[13] (Zernik, 2006, pp.104–105). But through the cinematic framing our horizon is restricted, we are made to focus on what matters to the construction of the film's world.

In particular we start to participate in the everyday life of others that so often eludes us. It ranges in scale from large scenes to smaller details, as any

> given film can bring something to our explicit attention within the framed image, and within the represented and fictional reality of a work, that would not normally be selected [...] in everyday life experience or, indeed in other films. [...] bubbles forming in a cup of coffee in a Parisian café (in Godard's *Two or Three Things I Know About Her*).
>
> *(Yacavone, 2015, p.177)*

Part 1 considered the various aspects of everyday life in relation to everyday environment with an emphasis on the dwelling, while Part 3 dealt specifically with a selection of the elements of architecture. But no straight transmission from film to architectural design was offered, only a series of observations on lived spaces. There are no possible literal translations; we cannot leave it to the raw filmic pictures to do the job of 'transference', as indeed 'while I am looking at an object I cannot imagine it' (Wittgenstein, 1981, p.108). We must therefore somehow evoke the power of images and bring 'the image to the very limit of what he is able to imagine' (Bachelard, 1964, p.227). We must find ways of transforming the unsolicited moving pictures into ephemeral oneiric images, we cannot simply follow what we see on the screen; that can only be a departure point. This is a complex and yet simple 'model', which opens new avenues, and one that pertains to the world of cinematic-assisted imagination. Or to put it another way, we may need to consider and 'restore the subjectivity of images and to measure their fullness, their strength and their transsubjectivity' (Bachelard, 1964, p.xix). The purpose of this book is to open new horizons, state novel problems and propose innovative conceptual tools. The consideration of what Lefebvre referred to as the 'minor magic of everyday life' will hopefully open up the path to an innovative reflection on the complexity of architecture as experience and the need for a more humanistic-based approach.

## Notes

1 We have to be wary of Keiller's remark: 'Critically significant architects such as Jean Nouvel and Bernard Tschumi have produced buildings informed by their readings of cinematic space, which seem

230 Cinematic aided design

to draw mainly on the idea of cinematic montage. In these, film space was considered as a model for architectural space, but more recently much of the discussion of film in architectural circles appears to have declined into an exploration of influences that the imageries of architecture and cinema exert on one another' (Keiller, 2013, pp.141–142).

2 Wenders rightly reminds us that 'Our contemporary life as it is would be completely different if the 20th century had happened without the cinema […] life now in the early 21st century is completely formed by the fact that the 20th century was the century of the moving image – the moving image changed our way of thinking, moving around and seeing things (Wim Wenders in Conversation on *Wings of Desire* Axiom Films DVD Bonus 2003).

3 In the high-profile digitally-animated renderings for rebuilding Ground Zero/the World Trade Center, McGrath and Gardner noted that 'The great outpouring of digitally animated renderings for the rebuilding of Ground Zero and the World Trade Center Memorial Competition showed dramatically that digital modelling and animation have entered the public sphere and imagination. In spite of the enormous expense, labour as well as technologies and talents involved, these presentations were uniformly boring and non-communicative. It is remarkable that the elaborate presentations lacked any depth of contact with either the robust history of architectural language representation techniques, or the power of moving cinematic images, the most universal of contemporary communicative languages' (McGrath and Gardner, 2007, p.8).

4 'AutoCad', first released in 1982, is still the dominant software package in architecture, engineering and construction, with an 85 per cent market share and over 8 million users worldwide: (www.wikinvest.com/stock/Autodesk (ADSK)).

5 Lawson notes that 'Increasingly, architects are using generic software that can address form only as abstract geometry' (Lawson, 2002, p.331), while Koolhaas remarks that 'Representation is more and more homogenous through the computer, which removes any part of authenticity'; […] 'if we don't do anything, we will be living in a virtual space – but built' (Koolhaas, 2008).

6 It is as if Negroponte was anticipating Deb Roy's research to come 40 years on: 'Imagine if you could record your life – everything you said, everything you did, available in a perfect memory store at your fingertips, so you could go back and find memorable moments and relive them, or sift through traces of time and discover patterns in your own life that previously had gone undiscovered. Well that's exactly the journey that my wife and collaborator Rupal and my family began five and a half years ago. It began on the day that we walked into the house with our first child, our beautiful baby boy. And we walked into a house with a very special home video recording system' (Roy, 2012).

7 Steadman added that '"Models in the material world" would thus be representations of buildings or artefacts in drawings, diagrams, photographs, in written or otherwise encoded marks on pieces of paper, or as solid material models made out of cardboard or wood; and "models in our heads" would of course be mental images or pictures of these same buildings and objects'.

8 See Chapter 2 for a discussion on film and realism.

9 Neuroscientists and psychologists have demonstrated that there was a deep cognitive engagement with film, thanks to our mirror neuron activities (Shimamura, 2013, p.20) that helps us to identify with the characters on the screen – a phenomenon often referred to as 'empathy'. Konigsberg in particular remarks that 'Most of the experiments on mirror neurons must, by necessity, require the subject to perceive the action or emotion in a picture, which is likely to produce some major distinctions from seeing an action or emotion on someone's face in actuality. Crucial differences also exist between looking at an image in a test situation and sitting in a movie theater watching the image on a large screen. And there are also the distinctions between my own emotional sensitivity and history and those of a person next to me […] part of the brain responsible for our sense of self shuts down when we are experiencing something like a film. I don't think we ever lose the sense of "me" when watching a film but our sense of self is certainly diminished and the barrier around us removed, allowing us at times an astonishing intimacy with the world and faces on the screen. Neuroscience in its study of the brain gives us insight into our most intimate moments in the theater' (Konigsberg,

2007, p.17). Phenomenology and cognitivism now share some common ground, as acknowledged by Hochberg: 'The theoretical proposal that perceptual experience be thought of as expectancies about sensorimotor contingencies, rather than as expressions of mental representations, is endorsed' (O'Regan and Noë, 2001, p.986).

10 Vesely adds that 'Practical situations are usually formed spontaneously. On the deeper level, they are shaped not only by our exploration of new situational possibilities, individual preferences, intentions, and desires but also by the given conditions of everyday life' (Vesely, 2006, p.375).

11 He continues as follows: 'The reasons for that resistance are not difficult to find, as Gadamer points out: "The very idea of a situation means that we are not standing outside it and hence are unable to have any objective knowledge of it. We are always within the situation, and to throw light on it is a task that is never entirely completed. This is true also of the situation in which we find ourselves with regard to the tradition that we are trying to understand"' (Vesely, 2006, p.382).

12 For an analysis of Zumthor's notion of atmosphere applied to film, I have attempted to apply his criteria to Deray's *La Piscine* (1969) – see Penz, 2014.

13 My translation from the French: 'Pour Merleau-Ponty, le champ perceptif est infini, car il s'inscrit sur fond de déploiement d'un horizon. Quel que soit l'objet que je fixe, c'est toujours sur la complétude du monde qu'il se détache'.

## References

Bachelard, G. (1964) *The poetics of space*. Boston: Toronto: Beacon Press; Saunders Ltd.

Becker, H. S. (2007) *Telling about society*. Chicago: University of Chicago Press.

Cardoso Llach, D. (2015) *Builders of the vision: software and the imagination of design*. New York, NY: Routledge.

Carpo, M. (ed.) (2013) *The digital turn in architecture 1992–2012*. AD reader. Chichester: Wiley.

de Baecque, A. and Herpe, N. (2016) *Éric Rohmer, a biography*. Berlin, Boston: De Gruyter.

Dovey, K. (1993) 'Putting geometry in its place: Toward a phenomenology of the design process', in David Seamon (ed.) *Dwelling, seeing, and designing: toward a phenomenological ecology*. Albany: State University of New York Press.

Eastman, C. M. (ed.) (2011) *BIM handbook: a guide to building information modeling for owners, managers, designers, engineers and contractors*. Second ed. Hoboken, N.J.: Wiley.

Ferro, M. (1983) Film as an agent, product and source of history. *Journal of Contemporary History*. 18 (3), 357–364.

Janson, A. and Tigges, F. (2014) *Fundamental concepts of architecture: the vocabulary of spatial situations*. Basel/Berlin/Boston: Birkhäuser.

Keiller, P. (2013) *The view from the train: cities and other landscapes*. Verso.

Konigsberg, I. (2007) Film studies and the new science. *Projections*. 1 (1), 1–24.

Lawson, B. (2002) CAD and creativity: does the computer really help? *Leonardo*. 35 (3), 327–331.

Lawson, B. (2007) *How designers think: the design process demystified*. Fourth ed. Amsterdam; London: Architectural.

Lefebvre, H. (2014) *Critique of everyday life*. The three-volume text. London: Verso.

Marks, L. U. (2000) *The skin of the film: intercultural cinema, embodiment, and the senses*. Durham: Duke University Press.

McGrath, B. and Gardner, J. (2007) *Cinemetrics: architectural drawing today*. Chichester: Wiley-Academy.

Mitchell, W. (1975) 'Vitruvius Computatus', in Dean Hawkes (ed.) *Models and Systems in Architecture and Building*. First ed. Hornby Eng.: Construction Press.

Murray, C. (2016a) *The Architectural Review: How the Internet Has Promoted the Banality of 'Notopia'* [online]. Available from: www.archdaily.com/791759/ar-issues-how-the-internet-has-promoted-the-banality-of-notopia (Accessed 6 February 2017).

Murray, C. (2016b) *The Architectural Review: On 'Notopia,' the Scourge Destroying Our Cities Worldwide* [online]. Available from: http://www.archdaily.com/789475/ar-issues-on-notopia-the-scourge-destroying-our-cities-worldwide (Accessed 6 February 2017).

Negroponte, N. (1970) *The architecture machine: toward a more human environment.* Cambridge, Mass: MIT Press.

Oatley, K. (2013) 'How cues on the screen prompt emotions in the mind', in Arthur P. Shimamura (ed.) *Psychocinematics: exploring cognition at the movies.* Oxford; New York: Oxford University Press. pp. 269–284.

O'Regan, J. K. and Noë, a (2001) A sensorimotor account of vision and visual consciousness. *The Behavioral and brain sciences.* 24 (5), 939-73-1031.

Pallasmaa, J. (2007) *The architecture of image: existential space in cinema.* Helsinki: Rakennustieto.

Penz, F. (2014) 'Atmosphère d'Eau Sauvage: Reflections on La Piscine (1969)', in Christopher Brown and Pam Hirsch (eds) *The cinema of the swimming pool.* New Studies in European Cinema. Bern, Switzerland: Peter Lang. pp. 101–119.

Roy, D. (2012) The data family. *Significance.* 9 (4), 34–37.

Schumacher, P. (2010) *The autopoiesis of architecture: v. 1: a new framework for architecture: a conceptual framework for architecture.* John Wiley & Sons.

Shimamura, A. P. (2013) 'Psychocinematics: issues and directions', in Arthur P. Shimamura (ed.) *Psychocinematics: exploring cognition at the movies.* Oxford; New York: Oxford University Press. pp. 1–26.

Sobchack, V. (1991) *The address of the eye: a phenomenology of film experience.* Princeton University Press.

Spiller, N. and Clear, N. (eds) (2014) *Educating architects: how tomorrow's practitioners will learn today.* New York: Thames & Hudson.

Steadman, P. (1975) 'Models in our heads, models in the material world, and models in the world of objective knowledge', in Dean Hawkes (ed.) *Models and systems in architecture and building.* First ed. Hornby Eng.: Construction Press. pp. 29–34.

Steadman, P. (2016) Research in architecture and urban studies at Cambridge in the 1960s and 1970s: what really happened. *The Journal of Architecture.* 21 (2), 291–306.

Trotter, D. (2008) Lynne Ramsay's Ratcatcher: towards a theory of haptic narrative. *Paragraph.* 31 (2), 138–158.

Vesely, D. (2006) *Architecture in the age of divided representation: the question of creativity in the shadow of production.* MIT Press.

Wittgenstein, L. (1981) *Zettel.* Second revised edition. G. E. M. Anscombe and G. H. von Wright (eds.). Oxford, England: John Wiley & Sons.

Zernik, C. (2006) 'Un film ne se pense pas, il se perçoit' Merleau-Ponty et la perception cinématographique. *Rue Descartes.* 53 (3), 102–109.

Zumthor, P. (2006) *Atmospheres: architectural environments – surrounding objects.* Birkhäuser GmbH.

# INDEX

Page numbers in *italics* refer to illustrations, those followed by n are notes, and those with a p in front are plates.

*Abigail's Party* 109
Adorno, Theodor 43–4, 48n19
'affective space' 225
AHRC 4, 7n5
Akerman, Chantal 40, 65–84, 84n25, 98n9; and Perec 71–4
Alberti, Leon Battista 138, 200
*Alice in Wonderland* 159
*All the Way Up* 109, *110*
*Alphaville* 184–5, *184*, *185*, 203–4
Amad, Paula 48n19
ambiguity and everyday life 93–4
*Amélie* 59, 111, 158, *158*
*Amour* 55
Anderson, Lindsay 21
Anderson, Stanford 89–90
Anderson, Wes 79–80
Andrews, Eleanor 179
'animated staircase section' 187–9
*Another Year* 110, 168–9
anti-realist approach and everyday life 42
Antonioni, Michelangelo 136, 144–52, 168
any-space-whatever 78
Apollinaire, Guillaume 151–2, 154n17
*Approches de quoi* [Approaches to what] 66
Aragon, Louis 81

architectonic of cinema 125–32
'Architects and research-based knowledge' 3
*Architectural Design (AD)* 22, 25–6
*The Architectural Review* 98n11, 220
*Architecture and the Built Environment* 27, 111
*The Architecture Machine* 221
'architecture of death' 23
*Architecture of the Everyday* 25
*Architectures d'Aujourd'hui* 33n39, 128–9, *128*, 141, 153n8, 192–3
*Les Archives de la Planète* 48n19
Aristotlean five-stage narrative arc 56, 63n14
*L'Arroseur Arosé* 56
'art of joining' 128
*The Art of Living* 118n14
As Found concept 20–1
As Found movement 5, 22
*As Found: The Discovery of the Ordinary* 20
atmosphere 228–9, 231n12
*Attempt at the Rhythmanalysis of Mediterranean Cities* 86
Augé, Marc 203, 214n6
Austen, Jane 56
'AutoCad' 230n4
*The Aviator's Wife* 226–7, *226*
*L'Avventura* 150–1, *150*, 161, 168

**234** Index

Bachelard, Gaston: ceilings 216n16; corners 212; doors 166, 168; *La poetique de l'espace* 16; oneiric house 105–7; outside and inside 137; rhythmanalysis 97n1; roof 134; stairs 194
*Badlands* 40–1
Bailey, Kenneth 117n4
*Ballet Mécanique* 189, *190*
Ban, Shigeru 26
banal 20, 26, 30n11, 42–3, 83n19, 116, 149
Banham, Reyner 32n32, 98n11
'baseline' 56–8, 62n13, 103
Bass, Saul 195n3
Bates, Stephen 24–5, 33n39
*Bâtir* 153n8
Battersea AHRC project 119n20
*The Battle of Algiers* 223
*Battleship Potemkin* 186–7, *187*, 195–6n7
Baudelaire, Charles 149
Bazin, André 83n20, 134, 173, 174n1
Becker, Howard S. 222
Beckett, Samuel 187
'bedroom film' genre 72–4
Bellos, David 30n11, 68
Benjamin, Walter 11, 127
Berke, Deborah 25
*Billy Liar* 109
BIM 221
*Birdman* 162–3, *162*
Bishop, Peter 27–8
Blanchot, Maurice 17, 59
*Bleak Moments* 109
Block, Bruce 157
Blondel, Francois 183–4, *183*
Bloomberg, Michael 200
*Blue Velvet* 57–8, *58*
'Bluebeard temptation syndrome' 166–8
bomb 56, 62n12
boredom and everyday life 59–60
Bourdieu, Pierre 28, 33n42
*Le Bourgeois gentilhomme* 7n2
*Boyhood* 116
Brand, Stewart 3
Brecht, Bertolt 42, 47n6, 47n9, 47–8n10
Bresson, Robert 95
*Bringing Out the Dead* 116
British Documentary Movement 21

British New Wave 21
Brutalism documentary 53–4
Burch, Noël 163–4, 165, 175–6n8

*The Cameraman* 187
Campbell, James W. P. 182–3
Carné, Marcel 134
Carroll, Noël 52–3, 61n6, 61n7
*Cause Commune* 16
Cavell, Stanley 39, 44, 45–6, 49n23, 56, 112
ceilings 212, 216n16
Center for Active Design 200
*La Chambre* 72–3, *73*
*chambre de bonne* 133
Chaplin, Charlie 42, 47n8, 157, 176n10
*Charlotte et son Jules* 73–4, *74*
Chenal, Pierre 128, 130, 153n8, 192–3
*Chevalier* 117n1
'chiaroscuro of everyday life' 43
Choisy, Auguste 192
*Choses, Les* 30n11
*Chronique d'un été* 39–40
CIAM 19–20
*Cinema, Gender, and Everyday Space: Comedy, Italian Style* 104
'cinema and everyday space' 104
*cinéma-écriture* 13, 67–8, 70–1
Cinematic Aided Design 220–32
'cinematic kitchen use of everydayness' 6
*Cinematic Musée Imaginaire of Spatial Cultural Differences* 7n5
cinematic typologies: of everyday life and architecture 100–22; house types 105–11; rhythmanalysis 104–5
'cinematic urban archaeology' 4, 119n20
*cinema-verité* 39–40
*Citizen Kane* 154n15
*The Clock* 98n13
*A Clockwork Orange* 53–4
'close the loop' 219–32, *219*
'closed system' 12
cognitivism 52–3, 223–4, 230–1n9
Cohen, Jem 115
Colomina, Beatriz 141
colours 208
*Coming up for air* 118n18

communal staircases 199, 212–13
Computer Aided Design (CAD) 220–2, 230n4
Connor, Steven 202, 205
*Construire pour Habiter* 17
*Les convoyeurs attendent* 158–9
corners 212–14, *213*, 216n18
*Coronation Street* 108
Corpet, Oliver 29n3
corridors 202–6, 214n4; and human drama 205–6; as non-places 203–5; as 'retarder' 202–3, *203*
*Cours du Soir par Jacques Tati* 183–4, *183*
Coutard, Raoul 184–5
*Le Crime de Monsieur Lange* 136, 172–3
*Critique de la séparation* 40
*Critique de la vie quotidienne* 12–13, 29n, 30n11, 42, 85–6, 92
*Critique de la vie quotidienne – Fondements d'une sociologie de la quotidienneté* 12, 18, 39
*Critique de la vie quotidienne – introduction* 18
Cronenberg, David 91
Cultural Studies 22

Daidalos 22, 33n39
*The Daily Mail* 99n18
*Damnation* 136–7, *137*, 169
dangerous stairs 181–2
Dardenne brothers 111, 170–1
De Certeau, Michel 207
de Sica 83n20
'deadpan' method 18
Debord, Guy 39–40
Decobert, Lydie 178, *179*, 185
'deep and shallow' spaces 172–3
defamiliarization 73, 158–9
Delaunay, Robert 151–2
Deleuze, Gilles 75, 83n20, 147–8, 149, 160
*Delicatessen* 199, *199*
DeLillo, Don 1
Delouvrier, Paul 17
dépaysement [defamiliarization] 73, 158–9
depth of field 139
*Deux ou trois choses que je sais d'elle* 53, 62n9
Diderot, Denis 190
Dielman, Jeanne 6
'The Dilapidated Dwelling' 25–6

*Disclosure of the everyday: The undramatic achievements in Narrative film* 44
*Discover Your Neighbour* project 32n33
'discovery of the ordinary' 20
disruption of the everyday 51–64; *Blue Velvet 58*; *La Piscine 57*; *Lost in Translation 59*; *Stunned Man 60*
*Divine Intervention* 116
*Do the Right Thing* 201
documentary 53–5, 110
*Dogville* 158
Doisneau, Robert 107
'door as an object' 209
'door-knob cinema' 156–7
'door-rich' 172
doors 156–177; *Amelie 158*; *Birdman 162*; 'Bluebeard temptation syndrome' 166–8, *167*; as a cut *163*; *Ed Wood 157, 164*; entrances 166; exits 166; farcical 131n6; as gaps between walls 209; of hope and expectations p6; *Le Mepris 209, 211*; *L'Eclisse 169*; linking time and space across the city *164*; as mental state *159*; with no middle *211*; as protection 171–2; of rejection 170–1; revolving *161*; *The Servant 163, 168*; *The Shining 172*; *Spellbound 159*; that reveal *168*; that unite and separate *158*; 'threshold as contested space' 168–70; *Two Days One Night 171*, p6
'double dimension of the everyday' 57
'double fiction' 90
Douchet, Jean 137–9, 139–41, 165–6, 179–80, 190–1
Douglas, Mary 79, 80
'Downtonising' tendancy 118–19n19
drama 103
*Drive* 162, 204–5, p7
*Le droit à la ville* 16, 22, 30n15
Durand, Jean-Nicolas-Louis 102, 103–4
Duvignaud, Jean 16

Eames, Charles and Ray 129, 130
*L'Eclisse* 144–52; doors 168, *169*; poster by Signac *145*; windows *144, 147, 148*
L'Ecole Spéciale d'Architecture, Paris 16
*l'écriture-cinéma* 13, 67–8, 70–1
*Ed Wood* 157, 158, 164, *164*

Eisenstein, Sergei 66, 81n2, 186–7, 195–6n7, 200
*Elements de rythmanalyse* 85
*Elements of Architecture* 6, 126–7, 130, 130–1n3; corridors 202, 214n5; doors 157; stairs 183, 200
Emerson, Tom 25
*l'endotique* 14, 70–1
entrances 166
*The Epilogue* 12
'equipment for living' 55
*Espace et représentation* 31n16
'espace quelconque' 78
*un espace sans fonction* 94–5
*Espèces d'Espace Perecquiens* 31n18
*Espèces d'espaces* 1, 13–14, 16, 70, 71, 72
*l'esprit d'escalier* 190
L'Esprit Nouveau 89–90, 93
*l'étranger* 149, 153n11
*l'étrangeté familière du rêve* 42
European-style architecture 200–1
Evans, Robin 125, 130, 173, 176n15, 198, 202
everyday: in film and its disruption 56–61; and the realism argument 41–4; UK 19–22; US 18–19
everyday and architecture: contemporary view 22–9; historical perspective 16–22
*The Everyday and Architecture* 25
*The Everyday and Everydayness* 32n27
*Everyday Architecture* 16
'Everyday architecture – in what style should we build?' 22–3, 25
'Everyday Architecture Re-made in Taiwan' 2
'everyday by stealth' 52
'everyday by synecdoche' 52
'everyday DNA' 52
everyday life 44–6, 221, 231n10; versus everyday environment 111–17; *Un homme qui dort* 69; in a non-everyday environment *115*; *Pulp Fiction* 103
everyday life and architecture 9–36; cinematic approach to 219–32; cinematic typologies of 100–22
*Everyday Life in the Modern World* 30n11
everydayness 11–36, 37–122, 205–6, 213
*Exhibition*: Melvin house 126, 142; ordinariness 46, 114; rhythmanalysis 5, 88–97, *91, 92, 93, 95, 96,* 98n, 104; stairs 180, *180*

exits 166
'experience' emotions 55

*Fahrenheit 451* 53–4, 192
'familiar realism' 44
*Family Life* 109
Farrell, Terry 27, 33n41, 111
Fausch, Deborah 18, 32n30
*La Femme de l'Aviateur* 226–7, *226*
la fenêtre en longueur 141, 142–4, 153n9
Les Fenêtres simultanées sur la ville 151–2
Ferro, Marc 53, 62n9, 223
'A few usages of the verb to inhabit' 17
film: as model of real world 221–3; and popular culture 62n10; as post-occupancy study *4*
*Film* 187
'film is part of reality' 53
film language metaphor 52
"film museum" 53
'film world' 90
'filmic thick time' 96
Finch, Paul 26–7
fire escapes 200, 214n1
*Fish Tank* 54–5
Five Points 128–9
floors 212
Foucault, Michel 114–15
Frampton, Kenneth 19, 128
France, everyday and architecture 16–22
Frankfurter Küche [the Frankfurt Kitchen] 125
*Die Frankfurter Küche* 125
Fraser, Murray 3
Free Cinema 21
French café *71*, 225–8, *226, 227*
French New Wave 20, 21–2, 47n5, 112–13
*Frenzy* 195n3
Freud, Sigmund 62n11
Friedberg, Anne 138
*Full Moon in Paris* 227–8, *227*
Fullwood, Natalie 104, 117n7
functionality 77–8
*Fundamental Concepts of Architecture: The Vocabulary of Spatial Situations* 102–3

Gabin, Jean 134
Gadamer, Hans-Georg 231n11

Gardner, Jean 230n3

Garrel, Philippe 193

Gehry, Frank 128, 131n8

*Gentleman's Agreement* 223

*Georges Perec's Scene of a Flight: Mnemotechnics on Screen* 7n1

Gilbreth, Frank B 125

Gilbreth, Lillian 125–6, 130n1

*A Giornata Particulare* 135

*The Girl Chewing Gum* 116–17

Godard, Jean-Luc: architectonic reading of 198, 206–14; 'bedroom film' genre 73–4; corridors 203; documentary 53, 62n9; everyday life 112; *Le quotidien* 40; rhythmanalysis 95; stairs 6, 184

*The Godfather* 52, *52*

*Gone with the Wind* 166, 191, *191*, 201

Goodall, Mark 7n1

*The Grand Budapest Hotel* 79–80

Greene, Graham 109

Grodal, Torben 46, 53, 61n, 61–2n8, 100

*Habiter l'inhabituel*, exhibition 117, p3

*habitus* 28

Halley, Peter 40–1

Hanson, Julienne 172, 176n13

'hard' world 55

Harris, Steven 25

Hattan, Eric 117, p3

*Helsinki, Forever* 116, 162

Henderson, Judith 32n32

Henderson, Nigel 19–20, 21, 32n32

*Her* 221

heterotopia 114–16, 120n30

Highmore, Ben 23–4

Hillier, Bill 172, 176n13

*Hiroshima Mon Amour* 66

*A History of Violence* 191

Hitchcock, Alfred: 'baseline' 103; corridors 203; disruption of the everyday 56; doors 156–7, 159; everyday life 113–14; oneiric house 105; stairs 179–80, 181–2, 183, 190–1, 194, 195n3, 200; windows 135

Hochberg, Julian 153n7, 175–6n8

Hogg, Joanna 5, 46, 88–97, 113–14, 126, 142

Holland, Charles 25

*Home* 54, p2

*Home Economics* 2

*L'homme d'à coté* 142–3, p5

*Un homme qui dort* 68–71, *69, 71*, 73–4, 133–4, *134*, 149

*Hotel Monterey* 72

*House after Five Years of Living* 129, *129*

house types 105–11

*How buildings learn: what happens after they're built* 3

*The Hudsucker Proxy* 136

Hughes, William 62n10

Hulot 54, *54*, 188, 202

Husserl, Edmund 48n16

hyperrealism 84n25

*I am Cuba* 135–6

'The Idea of the Home' 79

*If Buildings Could Talk* 3, p1

illusion theory 52

l'incontournable 13

Independent Group 19, 24, 32n32

'in-discipline' 2–3

indoor and outdoor 136, 164–5, 168–9

*l'infra-ordinaire* 14, 30n11, 58, 61, 70–1, 81, 117–18n9

*l'inhabitable* 16

*interroger l'habituel* 117

Intraub, Helene 153n7

*Introduction à la connaissance des rhythmes* 85

*Introduction to Modernity* 30n11

Izenour, Steven 18–19

*Jackie Brown* 47n4, 105, 114, *114*

Jacobs, Steven 156

James, Alison Sian 67

Janson, Alban 170, 192

Jarmusch, Jim 105, 112–13

*Jeanne Dielman*: architectonic of cinema 126; cinematography 76–81; and *Die Neue Wohnung* 79; everyday life 113; everydayness 71–2, 74, 75–81, *76*, *80*; versus Neufert's Architects' data *81*; rhythmanalysis 86–8, 91–2, 104; windows 134

Johnson, Mark 61–2n8

joining the dots 198–216

*Jour de Fête* 112

*Le Jour se Lève* 134
Jourdain, Monsieur 7n2
*Jules et Jim* 20

Kael, Pauline 57–8
Kafka, Franz 82n10
Kahn, Albert 48n19
Kazan, Elia 223
Keaton, Buster 187
Keiller, Patrick 25–6, 40, 220, 229–30n1
*Kill Bill 1* 59, 114
kino-pravda 40
*Kiss Me Deadly* 189–90
kitchen scenes 6, *52*
'Kitchen Sink' films 108, 111
Kitchen Sink movement 21–2
*Kitchen Stories* 100, *101*
Klevan, Andrew 44, 49n22, 51
Kofman, Eleonore 30n11
Konigsberg, Ira 230–1n9
Koolhaas, Rem: Computer Aided Design (CAD) 220, 230n5; *Elements of Architecture* 6, 126–7, 128, 130, 130–1n3; stairs 200
Kracauer, Siegfried 53
Krucker, Bruno 24
Kubrick, Stanley 62n11

Laforgue, Jules 1
*Las Vegas* exhibition 32n29
*Las Vegas in the Rearview Mirror* 32n28
*The Last Picture Show* 40–1
*Late Spring* 46
Lawry, Edward G. 44
Lawson, Bryan 220, 230n5
layers 173
Le Corbusier: and Fausch 32n30; films 130, 153n8; Five Points 96; La Ville Radieuse 131n3; modernism 84n24; and Perret 139–41; rhythmanalysis 85; stairs 192–3; Villa Savoye 89–90, 128–9; windows 142–3, 144, 188
Le Lionnais, François 30n9
*Learning from Las Vegas* 5, 18, 32n30
Lebas, Elizabeth 30n11
Lee, Spike 201
Lefebvre, Henri: *Critique* 29n1, 31–2n25; disruption of the everyday 51, 57, 58; *The*

*Everyday and Everydayness* 32n27; everyday and realism 41–5; everyday environment 119n23; everyday life 111, 117n8; everydayness 5, 11–22, 28–9, 41, 47n5; handout *15*; home 105; joining the dots 198; Le droit à la ville 30–1n15; leisure activities 82n5; 'lived' experience 39, 40; 'minor magic of everyday life' 229; 'moment' 224–6; objects 209, 215n8; and Perec 13–16, 30n11; rhythmanalysis 85–99, 104; *Saturday Night and Sunday Morning* 33n35, 48n11; windows 133
Léger, Fernand 43, 189
Leigh, Mike 109, 111
leisure activities 82n5
Lichtenstein, Claude 20
*Les Lieux* 82n7
*lieux de mémoire* 108, 186
'lieux de parole et des rencontres' 205
*Les lieux d'une fugue* 1, 2, 7n3
*Life, a User's Manual* 107
lifts 201, *201*, 202–6
*La Ligne Générale* 66, 81n2
*Limits of Control* 204
'limit-situations' 75
'lived architecture' 97
lived experience 40, 223–8
*Les Locataires* 107
London 27–8, 32n33, 41
*London* 41
*The London, Story* 174n3
Loos 140–1
Losey 179
*Lost in Translation* 59, *59*
'A love letter to an unloved place' 202
Lubitsch, Ernst 165–6
Lukács, György 43–4, 49n20, 67, 82n7
Lynch, David 57–8, 90
Lynch, Kevin 41

McDonough, Tom 39–40
McGrath, Brian 230n3
Mcleod, Mary 19, 26–7
'Magic of the Real' 228
'main street' 18, 28
La Maison Curutchet 142
Manfred Mann 118n18

Mangolte, Babette 71–3, 79–80
Marceau, Marcel 193
Marclay, Christian 93
Mass Observation movement 32n33
*matière brut* 14
Mazzeti, Lorenza 21
Meades, Jonathan 53–4
*Meaning of Contemporary Realism* 67
Mekas, Jonas 41, 47n3
Melvin, James 89, 96
Melvin house 89–97, *89*, 99n18, 126
'mental meandering' 224
*Le Mepris*: architectonic reading of 206–14;
    corners *213*; doors *209, 211*; joining the dots
    6, 198; objects *207, 208*; stairs *213*; walls *210*
Merleau-Ponty, Maurice 229
*Metric Handbook* 126
*metro-boulot-dodo* 69, 82n12, 92
*Micropsychologie et vie quotidienne* 3
*Midnight Cowboy* 40–1
Mielke, Friedrich 178, *178*–9, 185, 195n6, 200
'minor magic of everyday life' 229
Miralles, Enric 131n8
Mitchell, William 222
Mitchell, W. J. T. 3
'model' 221–22, 229, 230n3
'modern' 79–80
modernism 84n24
modernity 88–9, 98n10
Moles, Abraham 3, 160–2, 165, 174–5n5, 210,
    216n16
Molière, 7n2
'moment' 88, 224–5, 227
*Momma Don't Allow* 21
*Mon Oncle* 54, *54*, 187–9, *188*
Moneo, Rafael 100
montage 42–3
Montfrans, M. van 70
Moran, Joe 1–2, 107–8, 110
Morin, Edgar 39–40, *40*
movement-image 160
Mulvey, Laura 101
Murphy, Dudley 189
Murray, Christine 220–1
*Museum Hours* 115, *115*, 116
Musset, Alfred de 160, 174n4

National Film Theatre, London 21
naturalism 44, 52; 'radical naturalism' 44, 48n19
naturalist films 44, 47–8n10, 49n21
Negroponte, Nicholas 221–2, 230n6
*Die Neue Wohnung* 78–9, *79*
Neufert, Ernst 126
Neufert's Architects' data 6, 80, *81*, 126, 130–1n3
New Left 30n11
'new romanticism' 30n11
New York Tribeca 2015 Film Festival 2
*A Night at the Opera* 131n6
*Night of the Demon 181*
*Night on Earth* 105, 118n10
*Ninotchka* 176n9
*No Country for Old Men* 172
non-everyday environment *115*
non-everyday life *114*
'non-place' 203–5, 214n6
Nora, Pierre 108, 186
*A Nos Amours* 98n9
'Notopia' 220–1
*Notorious* 191
Nouvel, Jean 229–30n1
*La Nouvelle Vague* 20, 21–2, 47n5, 112–13
*Les nuits de la pleine lune* 227–8, *227*
*Number Seventeen* 179

*O Dreamland* 21
objects 206–8, *208*
objects, absence of 207–8, 215n8
observing the observed 101–4, *101*, 125–6
oneiric house 105–7, *106*, 194
'open system' 12
Ophüls, Max 135
ordinariness 44–6, 59, 109–10
'ordinary' 44–6, 49n25
'Ordinary Architecture' 25
Ordre des Architectes 2016 2
Orwell, George 109, 118n18
'other spaces' 114–16
Otway, Andrew 118n110
Oulipian constraint 68
*L'OuLiPo* group 14, 30n9
*Out of the Rubble* 110
outside and inside 176n11
Ozu, Yasujirō 46

**240** Index

paintings 138–9, 210–11, 215n14

Palladio, Andrea 140

Pallasmaa, Juhani: doors 130, 156, 169; emotions 55; situations 223–4; stairs 180, 185–6, 190, 196n10

Paolozzi, Eduardo 21

Paquot, Thierry 29n3

parametricism 221

Parc de La Villette 14

'La paroi mobile' 160–1

*La Partie de Campagne* 137–9, *138*

Partridge, John 90

*The Passenger* 136–7

*Paterson* 112–13, *113*

'Patio and Pavilion' 24

*Paysan de Paris* 81

Perec, Georges 1–2, 5, 7n3, 65–84; and Akerman 71–4; *Construire pour Habiter* 17; corners 216n17; doors 164–5, 171–2; *Espace et representation* 31n16; everyday life 23–4, 205; *interroger l'habituel* 117; and Lefebvre 13–16, 30n11; *Life, a User's Manual* 107; *l'infra-ordinaire* 58; rhythmanalysis 97–8n5; stairs 178; *un espace sans fonction* 94; walls and paintings 210–11, 215n14; windows 133–4, 149

Perret, Auguste 142, 143; and Le Corbusier 139–41

Peytard, Jean 67

phenomenological view of film 224, 230–1n3

photography 19–20, 32n32

*Pierrot Le Fou* 95, 99n17

*The Pilgrim* 176n10

*La Piscine* 56–7, *57*

*Le Plaisir* 135, *135*

*Plan Construction* (10th anniversary) 17

*Playtime* 112, 140, 202, 221

*La poetique de l'espace* 16

*Point Break* 160

Polanski, Roman 209–10

Pontecorvo, Gillo 223

*Poor Cow* 108, 109–10

'pop art' 19

la porte fenêtre 141, 142–4, *143*

post modernism 98n10

Post-Occupancy Evaluation 3, 7–8n7

'Pour une litterature réaliste' 67

Practice of Everyday Life 25

*Précis* 102

*Prénom Carmen* 158, 216n15

*Pride and Prejudice* 56–7

*Primer of Scientific Management* 125

Pritzker Prize, 2014 26

*The Production of Space* 16, 22, 86, 117n8, 215n11

*promenade architecturale* 188

*Psycho* 135, 182, *182*, 185, 194, *194*, 195n3

*Pulp Fiction* 103, *103*, 105, 201, *201*, 202–4, *203*

'purism' 79–80

Queneau, Raymond 14, 30n9

*Queuing for Beginners: The Story of Daily Life from Breakfast to Bedtime* 104

Queysanne, Bernard 68, 82n10

*Le quotidien* 13–14, 17, 19, 40, 70

Raban, Jonathan 55

'radical naturalism' 44, 48n19

Raith, Frank-Berthold 22–3, 25

Rancière, Jacques 136

Rapp, Davide 131n7

Rawlinson, Martha *106*

'reactivated circuit' 59

'real world' 222

realism 21–2, 41–4, 44–6, 47n4, 82n7

*Rear Window* 113, 135

*Rebecca* 156–7, 166–7, *167*

Regulier, Catherine 85

*Reinventing the everyday in the age of spectacle…* 112

Reisz, Karel 21, 48n11

Renier, Alain 31n16

Renoir, Jean 133, 136, 137–9, 139–40, 144, 165–6, 172

repetitive reactivation 60–1

*Repulsion* 209, 215n12

*Reservoir Dogs* 104–5

Resnais, Alain 66

*Le Révélateur* 193, *193*

'reverse image' of reality 42

Reversible Destiny/Shusaku Arakawa + Madeline Gins 23–4

rhythmanalysis 29n3, 85–99, 104–5

*Rhythmanalysis* 5
RIBA 3, 7–8n7
Richardson, Tony 21
Richter 78–9
right to light p5
right to the city 16
*The Rink* 157
Robertson, Manning Durdin 16, 31n19, 31n20
Rohmer, Eric 112, 226–8
Ropars-Wuilleumier, Marie-Claire 135, 148–9
Rosefeld, Julian 60
*Rosemary's Baby* 209, 215n12
Ross, Kristin 40
Rossi, Aldo 22, 151, 205–6
Rouch, Jean 39–40, 40
Roy, Deb 230n6
Ruscha, Ed 19, 32n31

*Salt of the Earth* 48n14
*Le Samourai* 189
Sanaa Architects p1
*Saturday Night and Sunday Morning* 33n35, 48n11
*Saving Private Ryan* 46
scalalogy *See* stairs
'scenario for human drama' 89
Schilling, Derek 14
School of Architecture, Lausanne 15
Schregenberger, Thomas 20
Schütte-Lihotzsky, Margarete 125
Scola, Ettore 135
Scott Brown, Denise 18–19, 32n28, 41, 98n10
Seeley, William P. 52–3, 61n6, 61n7
*Seen from the Window* 86
Seguin, Louis 172, 173
Sellars, Wilfrid 47n4
'Semi Detached Suburban Mr. James' 118n18
*Semi-Detached* 109
semi-detached houses, a cinematic typology 107–11, *110*
Sergison, Jonathan 24–5, 33n39
*Série noire* 67
*The Servant* 163–4, *163*, 166–8, *168*, 179
Seyrig, Delphine 76–81
Shand, Philip Morton 89, 98n11
Sheringham, Michael 13, 29n4, 31–2n25, 40

*The Shining* 55, 172, *172*, 185–6, 202
Shonfield, Katherine 209, 215n12
Signac, Paul 145–6, *145*
*Signs of Life, Symbols in the American City* 18
Sim, Lorraine 45
Simmel, Georg 158, 160
Situationist group 30n11, 111
situations 223–8
Siza, Alvaro 41
6A Architects 25
'skin deep' 228
Smith, John 116–17
Smithson, Alison and Peter 5, 19–20, 24, 32n32, 33n39, 46
Smithsonian Institute 18
'The social logic of space' 176n13
'sociologie de la quotidienneté' 14
'soft' world 55
space and emotion 228–9
*Spaces of the cinematic home* 105, 118n15, 179
spatial ambiguity 94
'spatial ambiguity of consciousness' 94–5
spatio-temporal passages 161–4
'the species of cinematic space' 13
*Spellbound* 159, *159*
Spielberg, Stephen 46
spiral stairs 184–5, *184*
'stair museum' 184–5, 187, 189, 195n6
'staircase wit' 190
stairs 178–97; *Alphaville 185*; ambiguous *193*; 'animated staircase section' 187–9; *Battleship Potemkin 187*; communal staircases 199, 212–13; corners 212–13; and cultural differences 200–1; dangerous 181–2; *Delicatessen 199*; directionality 190–5, *194*; end of 200–1; everyday life 190; *Exhibition 180*; fire escapes 200, 214n1; *Gone with the Wind 191*; *Le Mepris 213*; *Mon Oncle 188*; *Night of the Demon 181*; of our everyday 189–90; position of 198–206; *Psycho 194*, 195n3; spiral 184–5, *184*; straight *182*; Tati *183*; typology of cinematic 182–9; winding and straight 185–9
Stanek, Łukasz 16
Steadman, Philip 102, 221–2, 230n7
Steinberg, Saul 107, 118n14

Stierli, Martino 18, 32n28
*The Strange Little Cat* 113
*Stunned Man* 60, *60*, 63n20
*Sunset Boulevard* 201

Tarantino, Quentin 47n4, 104–5, 114
Tarkovsky, Andrei 55, 105
Tarr, Béla 136, 169
Tati, Jacques: Computer Aided Design (CAD)
   221; everyday life 3, 40, 111–12; stairs 183–4,
   *183*, 187–9; windows 140
Tawa, Michael 129–30, 131n10, 149–51,
   153–4n14, 154n16
Team 10 19–20
'tectonic' in architecture 128
Templer, John 181
terraced houses, a cinematic typology 107–11,
   *108*
*38 Témoins* 142, 143, *143*
*This is My Street* 108, *108*, 109, 191
Thomas, Maureen 63n14
*365 Day Project* 47n3
'threshold as contested space' 168–70
Tigges, Florian 170, 192
Till, Jeremy 25–6, 96
'time-image' 75
*The Tina Trilogy* 119n21
'To inhabit: the awakening of architectural
   thinking' 17
Tobe, Renée 179
Todorov, Tzvetan 63n14
*Together* 21
Toland, Gregg 154n15
Toubiana, Serge 111–12
*Traces* 160–1, *161*
'transference' 229
*transformations oulipiennes* 14
Trebitsch, Michel 30n11
*The Tree of Life* 116
*Trente Glorieuses* (1946–75) 17
*Trois Chantiers* 153n8
Trotter, David 44, 49n21, 172–3, 176n13
Truffaut, François 20, 47n5
Tschumi, Bernard 14, 134–5, 229–30n1
Turner, David 109
*The Twilight Zone* 159

*Two Days One Night* 170–1, *171*, p6

UK, everyday and architecture 16–22
*Umberto D* 75, 83n20
*Underworld* 1
*Un Unheimliche* 62n11
*Up the Junction* 108
Upper Lawn house 24
Upton, Dell 22, 115
urban studies 16
US, everyday and architecture 16–22

Vaizey, Ed 27, 33n41
"variable topological spaces" 160
Venice Biennale of Architecture 1980 98n10
Venice Biennale of Architecture 2010 8n8
Venice Biennale of Architecture 2014 126–7, *127*,
   p4
Venice Biennale of Architecture 2016 2
Venturi, Robert 18–19, 28, 32n30, 41, 98n10
*Vertical Promenade* 189
Vertov, Dziga 40
Vesely, Dalibor 192–3, 196n13, 199, 224–6, 231n10
*La Vie Filmée des Français* 65, 66–7
*La vie mode d'emploi* 67
*La vie quotidienne dans le monde moderne* 18
Villa Savoye 89–90, 128, *128*, 141, 192
La Ville Radieuse 131n3
Virilio, Paul 16
*The Vocabulary of Spatial Situations* 192
von Bagh, Peter 116

walls 208–11; 'as condensers of distance' 210; 'as
   condensers of emotions' 210, *210*; and
   paintings 210–11, 215n14
*Walls Have Feelings* 209
Ward, Elly 25
Welles, Orson 154n15
Wenders, Wim 3, 8n8, 230n2, p1
Whyte, William Holly 41
Wigglesworth, Sarah 25–6
Wilson, Colin 'Sandy' 189
'window onto the world' 138
windows 133–55; *Damnation* 137; indoor and
   outdoor 132n11; *La Partie de Campagne* 138;
   *L'Avventura 150*; *Le Plaisir 135*; *L'Eclisse 144*,

*147, 148*; onto the street *150*; of opportunities *138*; paintings as 138–9; Renoir and 137–9; *Un homme qui dort 134*
*The Wizard of Oz* 159
Wolff, Paul 125
Wollen, Peter 203–4
'Woman at the Window' 145–6
Woolcock, Penny 110, 119n21

Woolf, Virginia 45
Wright, Frank Lloyd house 164–5

Yacavone, Daniel 90

Žižek, Slavoj 51, 61n1
Zola, Emile 48n19, 49n21
Zumthor, Peter 168, 228, 231n12

# Taylor & Francis eBooks

## Helping you to choose the right eBooks for your Library

Add Routledge titles to your library's digital collection today. Taylor and Francis ebooks contains over 50,000 titles in the Humanities, Social Sciences, Behavioural Sciences, Built Environment and Law.

Choose from a range of subject packages or create your own!

**Benefits for you**
- Free MARC records
- COUNTER-compliant usage statistics
- Flexible purchase and pricing options
- All titles DRM-free.

**Benefits for your user**
- Off-site, anytime access via Athens or referring URL
- Print or copy pages or chapters
- Full content search
- Bookmark, highlight and annotate text
- Access to thousands of pages of quality research at the click of a button.

**REQUEST YOUR FREE INSTITUTIONAL TRIAL TODAY**

**Free Trials Available**
We offer free trials to qualifying academic, corporate and government customers.

## eCollections – Choose from over 30 subject eCollections, including:

| | |
|---|---|
| Archaeology | Language Learning |
| Architecture | Law |
| Asian Studies | Literature |
| Business & Management | Media & Communication |
| Classical Studies | Middle East Studies |
| Construction | Music |
| Creative & Media Arts | Philosophy |
| Criminology & Criminal Justice | Planning |
| Economics | Politics |
| Education | Psychology & Mental Health |
| Energy | Religion |
| Engineering | Security |
| English Language & Linguistics | Social Work |
| Environment & Sustainability | Sociology |
| Geography | Sport |
| Health Studies | Theatre & Performance |
| History | Tourism, Hospitality & Events |

For more information, pricing enquiries or to order a free trial, please contact your local sales team:
**www.tandfebooks.com/page/sales**

 | The home of Routledge books

**www.tandfebooks.com**

PGSTL 08/28/2017